DOWN TO EARTH

DOWN TO EARTH

NATURE'S ROLE IN AMERICAN HISTORY

TED STEINBERG

NEW YORK   OXFORD
OXFORD UNIVERSITY PRESS
2002

Oxford University Press

Oxford   New York
Auckland   Bangkok   Buenos Aires   Cape Town   Chennai
Dar es Salaam   Delhi   Hong Kong   Istanbul   Karachi   Kolkata
Kuala Lumpur   Madrid   Melbourne   Mexico City   Mumbai   Nairobi
São Paulo   Shanghai   Singapore   Taipei   Tokyo   Toronto

and an associated company in Berlin

Published by Oxford University Press, Inc.
198 Madison Avenue, New York, New York 10016
http://www.oup-usa.org

Oxford is a registered trademark of Oxford University Press

Text design by Cathleen Bennett

Library of Congress Cataloging-in-Publication Data

Steinberg, Theodore, 1961–
    Down to earth : nature's role in American history / Ted Steinberg.
        p.   cm.
    Includes bibliographical references and index.
    ISBN 0-19-514009-5 (cloth : alk. paper)
        1. Human ecology—United States—History.   2. Philosophy of nature—United
    States—History.   3. Human beings—Effect of environment on—United States—History.
    4. United States—Environmental conditions.   I. Title.
    GF27.S85   2002
    333.7'13'0973—dc21   2001047600

Printing number: 9 8 7 6 5 4 3 2 1
Printed in the United States of America
on acid-free paper

TO DONALD WORSTER

CONTENTS

This book will try to change the way you think about American history. It deals with some familiar topics—colonization, the industrial revolution, slavery, the Civil War, consumerism—and some not so well-known—the Little Ice Age, horse manure, pig sties, fast food, lawns, SUVs, and garbage. I will argue that the natural world—defined here as plants and animals, climate and weather, soil and water—has profoundly shaped the American past.

Historians of course have not completely overlooked nature. Virtually every U.S. history textbook, for instance, has an obligatory section on Theodore Roosevelt and the conservation movement. Sometimes there is also a brief discussion of the environmental reforms that began in the 1960s. Nature as politics—that has long been the main concern. You are unlikely to learn anything about the role of climate or soil fertility in history. Little about how Americans and Native Americans before them went about the task of feeding themselves. Virtually nothing about pigs, chickens, cows, and corn—or hamburgers, despite the fact that McDonald's plays a major role in the lives of so many people. Nothing about global warming or cooling. Not a word about volcanic eruptions across the world that led to hunger in America.

For most members of the profession and, almost by definition, for most Americans, history unfolds against a stable environmental backdrop. Nature is taken for granted and passed over in the rush to discuss what really mattered—wars, elections, and the other mainstays of political and intellectual history. Social history, pioneered during the 1960s and centered on exploring the lives of ordinary people, has proved no more receptive to the idea of nature as a dynamic force. Practicing history "from the bottom up," as some of the new social historians put it, meant digging down into the nitty-gritty of everyday existence, into work, family life, sexual orientation, gender relations, and race. But by and large, the social historians put away their shovels when they reached the land and soil itself.

And yet a shift as important as the industrial revolution, for example, did not take place in a setting from which nature was somehow magically excluded. Industrialization never would have unfolded in the way that it did were New England not blessed with the ample precipitation and water resources required to power the cotton mills—water that had to be controlled with dams, which in turn put an end to spring fish runs and ultimately brought factory owners into conflict with distant rural farmers for whom salmon and shad represented their next meal. Even a political and military event like the Civil War was shaped by ecological factors. Soldiers and horses needed to be fed, and for that to happen both the Union and the Confederacy had to turn to the land. Robert E. Lee may have been a brilliant military strategist, but between battles he was reduced to finding ample forage for the horses his troops depended on to fight. Likewise, the growth of modern auto-centered suburbs hardly liberated people from nature. Natural forces impinged on suburban life, at times dramatically, as homeowners confronted landslides, floods, fires, and outbreaks of insects and weeds. Nature was not nearly as passive and unchanging as historians may have led us to believe.

Writing history "from the ground up" means rethinking the time periods that have thus far defined how we approach the past. Three turning points, corresponding to the parts of this book, are worth our attention. Many people think of peaceful Plymouth Rock as the start of our nation's history. In fact, the European arrival in North America brought ecological tumult galore as two landmasses isolated for millions of years suddenly came into contact with one another. Disease, blight, cold, hunger, rats, weeds, and wolves, among other threats, confronted the Europeans in the first two centuries of settlement. It took time and plenty of hard work for them to make order out of the chaos, to transform the forests to meet their agricultural ambitions. But by 1800, they had created a world of fields planted with European grains and cash crops, of fences that shouted "Keep Out," a simplified landscape largely devoid of wolves, bears, and deer, where the woods, if they existed at all in the wake of the colonist's ax, were a good deal quieter than before.

The next turning point after the arrival of the Europeans occurred in the late eighteenth century. Thomas Jefferson was its architect. Well known as one of the nation's founding fathers, Jefferson spent a great deal of time thinking about the relationship between land and democracy. How should the land be allotted to give every farmer enough to pursue a life of economic independence? Jefferson turned to the Cartesian logic of the grid for an answer. In the Land Ordinance of 1785, surveyors gained authorization from the government to divide the land into perfectly square six-by-six-mile townships. The township itself was then laid out into 36 boxes, which when divided into quarters, yielded democracy's building block: 160 acres of land, an amount Jefferson and subsequent political leaders believed would ensure freedom for the American farmer.

The grid was to the rationalization of nature what the Declaration of Independence was to freedom. It allowed the land to be bundled up and sold in one of the most sweeping attempts on record to put nature up for sale, the legacy of which is still visible today as one flies across the nation's midsection. The grid, however, was just the opening stage in a century-long quest to bring nature into the world of exchange, as a price was put on everything from water and birds to trees and even buffalo bones, a vast transformation that left no region of the country—North, South, or West—untouched.

Turning point number three came with the rise of consumerism in the late nineteenth century with its automobiles and brand name foods such as Sunkist oranges and Sun-Maid raisins. Under this new economic order, production and consumption became physically divorced from each other. Nowhere was this clearer than in the way Americans went about feeding themselves. With fruits, vegetables, and meat no longer produced locally but on distant factory farms in such places as California, Arkansas, and North Carolina, where labor was cheap and sun abundant, people often failed to realize where their food came from, how it was made, and even who made it.

Nor, for that matter, did they realize the true costs of owning an automobile, perhaps the greatest symbol of the new consumer lifestyle. The profusion of cars in the 1920s and especially in the years following World War II resulted in a major transformation of the American landscape. With food coming from faraway factory farms, the land once planted with hay and crops gave way to roads and freeways paid for largely by the federal government. Ribbons of new asphalt and concrete brought in their wake the ubiquitous suburban development. Builders cleared the land of trees only to fill it with cookie-cutter tract housing and patches of lawn. A massive redistribution of financial resources from the city to the country was under way—a shift that had enormous ecological and social consequences.

The grid and the automobile may not have the drama of such political milestones as the American Revolution or the Civil War, but in terms of their impact on nature, not to mention people's daily lives, they were just as important. The trends bound up in these two symbols cut to the core of human existence, to how we go about feeding and sheltering ourselves, getting from one place to another, getting rid of what we no longer need—seemingly mundane issues that historians have for too long ignored.

Many historians dismiss the field of environmental history as made up of people who assume what they need to prove: that America's ecological health has been severely compromised. The question of what environmental well-being means is complicated. Even ecologists cannot agree on it. I consider a culture out of balance with the natural world if it is either undermining its present ability to sustain itself or foreclosing on its capacity to respond to future change. That is admittedly a very anthropocentric view. The loss of a plant or animal species may well be lamentable in its own right, regardless of its consequences for humankind. But since all cultures transform nature to some degree to survive, it is those maladaptive patterns that pose a threat to the very existence or future of a society itself that concern me most.

My intent is not to simply replace the triumphal view of history (as one march onward and upward) with a story of the environmental decline and fall of the American republic. Accounting for ecological change, not judging it, remains the main task of this book. What was the driving force behind the significant shifts in species diversity, soil fertility, and atmospheric conditions? Was it population growth? New technologies? My argument is that the transformation of nature—land, water, pine trees, pigeons, cows—into a commodity (a thing that can be traded for profit) was the most important single force behind these shifts. It was not the only factor, of course, but it was and remains the most important one.

Putting a price tag on the natural world and drawing it into the web of commerce led to sweeping changes in ecosystems throughout the nation.

Commodities have a kind of magical quality about them. When people conceive of something as simple as an orange or a piece of lumber, they tend to view its very essence as bound up in its price. Monetary value, in other words, is seen as being intrinsic to the commodity in question, ingrained within the object itself. Commodities thus often obscure from view the human labor—the work— that produced them in the first place. Karl Marx called attention to this phenomenon back in the nineteenth century. In this book I will show that more than simply social relationships between workers and owners became masked in the process of commodification. Human relations with nature—the logging of forests, damming of rivers, plowing of grasslands, and other attempts to significantly transform ecosystems—suffered a similar fate. The benefits of modern living, from fast food to flush toilets, for all their virtues, have come at the price of ecological amnesia.

What follows is an attempt to penetrate the mystifying forces at work in our economic culture. Environmental history centers on the examination of various relationships—how natural forces shape history, how humankind affects nature, and how those ecological changes then turn around to influence human life once again in a reciprocating pattern. The field's practitioners are thus well equipped to examine the ramifying effects and hidden costs of development, bringing previously obscure relationships into sharp relief in the process. Investigating the California Gold Rush, for example, we discover how it helped to trigger an ecological crisis far away on the Great Plains. Exploring the conservation of tourist-friendly animals in national parks, we can see its damaging effects on the survival strategies of poor whites and Indians. Examining an activity as mundane as eating a steak brings to light its drain on the West's underground water supply. Environmental history is full of many such surprises.

ACKNOWLEDGMENTS

This book began one day in 1999 when Bruce Borland, a freelance acquisitions editor working for Oxford University Press, called to ask whether I would be willing to write an environmental history textbook. My first answer was no. The thought of writing a comprehensive book largely devoid of argument made me shudder. Borland, I should say, is not your average textbook representative. He is a man with vision on a mission to see that college students receive books that convey the real excitement of learning. Here was an opportunity to introduce students to my field of expertise, a chance to shape how they thought about history and its place in the world today. What could be more important? I was sold. I thank Bruce for the education he gave me.

Douglas Sackman read a very early draft of the manuscript, slogging through the often dull and ungrammatical prose, pointing me in new directions and sending me back to the library time and again. His comments on the manuscript reflect not simply his intellectual breadth, but his commitment to first-rate teaching.

Jim O'Brien is not just my best critic and a dear friend, but the only person on earth willing to read three drafts of my work. Long live the Imperial Diner and its "boiled hamburger steak."

Michael Black and Bob Hannigan have, between them, two of the best pairs of eyes in the business. I can't thank them enough for their efforts. My thanks also to Tim Beal, Bruce Borland, David Morris, Helen Steinberg, and Joel Tarr for combing through the manuscript, in whole or in part, and showing me the path to clarity.

Peter Ginna at Oxford stepped in and placed a few chips on me. He is everything and more that an author could ask for in an editor. My thanks to Peter and his colleagues Peter Coveney and Gioia Stevens for believing and giving the book a shot with a larger trade audience. My gratitude too goes out to the terrific panel of anonymous and not so anonymous reviewers, including William Cronon and Adam Rome, who poured a great deal of time and energy into critiquing the manuscript. I know the book is better because of their trenchant criticism. It is also better because of the hard work put in by Oxford's Christine D'Antonio, Furaha Norton, and Robert Tempio.

My agent Michele Rubin, with her keen sense of fairness, taught me that there is in fact such a thing as a free lunch. My Case Western history colleagues, ever faithful and supportive, passed along information and commented on an early chapter draft. Jonathan Sadowsky offered his usual challenging read and many great laughs along the way. Peter Whiting and Norman Robbins contributed some critical information at various points. And Peter McCall patiently explained numerous ecological principles and lent me some very large books that I'm still not sure I fully understand. No one could ask for a better research assistant than Julie Digianantonio. And as for Elsie Finley of the Kelvin Smith Library, may she never retire.

A Burkhardt Fellowship from the American Council of Learned Societies financed a year's leave that was absolutely indispensable to the successful completion of this project. My thanks to Alan Taylor, James Boyd White, and Donald Worster for writing letters in support of my application. The College of Arts and Sciences and the School of Law at Case Western Reserve pitched in financially during the book's final stages.

I thank Nathan Steinberg for his work of art, "The Old Days, 200–1931," a constant source of inspiration, and Harry Steinberg for that gorgeous smile. And Salvatore, too, a man of the people who fought the good fight and gave us Maria. I loved him for all that.

Long ago a high school teacher named Fred Harrison taught me that history could really matter in life. It has taken me more than two decades to thank him. I hope he can forgive me. In the early 1980s, Bob Hannigan picked up where Fred left off. I'll never forget the kindness he has shown me over the years. Then there was Donald Worster, who led me to see both the forest and the trees, who made even gritty Waltham, Massachusetts, and its Charles River come alive in ways I never before imagined. This book is for him.

DOWN TO EARTH

PROLOGUE

ROCKS AND HISTORY

Open a U.S. history textbook and glued inside the cover is the familiar map of the nation, as if the place were simply a given. But land is a much less settled issue than those maps suggest. While historians have spent a great deal of time examining how various immigrant groups came to America, they have spent almost no time considering how America itself—the land—came to be where it is on the globe. In this sense, our nation's history began not in 1607 with Jamestown, in 1492 with Columbus, or even thousands of years before then whenever the first Paleoindians came here. Rather, American history got underway some 180 million years ago when the earth's only continent, a huge landmass known as Pangaea, began to break apart.

At first, Pangaea split into two parts. Then as the Atlantic Ocean expanded, North America separated from Africa and later from South America. Slowly, the continents began to take their present positions on the globe. By about 60 million years ago, North America—a discrete and contiguous landmass—had been born.

From this one momentous geological occurrence, a host of profound consequences followed. Separated from the so-called Old World of Eurasia, life forms in North and South America developed in isolation, explaining why Europeans who ventured to the New World for the first time were so struck, at times even horrified, by the continent's strange new plants and animals, especially its bison, moose, cougars, alligators, and rattlesnakes. Continental drift also explains why the Americas, severed from Eurasia by water, were the last of the habitable continents settled by humankind. When the Paleoindians did reach these places, they lived in isolation from Europeans and their diseases, a fact that had a stunning impact in post-Columbian times. Indeed, without the breakup of Pangaea, the entire rationale for Columbus's voyage simply would not have existed. Fourteen ninety-two would be a year of no particular importance, the Columbus national holiday just another ordinary autumn day.

3

Nowhere is it written that U.S. history must begin with the breakup of Pangaea. Beginnings are in themselves quite arbitrary. One could just as easily start the story with the emergence of life four billion years ago or even the development of the earth itself 500 million years before that. But beginnings do tell us a great deal about an author's underlying assumptions about the past. When textbook writers open their narrative of the American republic with Columbus or, more commonly today, with Paleoindians trekking across the Bering Strait, they put forth a very anthropocentric view of the past. History begins when people come onto the scene. But by dwelling, as most U.S. historians do, on such a relatively short expanse of time—1492 or even 12,000 B.C. to the present—it is easy to lose sight of the powerful natural forces that have played such a formative part in the history of this country. It becomes easy to forget that the earth's climate, geology, and ecology are not simply a backdrop, but an active, shaping force in the historical process.

History is structured by a vast array of natural factors: geological forces that determine if minerals will be available for mining, if the soil will be fertile enough for planting crops, and if ample water and level land exist to grow those crops with a minimum of effort; ecological forces that determine the range and diversity of plant and animal life, if corn or wheat, cows or llamas, will be available for domestication, and if there will be adequate forests to supply timber; and climatic forces that determine if enough frost-free days will be present for an ample harvest. Such natural factors—largely beyond the control of human beings— have had enormous impact on how the past has unfolded. People make history, but under circumstances that are not of their own choosing, Karl Marx once observed. He had economic forces in mind. But his statement applies as well to the world of nature, to the far-reaching climatic, biological, and geological processes that have determined the possibilities open to human beings on this planet.

Thus America's place on the globe, while often glossed over and forgotten, needs to be taken seriously. The land area of the United States is uniquely positioned to capture a relatively large amount of solar energy—the key ingredient for transforming inorganic matter and water into food through the process known as photosynthesis. Food crops such as wheat, corn, soybeans, and oranges, among others, flourish in the nation's temperate climate, rich soils, and abundant sunlight, explaining why California and the central part of the nation are in the front ranks of world food production.[1] Imagine for a moment how severely curtailed the food supply would be were the present continental United States rolled on its side. Such a move would make the nation's north-south dimension three times the distance from east to west, instead of the other way around. Spanning many more degrees of latitude and with much of its landmass now lying outside the temperate zone, America would be far less suitable for agriculture.

Continental drift is hardly the only geological episode to have far-reaching consequences on American history. Consider the birth of the Rocky Mountains and its effect on the biogeography of the world's breadbasket, the Great Plains. Before

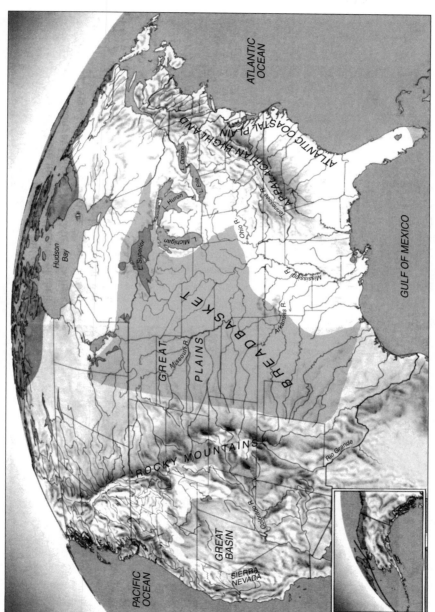

MAP OF NORTH AMERICA

Adapted from Out of Many, vol. 2, Brief 3rd ed., A History of the American People, by Faragher, Buhle, Czitron, and Armitage, © 2001, by permission of Pearson Education, Inc., Upper Saddle River, NJ.

the creation of the mountains, a process geologists refer to as the Laramide Orogeny, beginning some 80 million years ago, the Great Plains were a tremendous inland sea. The emergence of the Rockies, however, plugged the water's entry from the Pacific and Arctic oceans, creating conditions favorable to the eventual emergence of forest cover on the plains. The mountains also dried out the land by capturing the moisture of clouds on their windward side, creating a huge rain shadow that left the leeward plains in an even more arid state, precisely an environment suitable for the growth of grass. Meanwhile, the rain that did fall in the mountains washed away sediments and deposited them further east with each passing year, covering the old seabed with a layer of loose silt that was hundreds of feet thick and producing in the process one of the most level stretches of land on earth. The Rockies, by drying out the landscape of the plains, forced plant life to adapt accordingly. Grasses, which have complicated root systems that can exploit even the smallest amount of moisture, flourish in such an environment. Into these grasslands the American pioneer eventually forged, prepared to break the sod and replace it with another grass: the wheat so fabulously adapted to life in an arid locale.

That was not all the Laramide mountain-building episode did to contribute to America's rise to world economic dominance. It also broke up granite and metamorphic rocks, allowing metallic minerals to insinuate themselves into the faults left behind. Minerals such as gold, silver, zinc, lead, and copper settled that much nearer the earth's surface, where they could be mined with relative ease. Without this geological episode there would have been no Colorado gold rush in the 1850s, no mineral belt running through the state. The Laramide revolution was but one geological event on the nation's road to wealth. Taken together, the combined effect of the region's geological history accounts for North America's near total self-sufficiency in minerals. As one geologist has exclaimed, "No other continent has it so good!"[2]

One other event from the distant past is also worth our attention: the Pleistocene epoch that began 1.6 million years ago, the period commonly referred to as the Ice Age. During this time, huge glaciers, as much as one to two miles thick, covered the northern reaches of the continent (as well as Europe and Asia). Tundra stretched out over what is now Manhattan. The ice expanded south and then retreated on some 18 to 20 different occasions over the Pleistocene. The switch between these glacial and interglacial periods is not completely understood, but many attribute the shifts to changes in the Milankovitch cycle, named after the Yugoslav geophysicist who discovered this phenomenon back in the 1920s. From time to time, he observed, the earth's orbit around the sun changes, sometimes placing the planet closer to the star, where it can receive more heat, and sometimes further away, making the climate colder and producing a glaciation. Beginning about 10,000 years ago, the climate shifted and the ice sheet that covered much of Canada and the northern United States withdrew. It is no coincidence that American history has taken place during an interglacial period. Indeed, it is difficult to imagine the course U.S. history might have taken—or whether there would even be a United States—had the earth's orbit not changed and the ice not retreated. It is also sobering to note that although there is much concern today with global warming, in the long run it may be cold—that is, the return of another ice age—that will turn out to be our true nemesis.

Like the effects of continental drift and mountain building, glaciation too has had tremendous consequences for life on this continent. Animals and plants have adapted themselves to the glacial conditions that have prevailed for 90 percent of the last few million years. And again, U.S. agriculture seems to have benefited greatly from yet another geological event. When the glaciers retreated on several occasions from the Great Plains, they left behind a fine soil deposit called loess. The loess was eventually driven east by the prevailing westerly winds, finding its way to Kansas, Nebraska, Iowa, Wisconsin, and Indiana and providing the basis for rich, fertile soil—in some places 20 feet thick. Likewise, the soils of eastern Canada were scraped up and, in a generous moment, dumped by the glacier in the Midwest, again bolstering the fertility of our farms. It was not for nothing that the nineteenth-century geologist Louis Agassiz dubbed the glaciers "God's great plough."[3]

Without these soils, without the requisite sunlight and the right climate, America would no longer be the world's breadbasket. John Deere and his "singing plow," Cyrus McCormick and his famed reaper would become obscure tinkerers with projects of little practical importance, instead of icons discussed in virtually every American history textbook. Such are the implications of the really long view of the past. Suddenly the earth itself becomes an actor, a force to be reckoned with, instead of a simple line drawing inside a book's cover.

PART ONE

CHAOS TO SIMPLICITY

1

WILDERNESS UNDER FIRE

Although Christopher Columbus has a national holiday to honor his 1492 mission, on the basis of sheer exploratory drama we ought to celebrate something called Clovis Day instead.[1]

At least according to a much-honored archeological theory, the Clovis people trekked out of Siberia sometime before 11,000 years ago. Crossing the Bering land bridge (although "bridge" hardly does justice to the plain that purportedly stretched nearly 1,000 miles in width), they forged their way into Alaska, marking the first human settlement of North America. Within less than a millennium, they traveled the length of the continents, venturing to the Great Plains and the American Southwest (where their stone points were first discovered in Clovis, New Mexico), eventually ending up at the tip of South America. Two formerly uninhabited continents were quite suddenly—in geologic time at least—brought into the orbit of Homo sapiens. As discoveries go, this was a monumental journey that marked the greatest expansion across a landmass in the history of humankind. It can never be repeated on this planet.

That is, if it happened at all. In recent years, new evidence suggests the possibility that human beings arrived in North and South America earlier, perhaps as much as thousands to tens of thousands of years before the first Clovis hunters or Paleoindians crossed the Bering bridge. Using the technique of radiocarbon dating, archeologists have uncovered a site in southern Chile that goes back nearly 15,000 years. Even a human footprint exists to confirm the presence of these pre-Clovis people.[2]

Did these early settlers, whenever they arrived, walk lightly on the earth, extracting a living ever so gently from nature, leaving behind a pristine wilderness, as some environmentalists like to think? The notion that Indians acted out the ideals of the modern-day conservation movement has a long and enduring history. But such a view, however popular, has little basis in reality. Compared to the excesses of twentieth-century consumer culture, Native American life may well seem ecologically benign. But we must be careful not to romanticize the people and landscape in the period before European contact. Indians were intimately aware of and connected to the environment around them, and the rituals they took part in often emphasized their recognition of that dependence. They farmed the soil, hunted game, set fires, and gathered berries and nuts, engaging in a spiritually rich relationship with the land, while shaping it to meet the needs of everyday survival. Sparsely settled the land may have been, but a total wilderness it was not.

CRYING INDIAN

This advertisement, an American icon in the 1970s, helped popularize the idea of Indians as conservationists. (*Keep America Beautiful, Inc.*)

OVERKILL

When the Paleoindians arrived on the Great Plains, they found it teeming with large mammals, so-called megafauna, that included mammoths weighing between eight and nine tons (50 percent more than an African elephant), three-ton ground sloths, beavers the size of bears, 500-pound tapirs, plus exotic creatures like the pampatheres, akin to an armadillo but with the stature of a rhinoceros. Camels, saber-toothed cats, cheetahs, lions, antelopes, and horses all roamed the American West, and all were driven to extinction sometime before 10,000 years ago, near the end of the Pleistocene epoch.

Most of the available scientific evidence points to changes in global climatic conditions as the cause. Temperatures increased dramatically and the climate became more arid near the end of the Pleistocene. Even worse from the standpoint of living organisms was the onset of large swings in seasonal temperatures that resulted in much colder winters and hotter summers. Plant and insect communities sensitive to such shifts confronted a new and far less hospitable physical reality. The creation, in turn, of radically different habitats, goes the theory, had dire consequences for the megafauna as the animals found less food to eat. It is even possible that the growth of new toxic species of grass poisoned the mastodons and other large creatures.[3]

Not all scientists agree that climate played the pivotal role in the mass extinctions. Some researchers hold the Paleoindians themselves to blame, killing a mammoth one day, a ground sloth the next, as they expanded south down through the continents. Waging the equivalent of prehistoric "blitzkrieg," they argue, the Paleoindians exterminated animals unprepared to deal with being attacked by human beings. In this view, the continent's first settlers were hardly the low-impact stewards over the land that they are often made out to be. Nevertheless, over the course of the last 10 million years North America has experienced no fewer than six other such episodes of extinction, and in none of these events was humankind the culprit. That leaves the changing climate as a likely suspect.[4]

More important than precisely what caused the extinctions is the legacy left by this catastrophic annihilation. It is not too much to say that the Pleistocene extinctions altered the course of modern history, depriving America of valuable animal capital. Although the exact number of species exterminated remains unclear, unquestionably the vast bulk of North America's large mammals disappeared in the event. That left the continent in a state of biological impoverishment. It is no accident that of the 14 species of big domesticated animals relied on by cultures around the world for food, clothing, and transportation (the cow, pig, horse, sheep, and goat being the most important), only one, the llama, was domesticated in the Americas. The remaining 13 all came from Eurasia. The New World originally had a single species of horse, and unfortunately it was exterminated during the Pleistocene. History might indeed have unfolded differently if the European explorers of the sixteenth century had ventured to the Americas and found themselves face-to-face with a mounted cavalry.[5]

HIGH AND LOW COUNTERS

Although a great deal of ink has been spilled on the subject, we still have only a vague idea of North America's Indian population at the time of European contact. The native peoples themselves kept no records detailing their numbers, and with no direct demographic evidence available, researchers have had to devise various methods for estimating the continent-wide population from European observations recorded in diaries and other written sources. Early estimates done in the mid-nineteenth century—one by artist George Catlin, the other by missionary Emmanuel Domenech—concluded that the aboriginal population was roughly 16 to

17 million at the time of European arrival. When bona fide researchers got out their pencils and pads, however, the numbers plummeted. In 1928, the disciples of ethnologist James Mooney, the first scholar to study the problem, put forth a figure that was only slightly over a million. How did Mooney and his colleagues arrive at such a small number? Employing what some have labeled a "bottom-up" approach, Mooney calculated a total population for each tribe in North America, relying on historical evidence provided by European missionaries and soldiers. Only he chose to lower the figures given by these white observers. He reasoned that soldiers may have felt compelled to overestimate a given native population, and thereby enhance the magnitude of their own accomplishments. Victory over 10,000 Indians certainly looked better on paper than a triumph over half as many. After discounting the historical record, Mooney then simply added the numbers of the various tribes together. His million-person estimate endured for several decades and is still sometimes cited by conservative pundits eager to show that North America was largely virgin land populated by small bands of hunters before the Europeans arrived on the scene to pave the way for culture and civilization. Today, however, most researchers reject this extremely low number.[6]

In 1966, anthropologist Henry Dobyns created a huge stir when he proposed a figure in the 10- to 12-million-person range, revising that number upward in 1983 to 18 million. Employing a "top-down" approach, Dobyns used "depopulation ratios" based on his assessment of how various epidemic diseases—the most significant factor in the decline of the Native American people—affected the various Indian groups. He then broke up the continent into regions and multiplied the lowest figure for an area by the ratio, yielding the highest population total to date. Predictably, Dobyns and the so-called high counters have been accused of being pro-Indian.[7]

If the population in 1492 was indeed much closer to 18 million than to 1 million, then the rationale behind European conquest begins to unravel. The Europeans justified wresting the land from its aboriginal inhabitants on the grounds that the native peoples were not really using it. Compared to the population of Britain or Spain in the seventeenth century, the North American landscape must have seemed sparsely populated to the European eye. Those who did live on the continent, moreover, were seen practicing hunting and gathering, roaming the land like wild animals in the Europeans' view. Such small numbers of people living a mobile existence, in other words, had left the landscape in a wasted, unimproved condition. As the white settlers saw it—eventually taking their cue from philosopher John Locke—anyone entering such a wilderness who then set about making improvements was entitled to ownership over the property. Increase the size of the aboriginal population, however, and the Europeans begin to look like conquerors and thieves rather than "settlers" of virgin land.

To cite any population estimate, high or low, without rehearsing a litany of qualifications papers over the tremendous controversy that lies at the heart of the population debate. The temptation simply to throw up one's hands is enormous.

Anthropologist Shepard Krech, after reviewing all the currently available literature, argues for a figure in the range of four to seven million. Those inclined toward the highest numbers, he points out, have assumed that lethal European diseases emerged early, spread across wide expanses of the continent, and were always fatal to vast numbers of Native Americans. Yet the documentary record for these epidemics is extremely minimal, and some of the evidence that does exist undermines this set of assumptions. That said, whether Krech's estimate is indeed sensible, as he submits, remains open to debate. Probably the only sure thing that can be said is that the notion of a *true* figure for the precontact population is a chimera.[8]

MANY EGG BASKETS

To survive in North America, the Indians exploited the seasonal diversity of the various landscapes they inhabited. This was especially true in the far northern reaches of New England, where cold and frost, in addition to the stony soil deposited by the glaciers, made agriculture a risky and difficult venture. Compelled to adopt hunting and gathering, Native Americans found that in a temperate climate, the spring and summer months offered a plentiful supply of food. From March through May, the Indians used nets, weirs, and canoes to catch fish on their way to spawn upstream, while migrating birds such as Canada geese and mourning doves further bolstered the food supply. In the summer months, they also gathered various kinds of nuts and berries. By the fall, however, as the temperature turned colder and the region's plants began storing energy in their roots, the Indians ventured inland to find other sources of food. Eventually breaking up into small hunting groups, men set off after beaver, moose, deer, and bear, tracking the animals through the prints they left in the snow; women cleaned and prepared the meat, while tending to the campsites. In contrast to the summer, when food was in abundance, February and March often spelled privation, especially if a lack of snow made it more difficult to follow the animals. The Indians thus exploited various habitats, migrating across the landscape depending on the season of the year. As one European observer noted, "They move . . . from one place to another according to the richness of the site and the season."[9]

In the South, a warmer climate more conducive to agriculture allowed the Indians to combine farming with hunting and gathering to produce an even more secure subsistence diet. With the onset of warmer weather, late in February or early in March, men built fires to clear trees and ready the ground for planting. Women then formed the soil into small hills, sowing corn and beans, while planting squash and pumpkins in trenches between the mounds. Mixing such crops together had a number of important benefits that typically led to bumper agricultural yields. As the different plants competed for sunlight and moisture, the seed stock eventually became hardier. The crop mix may also have cut down on pests, as insects found it difficult to find their favorite crop in the tangled mass of stalks.

Meanwhile, bacteria found on the roots of the beans helped to replace the nitrogen that the corn sucked out of the soil, enhancing the field's fertility. But the so-called "nitrogen-fixing bacteria" were never able to add back all of the nitrogen lost, and fertility eventually declined, spurring the Indians to move on to find another area of trees to burn.[10]

Southern Indians scheduled hunting and gathering around their shifting agricultural pursuits. In the spring, after burning the trees, men set off to catch fish. In the summer, the Indians along the coast moved further inland to hunt turkeys and squirrels and gather berries, returning back downstream in time to harvest crops in the fall. The Indians were so attuned to the seasonal variation that characterized the forest that they often gave the months such names as "herring month" (March) or "strawberry month" (June) to describe the food they had come to expect from the landscape. Meanwhile, as the weather turned colder, nuts and acorns proliferated, attracting such game as deer and bears. As the animals fattened themselves on the food, their coats became thicker, making them inviting targets for Indians, who in the winter hunted them for meat and clothing.[11]

A similar seasonal subsistence cycle based on farming and hunting and collecting prevailed further west on the Great Plains. Apart from climate, which despite the potential for drought favored agriculture, soil on the midwestern prairies was as much as a full foot deeper than the two to four inches commonly found in New England. In the valleys of the Platte, Loup, and Republican rivers in present-day Nebraska and Kansas, Pawnee men and women capitalized on the excellent soil and favorable weather conditions by first burning areas during the early spring. Women then sowed corn, beans, and squash in small plots during April and May, hoeing them periodically. Women also spent the spring gathering Indian potatoes, an abundant root crop often relied on in periods of scarcity. In July and August the Pawnees packed the dry foods—wild and domesticated—that they harvested in the river valleys and used them to sustain themselves as they journeyed to the mixed-grass prairie west of the 98th meridian to hunt buffalo. (Buffalo thrive on the grasses—blue grama, buffalo grass, and red three-awn—primarily because they find them easy to digest.) In September, the Pawnees returned to the river valleys to harvest their crops, before leaving again in November for the plains to hunt buffalo. The primary goal of this system of hunting and horticulture—in existence for centuries before the coming of white settlers to the plains region—was to obtain a diversified set of food sources. It might be termed a "not-putting-all-your-eggs-in-one-basket" approach to deriving a living from the land.[12]

Obviously the Indians transformed the ecology of North America in their efforts to survive. But two points about their particular relationship with the land are worth underscoring. First, ample evidence suggests that in many instances, Native Americans exploited the landscape in a way that maintained species population and diversity. In California, for instance, Indians pruned shrubs for the purpose of basket making, but took care to do so during the dormant fall or winter period when the plant's future health would not be jeopardized. Similarly, shifting agriculture tended to mimic natural patterns in a way that modern agriculture, with its emphasis on single-crop production, does not. Second, dietary security, not the maximization of crop yields, was the most important element of Native American subsistence. At times this decision not to stockpile food could hurt them, even if it contributed to long-term ecological balance. It was common in northern New England for Indians to go hungry and even starve during February and March (when animal populations dipped), rather than to store more food during the summer for winter use. While this failure to maximize food sources may have jeopardized Indian lives, it also helped to keep population densities relatively low. The low density, in turn, may have contributed to the overall stability of these ecosystems, preserving the future prospects of the Indians' mode of food production. North America may well have suffered from a relative lack of biological resources (at least when compared with Eurasia), but the Indians managed to see in the land a vast expanse of possibilities for ensuring food security.[13]

PLEASE FORGIVE US

None of this is meant to suggest that the Indians viewed the land and its plant and animal life in only a practical light. In fact, Native Americans invested nature with a great deal of symbolic value, engaging in ritual behavior and telling stories that tended to complicate the relationship they had with the natural world.

Indian understandings of animals are a case in point. Among the Northern Algonquians, for example, the boundary between people and game animals appears to have been quite fluid and porous. Beavers were seen as participating in social relationships with human beings. One account from the 1760s, written after the killing of a bear, observed that Ojibwa hunters took the animal's head "in their hands, stroking and kissing it several times; begging a thousand pardons for taking away her life; calling her their relation and grandmother."[14] Unlike the Europeans, who tended to uphold a clear and distinct difference in their minds between themselves and the animal world, some Indian groups seemed inclined to blur such boundaries.

The Cherokee Indians in the South, who hunted deer, believed that the animals experienced emotions just as human beings did. Were they to fail to treat deer with the proper respect, the animals, as the Indians saw it, would become angry and act out their feelings on the hunters. According to one Cherokee myth, if a hunter forgot to ask forgiveness for killing a deer, he might make the animal so vengeful that it would retaliate by inflicting disease. The emotional bond they had with animals, in combination with the fear of retaliation, may have led the Indians to refrain from killing more creatures than they needed to survive, creating in the words of one anthropologist a kind of "natural balance" based on the idea that "nature is capable of striking back." But that said, Cherokee myths say nothing about the consequences that might befall them if they killed too many deer. Indeed, any such conservation impulse might well have been undermined by their belief in the reincarnation of animals.[15] Whether they were ecologically minded or not, one thing is clear: In general, Native Americans had a far more symbolically rich understanding of nature than the later Europeans, who generally embraced a utilitarian stance toward game.

FIRE AND FOREST

No Indian practice has done more to undermine the view of precontact America as a wilderness than the native people's use of fire. By the eve of European settlement, large parts of the continent had been radically transformed from forest into open ground—a point underlined by European observers. Of the area near Salem, Massachusetts, the Rev. Francis Higginson wrote in 1630, "I am told that about three miles from us a man may stand on a little hilly place and see diverse thousands of acres of ground as good as need to be, and not a Tree on the same." Puritan Edward Johnson remarked about New England that it was "thin of Timber in many places, like our Parkes in England."[16]

Similar observations about the openness of the landscape applied further south as well. One Andrew White, on a trip along the Potomac in 1633, remarked that the forest was "not choked up with an undergrowth of brambles and bushes, but as if laid out by hand in a manner so open, that you might freely drive a four horse chariot in the midst of the trees." After arriving in Florida in 1538, Hernando De Soto and his party of 600 men spent three years exploring a large section of the South, including parts of present-day Georgia, Alabama, Mississippi, Arkansas, and Louisiana. On their extensive travels they found the land—save for swamps—to be eminently unobstructed.[17]

Besides a source of ignition, it takes favorable weather in combination with fuels dry enough to burn for a wildland fire to start. Some parts of North America—Florida, for example—are more conducive to fire than others—such as New England—are. But within these geographic parameters, the Indians seem to have burned the land for a number of different reasons. In the South especially, burning provided a frontline defense against fleas, biting flies, mosquitoes, and ticks. By thinning the forest, burning also facilitated travel and hunting and made it easier for Native Americans to avoid surprise attacks from human and animal enemies. On the Great Plains, they lit fires to signal the discovery of buffalo herds or the approach of whites.

Fire also played an important role in Indian subsistence strategies. It was especially useful in creating environments attractive to game animals such as deer, elk, turkey, and quail. At various places in the East, burning the land fostered the so-called edge effect, creating an area of open meadowland on the border of a forest. A variety of wildlife flocked to such edge habitats, where Indian hunters easily dispatched them.[18]

Indians also employed fire more directly to improve their hunting prospects. Across the continent, Native Americans used fire to surround animals such as deer

PRAIRIE ON FIRE

Indians set fire to the land, as shown here in Alfred Jacob Miller's 1836 painting, to shape it to meet their subsistence needs. Not all parts of the continent experienced such anthropogenic burning. (National Archives of Canada/c-000432)

and buffalo, killing them as they passed through the one possible path left open (on purpose) for escape. The Sioux, for example, were known to set fire to the plains during their buffalo hunts. According to one observer, the buffalo, "having a great dread of fire, retire towards the centre of the grasslands as they see it approach, and here being pressed together in great numbers, many are trampled under foot, and the Indians rushing in with their arrows and musketry, slaughter immense numbers in a short period."[19]

After tribes such as the Pawnees adopted the horse, they too employed fire, managing the grasslands of the plains to help feed the creatures. Burning the land removed ground mulch and allowed sunlight to penetrate the earth more directly, accelerating the growth of grass and, more importantly, increasing yields during the spring and summer when the horses needed food most. Whites traveling out to the plains, for their part, remained quite aware that venturing through unburned sections of the prairie risked the possibility of inadequate feed for their mounts.[20]

Further west in California, fire had long played a vital role in the ecology of the region. Indeed, much of the state's plant life evolved in response to fire, incorporating the periodic burnings into their life cycles. Native people such as the Wukchumni Yokuts and Timbisha Shoshones set fire to freshwater marshes, thereby fostering the growth of forage for livestock, providing more space for waterfowl nesting, and increasing overall species diversity.[21] The Indians thus harvested food that they themselves played a key role in creating. In this sense, many coastal California environments were human artifacts, the product of Indian burning, and would have reverted to woody vegetation had the native peoples not intervened. The notion of a precontact "wilderness" certainly has no place here.

Although burning played an important positive role in Indian survival, it also had some negative effects. First, fires (especially those that raged out of control) destroyed trees, creating at times a shortage of timber in the grasslands, where such vegetation was scarce to begin with. Second, in upland areas of the South, repeated burning increased erosion and destroyed the mineral content of the soil. Finally, setting fire to some forests, notably oak ones, reduced the nuts and acorns available for human and animal consumption, again potentially undermining a subsistence regime.[22]

The Indians clearly left their mark on the North American landscape. Fire, from both lightning and deliberate Indian practice, produced the open, grassy expanses that dominated large sections of the continent. Such fires also simplified the forest cover. In the South fire encouraged the growth of various species of pine trees, at the expense of such hardwoods as hickory and oak.[23] To call North America on the eve of European arrival a pristine wilderness is to deny the very powerful role that the Indians, with fire as their principal tool, played in shaping the landscape.

CONCLUSION

The native people carried on a complex dialogue with the natural environment, made even more difficult to discern by the limitations of available evidence. But this much we can say: Indians certainly had a deep understanding of the various places in which they lived. Unlike the Europeans who followed them, they experienced the environment on a number of different levels—moral, spiritual, and practical—exploiting the seasonal diversity of various terrains through agriculture and hunting and gathering and producing a great deal of ecological security for themselves in the process. This was a culture founded on attaining day-to-day needs, not on the maximization of production.

Indians unquestionably left their mark on the landscape. In southern New England, for instance, the Indian population may have surged so much in the period immediately before European arrival that it even undermined the subsistence base, degrading the available supply of arable land and bringing on a food shortage.[24] In the end, deriving a living from a place is a complex process, and all cultures are capable of miscalculations, even the earliest ones, who clearly took their cue from daily needs and not from the logic of the market.

To see the Indians as the continent's "first environmentalists," living in harmony with the natural world until the Europeans set foot on the land and destroyed it, is a view that is at best inaccurate. At worst, it is demeaning to Native Americans. It turns them into savages incapable of making aggressive use of the environment and thus unworthy of any rights to the land in the first place.[25] In this sense, it is misleading, if not downright wrong, to term most of what the European colonists encountered when they stepped ashore a wilderness.

2

A TRULY NEW WORLD

It was perhaps the most ill-timed expedition in the history of exploration. In 1587, Sir Walter Raleigh, the English courtier and navigator, recruited 117 people—men, women, and children—to venture to the New World under the command of John White. Their destination: a spot of land roughly ten miles long and two miles wide off the coast of North Carolina now named Roanoke Island. White put the settlers ashore and a few weeks later returned to England to find supplies and additional recruits for the venture. War with Spain, however, delayed his return. In 1590, when he finally managed to make his way back to Roanoke, he found not a bustling plantation, as he had hoped, but utter desolation. Not a trace of the colonists could be found. No one can say definitively what happened to the "Lost Colony." Some suspect an Indian attack; others, that the settlers decided, on their own, to go off to live with the Native Americans. One thing, however, seems certain: Scientific analysis of tree rings reveals that the colonists at Roanoke lived through the worst drought in 800 years (1185 to 1984). Even the most foresighted and resourceful of explorers would have found the task of survival on the island a monumental challenge.[1] Raleigh could not have picked a worse time to launch his undertaking.

Until the voyages of the Vikings beginning in the eleventh century, North America remained isolated from Europe, two worlds going their own separate ecological ways. With the expeditions of the Norse and the subsequent ventures of Spain, Portugal, and Britain, however, the human will to unite the continents triumphed over age-old geologic forces.

As Raleigh's misadventure shows, the colonists encountered a new and potentially life-threatening world on the other side of the Atlantic. North America is a place of climatic extremes, the product of the continent's unique physical configuration. It is the only landmass in the world with both a wide base in the sub-Arctic and mountain ranges running in a north-south direction. Cold air from the Arctic can thus plunge south, where it often meets warm, moist air surging north from the Gulf of Mexico.[2] The result is a turbulent set of climatic conditions that make the land prone to weather extremes such as tornadoes, droughts, and floods. How did the colonists adjust to life in a brand new physical environment? What dilemmas did living in a truly new world impose on them? How did they revamp it to conform to the landscape and customs that prevailed in their European homeland?

CLIMATE SHOCK

One of the hardest problems the colonists confronted was the gap between their preconceived ideas about the natural environment and the reality that faced them on the ground. European views on climate and latitude are a case in point. The colonists believed, mistakenly, that latitude determined climate. They thus expected that Virginia, which has the same latitude as Spain, would also have conditions suitable for growing such crops as oranges, lemons, sugarcane, and grapes. European settlers persisted in this fantasy into the mid-seventeenth century. A pamphlet promoting the virtues of settlement in Maryland from the early 1630s assured newcomers of the likelihood "that the soil will prove to be adapted to all the fruits of Italy, figs, pomegranates, oranges, olives, etc."[3]

It took the colonists until the late eighteenth century to learn that their ideas about climate in America bore little relationship to reality. South Carolina was positioned "in the same latitude with some of the most fertile countries on the globe," wrote historian Alexander Hewit in 1779. "Yet he is in danger of error who forms his judgement of its climate from the latitude in which it lies."[4] As Hewit correctly surmised, latitude, although a factor in determining climate, is not all there is to the story. How a landmass is oriented with respect to the ocean also figures prominently in a region's weather. Because weather comes from the west, the Atlantic Ocean plays a major role in determining the climate of Western Europe. By heating up and cooling down more slowly than land, the Atlantic has had a moderating effect on the region's climate. Marked by relatively small variations in temperature and with adequate rainfall spread throughout the seasons, the humid environment found between 35 and 45 degrees north favors the production of citrus fruits and olives. The eastern part of North America, at that same latitude, does not benefit from the moderating effect of a huge ocean. Instead, a continental climate dominates, one subject to temperature extremes and with rainfall mainly concentrated in the summer, when the hot weather aids evaporation. Growing olives in Virginia is all but impossible.

Despite such misunderstandings, climate figured prominently in the thoughts of the Europeans, especially the British. Climate mattered to them not simply because of its connection to agricultural production and survival but also because the British identified climate as a key element in the character of their people. The English thrived, it was believed, in a moderate climate. They feared tropical heat, holding that such an environment was more suited to the French and Spanish. Travel to the southern part of America was thus perceived as carrying a great risk to life and health.[5]

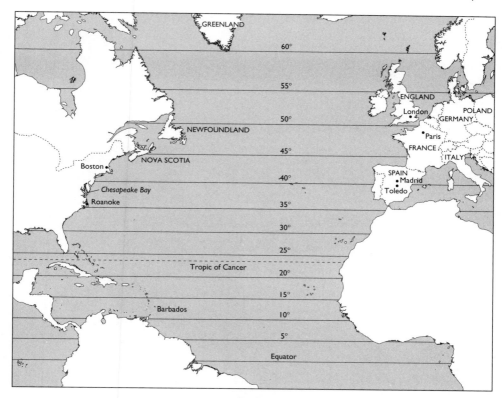

MAP OF COMPARATIVE LATITUDES

In this last respect at least, the perceptions of British colonists matched up well with reality. The hotter the climate, the higher, generally speaking, the death rate. The settlement of the American South is a case in point. Jamestown, Virginia, was the first area in North America to be *permanently* settled by the English, although all the attention devoted to the Pilgrims and Plymouth Rock might easily lead one to think otherwise. The colony of Jamestown is easily overlooked because its checkered history serves as a poor starting point for a great nation. Late in 1606, three ships carrying 144 people left Britain and by the following spring had entered Chesapeake Bay, establishing a colony on the James River, roughly 50 miles from where it empties into the bay. This was a prime agricultural area, with a growing season roughly two months longer than New England's. Although the colony got off to a fine start, its prospects had turned sour by the summer when, according to one observer, "our men were destroyed with cruell diseases, as swellings, Flixes, Burning Fevers, and by warres, and some departed suddenly, but for the most part they died of meere famine."[6]

MAP OF AMERICAN COLONIES

By January of the following year, the colony edged toward the brink of extinction, with only 35 of the original settlers still alive. Indeed, between 1607 and 1625, some 4,800 out of 6,000 colonists perished at Jamestown. "Meere famine," however, does not do justice to the complex set of environmental factors that may have played a role in the staggering death toll. It seems, based again on tree ring analysis, that like their predecessors on Roanoke Island, the colonists at Jamestown confronted extraordinary drought conditions. Drought stalked the Virginia landscape between 1606 and 1612, the worst seven-year dry spell in 770 years (from 1215 to 1984). Malnutrition may well have been the cause of the high death rate, but it would be remarkable if such a severe drought did not bear on the colonists' inability to find an adequate amount of food.[7]

Poor water quality—a situation made worse by the drought—also contributed to the settlers' woes. The colonists relied heavily on the James River, a supply that proved safe for most of the year. But when the summer arrived, the flow of the river lessened considerably. Pools of stagnant water contaminated with human waste created conditions favorable for the spread of typhoid fever and amoebic dysentery. Worse still, the decline in the flow of freshwater allowed saltwater from the bay to intrude further upstream. As a result, the colonists found themselves drinking water laden with salt in concentrations five times the amount recommended for drinking today. Salt poisoning was what plagued them. By sticking close to the river's estuary (the zone where freshwater and saltwater meet) during the summer, the colonists were killing themselves, yet they continued this suicidal behavior until Captain John Smith intervened. Smith noticed that the Indians left the estuarine zone in July, heading for high ground where freshwater springs could be found. Mobility thus ensured the Indians' good health. In the spring of 1609, Smith urged his comrades to scatter into the countryside, and the summertime death toll declined. Unfortunately, Smith soon left the colony to return to Britain and when he did so the colonists again congregated like sitting ducks in Jamestown—victimized by their failure to understand their surroundings in anything approaching the detail of their Indian neighbors.[8]

Malaria also flourished in the warmer southern climate. Once again, the colonists found themselves caught between their erroneous landscape perception and the tragic reality. Europeans first introduced malaria into North America; later a more lethal form of the disease arrived from Africa. High mortality rates plagued the South, but particularly the colony of South Carolina, where some parishes failed to see a natural increase in population until the American Revolution. A common proverb circulating in Britain in the revolutionary period went: "They who want to die quickly, go to Carolina."[9] It was an apt prophecy, in part because the colonists wrongly believed until well into the eighteenth century that swampy areas were relatively healthful. They preferred swamps to cities, where, they believed, arriving ships brought diseased passengers ashore. In fact, the swampy Low Country was precisely the best breeding ground for mosquitoes, explaining the recurrent summer and fall malaria problem.

While colonists in the South faced the problem of heat and its implications for disease, settlers in the North struggled with the reverse situation: persistent cold. If few remember Jamestown in the rush to glorify the success at Plymouth Rock, virtually no one recalls the colony of Sagadahoc in Maine, founded the very same year (1607) that Virginia Company ships landed in the Chesapeake. Bad management, in part, led to the settlement's demise within less than a year. But a bitterly cold winter also played a part. The prospects for settlement, wrote one observer some years later, were literally "frozen to death."[10] It would be more than a decade before the Pilgrims—perhaps discouraged by this miserable initial effort—again tried to establish a beachhead in the region. Focusing only on the successful efforts of the colonists has thus obscured the very real struggle they faced in coming to terms with the environment in the northern reaches of this new world.

Larger climatic forces also may have contributed to some of the problems the New England colonists encountered. History in North America has thus far unfolded, as noted earlier, during an interglacial period. But the ice and cold have already made one major return visit. A Little Ice Age intervened from the mid-fifteenth century to the mid-nineteenth century (although some scientists believe the trend began as early as 1300). Although dubbed an ice age, the period is best viewed as one made up of a series of intense climatic shifts—cold winters, giving way to more mild ones with heavy rains in the spring and summer, switching to droughts and summer heat waves. The exact cause of the schizophrenic climate is still not completely understood. But a change in the relationship between the ocean and atmosphere may be to blame.[11] Nevertheless, there is little doubt that the most severe cold was felt in the northern hemisphere between 1550 and 1700. During the seventeenth century, the temperature of the water off the coast of New England rivaled that found in the Labrador Sea today.

During the most severe part of the Little Ice Age, the New England colonists experienced one of the most significant early challenges to their survival: severe food shortages in the years 1696, 1697, and 1698, precisely the years when the cold was at its worst. The winter of 1697–1698 was probably the coldest winter on record in the seventeenth century. Near winter's end, the Puritan Samuel Sewall lamented the consequences of the extreme cold:

> To Horses, Swine, Net-Cattell, Sheep and Deer
> Ninety and Seven prov'd a Mortal yeer.

By this time, New England's population—which may have increased as much as four times between 1640 and the end of the century—had already strained the available resource base, turning the region into a net importer of corn, wheat, rye, and other grains. The severe cold in the latter part of the 1690s raised the even worse possibility of famine. In 1696, prices for wheat and maize were one and a half to two times what they were normally. There were reports of people in Boston having to do without bread for weeks at a time.[12]

Focusing on the darker underside of early American history—the famine, disease, and failure—does much to challenge the view that the past has been one direct march onward and upward. But more than undermining the triumphalism that has so marred our understanding of this nation, these examples demonstrate that, like the Indians, the Europeans needed to figure out a way to survive in a literally new world that was as unforgiving as it was unfamiliar.

BIOLOGICAL REVOLUTION

Just as long-term climatic forces such as glaciations shaped agricultural prospects in the New World, so too did ecological changes. The Pleistocene extinctions some 13,000 years ago might seem barely relevant to the European arrival. But without those extinctions the colonists probably never would have succeeded to the degree that they did in dominating North America.

In the first place, the Pleistocene mass death, by eliminating most of the big mammals in the Americas, helped to remove a major source of disease. Unlike Eurasia, the New World's lack of cows, pigs, horses, and other domesticated species (capable of transmitting disease to human beings) insulated it from epidemics. And if the first human settlers, the Paleoindians, did indeed journey to the continent by passing across the Bering land bridge, the cold environment would have filtered out diseases and killed off the sick, preventing illness from being passed along to descendants. Prior to the end of the fifteenth century, the Native Americans had acquired no immunity from a variety of illnesses that Europeans had lived with since they were children. Smallpox, measles, whooping cough, chicken pox, malaria, typhoid fever, cholera, yellow fever, influenza, and amoebic dysentery were all unknown to the Indian immune system and would have remained foreign to them had not the European Age of Discovery reunited what geological forces had rent asunder hundreds of millions of years before.

The epidemiological upheaval created by European contact with the New World is difficult to fathom. Precisely how many Indians lived on the continent before the arrival of the colonists is, as we have seen, the point of some contention. But whatever the exact population figure, no one disputes that the Native American population loss by 1900 was truly monstrous. Even assuming that a million people inhabited the continent—an implausibly low number—some two-thirds of them were gone after four centuries of European contact. The higher initial population figures, which seem more likely, yield a rate of attrition between 95 and 99 percent, one of the most dramatic population reductions in the history of the world.[13]

Smallpox, a horrific disease once described by British historian Thomas Macaulay as "the most terrible of all the ministers of death," was one of the greatest killers. Merely breathing air contaminated by a smallpox victim who had coughed or sneezed could result in infection. Since the virus often survived in dried-up bodily secretions that clung to bedclothes or blankets, an activity as mundane as sweeping the floor could cause contaminated particles to float through the air and be inhaled. And with a 10- to 14-day incubation period, smallpox was easily spread, as seemingly healthy people exposed to the disease infected others in their travels.[14]

The Spanish first introduced the disease into Hispaniola in 1519. Eventually, the deadly virus worked its way across Puerto Rico, Cuba, and Mexico before landing in what is today the United States. The first recorded epidemic occurred in the 1630s among the Algonquians of Massachusetts. "Whole towns of them were swept away, in some not so much as one soul escaping Destruction." The disease wreaked havoc in New England and ultimately spread west to the St. Lawrence and Great Lakes region, devastating the Huron and Iroquois of New York in the 1630s and 1640s. Mortality rates ranged as high as 95 percent. When a sailor suffering from the disease set foot in Northhampton County, Virginia, in 1667, smallpox began its march through the South. According to one report, Indians in Virginia "died by the hundred."[15]

Some colonists did not regret the demographic collapse, using it as a pretext to assert their claims of sovereignty over the land. John Winthrop, governor of the Massachusetts Bay Colony, observed in 1634, "For the natives, they are neere all dead of small Poxe, so as the Lord hathe cleared our title to what we possess." Others, realizing their dependence on the native people and their knowledge of the land, extended help in times of sickness. When the Plymouth colonists learned of the Indian Massasoit's illness, they "sente him such comfortable things as gave him great contente, and was a means of his recovery."[16]

Seeing the enormous advantages that accrued from the decimation of the Indians by disease, some colonists may have taken matters upon themselves. During Pontiac's Rebellion in 1763, British soldiers, under the command of Gen. Jeffrey Amherst, distributed smallpox-infected blankets to the Indians. Whether Amherst ordered his subordinates to employ the virus against the Indians surrounding Fort Pitt or not (and the evidence suggests that he was not the first person to dream up the plan), the move coincided with a major epidemic in the spring and summer. Although the blanket affair has gone down as one of the most notorious efforts to employ disease as a weapon, biological warfare was by no means uncommon in the eighteenth century. At the time, such behavior even conformed to customary codes of conduct during European wars.[17] Still, most of the smallpox epidemics spread mainly without design.

The Europeans imported far more than disease into America. They also brought Old World plants and animals with them, species that had never before been introduced into the New World: plants such as wheat, rye, and bananas and animals such as horses, sheep, pigs, and cattle. Old World plants and animals expe-

HOW HORSE WILL TRAVEL

Transporting large animals such as horses to North America necessitated special devices and extreme care. Despite such measures, many of the animals died en route. (Robert M. Denhardt, The Horse of the Americas *[Norman: University of Oklahoma Press, 1975])*

rienced such amazing success that historian Alfred Crosby has deemed this development a "biological revolution." The Pleistocene is an excellent place to go looking for an answer to the enormous biological success the Europeans experienced. Once again, the massive animal extinctions some 13,000 years ago shaped the course of modern history. The elimination of the bulk of the continent's large mammals may have created huge, empty eco-niches into which European livestock entered with spectacular success. Meanwhile, the introduction of Old World plants may have doubled or perhaps even tripled the number of food crops available for cultivation in the Americas.[18]

More than just seeds came to the Americas. An entire knowledge base too had to be imported. Rice is a case in point. Of the 20 or so species of rice found on earth, only two ever became domesticated. One of those species originated along the Niger River in Mali. Although it is commonly believed that Europeans brought rice to the Americas, in truth, Africans played the key role in this particular intercontinental biological exchange. Only West Africans, enslaved and shipped across the Atlantic from their homeland along the "Rice Coast" from Senegal to Liberia, knew how to cultivate the crop productively. African women, in particular, possessed the detailed knowledge of soil and water conditions and the ins and outs of processing and cooking rice necessary for success with this staple. Racist notions, however, seem to have kept scholars from recognizing the truly fundamental role played by Africans in the biological revolution that swept across the New World.[19]

In some respects, Eurasian biology succeeded all too well. In 1609, rats stowed aboard British ships overran the Jamestown colony, while black flies, cockroaches, and a host of plant weeds—dandelions, chickweed, and stinging nettles—found their

"TO BE SOLD"

Slaves from the west coast of Africa, where tidal rice cultivation had long been practiced, provided indispensable knowledge to southern planters. This late-eighteenth-century advertisement calls attention to the homeland of newly arrived slaves being auctioned outside of Charleston, South Carolina. (Library of Congress)

way across the Atlantic, much to the chagrin of the colonists. Even the Indians commented on the weeds. They dubbed plantain "Englishman's Foot" after watching it repeatedly sprout wherever the colonists ventured. As one Indian source observed, the weed "was never known before the English came into this country."[20]

On balance, the European settlers greatly benefited from the biological exchange that accompanied the journey to America. Perhaps the most important payoff came as New World plant foods such as maize, potatoes, beans, and squash crossed the Atlantic in the other direction, allowing farmers to optimize the use of European soil and weather conditions. The importance of maize alone, which can flourish in areas that are too dry for planting rice and too wet for planting wheat, cannot be overstated. The plant went on to become one of the world's premier food crops. "The Indian Corn, or Maiz," wrote one colonist in 1701, "proves the most useful Grain in the World." Maize could grow in a large number of different environmental settings. "It refuses no Grounds, unless the barren Sands, and when planted in good Ground, will repay the Planter seven or eight hundred fold."[21] It is unlikely that the population of Europe could have surged to the extent that it did in the two and a half centuries after Columbus without the New World crops.

KEEP OUT

Apart from the biological baggage, the colonists also brought a variety of cultural beliefs and practices that profoundly affected the land. Chief among these was a commitment to private property—the idea that people could erect boundaries and claim exclusive use of a parcel of earth. But first the colonists had to gain possession of the land itself. The Indians, as already noted, engaged in a complex relationship with the land, relying on mobility to exploit the natural environment's seasonal diversity. Thus they did not settle permanently and improve property in the way that the English expected. According to one seventeenth-century British observer, Indians had "no particular property in any part or parcell of the country, but only a general residencie there, as wild beasts have in the forest."[22] In other words, Indians did not establish private property in land. They did not improve the land by fencing and farming the soil in the way the English expected, choosing instead, as the Europeans saw it, to merely roam the landscape like wild animals. This view of Indian subsistence thus served as a convenient means for dispossessing the Native Americans. What the Indians did not improve and own the colonists were free, they reasoned, to take and use for themselves.

Instead of establishing exclusive rights to ownership, the Indian concept of property was far more fluid. Native Americans claimed not the land itself, but what existed on it, such as wild berries, acorns, fish, or game animals. The names the Indians gave to different parts of the landscape are suggestive. It was common for Indian place names to describe the kinds of plants or animals that could be found in a particular locale. Abessah in Maine, for example, translated as "clam bake place."[23] Other place names described locales where eggs could be gathered, where fish could be caught, and so on. In contrast, the colonists tended to use more arbitrary language to describe the landscape, naming places after people and places in their homeland. When the British seized New Amsterdam from the Dutch in 1664, they named it New York in honor of King Charles II's younger brother, James, Duke of York.

Not surprisingly, given their different views of how to relate to the land, the Indians and colonists clashed over the question of ownership. Indians often conveyed land to the colonists. But what the Indians thought they were giving and what the colonists thought they were getting were two different matters. Native Americans commonly believed that they were simply supplying whites with the same rights to land that they themselves had: to use it for planting corn, hunting, or whatever other subsistence activity was possible there. The colonists of course thought they were being given the exclusive right to own the property.

Although they had a less fixed understanding of property, the Indians were not at all cavalier about their land rights. In fact, they were quite aware of the limits and boundaries of their claims. Roger Williams noted that the Native Americans were "very exact and punctuall in the bounds of their Lands, belonging to this or that Prince or People."[24] Although it is tempting to assume that only the colonists possessed the requisite cartographic knowledge to dominate the land, in truth the Indians used their knowledge of the continent to map it, and even to contest the Europeans' efforts to dispossess them. Some deeds even included graphic renderings of the landscape drawn by Indians themselves that reserved for them rights to continue their subsistence practices. In 1703, for example, the Weantinock Indians, who lived and fished for shad and eels along the banks of the present-day Housatonic River in Connecticut, conveyed land to white settlers. But in a map accompanying the deed, the Indians explicitly reserved the right to continue fishing.[25]

Nevertheless, the colonists did ultimately manage to convert the landscape into private property. Eventually, the land would be bought and sold for the purposes of profit, a development that has had enduring ecological consequences. "More than anything else," historian William Cronon has written, "it was the treatment of land and property as commodities traded at market that distinguished English conceptions of ownership from Indian ones."[26]

THE FUR TRADE

Private property had a profound effect on human relations with the natural world. But it was not alone among European institutions in terms of its far-reaching ecological consequences. European commodities markets, and North America's incorporation into them, also had tremendous impact on the continent. Animals such as deer and beaver that Indians had hunted to survive were swept into a burgeoning fur trade and, in places, annihilated.

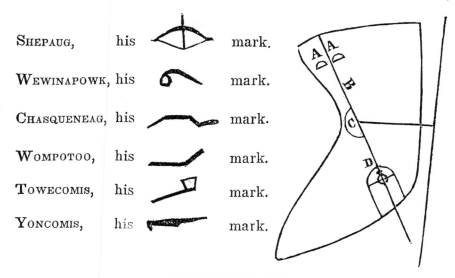

SHEPAUG, his   mark.

WEWINAPOWK, his   mark.

CHASQUENEAG, his   mark.

WOMPOTOO, his   mark.

TOWECOMIS, his   mark.

YONCOMIS, his   mark.

WEANTINOCK DEED

Although the original deed, drawn up on February 8, 1703 is lost, this rendering in Edward R. Lambert, History of the Colony of New Haven (1838), shows the graphic Indians drew to reserve their right to fish at the falls. (Kelvin Smith Library, Case Western Reserve University)

Prior to the emergence of a full-fledged market in game in the seventeenth century, beavers existed in huge numbers. These creatures were (and are) herbivores, meaning that they survived chiefly on plant species. They also constructed dams and canals as a way of creating a suitable habitat near their food sources. Their projects—and they have been known to erect dams 18 feet high and 4,000 feet long—radically altered ecosystems, creating ponds and changing streamflows. The Europeans chiefly valued beavers because their underhairs made excellent felt hats. In the late sixteenth century, such hats were all the rage in England and France, a trend that led to the eventual annihilation of Europe's beavers and the shift in focus toward America. As early as the end of the seventeenth century, overhunting in response to the rise of a market in furs caused the beaver population of southern New England to crash.

Some have held that Indians killed beavers, deer, and other game animals because the Europeans had tricked them into giving up the conservation impulse implicit in their elaborate game taboos. In this view, the Indians saw game animals as family members and only killed what they needed to survive. Then the Europeans entered the picture and perverted this relationship by seducing Indians with various trade goods. One historian has even put forth the controversial view that the Indians blamed beaver and moose for the epidemics that raged through their society, a development that undermined their spiritual relationship with such creatures. This belief then spurred them on an extermination campaign.[27]

One thing we can be sure of: When epidemic disease led to the collapse of the Native American population, the stage was set for a change in the way these people related to game animals. Whether Indians blamed such animals for their illnesses or not, when Europeans arrived bearing trade goods, many Indians willingly accepted them in return for beaver pelts, in part at least to enhance their battered political prospects in a period of extreme stress and demographic upheaval. Wampumpeag, or wampum, beads made from the shells of whelks and quahogs, soon took on enormous symbolic significance among the Indians of southern New England, playing a central role in the fur trade. Eventually, Indians realized that beaver pelts could command a price on the market. By killing the animals and exchanging them for wampum they could bolster their personal power and political prospects.[28]

The decline in beaver had ecological effects that radiated out across the New England landscape. Ecologists consider the beaver a "keystone species," an animal that many other life forms rely on to survive. Beavers create ponds and in the process furnish habitats for turtles, frogs, fish, and waterfowl. Woodpeckers and chickadees nest and forage in the trees downed by these creatures. Thus the decline in the beaver population presaged important changes for species throughout the ecosystem. From the standpoint of humankind, however, the decline had at least one positive effect. With the animals no longer around to tend to them, beaver dams throughout New England collapsed, exposing soils rich in organic matter and creating an ideal environment for grass, which the colonists used as forage for their livestock.

In the South, deer more than beavers played the key role in the emerging fur trade. The warmer climate prevented southern beavers from developing the thick furs so common further north. That fact made the animals far less viable commodities. Europeans used deerskins, however, to make leather—fashioning gloves, saddles, bookbindings, and other items out of them. Until the early eighteenth century, leather workers relied on European cattle for their raw material. But when disease broke out among the French cattle herds, they turned to America's deer to make up for the shortfall.

Southern Indians, like tribes in the North, were initially swayed to kill more deer in exchange for a range of goods, including guns, metal kettles, knives, hoes, linen, and silk. As early as 1699, overhunting spurred the Virginia legislature, in an early preservation effort, to ban the killing of white-tailed deer between February and July. Other efforts to regulate hunting followed. Beginning in the eighteenth century, market forces combined with the Indians' appetite for alcohol to put even heavier pressure on the southern deer population. By 1801, Mad Dog, a Creek chieftain, remarked, "our deer and game is almost gone." In all probability, however, the species never went extinct in the southern colonies. That was because Europeans, concerned about the safety of their livestock, were also killing wolves and other animals that preyed on deer.[29] In this respect, at least, ecology may have gotten the better of capitalism and its markets.

IN THE WOODS

New World timber, like fish and fur-bearing animals, also entered very early into the web of transatlantic commerce. By the late sixteenth century, a wood shortage had descended across Britain, a nation that was heavily dependent on this commodity for meeting its industrial, naval, and energy needs. Indeed, the demand for wood had never been greater. The British fishing fleet, with its sights set on Newfoundland, expanded rapidly in this period, requiring large amounts of wood for building the new vessels. Carpenters used huge quantities of timber for mine shafts, factories, and furnaces. Coopers required staves and hoops in an age when nearly everything of importance was stored and shipped in barrels. Brickmakers, glassmakers, ironmakers, and even bakers used wood for fuel. Producing a single ton of iron required burning all the trees on a two-acre piece of woodland. The late sixteenth-century timber shortage thus struck at the very heart of British economic dominance, and its effects trickled down the social scale. As the price of firewood doubled between the 1540s and the 1570s and then tripled again in another six decades, Britain's poor found themselves shivering through the winter. The development of a transatlantic timber trade would do little to ease this burden, but it did play a major role in bolstering British naval power and in serving commercial needs throughout the Atlantic world.[30]

British shipbuilders had for some time been relying on the forests of northern Europe. But war in the 1650s had severely interfered with this trade. Moreover, these forests rarely had trees that were tall enough to completely satisfy the requirements of British shipwrights. New England's supply of white pines proved especially enticing. Reaching as high as 150 feet and commonly three to four feet in diameter, the trees—more because of their sheer numbers than their actual size—impressed the British colonists.

Beginning in the 1640s, New England's forests also played a vital role in facilitating trade across the Atlantic Ocean. Merchants in heavily deforested Atlantic and Caribbean islands desperately sought wood for shipping wine and sugar. For them, the forests of New Hampshire and Maine were a godsend, supplying the raw material they needed for making the barrels and casks so crucial to the free flow of commodities.

It was not just the forests of New England that suffered to pay for Europe's commercial and naval expansion. The pinelands of the South also experienced significant change. A nearly unbroken 100-mile-wide band of longleaf pines stretched all the way from southeastern Virginia to Texas, a distance of some 1,500 miles. Among the first of the trees to grow in a recently burned or cleared forest, pines produce strong and durable wood perfect for a variety of building purposes. They are also an important source of pitch and tar. Tar helped to preserve wooden fences, and when smeared on the rigging of ships it prevented fraying. Pitch is an even heavier and stickier substance, often painted onto a boat's hull to prevent leaks. War between Russia and Sweden in the early eighteenth century had severely curtailed Britain's access to these products, known collectively as "naval stores" because of their role in maritime pursuits. Conveniently, increased settlement in the Carolinas put the longleaf pine belt near at hand. By 1715, American lumber supplied about half of Britain's naval needs.[31]

At the same time that the forests of the East catered to European economic and military pursuits, cities began to sprout in America, placing an added burden on the continent's woodlands. Within 10 years of Boston's founding, the nearby woods were so depleted that wood had to be imported from as far away as Cape Ann, 30 miles to the north. By the late eighteenth century, one observer near Philadelphia noted that "the forests are everywhere thin." In 1745, Benjamin Franklin bemoaned the depletion of the wood supply, which had once been "at any man's door" but now required shipping of up to 100 miles from hinterlands to coastal cities.[32] And the problem was not confined to the North alone. Just a handful of years after the founding of Georgia in 1732, the city of Savannah was already importing firewood from distant plantations. The scarcity of wood in urban areas became so acute that the colonists felt the need to appoint official "corders," who helped prevent firewood suppliers from shortchanging customers. New York appointed its first corder in 1680, and Boston shortly thereafter.

The depletion of the forest had three main ecological consequences. First, by destroying animal habitat, it affected species diversity. Animals such as bears, dependent on the acorns supplied by oak trees, found it far more difficult to survive in a world without woods. Panthers and wolves also felt the effects of the decline. But like many ecological changes, the results were not always simple. Some species of birds actually flourished as the forests disappeared. Foxes and wolves adversely affected by the clearing trend could no longer prey on bobwhite quail, for example. Other animals such as opossums even preferred the new, cultivated habitat created by the colonists in the South.[33]

Second, cutting down trees also changed the climate. Tree canopies shaded the land from sunlight and kept down summer temperatures on the ground. In the winter, even though the leaves in an oak and hickory forest would be gone, the trees themselves helped to insulate the soil below, moderating the effect of the cold. Felling forests made the landscape more vulnerable to weather extremes, creating soils that in the summer were drier and less conducive to plant growth.

Third, deforestation played havoc with rivers. Trees helped to ensure that streams flowed steadily because their roots absorbed and released water throughout the year. Clearing the forest, however, generally increased the amount of water that ran off into streams. And without tree roots to hold the ground in place, soil too was sent barreling down hillsides. The increase in river sediment left less space for the water and increased the possibility of flooding. Meanwhile, the rapid runoff that followed in the wake of deforestation also made the landscape significantly drier for much of the year.[34] Cutting down large sections of the continent's forests thus helped to set the stage for disaster: droughts and floods that emerged directly from the sharp edge of an ax.

CONCLUSION

What motivated Europeans to journey to North America given the huge risks attached to such a project? The hope for new religious converts, simple curiosity, and, the most commonly cited reason, the search for precious minerals are the factors most often given. But the glitter of gold has obscured from many students of American history the full story behind Europe's quest. Treasure was indeed an important motivating factor, but so was the craving for such resources as fish, timber, whale oil, and land on which to grow wheat, sugar, and grapes. What the Europeans actually found on their travels, and indeed even set out to find, was not so much mineral resources as *biological* ones. By bringing the temperate climate of North America and its rich expanse of land and biota into the orbit of their economy, the Europeans secured for themselves an extraordinary share of the earth's natural capital. Europe, as historian E. L. Jones once put it, experienced a stunning "ecological windfall."[35]

Europe's tremendous good fortune, however, came at the expense of the land and native peoples of North America. Vast changes ensued as the explorers brought the two continents together for the first time in millions of years. Transformations ramified across the landscape: a horrifying decline in the native population resulting from exposure to Old World diseases, the devastation of fur-bearing an-

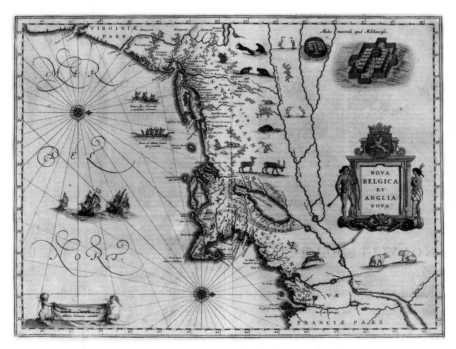

NEW BELGIUM AND NEW ENGLAND
This 1635 map, published in Willem Janszoon Blaeu's Le Grand Atlas, showed animals to be found in the New World. (Bancroft Library)

imals and forests as both became incorporated into European markets, and changes in the very meaning of land itself as the colonists imposed the strictures of private property across the continent. The white settlers encountered a literally new world and then proceeded—perhaps naturally enough—to reinvent it in conformance with the image they had of their European homeland.

Yet despite such enormous ecological success, the Europeans in no way liberated themselves from the constraints imposed by the natural world itself. They too, like the Indians, had to figure out how to wrest a living from the land without undercutting the resource base that made possible their way of life. And even then, the colonists were hardly in complete control of their ecological destiny. Natural forces could intervene to upset the best-laid plans and wither dreams into dust and death in this new and foreign place.

3

REFLECTIONS FROM A WOODLOT

In 1845, nature writer Henry David Thoreau (1817–1862), seeking to escape the hustle and bustle of daily life, went looking for a quiet little piece of land free from the intrusions of New England's thriving agricultural economy. Ironically, he had to settle for an old woodlot in Concord, Massachusetts, a place where farmers routinely ventured to find fuel to heat their homes. One of the nineteenth century's leading critics of progress and its impact on the natural world, Thoreau came of age in a region thoroughly transformed by human action, a place of fields and fences so devoid of forest and animal habitat that the largest mammal commonly encountered was the muskrat.[1]

In Concord, near the legendary Walden Pond, Thoreau built himself a cabin and lived in it for about two years. The journal he kept while there formed the basis for his most famous book, *Walden, Or Life in the Woods*. "When I first paddled a boat on Walden," he wrote, "it was completely surrounded by thick and lofty pine and oak woods." Relishing that fond memory, he continues: "But since I left those shores the woodchoppers have still further laid them waste, and now for many a year there will be no more rambling through the aisles of the wood, with occasional vistas through which you see the water. My Muse may be excused if she is silent henceforth. How can you expect the birds to sing when their groves are cut down?" At roughly the time that Thoreau headed to Walden, some 60 percent of the New England landscape had been converted from forest into open fields, almost the exact opposite of today, where the reverse ratio of forest to open space prevails. The incessant cutting of trees to create new farmland and supply households with fuel drove Thoreau to distraction. As he put it: "Thank God, they cannot cut down the clouds."[2]

The domesticated countryside Thoreau confronted was the product of endless hours spent cutting down trees, planting fields, and tending fences, as the colonists and their descendants entered into battle with the earth and its ecosystems. In simple terms, an ecosystem is a collection of plants, animals, and nonliving things all interacting with one another in a particular locale. Left undisturbed by humankind, the New England landscape would eventually revert largely to inedible woody matter, to forest. Ecosystems in such "climax" states contain only small quantities of human food. Agriculture tries to stop nature from evolving toward this food-scarce condition and instead guides the land into yielding a supply of crops suitable for human consumption. Tillers of the soil seek to turn the landscape into an agroecosystem, a collection of domesticated plants for feeding people. Farming is always a battle with the natural world, a struggle to keep nature from doing what comes naturally.

How did the landscape Thoreau sought to escape come to be? What kinds of threats emerged to stymie farmers in their quest to simplify the region's diverse set of habitats? What was gained and lost, ecologically speaking, as the woods, to paraphrase Thoreau, went prematurely bald?

FROM FORESTS TO FIELDS

When the colonists arrived in New England, forest was the dominant form of vegetative cover. It was the main obstacle standing between them and their quest to remake the region into an agricultural utopia. Initially, the Europeans went in search of cleared areas suitable for planting crops, appropriating Indian fields and thereby saving themselves from the backbreaking labor involved in clearing forestland. Plymouth and many other New England towns, for instance, were established on old Indian fields. One early settler was even confident that enough "void ground" existed in New England to serve the short-term needs of all those who chose to venture overseas.[3]

Eventually, however, population growth outstripped the supply of Indian land, forcing the European settlers to cut down more forest themselves. For most of the

WALDEN POND

In 1845, Henry Thoreau moved into a cabin on this spot in Concord, Massachusetts, a place where local farmers cut wood for fuel. (Library of Congress)

colonists, cleared, arable land was the landscape most familiar to them from life back across the ocean. It took time to become accustomed to the hard labor involved in cutting down the woods. In the northern colonies, trees were usually chopped down, although sometimes a technique known as girdling was used. Girdling, a practice far more common in the South, involved cutting a horizontal channel all the way around the tree, which stopped the vertical flow of sap. Deprived of sap, the leaves would die and the branches eventually fell off, leaving the surrounding land dry and suitable for planting.

New Englanders, however, generally clear-cut the forest, in part because the demand for fuel wood and lumber encouraged it. The market for potash, an alkaline substance that came from burning hardwood trees, also drove farmers to cut and burn the woods with a vengeance. Used to manufacture soap, glass, and gunpowder and to bleach linens and print calicoes, potash served a range of industrial uses but at the expense of farms, which lost the nutrients that the ashes would otherwise have released back into the soil had they not been exported to market.

With their very existence dependent on the successful production of food, farmers had little if any time for removing stumps and stones. Instead, they adapted to the half-cleared fields by planting Indian corn (maize) and grass; both grew well in such an environment. A pattern of "extensive" farming began to emerge. Rather than carefully tending arable land, engaging in crop rotation, manuring, and the thorough removal of stumps and stones—all recognized as part of proper agricultural practice in Europe—New England farmers simply exploited the soil and then forged ahead with the clearing of new land. Cutting down trees remained hard work, but it was easier to partially clear the land, plant it, and then move on to another small plot than to constantly improve the soil on one field to the high Old World standards. The colonists were too busy figuring out how to produce food rapidly to worry about efficient agricultural practices. Disheveled-looking their fields may well have been—indeed, many travelers commented on the rather sorry shape of the colonial landscape—but they were also serviceable and well adapted to surviving in a new, land-rich environment.[4]

Early on, the colonists adopted the Indian practice of planting corn along with beans and pumpkins or squash. These plants reinforced one another, resulting in high agricultural yields. The stalks of corn facilitated the growth of beans by giving them a structure to climb. The beans, as noted earlier, replenished the nitrogen that the corn drained out of the soil, bolstering fertility. And the pumpkins were a valuable source of food in the pioneer environment. "All kind of garden fruits grow very well," wrote Puritan Edward Johnson in 1654, "and let no man make a jest at pumpkins, for with this fruit the Lord was pleased to feed his people to their good content, till corn and cattle were increased."[5] After a few seasons, however, the colonists slowly began the process of transforming New England into an image of the Old World, planting European grains such as wheat and rye alongside the maize, a crop they never abandoned in part because it proved a more reliable source of food.

New England, unlike the South, did not center its economy around an export crop like tobacco. Nor were its soils as fertile as those in the mid-Atlantic area—by the eighteenth century, the great grain-producing region of the colonies. Instead, New England's soil had a moisture content that made it especially suited for growing grass to support livestock. Grass played the pivotal role in the region's farm ecology. "To what produce is your climate best adapted?" George III asked Massachusetts Governor Thomas Hutchinson in 1774. "To grazing, Sir," responded Hutchinson. "Your Majesty has not a finer Colony for grass in all your dominions: and nothing is more profitable in America than pasture, because labour is very dear."[6]

The grass fed cattle that, in turn, produced manure that was spread over the fields as fertilizer for growing corn and other crops. Grass and cattle helped to maintain soil fertility—the key to reproducing a sustainable form of farm life—by recycling nutrients back into the fields. It is no wonder then that the colonists especially valued the region's meadows—grassy, uncultivated lowlands found along rivers or salt marshes. Old beaver ponds, the Europeans no doubt delighted in realizing, often became meadows, especially as the species was hunted to extinction. Meadow grass (hay) grew every year in these areas—no planting or cultivation needed. For the first two centuries of European existence in New England, meadows provided a crucial source of winter fodder. And best of all, they required little work on the colonists' part. Early New Englanders settled such river sites as Concord, Sudbury, Dedham, and Medfield, Massachusetts, precisely to partake of the free grass. The hay supported the livestock, while animal manure regenerated the soil. In effect, the colonists maintained soil fertility and food production by relying on the nutrient subsidy provided by such natural meadows.

Farming the land in this way was a delicate balancing act, made even more unpredictable by an assortment of threats from predators and plant disease. New England's wildlife had long been a problem for those practicing agriculture, affecting not just the colonists but also the original farmers in the region. Crows and blackbirds (probably redwings and grackles) attacked seeds sown by Indians, forcing them to erect platformlike watch houses, often staffed by children, for scattering the birds. Although not nearly as simplified in terms of species diversity as the fields the Europeans tended, the agroecosystems maintained by Native Americans required this energy expenditure—the work involved in fending off birds—to return satisfactory yields. Generally speaking, as the landscape strayed from its diverse forest state, the more open it became to pests and disease and the more work and energy it took to maintain it in an agricultural form.

As the colonists remade New England into a replica of the Old World landscape, abandoning corn, beans, and squash for fields planted with European wheat and rye, they ran into trouble. Passenger pigeons posed an early threat. Known to fly in flocks ranging in number from hundreds of thousands to millions—reportedly taking hours to travel by and leaving dung several inches thick on the forest floor—the birds descended in droves on grain fields. In 1642, the pigeons attacked grain in a number of Massachusetts towns. They also fed on the acorns and chestnuts in the surrounding forest, driving the settlers' hogs (set free to feed in the woods) to the brink of starvation.[7]

Native species of insects also found the new sources of plant food a major attraction. So many grasshoppers converged on the grain crops of the first Massachusetts settlements that the colonists were reportedly forced to use brooms to sweep them into the ocean. In 1646, caterpillars swarmed the region, becoming fairly regular visitors to the colonists' grain fields in the ensuing years. The Indian practice of burning the land held down these insect populations. But with the Native Americans largely driven from the land and the prospect of a brand new source of concentrated food—the wheat and rye—insect populations reached new heights.

Livestock too was threatened, especially by wolves. It took only a decade after the Pilgrims first arrived for a bounty to be placed on the gray wolf, with all the colonies eventually following suit. Sometimes especially rapacious animals might elicit stronger measures. In 1657, New Haven, Connecticut, posted a sum of five pounds for anyone who could kill "one great black woolfe of a more than ordinarie bigness, which is like to be more fierce and bould than the rest, and so occasions the more hurt."[8]

Some of the threats to agriculture were of the colonists' own making. A fungus known as the black stem rust (or "blast") proved devastating to rye and especially wheat. When the colonists brought barberries from Europe to North America to make jam, they also imported, unwittingly, this fungal parasite that used the barberry as a host. In the eighteenth century, a number of New England states passed laws aimed at eliminating barberry bushes, but with penalties rarely assessed, their effect remains open to question. The blast proved so insidious that in some areas of New England it came close to completely annihilating the wheat crop.

By arresting forest growth and replacing it with an abridged form of plant life, the New England colonists found themselves locked in a battle with various pests and diseases. Simplifying nature had its costs. Sustaining this streamlined agro-ecosystem required the input of a great deal of human energy—whether that meant sweeping insects into the sea or pursuing wolves through the forest—to achieve the desired results.

MALTHUSIAN CRUNCH

Even if pests and disease could be fended off, there was still the threat posed by too many people pressing against a limited resource base. In much the way that the British economist Thomas Malthus (1766–1834) would later outline, population began to outstrip New England's land supply as early as the 1720s. This trend, combined with an economic slump that began at the outset of the century, presented a serious challenge to the farm economy.

The Malthusian crunch hit the older towns of eastern Massachusetts first. As population expanded against the limits of a finite supply of land, these settlements became more crowded. Inheritance customs added to the problem. Typically the eldest son received a double share of the estate left by the deceased; the remaining shares were divided evenly between both sons and daughters. During the first few generations, the division of land in this way still allowed each succeeding generation a sizable enough piece of property to operate a successful farm. But as the eighteenth century unfolded, the repeated division led to progressively smaller estates. In the 1600s, land holdings commonly ranged between 200 and 300 acres; by the second half of the 1700s, farm size plummeted to the point where the average holding may have been as small as only 40 to 60 acres. Reverend Samuel Chandler of Andover, Massachusetts, who had seven boys to take care of, wrote in the 1740s of being "much distressed for land for my children."[9] Relentless population pressure also forced up the price of land in older towns outside of Boston, such as Concord and Dedham, Massachusetts. Malthusian pressures may even have compelled New Englanders to rethink their views on inheritance. By the 1720s, some Massachusetts farms were being passed down intact to the oldest son, with the other siblings left to either migrate or find some other means of support. America, the land of opportunity, was in trouble.

The ecological effects of the rise in population are difficult to pin down. Some historians have blamed the population and land imbalance for soil exhaustion and a consequent lowering of agricultural production. New England agriculture was beginning to unravel. Increasing population and prevailing inheritance patterns ran up against the ecological wall created by worn-out soils. "Patriarchy," historian Carolyn Merchant writes, "had come into conflict with ecology."[10] But whether the declining yields stemmed from soil exhaustion or some other factor is unclear.

Population growth alone does not wear out the soil; certain agricultural practices do. Some historians have argued that New Englanders bankrupted the soil by suspending efforts to recycle nutrients back into it. They planted year after year but failed to properly use the manure necessary to keep the soil in good shape. Colonial farmers remained wedded to an extensive mentality—looking for new fields instead of improving the yields of the ones they had—that kept them from employing any of the basic reforms necessary for ecologically sustainable agriculture. Inefficient farming meant declining soils and falling agricultural yields, a pattern made all the worse by population growth.

A more satisfying interpretation of New England's demographic dilemma and its ecological consequences emerges when we focus on natural hay meadows—the heart of the region's agriculture. Meadowland provided a vital source of food for livestock and, through the manure the animals generated, a nutrient boost for the soil. Farming under this system required just the right amount of land suitable for crops, livestock, and hay. Achieving the correct balance between these various types of land uses held the key to putting agriculture on a solid ecological footing. When the demographic crunch emerged in the eighteenth century, it made life for the younger generation difficult in at least one major respect. It now became harder for them to gain access to the right configuration of landed resources, that is, cropland, pasture, and especially meadowland. Soil exhaustion, per se, may not have been the main problem in Concord and other older New England towns, places where farmers lived and died by the availability of natural meadows. Access to meadowland and marsh grass attracted the early colonists and contributed to the birth and longevity of these settlements. Perhaps it can explain their downfall as well.[11] When population pressure and inheritance customs made meadowland inaccessible to increasing numbers of young farmers, the diversified basis of the agroecological system suffered. America's experiment as the land of opportunity foundered on the limits of meadow grass.

Into this distressing and delicate social and ecological context marched the British with their challenge to the autonomy of the 13 colonies. On four occasions between 1764 and 1773, Parliament asserted its right to tax the Americans, with the last attempt ending in the famous Boston Tea Party. Land pressures alone did not cause the colonies to break with Britain, but they certainly provided a context that made Parliament's attempt to subordinate the colonies all that more intolerable.[12] That Concord, Massachusetts, a town buffeted by the changes outlined here, would serve as the starting point of the American Revolution was no accident.

THE VOLCANIC SHADOW

Population pressures aside, New England farmers did have to deal from time to time with conditions of scarcity. To some extent, this problem was an annual event. For centuries, the changing of the seasons exerted one of the most important constraints on food supply and diet. Climate change added to the problem, creating, if not a systematic food crisis, then periodic shortages that left some New Englanders hungry.

Although they did not move through the landscape to exploit its seasonal diversity, New Englanders found that the time of year determined the availability of certain critical foods. The fall harvest provided the greatest variety of things to eat, as the last of the fresh food from summer was combined with winter provisions. Rye and wheat were harvested in the summer. Apples were also gathered late in that season, and soon thereafter corn and beans were brought in from the fields. Meanwhile, pigs and cattle were slaughtered and salted down for winter use. Following this period of ample food came the winter season, when the diet of the average New Englander was at its most monotonous, consisting often of little more than pork, peas, and bread. But the toughest dietary challenge occurred in the early spring when many families had reached the end of their stored provisions and found themselves scraping the bottom of the grain bag and meat barrel. In April 1803, one New England man described his family's dire dietary straits:

"At breakfast my wife gave me an account of our family—asked me if I had brought home any money to buy provisions for us. I told her I had but very little. 'Well,' she said, 'our meat and meal, and about every other article are nearly gone, and what shall we do?' I reminded her that the Lord had provided for us when we were in great straits, and I doubted he would not now. I told her she must pray for what she wanted, but this did not satisfy her; she wept bitterly." Only with the advent of warmer weather did the threat of scarcity recede as seasonal foods such as fish, which annually ascended New England's streams, became more readily available. As one proverb had it, "We hope meat will last 'till fish comes, and fish will last 'till meat comes."[13]

Climate change may have posed an even more significant threat to diet and agriculture. The period from 1750 to 1850 marked a transition away from the cooler temperatures of the Little Ice Age toward a warmer climate. Such change, however, brought with it unpredictable weather. That posed a problem for farmers, who relied on set patterns to know when to plant and harvest their crops. During any given year, a Massachusetts farmer faced the threat of a killing frost— which might destroy as much as half of the fall crops—at any time between August 29 and November 17. Late spring frosts were equally hard to predict. In May 1773, farmers near Portland, Maine, sowed their fields with wheat and rye; by the middle of the month, potatoes and maize had been planted and were beginning to sprout. The prospects for a good harvest looked excellent—that is, until frosts on May 19 and May 22 killed the burgeoning crops. An entire month's worth of labor evaporated, literally overnight.[14] With the weather changeable and prone to extreme conditions for so much of the growing season, farmers found it hard to plan ahead.

On at least two occasions, global climate change, connected to volcanic eruptions around the world, teamed up with various other factors to create food shortages. Hunger became a serious issue during the spring and summer of 1789 throughout New England, upstate New York, Pennsylvania, and Canada. A visitor to the Green Mountains of Vermont observed: "The year 1789 will be remembered by Vermont as a day of calamity and famine. . . . It is supposed by the most judicious & knowing that more than $\frac{1}{4}$ part of the people will have neither bread nor meat for 8 weeks—and that some will starve."[15]

The causes of the calamity were severalfold. Some contemporary observers blamed the Hessian fly—a pest purportedly brought by German mercenaries recruited to fight in the Revolutionary War—which attacked the wheat crop. (In truth, the fly had troubled American farmers for some time before 1776.) The plant and the insect, as it turns out, originated together in Asia. The fly, which thrives in cool, damp weather, invades the wheat and its larvae feed on the crop, in the end destroying it. Inclement weather conditions conducive to the spread of the fly surfaced in 1788 and 1789 because of an unusual global climate pattern. Volcanic eruptions in Japan and Iceland sent millions of tons of dust into the atmosphere, reducing the amount of sunlight reaching the earth, lowering global temperatures, and adversely affecting the food supply.

The extended winter weather compelled many farmers to exhaust their winter fodder, leading them to slaughter their cattle rather than see them starve. The cold weather also forced them to postpone planting. Given the especially short growing season in northern New England, any such delay raised the prospect that the crops might not mature before a frost killed them in the fall. Farmers became alarmed and some at least began hoarding grain, driving up prices.[16]

Just how unpredictable the weather could be was demonstrated again in the early years of the nineteenth century. Another period of extraordinary volcanic activity between 1811 and 1818 brought more unstable weather. Agricultural prospects declined and soon a dearth prevailed. On April 13, 1815, the eruption of Mount Tombora in Indonesia lifted huge amounts of rock and ash into the sky. It was the greatest volcanic event in over 300 years. "The bright sun was extinguish'd," wrote poet Lord Byron from Britain 16 months after, "and the icey earth/Swung blind." On a "dust veil index" designed to measure the obscuring impact of volcanic ash on global weather patterns, the famed 1883 Krakatoa eruption registered a 1,000. Tombora rated three times that.[17]

By 1816, the Tombora eruption resulted in severe cold across New England, as well as in much of the western world. Snow and ice were reported in parts of New England for all 12 months of the year. "I presume the oldest person now living knows of no such weather the 8th of June," wrote Joshua Whitman, a farmer from Maine, in 1816 after a three-hour snowstorm. "Many of the leaves of the trees are blown off and to pieces by the roughness of the weather." The exceptionally cold conditions unquestionably affected New England agriculture. Assessments of the 1816 harvest from every part of the region confirm that the corn crop was nearly a total loss. The hay crop was small, and the harvests of wheat and rye were anywhere from fair to normal. (The effects of the cold were felt even in the South, with crop deficiencies reported in South Carolina.) The rise in corn prices created a dearth in New England. In the interior parts of New Hampshire, "the cattle died for want of fodder, and many of the inhabitants came near perishing from starvation." In Vermont, families reported being forced to subsist on hedgehogs and boiled nettles.[18]

What was happening in New England was part of a much larger calamity that historian John Post has dubbed the "last great subsistence crisis of the western world," a transnational disaster that may have spawned social and economic upheaval throughout Europe and North America. The volcanic activity serves as a reminder that seemingly irrelevant natural processes in far-off lands can shape the course of American history. Despite the efforts of historians to view it as a self-contained region with its own unique history, New England remained part of a globally interdependent environment with its fortunes tied to whatever distant fires happened to be brewing in the earth.

GO WEST, COLD MAN

Climate may also have played an important role in spurring westward migration. With the Indians and British forced by the 1790s out of New York, New Englanders had an unobstructed path westward. In 1795, an observer in Albany, New York, counted some 500 sleighs loaded with the personal effects of entire families. As a result of the migration west, the population of New York rose fourfold between 1790 and 1820 to 1.4 million, making the state the most populous in the nation.[19] Why did people suddenly become so footloose?

Many factors were involved. Increasing population pressing against limited land, especially meadowland, certainly played a role. In 1825, the completion of the Erie Canal facilitated the transport of produce from the Midwest to the East, a trend that tended to undermine New England's agricultural prospects. But it is difficult to fully comprehend the particular timing of the exodus, especially the logic behind its ebb and flow, without examining climate. Colder weather accounts in part for the steady stream of migrants between 1810 and 1820. Over 60 towns in Vermont recorded a loss in population during this time. The years from 1816 to 1817, corresponding to the cold and dearth, witnessed a veritable flood of travelers. "In the pressure of adversity," one observer noted, "many persons lost their judgment, and thousands feared or felt that New England was destined, henceforth, to become a part of the frigid zone." The result was "a sort of stampede" out of "desolate, worn-out New England" to the rich farmlands of Ohio.[20]

Significantly, the push westward abated in the 1820s, precisely the decade when a temporary respite—a trend to warmer temperatures—occurred. Migration out of New England picked up again during the following decade, as temperatures moved significantly downward, perhaps the result of another massive volcanic eruption in Nicaragua.[21] It is obvious that more than weather alone was at work in these migration patterns. But its role should not be ignored.

OFF TO MARKET

For those who stayed behind, the challenges of weather, climate, and demography demanded new agricultural techniques. The trend toward market farming was perhaps the most important development in this respect. Colonial farmers had always engaged in production mainly to meet the needs of their families. In general, farmers frowned on any marketing activity that might put a family's welfare in jeopardy. Still, from as far back as the seventeenth century, some farmers, generally those located near port towns, grew crops for sale elsewhere. After 1650, farmers near Boston supplied grain for trade with the West Indies. During the eighteenth century, market farming expanded further inland in Massachusetts. One study of Massachusetts farm households revealed that in 1771 most were unable to meet all their needs for corn, fuel, and hay without turning to exchange.[22]

The shift toward commercial agriculture was clearly a complex and multifaceted process. Why market production emerged when it did is susceptible to no single answer. But it may have been linked to climate change. The trend toward more erratic weather between 1750 and 1850 coincides with this important economic transformation. Farmers may have increasingly viewed trade as a way of adapting to the unpredictable spates of extremely cold weather, using market transactions to insulate themselves from the vagaries of nature.[23] Even if we do not accept the rise of market farming as inevitable or "natural," we can credit that nature (in the form of climatic forces) played a role in the emergence of this new form of economic organization.

How exactly did the market help farmers deal with bad weather? The sale of livestock was one way. In early New England, settlers commonly allowed their cattle to roam free in the woods, grazing on whatever plant matter they could find. But beginning in the late eighteenth century, farmers began raising cattle with an eye to their market value, herding them off the open range and into fenced pastures and barns. In Brighton, outside of Boston, a cattle market began about 1776 (in response possibly to the need to feed the Continental army). Now when cold weather damaged the hay crop, farmers could sell their cattle before the animals starved.

Livestock helped farmers through hard times in other ways as well. During years of ample grain and hay yields, the surplus food could be used to fatten cattle and swine. In periods of grain scarcity, the animals could be slaughtered to supplement the family diet. During the dearth of 1816, grain was in such short supply in one New England town that no family had enough to board a schoolteacher. Farmers, strapped for fodder, found themselves unable to feed their livestock, a dilemma that ultimately provided a way out of the schooling problem. A farmer with a heifer he could no longer feed stepped forward and offered to slaughter the animal. Cut into pieces and then salted down, the meat provided food for the teacher and education for the students.[24]

Market-oriented agriculture meant that farmers focused increasingly on the production of cattle, hay, and wood, commodities that could earn them money. Farming became more commercial as well as more rationalized. Agricultural reforms, viewed in the early years of settlement as too labor intensive, now proved attractive to a people more concerned with economic efficiency than survival. To increase production, farmers developed artificial meadows, sowing their land with English grasses such as timothy and clover rather than relying solely on the natural grass along rivers and marshes. Between 1801 and 1840, Concord farmers doubled their English hay output from four to eight tons. English grasses entered New England in the mid-seventeenth century, but the colonists, seduced by the "free lunch" provided by natural meadows, had paid them little attention. Evolved to survive on soil compacted by grazing animals, the British hay provided a much higher nutritional content than the species indigenous to the eastern part of North America, and thus was a better source of fodder. Farmers throughout New England rushed off to drain swampy land and sow it with foreign grass, hiring work-ers to help them in their efforts.[25]

New England farming was gradually moving away from extensive cultivation—involving the application of scarce labor in a land-rich environment—toward an intensive regime that bolstered yields by employing far more labor, technology, and capital. Under the newly intensified system, farmers began to show more con-cern with fertilizing the soil and with crop rotation. They also adopted better tools. Harvesting small grains had always been a high-stakes gamble, with no more than a two-week window before the grain became overripe and prone to damage from rain and wind. Farmers needed to hurry, but as late as the early nineteenth cen-tury the relatively primitive scythes available slowed them down. In the decade and a half after 1830, however, improved scythe blades, grain cradles, and hay rakes raised the prospects for success.[26]

Ultimately these agricultural improvements produced a more reliable and di-verse source of food. By the late eighteenth century, New England's food supply became less dependent on seasonal changes. The threat of springtime scarcity re-ceded as grain yields rose in response to ample English hay and improved soil conditions (in part the product of more cattle and manure for transporting nutri-ents). Farmers also turned to kitchen gardens, growing vegetables that could be stored for winter use and increasing the diversity of the household diet. More cat-tle also meant the potential to preserve larger quantities of salt beef, tiding farm-ers over until summer. The seasons—formerly a powerful force in both Indian and colonial subsistence strategies—slowly loosened their grip on everyday life.[27]

CONCLUSION

Thoreau's death in 1862 corresponded with the end of the story that had been unfolding in New England for over two centuries. By the 1860s, the region's long-standing battle to conquer the forest was coming to a close as farmers migrated out of the region to richer soils in the Midwest. Trees began to encroach on the abandoned farmland. But it was a unique new forest environment that developed. The oaks, hickories, and chestnuts that had carpeted southern New England when the colonists arrived did not return right away. A new kind of forest arose, one composed of tree species adapted to life in a landscape filled with fields. It was a simplified woodland, made up largely of white pine trees, a drought-tolerant species with seeds easily dispersed by the wind. The reincarnation of New En-gland as a white pine region was an artifact of its earlier creation as a land of fields and farms.[28]

As the war against the woods ended, a new front in the struggle with nature was beginning to open. Thoreau lamented many aspects of what agriculture had done to New England but saved his greatest ire for the factories and railroads that soon intruded on the landscape. And yet, how ironic that this critic of progress should have earned a living as a surveyor, measuring the land into discrete parcels

HENRY DAVID THOREAU
Although little known outside of a small circle of philosopher colleagues during his life, in the twentieth century Thoreau emerged as the very personification of the wilderness ethic. (Library of Congress)

so it could be bought and sold. Indeed, he had surveyed Walden Woods so extensively that he once wrote, "I now see it mapped in my mind's eye . . . as so many men's wood lots."[29] When he lugged his surveying equipment out to mark off the land, he participated in what became a major preoccupation for nineteenth-century Americans: the transformation of the earth—its soil, trees, and even water—into a set of commodities. Next we explore that shift in detail.

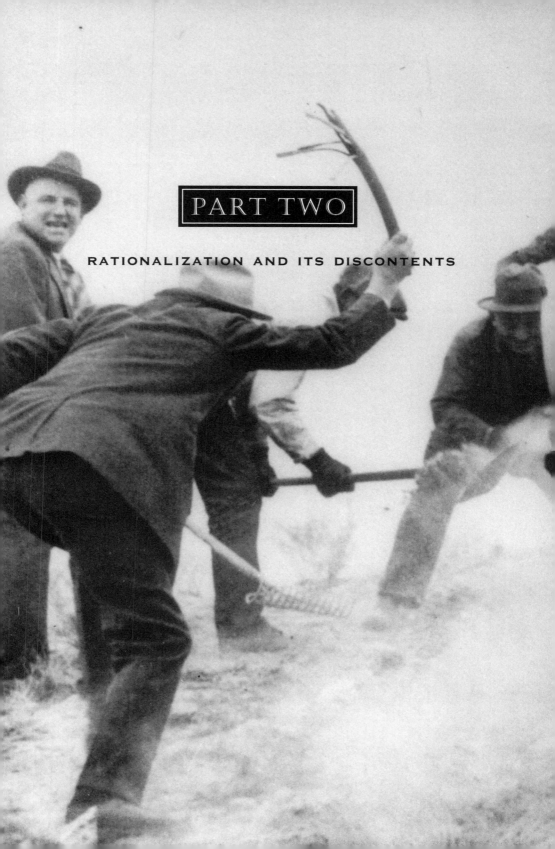

PART TWO

RATIONALIZATION AND ITS DISCONTENTS

4

A WORLD OF COMMODITIES

Henry David Thoreau, despite his work as a surveyor, never believed that landown-ership conferred any true claim to nature. Indeed, he remained, in his writing at least, dead set against the worlds of both property and exchange. In one of his journal entries, he wrote of an encounter with a townsman where he condemned the idea of putting a price tag on nature: "Remarking to old Mr. B——— the other day on the abundance of apples, 'Yes,' says he, 'and fair as dollars too.' That's the kind of beauty they see in apples."[1] Thoreau, for his part, saw in ap-ples, not dollar signs, but the wondrous glories of life on earth. The bard of Walden, however, was out of step with one of the ruling passions of his time.

The most striking thing about the century following 1790 was the way that new technologies and social innovations helped to redistribute natural wealth—water, soil, trees, and animals—among regions. This recycling of natural capital, more than anything else, sets apart the industrial age. The single most powerful tool for parceling out resources was the concept of a commodity. By conceiving of such things as water and trees as commodities, rather than as the face of na-ture, and putting a price on them, it became possible to efficiently manage and reallocate what had now become resources. Reduced to economic units, elements of nature were moved about the country like pieces on a chessboard, redressing resource deficiencies wherever they arose and contributing to one of the greatest economic booms in the nation's history.

FACTORY WATERS

In 1790, the United States was a reasonably prosperous nation of four million people—mainly farmers—packed into a narrow strip of land stretching from Maine to Georgia. Seventy years later, the country had become one of the world's lead-ing economic powers, with a population of 31 million. It led all nations in the amount of wheat it exported and ranked third in manufacturing behind only Britain and France. Average per capita wealth boomed in the first half of the nineteenth century; goods once available only to the wealthiest Americans became ordinary, everyday items. Economic development, in turn, led to the expansion of cities. Between 1790 and 1860, the urban population increased more than 30-fold from 202,000 to 6,217,000. An industrial revolution swept across the North, trans-forming the nation into an economic powerhouse.

Factories, machines, railroads—these are the images that typically come to mind when we think about this new economic order. But industrial capitalism was not simply a techno-economic system; it was also an ecological regime based on the streamlining of nature. One of the earliest efforts at rationalization involved a shift in the use of rivers.

Long before water became a commodity for powering New England's factories, before the dams and canals produced energy, farmers relied on rivers and streams to provide food for the family economy. In the spring, when winter stores ran low, the colonists went fishing for shad, alewives, and salmon, species of fish that return from the ocean to freshwater streams to reproduce. Salmon were so plentiful during the colonial period that as late as 1700 they sold for only one cent a pound. Shad were even more copious, so much so that some felt embarrassed to be caught eating them. As one observer recalled, "it was discreditable for those who had a competency to eat shad." One New Hampshire farmer visited a fishing place on the Merrimack River for six straight days in June 1772 and returned with a remarkable 551 shad for his efforts. The spring profusion of fish brought farmers descending on the region's rivers, turning the most productive fishing spots into veritable carnivals, replete with drinking and card playing. Securing an important supply of dietary protein at precisely the point in the seasonal cycle when they needed it most, farmers may have also turned to fishing to relieve feelings of loneliness brought on by a long, hard winter.[2]

In the middle of the eighteenth century, when Malthusian strains surfaced in New England, fish took on even more importance in the family economy. By this time, inhabitants had lost their embarrassment over eating shad, and the fish sold for a penny apiece in the Connecticut River valley. It is quite likely that the intensification of fishing led to a decline in the stock of migrating fish even before industrialization and the damming of rivers delivered the finishing blow to such species.

With farmers more dependent than ever on fish, economic change and the rise of a new group of river users set the stage for a bitter and protracted conflict over the handling of New England's waters. By the late eighteenth century, the owners of blast furnaces and textile mills forged their way onto rivers, erecting dams to supply factories with power for production. The move, combined with the harmful effects of farming on spawning grounds (as soil from plowed fields ran off into rivers), led to the eventual decimation of the spring fish runs.

Located on the banks of streams at the point where the water descended most steeply, mills for grinding grain and sawing logs had existed since the early colonial period. Noisy and cumbersome wooden wheels captured the energy of the water as it rushed downstream and put it to work. The sounds of progress, however, could only be heard on a seasonal basis. The grinding of grain took place mainly in the fall, so it was hardly a problem for mill owners to open the dam gates in the spring when the fish runs began. But the new breed of factories required a continuous supply of water. Blast furnaces relied on a large leather bellows, powered by a waterwheel, to stoke the fire needed to remove the impurities from iron ore. Such furnaces for producing pig iron ran all day. With winters too cold for working out-of-doors and summers too hot and with fall a time of low river water, spring proved the ideal season to put a furnace in blast. Fishing suffered as a result.

Textile factories were another story altogether. They raised high dams to create enough energy to power large numbers of machines and presented an even greater barrier for fish. The Englishman Samuel Slater, builder of what is reputed to be the first textile factory in America, constructed a dam in the early 1790s in Pawtucket, Rhode Island, that blocked the passage of fish upstream. In 1792, backcountry farmers petitioned the Rhode Island General Assembly to force Slater to remove the dam. But one of Slater's partners used his political muscle with the legislature to head off the opposition.[3]

In its scale, even the Slater mill was nothing compared with the factories that followed along New England's more powerful Merrimack and Connecticut rivers. These enterprises had vast energy needs and, in the quest for greater production and profit, eventually transformed water itself into a commodity. The construction of mills at Lowell, Massachusetts, on the Merrimack River helped lead to this new conception of water. In 1821, a group of New England capitalists known as the Boston Associates purchased land and water rights at Pawtucket Falls. Over the course of the next 15 years, they built an elaborate waterpower labyrinth consisting of seven power canals and a supporting network of locks and dams for providing the energy to make cotton cloth. The Boston Associates formed highly capitalized corporations with the money to build impressive waterpower systems. This new generation of business enterprises outstripped all earlier attempts to control water. But as impressive as the physical infrastructure was, the corporations showed even more creativity and drive when it came to selling the water itself.

In early America, the English common law (a body of legal principles based on court decisions and customs, as opposed to law created by legislative enactments) guided the colonists in their relationship with water. Landowners along a river had rights (not outright ownership) to use the water for fishing or other purposes as long as they did not impede the natural flow to the detriment of others along the stream. When mill owners sold their property, they rarely, if ever, provided precise figures on the amount of water that flowed through it. They simply sold the land with the understanding that the new owner would have whatever rights that the law allowed.[4]

The corporation responsible for distributing water at Lowell, however, disposed of the resource in a completely different manner. One of its chief innovations was the "mill-power" concept. A mill-power equaled the amount of water necessary to drive 3,584 spindles for spinning cotton yarn—the capacity of one of the Boston Associates' earliest factories—plus all the other machinery necessary for transforming the yarn into cloth. The concept enabled the company to easily package water and put it up for sale. By the 1830s, companies at Lowell were even able to purchase water without buying any land, breaking with past tradition. Water itself had become a commodity.

This trend went hand in hand with increasing ecological change, especially in the 1840s as plans accelerated to build a new textile city downstream from Lowell in Lawrence, Massachusetts. With only a five-foot drop in elevation at the river site—compared with a 30-foot fall at Lowell—a dam some 32 feet high had to be built to supply enough energy to the Lawrence factories. The completion of this monumental structure sealed off the Merrimack River, providing the finishing blow to the already severely compromised spring fish runs. What had once been a free-flowing body of water open to salmon, shad, and alewives had been transformed into one long power canal.

With Lawrence rising along the lower Merrimack and the mills at Lowell already running more machinery than ever before, waterpower became an increasingly precious commodity. The unpredictability of rainfall and the increased demand for waterpower eventually spurred the corporations along the lower Merrimack to seek control over the entire river itself, from its headwaters in New Hampshire down to the sea. By 1859, the factories at Lowell and Lawrence had, by virtue of an elaborate series of land purchases, secured the rights to New Hampshire's largest lakes, an empire amounting to 103 square miles of water.

Using a set of dams placed at the outlets of the lakes, agents employed by the Massachusetts factories stored water in the winter and spring for use between July and October when a lack of rain often made water scarce. In the past, the mills were at the mercy of the seasons, with dry conditions dragging down production. The New Hampshire acquisitions, however, liberated the factories from nature's calendar and allowed them to hum all year round.

This grand scheme for controlling the entire river amounted to a massive redistribution of water wealth from New Hampshire to Massachusetts. Some considered what the Boston Associates had done to be tantamount to theft, and they rose up to defy them. In 1859, a group protested by trying to destroy a dam in Lake Village, New Hampshire, a key structure in the Boston Associates' designs for water. The mob was led by a man named James Worster, who in the decade or so leading up to the attack either threatened or destroyed no fewer than three different dams owned by the Boston businessmen. In 1847, Worster ripped off an abutment and chopped down planking belonging to a dam managed by the Great Falls Manufacturing Company in Somersworth, New Hampshire. He believed, probably correctly, that the structure was flooding his property. In 1859, Worster and his compatriots arrived at the dam in Lake Village and proceeded to try to level it using axes and iron bars, but evidently they caused no serious harm.

The attackers were a varied group. Some were farmers angry that their meadows were flooded to convenience out-of-state factories. Others were upstream mill owners who resented being forced to follow the waterpower schedule of the lower Merrimack corporations. Yet more were loggers who wanted the gates lowered to send timber downstream. Some were simply poor and dispossessed—folks who were angry that the economic transformation pulsing through the region had left them behind.

Others eschewed axes and iron bars and turned to the law to redress their grievances. What they found was that the law too was changing, evolving in a direction that conceived of water as a tool for bolstering the new industrial order. In deciding disputes over access to water, the courts had long held to a so-called natural-flow rule: Water had to flow as it had customarily flowed. In the nineteenth century, however, as large manufacturing establishments filled in along the rivers of the North, the courts shifted toward the doctrine of reasonable use. Under this new rule, courts weighed the different interests at stake in the use of water, sacrificing the wishes of some for the larger good of a community. "The rule is flexible, and suited to the growing and changing wants of communities," wrote one New Hampshire judge.[5] Because no one could say exactly what was in the best interests of any community, the rule tended to favor those who used the river to generate the greatest economic prosperity. The doctrine rested on an understanding of water as a commodity in the service of economic growth. Such a view meshed nicely with the needs of the Boston Associates, who in the end had their way with the river.

The industrial revolution meant more than simply the rise of factories, railroads, and new forms of work and social life. It brought about class conflict under the factory roof, to be sure—strikes and walkouts over wages and hours—but it also involved a struggle over nature, over who would control it and for what ends. The mills along the lower Merrimack incorporated the natural wealth available in the countryside into their designs for production and in so doing produced more than just cloth. They generated a chain of ecological and social consequences that spilled out beyond the factories, affecting places and people more than 100 miles away in a completely different state. Nothing better demonstrates the ways in which industrialization led to a major reallocation of natural resources, enriching some at the expense of others.

GRID AND GRAIN

Efforts to commodify water paled beside the far more sweeping attempt to package and impose order on the fertile lands of the Midwest and beyond. Beginning in the 1780s and continuing into the next century, the rich soil of the prairie was neatly divided and sold to farmers. They planted grain and then marketed it throughout America (and Europe), in effect spreading the West's soil wealth throughout the nation.

More than anyone else, Thomas Jefferson initiated the makeover of the West into a checkerboard. Jefferson believed that small freeholding farmers—yeomen, men who could care for their families on their own without the need for hiring hands—formed the basis of a democratic society. "Cultivators of the earth are the most valuable citizens," he wrote in 1785. "They are the most vigorous, the most independent, the most virtuous & they are tied to their country & wedded to liberty & interests by the most lasting bonds."[6] Just the right amount of land was needed to ensure the yeoman's independence and virtue. Too much land would create a nation of tyrants; too little, a country of paupers. Striking the perfect balance between western soil and the people who would farm it became a major preoccupation for this founding father.

To execute his plan for democracy, Jefferson proposed something called the U.S. Rectangular Land Survey—familiarly known as the grid. Under the plan, surveyors were first sent to eastern Ohio with instructions to divide the land into boxes that would measure six miles square. Then they were instructed to divide these larger boxes into smaller ones, one-mile square, which were divided, yet again, into quarter sections measuring 160 acres each, considered to be the approximate size for a single farm. In 1785, Congress passed the grid into law and from that point on this same checkerboard pattern was etched across the West—one of the most far-reaching attempts at rationalizing a landscape in world history.

The grid was the outward expression of a culture wedded not simply to democracy, but to markets and exchange as well. It would aid in the rapid settlement of the country, turning millions of Americans into independent landowners, while at the same time transforming the land itself—its varied topography, soil, and water conditions—into a commodity, a uniform set of boxes easily bought and sold. But the grid was only the first step in the prairie's journey to distant markets.

Once farmers purchased land they needed to plow up the existing vegetation. The prairie grasses that thrived on the organically rich, deep soil laid down by the

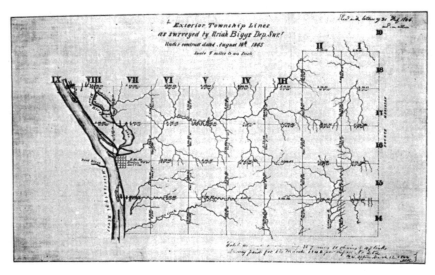

THE GRID

Surveyors finished imposing the geometric logic of the grid on the area east of present-day La Crosse, Wisconsin, in 1845. (Hildegard Binder Johnson, Order upon the Land [New York: Oxford University Press, 1976])

glaciers thousands of years earlier were at first a challenge to cut. Wooden plows with edges made of iron proved virtually useless. Only with the development and spread of the steel plow—invented in 1837 by John Deere, an Illinois blacksmith— did the dense sod succumb. In place of the native vegetation, farmers planted corn and wheat, domesticated species of grass that grow best in a monocultural environment, that is, in fields by themselves. These crops tend to grow quickly, socking away carbohydrates in their seeds. With bread constituting a major component of the American diet, wheat would eventually emerge as the West's major cash crop; acres and acres of some of the world's best agricultural land in states such as Ohio, Indiana, Illinois, Iowa, and Kansas were plowed up and given over to the plant.

In the early years of settlement, farmers grew a variety of crops, including wheat, corn, oats, rye, and barley. Increasingly, however, farmers became more specialized, as commercial agriculture, aided by improved railroad transportation, proceeded apace. Much of the grain ended up in the Northeast, where, by the 1840s, population growth had outstripped the local farm economy's ability to provide. In effect, the West's surplus of soil wealth underwrote industrial development further east.

The railroads not only delivered the products of the rich soils of the prairie into the bellies of easterners. They also changed the meaning of the crops themselves. With water-borne transportation, farmers put their grain into sacks so they could be easily loaded into the irregularly shaped holds of steamboats. The advent of the railroads and steam-powered grain elevators (first developed in 1842) spurred farmers to eliminate the sack altogether. Now grain would move like a stream of water, making its journey to market with the aid of a mechanical device that loaded all the wheat from a particular area into one large grain car. Sacks had preserved the identity of each load of grain. With the new technology, however, grain from different farms was mixed together and sorted by grade. The Chicago Board of Trade (established in 1848) divided wheat into three categories— spring, white winter, and red winter—applying quality standards to each type. Wheat was turned into an abstract commodity, with ownership over the grain diverging from the physical product itself. By the 1860s, a futures market in grain had even emerged in Chicago. Traders could still buy and sell grain in the city as they had long done. But it was now possible to enter into a contract to purchase or sell grain at a particular price. What was being marketed here was not the physical grain itself so much as an abstraction, the right to trade something that may not have even been grown as yet.[7]

The grid helped draw the land into the world of exchange. Then the railroads and the advent of grain-grading systems turned the products of the soil itself into something that could be packaged and sold. It would be hard to overestimate the importance of commodities in nineteenth-century America. They played a key part in mediating the relationship between people and the natural world.

THE BUSINESS OF TREES

Although the farmers who settled the prairie found a surplus of soil wealth, there was one natural resource missing from the landscape, and it was a critical one: wood. Wood played a role in nineteenth-century America akin to that of plastic and steel in our own time. Just about everything that was built, from homes to roads and bridges, involved wood. Its greatest use was in homes for heat. But it also served as fuel for powering railroads and steamboats and to make charcoal for the iron industry. In 1839, Americans consumed some 1.6 billion board feet of lumber. Thirty years later that figure had risen steeply to 12.8 billion board feet. After 1860, much of that wood came not from New England and New York but from the vast forest reserves of the Great Lakes states of Michigan, Wisconsin, and Minnesota. Yet another major reallocation of the nation's natural resources was under way.[8]

The explosive growth in the population of the central United States, almost a fivefold increase between 1850 and 1890, spawned much of the demand for wood. As one early observer put it, the Illinois prairie, "which strikes the eye so delightfully, and where millions of acres invite the plough, wants timber for building, fencing, and fuel." Urban and industrial change in the Northeast also brought about an equally significant demand for wood. New York City alone, which rose to become what one British newspaper called "the London of the New World" after the opening of the Erie Canal in 1825, required huge amounts of lumber. At first the city drew on the Adirondack Mountains to supply its building and energy needs. But rapid economic growth stimulated the need for more distant sources. Canals such as the Erie and others that linked eastern rivers with the Great Lakes opened up the pine forests of the central states to consumers in New York City.[9]

Pine is a durable and strong wood that is soft enough to be easily worked with even the simplest of hand tools, making it especially attractive for building purposes. It also floats nicely on water, which allowed it to be transported to distant markets across the nation. The central and northern reaches of Michigan, Wisconsin, and Minnesota all contained extensive pine forests as well as many large rivers for floating logs into the Great Lakes. What the Erie Canal did for opening the pine forests to markets in the East, the Illinois-Michigan Canal (opened in 1847, connecting the Chicago and Illinois rivers) did for markets in the West. The canal put an end to the log cabins that dotted the plains. Balloon-frame houses replaced them, structures whose lightweight, milled lumber drew down the forest reserves of the Great Lakes states.[10]

The Illinois-Michigan Canal further solidified Chicago's position as the dominant wholesale lumber center in the country. In 1847, some 32 million board feet of lumber passed through the city; in 1851, after the opening of the canal, the figure rose to 125 million, reaching more than one billion in 1869. Chicago was well positioned to mediate exchange between the forested regions north of the city and the largely treeless prairie to the south and west. The city acted like a

huge magnet for timber originating along rivers such as the Peshtigo and Menom-
inee in eastern Wisconsin and the Muskegon, Grand, and Manistee in western
Michigan. These rivers carried lumber directly into Lake Michigan. From there the
wood made its way to Chicago, where wholesalers sorted it and sent it west as
far as Colorado and south as far as Texas.[11]

By 1860, the settlement of the West along with timber shortages in the East
converged with ever widening impact on the pine forests of the Great Lakes
states. Over the next 30 years, lumbering became a full-fledged industrial enterprise in Michigan, Wisconsin, and Minnesota. Instead of simply cutting down
individual trees and sending them to market, something the colonists had done
as far back as the seventeenth century, newly formed lumbering corporations
bought up huge tracts of pineland and set about systematically cutting the trees.
Both the colonists and the later industrialists saw timber as a commodity, but
the latter group adopted a far more thorough and calculating approach to removing trees. In this sense, what happened between 1860 and 1890 represented
a significant break with the past. No longer were farmers in search of extra income the main source for shingles, firewood, and other wood products. By the
1870s, farmers and city dwellers alike purchased forest products from large manufacturing concerns located in the Great Lakes states rather than chopping wood
themselves or buying it locally.[12]

The commercialization of lumbering was in part the product of technological
change. The early, thick saw blades tended to waste a large quantity of wood,
with perhaps as much as a third of the log left behind on the floor as sawdust or
scrap. In the 1870s, however, the British-invented band saw, with its thinner
blade, became standard issue in the Great Lakes states' lumber factories. Meanwhile, the rise of steam-powered mills streamlined production by allowing for
the more efficient, centralized, and continuous cutting of lumber. Steam helped
to automate a variety of tasks, from cutting to the carrying away of waste. Friction feeds, for instance, automatically sent the logs directly past the saws. Mills
also employed steam to heat log ponds, preventing them from freezing and making possible year-round lumber production.[13]

For industrial lumbering to succeed, a way had to be found to neutralize the
effects of the seasons on production. Traditionally, cutting took place in the winter, when snow and ice made it easier to drag logs to the banks of streams. Once
the streams and lakes thawed, workers rafted the logs to mills, where they were
cut into lumber in the summer. If nature did not cooperate—if the winter proved
dry and warm, if the spring thaw was delayed—production would suffer. To
counter the effects of climate on lumber production, loggers experimented with
a variety of techniques for transporting trees out of the woods. In the 1870s, loggers in the Great Lakes states began sprinkling water on sleigh roads, giving them
an artificial ice coating to facilitate travel. The ice reduced the friction and allowed
workers to move larger and heavier loads, with some sleighs capable of carrying
over 100 tons worth of timber.[14]

But all the sprinkling in the world would not save a logger from the threat of a warm winter. Without snow the sleigh roads turned to mud. In the 1870s, a set of snowless winters left lumber companies to ponder ways of liberating themselves from the seasons. Railroads were one possibility. At first, the remoteness of the pine forests discouraged common carriers from laying track. But increasing lumber prices in the late 1870s combined with periodic warm, dry winters compelled loggers to turn to iron rails. By 1887, 89 logging railroads crisscrossed Michigan, transforming logging from a winter activity into a year-round one.[15]

Once the logs arrived at a river, the trip downstream to a mill could be a long and tortuous one. Logjams were common—at times stretching for 10 miles—and became even more frequent as pressure on the northern Midwest pinelands increased in the 1860s. To help keep the logs moving efficiently, barriers called booms (essentially a chain of floating logs) were constructed to control the direction of the timber. By the 1870s, booming companies existed in all the major logging areas of the northern Midwest.

Frederick Weyerhaeuser of Rock Island, Illinois, epitomized the new industrial approach to lumber. Weyerhaeuser had a stake in some 18 lumber manufacturers and oversaw the cutting of timber throughout a large part of the Chippewa, St. Croix, and Upper Mississippi watersheds. By buying up other milling companies and controlling all the processes of production from the felling of the tree to the making of mass-produced lumber, Weyerhaeuser and his associates achieved

LOGJAM

Logjams often developed in the spring as workers floated logs downstream to mills. Men risked their lives trying to dislodge what sometimes amounted to tens of thousands of logs stacked as much as 10 feet high. The jam pictured here occurred on Wisconsin's Chippewa River in 1869. (Library of Congress)

a large degree of both horizontal and vertical economic integration. "In his way," writes geographer Michael Williams, "Weyerhaeuser was the counterpart of Rockefeller in oil or Carnegie in steel."[16]

Lumber barons like Weyerhaeuser could not have succeeded to the degree that they did were it not for the help of the federal government. The government subsidized large-scale lumber production mainly through the sale, at bargain prices, of federal timberland. By allowing lumber companies to amass huge quantities of inexpensive land, it underwrote the industry's growth. Even land granted to railroad and canal companies eventually came under the control of large lumber interests. Perhaps most surprising of all, this enormous giveaway of what one commissioner of the General Land Office in 1876 called our "national heritage" took place without any deliberate decision on the part of Congress.[17]

Of course the lumber companies really had no interest in the land per se. What they wanted was the right to cut the timber. Once the trees were gone, the companies were quite willing to relinquish their land claim, often defaulting on their taxes or selling it cheaply to anyone wishing to farm it. What the lumber barons sought was simply the ability to cut wood. They received, in effect, unconditional licenses to fell timber.[18] The forest and the soil parted ways, as the objectification of trees brought them even more squarely into line with the abstract world of prices and markets.

This calculating and systematic approach to the removal of trees went on with little if any regard for future yields. The end result was predictable: the eventual destruction of the forest. By 1900, the pinelands of the northern Midwest had been logged out. With the consuming public more reliant on pine than ever before, it would not be long before the timber capitalists of the Great Lakes states set off in search of new woods to cut. By the 1890s, they fixed their eyes on the American South, and a decade later the far West, where the name Weyerhaeuser would soon become synonymous with timber.

As the lumber barons headed south, they gave over their abandoned stumplands to settlement companies, which tried to entice immigrants into farming the cutover land. But the land, so full of stones and stumps, proved difficult if not impossible to plow. And in any case, the climate was too cold for agriculture to be successful. But none of this gave speculators such as the infamous James Leslie "Stump Land" Gates reason for pause as they misled prospective settlers into thinking that financial success lay just around the corner.[19]

The wholesale logging of the northern woods created the perfect setting for fires. The loggers, in their haste to remove those trees with commercial value, produced an incredible amount of slash, the branches and other debris left behind in the cutting. In 1871, a Port Huron, Michigan, man reportedly walked for an entire mile stepping from one branch to the next without ever setting foot on the ground. When the farmers moved into the region they set fire to the slash to remove it. Only the fires burned out of control. In the 50 years after 1870, massive conflagrations swept across the landscape. In 1871, referred to as the Black

Year, fires scorched Illinois, Wisconsin, Michigan, and Indiana. Indeed the word "firestorm" was actually coined in response to these disasters, only to be rediscovered during World War II. Fifteen hundred people may have died in a fire around Peshtigo, Wisconsin. Many were asphyxiated in their cellars, where they fled to escape the smoke and heat. Other major fires singed Michigan in 1881 and Minnesota, Wisconsin, and Michigan in 1894.[20]

PESHTIGO FIRE, 1871

The late nineteenth century witnessed some of the worst wildland fires in American history, as steam locomotives, throwing sparks, wound through logged-out landscapes littered with downed branches. (Harper's Weekly, December 2, 1871; Western Reserve Historical Society)

One survivor of the 1871 Peshtigo fire recalled that many people saw the event as proof that judgment day had come, falling to the ground and prostrating themselves before God. "Indeed this apprehension, that the last day was at hand, pervaded even the strongest and most mature minds."[21] But far from being acts of God, the fires were, in fact, a testament to the unintended ecological consequences that derived from the systematic attempt by timber capitalists to bring the natural wealth of the northern forests into the economic mainstream.

PIGEON FEVER

The transformation of the northern woods into stumpland was rivaled by another equally impressive vanishing act: the sudden extermination of the most prolific bird on the face of the earth. In early America, flocks of passenger pigeons—a 16-inch-long, slate-colored bird with violet, gold, and green about the neck and a wedged-shaped tail—literally darkened the sky. "It extended from mountain to mountain in one solid blue mass," wrote James Fenimore Cooper in his 1823 novel The Pioneers about a swarm of pigeons passing near Cooperstown, New York, "and the eye looked in vain over the southern hills to find its termination." A decade later, ornithologist Alexander Wilson from a site near the Ohio River wrote of being "suddenly struck with astonishment at a loud rushing roar, succeeded by instant darkness." He likened the pigeons passing overhead to a tornado and calculated the entire flock to be about two billion birds.[22]

Periodically, the birds made a nuisance of themselves, feasting on the colonists' grain fields. But sometimes the pigeons arrived during a period of scarcity and the colonists managed to kill enough of them to stave off famine, as happened in 1769 during a Vermont crop failure. By the mid-nineteenth century, however, the birds were being pushed to extinction. A number of factors contributed to their decline. The growth of cities played a role. Farmers, who had long been in the habit of killing the birds for food, took to packing them up in barrels and shipping them off to urban areas. Meanwhile, deforestation destroyed habitat and nesting areas. Even the pigeons themselves played a part in their own demise. The birds produced only one egg, limiting their reproductive potential. They also tended to roost in such great numbers that they caused tree branches to snap off, killing their young. The last significant nesting in New England happened in 1851, near the town of Lunenburg, Massachusetts. The following year, Henry David Thoreau wrote: "Saw pigeons in the woods, with their inquisitive necks and long tails, but few representatives of the great flocks that once broke down our forests."[23]

By the second half of the nineteenth century, the northern Midwest had become the pigeon's last refuge. In 1871, south central Wisconsin witnessed an immense nesting; perhaps as many as 136 million pigeons fanned out over a 750-square-mile area. Seven years later, another huge nesting took place, this time near Petoskey, Michigan. Then, quite suddenly, over the course of just a single gener-

HUNTING PARTY

Sportsmen took special trains, like the one pictured here in Minnesota in 1880, to wetlands and other environments, where they hunted various kinds of birds. (Minnesota Historical Society)

ation, the great flocks disappeared completely. In 1890, one observer wrote: "I have often stood in the farm-yard, gazing in rapt admiration, as the setting sun was darkened by the traveling flocks. We miss them more than any other birds."[24]

Why the end came so rapidly remains something of a puzzle. Certainly the rise of market hunting aided by the spread of the railroad and the telegraph played an important part. Where colonial farmers had relied on the pigeon to supplement their own diets, shipping the occasional barrel to the city, the market hunters reduced the pigeons to a pure commodity, with little meaning beyond the price it would bring. Alerted by the telegraph to the start of a major passenger pigeon nesting, market hunters piled into railroads, which by the 1850s expanded throughout the northern Midwest. The trains also allowed the hunters to ship the pigeons back to consumers in various cities, including Chicago, St. Louis, Philadelphia, Boston, and New York.[25]

But technological change and commodification alone probably would not have led to the pigeon's demise had not ecology also intervened. The pigeons fed on the nuts produced by beech, oak, and hickory trees and congregated in huge colonies; they were living proof of the dictum that there is safety in numbers, at least against such predators as hawks and raccoons. Such immense numbers of birds ensured that at least some eggs and young birds would always survive. But when market hunters severely thinned out the flocks, the last remaining pigeons may have been unable to stave off their predators.[26]

Measuring the ecological effects of the pigeon's decline is difficult to gauge. Pigeon dung may seem like an inconsequential thing. But the immense quantities of it produced by the vast flocks of birds had the power to influence the ecology of entire regions, providing an important source of nutrients in roosting areas. The pigeon's demise cut off this fertilizer source with potentially far-reaching effects on plant and forest life.

The bird's extinction may have had an even more profound effect on the relationship Americans had with the land's natural rhythms.[27] We can only imagine how it felt to have spring arrive and look up into the sky at thousands, even millions of birds. When the birds vanished, there was one less natural event to mark the onset of this season, as the passenger pigeons joined the spring migrations of salmon and shad in the annals of extinction. Farmers and urbanites alike became further detached from the cycles of nature as yet another group of animals that had formerly heralded the coming of spring met its end.

Industrial change involved a kind of war waged against seasonal variation. Whether this meant getting water to flow when industrialists, not nature, demanded, or whether it meant building tram roads so that loggers could cut and transport trees all year round and not just in the winter, the result was the same: Seasonal change gave way to the mechanical ticking of the clock.

CONCLUSION

The passenger pigeon's decline was simply one example of the power of industrial capitalism to systematically rearrange the components of an ecosystem, packaging them up and delivering them to where demand was greatest. In the process, resources such as cotton cloth, pigeon meat, and lumber lost binding ties with their place of origin and the human and natural processes responsible for their existence. When the cotton cloth produced at Lowell found its way into a shirt, who, aside from perhaps a mill agent or disgusted fisherman, would ever think to inquire about the true costs of the energy that went into the item, the water that was literally drained away from farmers in one state and made to flow according to a production schedule dreamed up by industrialists in another? Who would possibly see in a roofing shingle the complex set of processes—the federal government's land subsidies, the fires that plagued the land—bound up in this small but essential piece of wood?

Conceiving of things as commodities allowed people to reduce all that was complex and unique, whether pigeon meat, lumber, apples, or oranges, to a single common denominator: price. In a world moving toward such a state, where something as elusive as water could be owned and sold, where grain that did not even exist yet could be purchased, where so many aspects of the natural world were being rendered equal before the almighty dollar, it was easy to overlook what separated one thing from another. Commodities have a special ability to hide from view not just the work, the sweat and blood that went into making them, but also the natural capital, the soil, water, and trees, without which they would not exist. Money, to quote nineteenth-century German sociologist Georg Simmel, had become the "frightful leveler," reducing the uniqueness and incomparability of objects to a state of "unconditional interchangeability."[28]

5

KING CLIMATE IN DIXIE

April 15, 1849, was one of the strangest spring days on record in Dixie. To the disbelief of many, it snowed. For three hours a blizzard raged across Marietta, Georgia. From the southeastern coast west to Texas, the storm and subsequent frost killed cotton, corn, and other crops, as winter refused to relinquish its grip on the land. "The damage done by the late frost you can hardly form an idea unless you were here to see," lamented one South Carolina planter. By all measures, the cold spell was an exceptional event, although it seemed to confirm what James Glen, colonial governor of South Carolina, said about a century before: "Our Climate is various and uncertain, to such an extraordinary Degree, that I fear not to affirm, there are no people on Earth, who, I think, can suffer greater extremes of Heat and Cold."[1]

It has long been realized that climate played an important role in southern history.[2] Growing such staple crops as tobacco, rice, and cotton would have been impossible were it not for the region's long growing season, its ample rainfall, and its warm weather pattern. Beyond this obvious and important insight, however, climate is taken for granted, with most students of the South viewing it as a largely stable and unchanging aspect of life in this region. And yet, it bears noting that slavery and the plantation economy emerged during the Little Ice Age, a period of erratic weather conditions. Growing any kind of crop is a chancy enterprise, made even more unpredictable by a volatile weather regime, a point not lost on the antebellum South's planter class, people who suffered through the 1849 freeze and other cold weather outbreaks, including a devastating one in February 1835, which killed Florida's entire citrus crop.

One does not have to accept the inevitability of the slave-based plantation economy to recognize the important role that natural forces played in it. It is the place of nature—climate, soil, and water—in the history of this brutal system of racial and labor exploitation that is our subject in this chapter.

A MATCH MADE IN VIRGINIA

Located at the northern end of a plantation region stretching as far south as Brazil, the southeastern United States was part of a set of tropical and subtropical environments well suited to growing commodities for European consumption. In Virginia the commodity of choice was tobacco.

From the start, a business mentality informed life in the colony. While the New England colonists had lofty religious ambitions in mind as they ventured across the Atlantic, Virginia's colonists set their sights much lower. Their goal was to create a comfortable rural existence that improved on their more meager prospects back home. New Englanders wrote sermons; Virginians published promotional tracts. They tried to sell their newfound home to those seeking to rise up in the world to the status of gentlemen. To secure a decent standard of living, the southern colonists had to import a variety of foods and finished goods from their homeland. And to generate the money needed to purchase them, they centered their economy on the production of tobacco, a crop of New World origin demanded by smokers in Europe.[3]

In growing tobacco, southerners, like all good farmers, tried to load the dice as much as possible in their favor, before rolling them and taking their chances with nature. In the first stage of cultivation, they planted many different beds with the crop, often separated by great distances, in order to ensure that pests, disease, or cold weather did not rob them come harvest time. But some important aspects of tobacco cultivation were beyond the planter's control. In order for the seedlings to be successfully transplanted, for example, a good, soaking rain was needed to permit farmers to uproot the tiny plants without damaging their root structures. In the decision as to when to cut tobacco, planters again gambled with nature. To fail to cut before a frost would lead to the crop's destruction, yet cutting too early to beat the cold could mean harvesting an unripe crop that might fail to cure properly. Successful tobacco planting thus demanded a great deal of luck, a point not lost on eighteenth-century Virginia planter Landon Carter, who in 1771 lost his tobacco to drought, despite his best efforts to ward off disaster. "Had I not been honestly sensible that no care had been wanting nor diligence neglected," he wrote in his diary, "I should be uneasy more than I am; but as I have nothing of this sort to accuse myself with, I must and do submit."[4]

As crops go, tobacco is extremely demanding of the soil. Even the slightest deficiency in a single element—and the crop required substantial nitrogen, potassium, and phosphorus—tended to result in small yields. The problem, however, was that although the South offered ample rain and a long growing season, its soils left much to be desired. The region had escaped the most recent glaciation and thus failed to benefit from the minerals pulverized by the large masses of moving ice. In addition, the area's abundant precipitation tended to cause minerals to leach from the soil. Worse yet, the soil, especially in the Piedmont section (the rolling hills between the Appalachian Mountains and the Atlantic coastal plain), was weathered and extremely susceptible to erosion. The poor soil was no match for the tobacco plant's tremendous mineral appetite. As one observer put it in 1775, "there is no plant in the world that requires richer land, or more manure than tobacco." Faced with a crop especially demanding of nutrients, the colonial tobacco planter was "more solicitous for new land than any other people in America," moving on to fresh soil once the old land became exhausted.[5]

Tobacco demands much of the soil, but it also asks a lot of those who cultivate it. Few crops are quite as labor-intensive. That was a serious problem in land-rich America, where the price of free labor was high. To deal with this dilemma, planters tried to legally bind laborers to their masters to prevent them from seeking out their own land. White indentured servants, bound by contract, worked to clear the land, using hoes to make small hills for planting tobacco or corn. The soil was used continuously until it became exhausted; then servants went about the laborious task of clearing more land. The system worked reasonably well until the latter part of the seventeenth century, when the price of servants rose while tobacco prices fell. As labor for felling trees became scarcer, the supply of fresh land dwindled. Planters continued to cultivate the same plots of soil. By the last third of the century, the older colonial settlements entered an ecological decline.

Trapped by the reality of failing soils, planters eventually exercised their imaginations. Beginning in the 1680s, Chesapeake tobacco planters turned to their Indian predecessors for inspiration, adopting a system of land rotation. Servants cleared a handful of acres in a haphazard manner. They then planted corn or beans (in between the leftover stumps) during the first year of cultivation, followed by two to three successive years of tobacco. After that, corn combined with beans or peas in years four through seven, followed often by a year devoted to wheat. They then abandoned the field for a generation to restore its soil fertility.[6]

The success of this system—in widespread use throughout the Chesapeake region by the 1740s—depended on the clearing of new tobacco lands every three to four years. A servant might be available to do the initial work, but once his contract expired, planters scrambled to find labor to clear more land. It is perhaps not coincidental that this more ecologically sustainable form of farming arose at roughly the same time that southern planters were replacing their indentured servants with black slaves from Africa. Slavery and shifting cultivation made a perfect match from the planter's standpoint. The land rotation system required the clearing of new tobacco land every three to four years in perpetuity; slavery offered planters a guaranteed labor supply.[7]

The ecological virtues of this new way of relating to the land extended beyond its regenerative effect on soil fertility. It also helped to ward off soil erosion. Slowly the landscape evolved into a patchwork—with some land in cultivation, some in various stages of abandonment, and some filling in with grass and eventually pines and other trees. With no large expanses of open fields, the soil did not fall victim to wind erosion. The fields also contained leftover stumps that acted to check erosion. And with field hands using hoes (not plows) to form hills for planting, the uneven surface trapped water before it disappeared with even more soil. In all, this labor-intensive system of land use remained ecologically sound. Eighteenth-century plantations clearly were commercial ventures designed to capitalize on upswings in the price of tobacco, as well as highly exploitative systems organized around indentured servitude and slave labor. But they were also living proof that occasionally business and ecology could go hand in hand.

ORDER ON THE LAND

Although the land rotation system proved a success in the short run, it eventually broke down under the pressure of population growth. By the last quarter of the eighteenth century, as population densities increased in the Chesapeake region, planters ran short of land and had to shorten the fallow period. The move hindered the land's ability to replenish itself. Shifting agriculture would soon give way to a more intensive form of farming that proved considerably less stable from an ecological perspective.

The imbalance between population and land generated a number of responses. Some men migrated. Some deferred marrying until they had amassed enough land to raise a family. Others believed that agricultural reform was the answer. People such as John Taylor of Caroline and Edmund Ruffin urged the adoption of a more modern and enlightened set of farming practices. Put aside hoes and axes, they advised, and replace them with plows. Remove stumps and other debris from fields and give them a clean and ordered appearance. Fertilize those fields with manure and plaster of Paris and use the land continuously rather than abandoning it to fallow. Above all, they called on planters to use the land intensively and to profit from every last ounce of fertility that the soil had to offer.

Dramatic results ensued as planters acted on this advice. With the soil no longer allowed to rest for 20 years, the amount of land in cultivation increased markedly. Land planted with crops in southern Maryland rose from roughly 2 percent in 1720 to almost 40 percent by the early 1800s. When their lands became exhausted, some planters sold their tidewater plantations and ventured into the Piedmont. There they cleared fresh land and then broke out plows to ready the ground for planting tobacco and corn. But farming the Piedmont, with its steep slopes and soils susceptible to erosion, had significant ecological consequences. Sediment soon sluiced into rivers and streams. During a 1779 flood, one observer described the James River as a "torrent of blood." Beginning in 1780, the port at Baltimore had to be dredged on a regular basis to combat all the silt. The sediment must have destroyed spawning grounds frequented by migrating fish and, with its high concentrations of phosphorous and nitrogen, probably affected other bottom-dwelling organisms as well.[8]

Ironically, as agriculture became more rationalized, as fields became tidier and subject to continuous cultivation, the entire farm system became less "rational" from an ecological vantage point. The fertility was literally mined out of the soil, as planters, in the words of one scholar, "bought land as they might buy a wagon— with the expectation of wearing it out."[9] Business farming and ecology had, for the moment, parted ways.

HARNESSING THE TIDES

While the Upper South turned increasingly to plows and continuous cultivation in the years after the American Revolution, planters along the coasts of South Carolina and Georgia experimented with other means of making the landscape bear fruit. Beginning in the 1720s, South Carolinians focused their energies on rice, growing the lucrative crop on dry soil and relying on rainfall for moisture. They soon discovered that yields increased dramatically if the rice crop was grown on marshlands near the coast, where it could be irrigated with reservoirs and ponds. Slaves imported into the colonies from West Africa, where the rice had long been grown, played the pivotal role in helping southern planters organize their economy around the grain.

However, rice farming seldom went easily. Floods and droughts in the Low Country upset planters' designs for water control. Weeds fed off the rich supply of nutrients and water and posed an even more significant threat. By late spring, slaves could be found toiling away in mud knee-deep in an effort to keep the weeds at bay. Slaves commonly ran away to escape the backbreaking work. At times, plantation managers even resorted to bribery to secure the necessary labor, lest their fields be overrun with unwanted vegetation. South Carolina planter Josiah Smith, Jr., found himself forced to offer his slaves the enticements of beef and rum to keep them from fleeing when "the Grass was very bad."[10]

Then, in the 1740s, planters tapped the know-how of their West African slaves and discovered a means of recruiting nature to their cause. Huge numbers of blacks

SOWING RICE

Although we tend to associate rice with Uncle Ben, in reality it was African women who played the main role in showing Americans how to plant and raise the crop. (Patience Pennington, A Woman Rice Planter *[Cambridge, MA: Harvard University Press, 1961])*

skilled in the cultivation of rice in wetland environments came to South Carolina in the 20 years following 1750. Together they reengineered the landscape to make use of the ebb and flow of ocean tides for flooding and draining rice fields. The tidal flow was helpful in at least two ways. First, it was used to kill weeds. Second, it drastically reduced the need to hoe the fields. Tidal irrigation amounted to one huge energy subsidy for rice planters. The energy came courtesy of the gravitational attraction of the sun and moon, and it lowered the workload demanded by rice cultivation. In 1802, one observer wrote, "River swamp plantations, from the command of water, which at high tides can be introduced over the fields, have an undoubted preference to inland plantations; as the crop is more certain, and the work of the negroes less toilsome."[11]

Although the technique had been discovered in the mid-eighteenth century, it was not until after the American Revolution that tidal irrigation spread widely over the Low Country. Rivers such as the Ogeechee and the Altamaha in Georgia, with large watersheds and deep enough channels to create the right combination of freshwater and saltwater flow, provided ideal locations. The technique was usually practiced by wealthy planters, mainly because of the huge expense in time and money involved in building the proper water control system. Planters had to attend carefully to the direction and flow of the water since the intrusion of saltwater onto the rice fields would spell disaster for the crop. In the 1790s, a group of South Carolina planters made the mistake of building a canal to connect two rivers and inadvertently caused saltwater to encroach on the rice fields, causing the value of some of this land to plummet to a mere fraction of its original price. To avoid such calamities, planters relied on their slaves to erect elaborate systems of embankments and canals, a costly and labor-intensive process. For those who could afford the expense, however, the dividends were great. While inland rice plantations produced roughly 600 to 1,000 pounds of rice per acre, tidal plantation yields were in the 1,200- to 1,500-pound range.[12]

The blossoming of tidal rice cultivation in the years after the American Revolution is best understood as part of the larger national trend toward rationalizing agriculture. Just as the U.S. government employed the grid in the Midwest to divide up the land into tidy little boxes so it could be sold and converted into farmland, surveyors with the same rectangular logic in mind descended across the Low Country, parceling it out into quarter-acre squares. Slaves leveled the ground and built embankments around these squares as well as trunk lines to carry the water from the river to the fields. A staggering amount of work went into reshaping the land for tidal rice cultivation. By 1800, the rice banks on a plantation located on a branch of South Carolina's Cooper River extended for some 55 miles and consisted of more than 6.4 million cubic feet of dirt. In other words, slaves with nothing but shovels and hoes hauled approximately the amount of earth it would take to fill the planet's largest pyramid, Egypt's Cheops, three times. The end result of the slaves' efforts was a reengineered landscape designed to maximize rice production—a "huge hydraulic machine" in the words of one planter.[13]

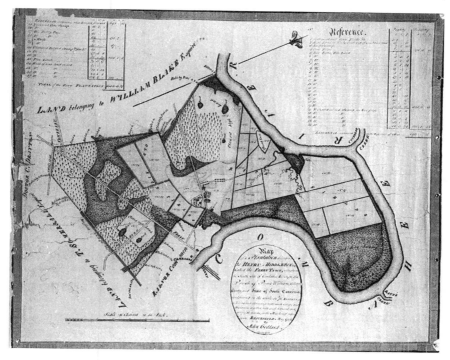

RICE PLANTATION

Using the grid as their guide, planters and slaves carved out this tidal plantation along the lands adjacent to South Carolina's Combahee River in the late eighteenth century. (South Carolina Historical Society Collections)

The impact of the hydraulic grid extended beyond the land into the realm of labor. Slaves on rice plantations worked under a code of conduct known as the task system. Unlike tobacco and sugar plantations, where gangs performed a specific job under the watchful eyes of an overseer, blacks who produced rice received a certain amount of work, a "task," for each day. After completing the assigned job, slaves could do as they liked with their time. Why the task system emerged in the Low Country is not entirely clear, but the unique demands involved in growing rice may account for its rise. Tobacco required meticulous care, while rice, a hardier plant, demanded somewhat less attention. More important, much of the work in rice cultivation centered on the digging of ditches and embankments—discrete, easily measured tasks. And with the aid of the grid, which imposed geometric order on the landscape, plantation managers could assign slaves the job of weeding and hoeing in a self-contained area. A slave could generally perform any operation to completion on a quarter-acre piece of land. As one master put it in the late eighteenth century, "a Task was a quarter of an Acre to weed p. day."[14]

The task system clearly predated the emergence of tidal irrigation. But the development of this new energy source spurred planters to impose even more order on the landscape, as they enlisted geometry to help them get the maximum work from slaves. Tidal energy relieved field hands from hoeing during the summer, but then planters turned around and raised the amount of land a slave was responsible for to half an acre. As the summer workload declined, winter chores increased, with slaves pressed into service maintaining ditches and canals. The surplus energy supplied by the tides did little to improve the quality of slave life, but instead went to fatten the profits of the already wealthy planter class. If anything, working conditions in the fields declined. "No work can be imagined more pernicious to health," wrote South Carolina historian Alexander Hewit, "than for men to stand in water mid-leg high, and often above it, planting and weeding rice; which the scorching heat of the sun renders the air they breathe ten or twenty degrees hotter than the human blood."[15]

If tidal irrigation offered less in the way of freedom for slaves, it also imposed strictures on the planters themselves, tying them more closely to a schedule not of their own making. Georgia planters, for example, had their slaves plant the rice seeds in March, just before the first full spring tide. Later plantings were timed to coincide with the new and full moon, when tides provided enough water to make the seed wet.[16]

As it was, even before the rise of tidal irrigation, rice planters felt compelled to organize their production schedule around the rhythms of nature. Like one-crop agriculture anywhere, rice remained susceptible to attack by predators. No animal presented more problems than the bobolink. These birds swarmed over the rice fields as they migrated north in the spring, returning south for yet another visit in August and September. Planters who were late in getting their rice in the ground used water to help the rice ripen more quickly, before the birds descended again in the summer. But this technique cost them by reducing yields.[17]

Reengineering the landscape to produce rice also spawned at least one unintended ecological consequence. Tidewater areas were already excellent breeding grounds for mosquitoes. Rice plantations, with their carefully designed systems for flooding and draining the land, made the habitat even better for mosquitoes, especially for the malaria-carrying *Anopheles* species. The connection between the cultivation of rice and the increase in malarial conditions did not escape notice among contemporary observers. "These exciting causes of disease lie dormant in the native state of new countries, while they are undisturbed by cultivation," wrote one, "but when the ground is cleared and its surface broken they are put into immediate activity." Although a substantial percentage of Africans were immune to one common strain of malaria, European Americans were not, a fact that compelled many masters to flee the plantations during the warm months.[18]

Despite some disadvantages, tidal cultivation proved enormously successful in boosting rice yields. In part, the surplus energy provided by the tides increased output by allowing slaves to tend to as much as five times the amount of rice they had customarily cultivated on inland plantations. But the success of tidal agriculture stemmed from more than simply an increase in energy. Low Country rice planters were also the secret ecological benefactors of changes afoot in the Up Country, shifts explaining why soil exhaustion was rarely an issue for those in the tidal zone. The settlement and clearing of forest from the steeply sloped Up Country sent fertile topsoil into rivers and eventually on to the rice plantations. As one South Carolina geologist put it in 1860, "the Up-country since its cultivation was first commenced, has been going steadily downstream."[19] Low Country planters, aware of the sediment-rich water being sent to their doorsteps, would use a full tide to flood their land, causing the river water from upstream to deposit its load of fresh soil on their fields.

But the same forces at work redistributing the Up Country's soil wealth—the clear-cutting and settlement of the forest—also increased the threat of floods. Indeed, Georgia rice planters lamented the increasingly severe deluges that damaged their bank and canal systems—and of course their crops—in the years after 1830, especially the devastating inundations of 1833, 1840, 1841, and 1852. On balance, however, the settlement of the Up Country was a nice bonus to the downstream planters, providing a new source of soil wealth to accompany the infusion of energy they received courtesy of the earth's relative position in the solar system.

THE OTHER SOUTH

The steady disappearance of the Up Country's soil into the account books of the Low Country is perhaps an apt metaphor for the divergent economic courses these two regions took in the antebellum period. Although large-scale plantation agriculture was a major component of the Low Country economy, as of 1850 such plantations made up barely a fifth of all the farmsteads in the South. While rice and tobacco planters were engaged in single-crop agriculture for market, small farmers in the Georgia and Carolina highlands practiced a more diversified form of agriculture centered on family survival. Yeoman farmers, who had few if any slaves, worked hilly and sandy soils and often had little choice but to put the safety of their family ahead of exporting products for market. The yeomen and planters thus had two entirely different goals and approaches for relating to the land, a situation that at times brought them into conflict. Although there were many fewer planters than yeomen, the former had far more power and political muscle. As a result, more than just soil disappeared from the Up Country landscape.

Consider what happened to the fish that once swarmed upstream in southern rivers. Although the use of water to power mills occurred on nowhere near the scale that it did in the North, in the period leading up to the Civil War, the South flirted with industrial transformation. Traditional sawmills and gristmills, in existence since the colonial period, became better capitalized and began producing for more distant markets. Rice planters used some of their newfound wealth to build rice mills. Even textile mills, that staple of northern factory production, showed signs of expanding throughout the South beginning in the 1810s. Much as had happened in New England, conflict broke out as mill owners, many of them serving the needs of the slave-based plantation economy, dammed rivers for power, blocking the fish and cutting off upstream farmers from an important food source.

Shad and herring, the main species taken by farmers, normally spend most of their lives at sea, returning in the spring to freshwater rivers to deposit and fertilize their eggs. When they returned, they became easy prey for farmers throughout the southern Piedmont. Reaching at points hundreds of miles upstream from the ocean, the fish, once salted down, composed a major component of the southern diet, especially for the poor. During the eighteenth century, the fish were readily available, easy to catch, and, according to one source, "cheaper than bacon."[20]

Farmers in the Up Country turned to the annual spring shad and herring runs to round out a diet based mainly on corn, deer, rabbit, and squirrels. But in the period after the American Revolution, the intrusion of market relations undermined the pioneer's subsistence as the damming of rivers to aid transportation and industry cut off fish from spawning grounds and led their populations to decline. In Virginia, for instance, tobacco planters in the Roanoke valley petitioned the state legislature for help in making rivers into a means for transporting crops to market. In South Carolina, defenders of a mill along the Tyger River complained of the lack of streams for grinding grain to meet local needs, "much less to manufacture Flour for market."[21] In both these cases, fishing interests came second to commerce and industry.

As market relations made further inroads, those who depended on the fish cried out. In 1787, a group of South Carolina yeoman farmers opposed a milldam across the Edisto River that left them "totally cut off from availing themselves of the common Rights of Mankind." The mill, which cut lumber for sale to Sea Island plantations, blocked the passage of fish, depriving people upstream "of *a necessary of Life*, which their fellow citizens living upon other water courses 200 miles above the said Mills enjoy in the Greatest plenty."[22] Such rhetoric resonated among citizens across the nation in the supercharged atmosphere of the revolutionary era. Up Country yeomen readily employed it to protest the market forces, propelled by slavery, that were slowly coming to the fore.

The southern farmers, much like their counterparts in New England, argued that their common rights were being trampled in the rush to preserve the economic interests of mill owners. Fish, the farmers declared, derived from either God or nature and by right existed to serve the public good. Shad and herring were central to what the historian E. P. Thompson has labeled a "moral economy." By this he meant an economic regime where people had reciprocal rights and responsibilities toward one another, where the self-regulating market based on money did not as yet rule material life, where a code of behavior existed that preserved the welfare of a larger community, even if this proved unprofitable to an individual. In such a moral economy, fish amounted to sacred necessities of life that no one would possibly even dream of destroying.[23]

In fact, the fish did not owe their existence to the abstractions of nature or God. Ecological factors, more than religion, determined whether the fish would lay eggs, as well as whether a river system remained healthy enough to support such reproductive efforts. Changes were occurring in the ecosystem at large, some of which could have affected the ability of shad and herring to reproduce. Ironically, the yeoman farmers themselves may have played a role in causing their own troubles, undermining the fish that formed the basis of their moral economy by chopping down the forest and settling more of the Piedmont. Extensive deforestation took place in the South between the American Revolution and the Civil War, especially in the decade of the 1850s. Erosion increased, as did the sediment load of rivers, benefiting tidal rice plantations, but also burying fish spawning grounds.

The final blow to the fish runs came during the mid-nineteenth century. Commercial fishermen threw huge seines across rivers, systematically exploiting the catch to where it could no longer reproduce. As far as migrating fish were concerned, both the North and South wound up with rivers that were, for all intents and purposes, dead. The moral economy of water had given way to a far more market-oriented calculus, as rivers became biologically impoverished power and navigation canals. Those who had formerly depended on water for food turned to new ways of earning a living from the land. In New England, the possibility of factory employment provided farmers with one way out of this dilemma. But few such opportunities existed for their southern counterparts. There the rise of a market culture meant further expansion of slavery, not more wage work in factories.[24]

SOIL MINING

In the late eighteenth century, when Britain entered its industrial revolution, Low Country planters began searching for a variety of cotton to meet the needs of British textile mills. Georgia planters eventually discovered a kind of long-staple cotton (perhaps brought to the United States from the Bahamas) that flourished along the coast in an area known as the Sea Islands. Extending from South Carolina all the way to northern Florida, the islands proved an ideal cotton environment. The long-staple variety required an exceptionally long growing season, in excess of 250 days without frost, and grew best when nurtured by moist ocean breezes. In both these respects the Sea Island environment cooperated. Between 1785 and 1795, island planters saw their profits from long-staple cotton rise dramatically.

In an effort to cash in on the burgeoning cotton market, planters further inland tried to plant the crop but found that only the short-staple variety grew away from the coast. Short-staple cotton, however, had one serious drawback: The cotton seeds had an annoying habit of clinging to the lint, requiring as much as an entire day to clean a pound of the crop by hand. In 1793, however, Eli Whitney invented the famed cotton gin for separating the cotton fibers from the seeds. From this point forward, the South's fortunes remained tied to the textile-driven industrial transformation that eventually spread from Britain to America.

While northerners moved toward abolition in the 1790s, southerners headed in precisely the reverse direction: a marked expansion in slavery, fueled by the booming cotton economy. Short-staple cotton could be successfully grown in nearly all of the South located below the 77-degree summer isotherm (a line drawn on weather maps to connect places with the same temperature). That fact allowed the slave system to emerge from its coastal confines and spread throughout the Piedmont and eventually as far west as eastern Texas. Cotton could be grown at some distance from the rivers required to transport the crop to market because it was a nonperishable item and relative to, say, grain, far more valuable per unit of weight. It was also a crop perfectly suited to single-crop plantation agriculture with its slave laborers, who carried out the necessary planting, hoeing, and picking under the supervision of an overseer.

Apart from having the requisite number of frost-free days (roughly 200), the South also possessed enough rainfall (approximately 20 inches) and the right precipitation pattern for growing cotton. Too much spring rain and the crop's root system might not take properly in the soil; too much rain at harvest time and the boll might fall off before being picked. With their gentle spring rains, increasing through the middle of the summer and then tailing off, the southern states made for perfect cotton country. Climate helped to forge the cotton South, as the region rose to become the world's leading supplier of the fiber, bolstering the industrial transformation of the North and Europe in the process. By 1860, the United States accounted for two-thirds of the world's supply.

Cotton planters, like their counterparts who grew rice, tried as much as possible to streamline the production process. One of the greatest advances involved a shift in the species of cotton grown. By the early nineteenth century, planters moved from black- and green-seed varieties to Mexican cotton. Unlike these earlier types, the Mexican cotton had large bolls, allowing slaves to pick as much as five times more per day than with the inferior black-seed kind. Economically speaking, this development nearly rivaled the invention of the cotton gin.[25]

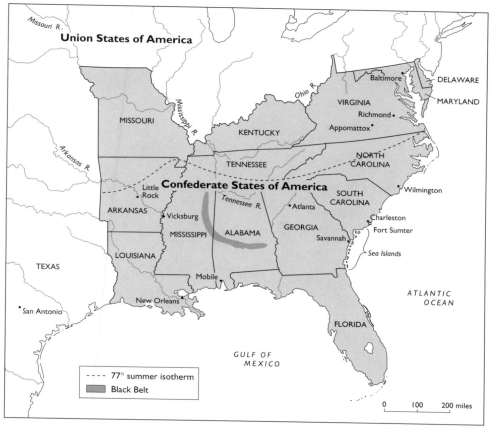

MAP OF THE AMERICAN SOUTH

The region south of the 77-degree summer isotherm is the part of the eastern United States best suited climatically for growing cotton. Within that region, The Black Belt—an area noted for its dark and especially rich soil—led the nation in cotton growing during the antebellum period.

Planters also standardized many of the routines and tasks associated with cotton production. In the early years, slaves used their feet or a wooden tamper to stuff cotton into bags of different sizes. In 1779, a lever press was invented in Mississippi that produced neat, square bales. By the mid-nineteenth century, large plantations with the latest equipment packed anywhere from 40 to 50 bales per day.[26]

But the rise of the Cotton Belt—the name for the vast stretch of South Carolina, Georgia, Alabama, Mississippi, and Louisiana devoted to the crop—rested on more than simply climate and efficient production. By 1800, cotton had spread very little from its initial coastal confines, blocked in large part by the presence of 125,000

"IN THE COTTON FIELD"
The early-nineteenth-century introduction of Mexican cotton, with its large bolls, vastly increased the amount of crop a slave could pick in a day. (Library of Congress)

Indians who still occupied land east of the Mississippi. This fact led many of the South's leading planters to push for their removal. European and American traders had since the late eighteenth century helped to weaken these southern tribes, introducing disease, liquor, and a market for deerskins—undermining their subsistence economies. In the quarter-century following 1814, Andrew Jackson delivered the finishing blow. Jackson, in his capacity first as military officer and later as president, masterminded a systematic removal campaign. The treaties he had written up between 1814 and 1824 alone aided the United States in acquiring three-fourths of Alabama, a third of Tennessee, and a fifth of Mississippi and Georgia.

Jackson succeeded in transforming the communally held lands of the southern tribes into private property available for sale. "No one will exert himself to procure the comforts of life," Secretary of War William Crawford explained in 1816, "unless his right to enjoy them is exclusive." By 1844, only a few thousand Indians remained east of the Mississippi and even they had, in large measure, been forced to accept life under a society based on private property. In the process, they abandoned the communal obligations toward the environment that once undergirded their culture. By the 1840s, the few remaining native people found themselves surrounded by profit-maximizing cotton growers. Unlike their Native American predecessors, the white planters were content to farm hillsides, a trend that over time led to an increase in soil erosion.[27]

Southern whites intent on growing cotton streamed into Alabama, Mississippi, and Tennessee in the 1820s and 1830s, but whether they were pushed or pulled westward defies an easy answer. Clearly, the superior soils available in parts of what was once the nation's old Southwest attracted the attention of settlers. Some people may have abandoned perfectly adequate farmland in search of the greater returns to be found in the Black Belt, a land of dark, fertile soil extending from central Alabama northwest into Mississippi. But far more evidence suggests that between 1780 and 1840, many cotton planters were pushed into such regions by the growing problem of soil depletion.

Buoyed by sharply higher cotton prices, especially in the 1810s, planters in the eastern parts of Georgia and South Carolina became mired in a profit-driven cycle of clearing and land abandonment that left the landscape in a state of disarray. "Tens of thousands of acres of once productive lands are now reduced to the maximum of sterility," wrote one resident of South Carolina's Piedmont in the 1850s. "Water-worn, gullied old fields everywhere meet the eye." In the Georgia Piedmont, some of the gullies on old cotton lands extended 150 feet in depth.[28]

Some abolitionists attributed the South's problem with soil depletion to slavery, arguing that bondsmen had little motivation to sustain the fertility of the land. In the period leading up to 1860, the Piedmont's slave population density correlated nicely with the worst areas of soil erosion. But the problem, according to geographer Stanley Trimble, stemmed not from slavery as much as from single-crop agriculture and the lack of a "land-ethic" among profit-driven southern planters.[29]

It seems unlikely that slavery alone was to blame for the depletion of southern soils, if for no other reason than that family farms in the North also severely depleted the soil. But slavery did create a context for soil exhaustion to take place. With slaves themselves (a form of personal property) constituting over half of the agricultural wealth of the cotton South, land took on secondary importance to planters. Slavery and soil erosion correlated: Planters had few incentives to maintain the fertility of the land when they could just as easily head off toward fresh soil, with their most valuable personal property (their slaves) in tow.[30]

Thus planters failed miserably when it came to maintaining the land's fertility. Very little nutrient-rich manure made it back to the soil for two reasons. First, it required a significant amount of labor to stockpile and spread over the fields. One source summarized the dilemma confronting planters by noting that northern farmers "can well afford to fertilize their little spots of ten or a dozen acres; but a Southern plantation of 500 or 600 acres in cultivation would require all the manure in the parish and all the force to do it justice."[31]

Second, there was not much manure to spread around in any case. As South Carolina state geologist Oscar Lieber put it in 1856, "no manure worth mentioning is saved under the present system." The shortage resulted from a combination of climate, soil, and epidemiological conditions. Unlike the North, the South was not a good environment for growing grass. And without it, there was little feed for cattle, a major source of manure. Acidic soil, combined with the persistent threat of rain at precisely the point in time when fodder crops such as timothy and red clover needed to be cut, made raising grass difficult. Even worse, a parasitic animal infection (babesiosis) spread by ticks further dampened southern cattle-raising prospects. With labor dear and the supply of livestock limited, manure played a minimal role in antebellum southern agriculture.[32]

For a brief period, southern planters had high hopes for Peruvian guano, a fertilizer made up of bird droppings found in various coastal reaches of South America. In the 1850s, declining agricultural prospects and high guano prices caused southern farmers to clamor for federal intervention. It is hard to imagine a U.S. president being preoccupied with bird feces, but in 1850 Millard Fillmore made it a subject of his state of the union address. Six years later, Congress passed legislation allowing anyone who discovered the much-sought-after excrement on an unclaimed island or rock, anywhere in the world, to receive government protection of the claim. The legislation set off a veritable bird-droppings rush, with Americans laying claim to some 59 rocks and islands in the Caribbean and Pacific in the seven years following the act's passage. But in the end, guano failed to rescue the South from soil degradation. Guano imports peaked in 1854 and then experienced a rapid decline due to the expense of the material combined with the massive quantities needed to revitalize exhausted cotton fields.[33]

Slavery, monoculture, climate—all these factors help explain why soil exhaustion threatened southern agriculture in the period before 1840. But to some extent, the focus on cotton at least is misplaced. Cotton was not particularly demanding of soil nutrients, certainly not when compared with corn. By the 1840s, as the North moved toward a more diversified diet (aided by an integrated transportation system), corn remained a mainstay of southern cuisine. Corn is a very versatile crop that can flourish in a variety of different settings. It meshed well with cotton, requiring little care during the season when the cash crop needed harvesting and making up as much as 40 to 50 percent of a plantation's farm value. Its only drawback was that it made great demands on the soil, requiring as many as 13 nutrients to thrive. Planting so much of it thus only added to the South's soil woes.

By the 1840s, the South may even have been shedding its commitment to the single-crop cultivation of cotton. Planters began to devote just two-thirds of their land to cotton and a third to corn and cowpeas, the latter a nitrogen-fixing leguminous plant used to maintain soil fertility. When the cotton lands declined after a couple of years, planters shifted the crop to the soil improved by the peas. This seemingly mundane shift in crop choice, more than the Peruvian guano craze, may have briefly liberated the South from the vicious cycle of land abuse that prevailed for most of the period leading up to the Civil War.[34]

CONCLUSION

What is the relationship between slavery and the environment? One does not have to be a Confederate sympathizer to observe that, historically speaking, slavery has not flourished in very cold climates. There is nothing the least bit natural about slave labor, but in the antebellum South, at least, it owed its rise to a climate that favored the growth of short-staple cotton. The development of the Cotton Belt rested on a set of climatic conditions; without them it is hard to imagine slavery taking on the role that it did in southern political culture.

If nature shaped the evolution of slavery, the reverse proposition—that the slave system had significant environmental implications—seems even more persuasive. Land played a secondary role in a society in which so much wealth remained tied up in owning and trading slaves. It followed that little incentive existed for planters to maintain soil fertility, especially when an expanse of fertile land was always available further west. Thus the stage was set for the brutal cycle of clearing, ecological degradation, and eventual abandonment that characterized southern agriculture in the 60 years after 1780.

Slavery created favorable conditions for this abusive pattern of land use to emerge. But it was the market orientation of planters, especially the great profits that could be made by growing cotton, that drove them forth on a reckless tear through the land, leaving a trail of gullies to show for their efforts. In this respect, the South and the North were not all that dissimilar. In both regions, agriculture answered to a higher force, be it the price of wood, furs, tobacco, or cotton. Southern land and soil came to be looked upon less as a meal ticket and more as a resource organized around the profit motive, with the planter elite content, some exceptions aside, to mortgage Dixie's ecological future.

In the end, however, the South's ultimate ecological legacy rested on its path-breaking role in the emergence of specialized, one-crop agriculture. The commercial farming of staples split production off from consumption, making it difficult, if not impossible, for the end users of these commodities to grasp the enormous social and environmental costs involved in devoting vast areas to growing a single set of plants. Here the southern states did diverge from the northern ones. By focusing so intensively on producing tobacco, rice, and ultimately cotton, the region forged a new, more modern relationship with the land the consequences of which are still felt today.

THE GREAT FOOD FIGHT

Spring 1865 brought misery and death to the beleaguered Confederacy. All that remained of the formerly invincible Army of Northern Virginia was 55,000 desperate and starving troops, men battered by four years of war, their pride melting before thoughts of desertion. The indignities of war mounted. In April, the men trudged toward Amelia Courthouse, Virginia, driven on by the prospect of a rendezvous with rations arriving by train. But a snafu caused ammunition to be delivered mistakenly. As the men dragged themselves forward, they were reduced to eating horse feed—the corn on the cob commonly fed the animals. "Two ears were issued to each man," one soldier wrote. "It was parched in the coals, mixed with salt, stored in the pockets, and eaten on the road. Chewing the corn was hard work. It made the jaws ache and the gums and teeth so sore as to cause unendurable pain." Thus it was that one of the first things Gen. Ulysses S. Grant did after the South surrendered was send three days of rations to the former Confederate rebels, taking the edge off their hunger and welcoming them back into the United States.[1]

The Civil War interrupted many of the normal routines of daily existence. But one basic fact of life remained the same: The nation's citizens, like all human beings, still had to figure out how to feed themselves and the animals on which they had come to depend. The eternal quest to survive biologically, to derive the requisite number of calories from food, was as relevant for soldiers on the battlefield as it was for plantation slaves and factory workers. Biological existence, in turn, depended on agriculture, on the land, soil, weather, and countless other natural factors that went into getting the earth to yield fruit. Even the fate of military actions sometimes hinged on forces beyond human control. Campaigns bogged down along mud roads made impassable by winter precipitation. In one case, rain led a Union commander to call off an assault altogether. Nature did not take a vacation when the nation—wrenched apart by two vastly different political frameworks, one based on free labor, the other on slavery—went to war.

MUD WRESTLING

"After four years of arduous service marked by unsurpassed courage and fortitude, the Army of Northern Virginia has been compelled to yield to overwhelming numbers and resources."[2] Those were the words of Gen. Robert E. Lee, summing up the reasons behind the South's defeat. With 22 million people to the Confederacy's nine million, with 70 percent of the nation's railroad mileage, plus

110,000 factories (to the South's 18,000) producing nearly all of the firearms available in the country, it may well have seemed predestined that the North, with moral reason on its side to boot, won the war. But in 1861, as the first shots went off, the outcome seemed far less certain.

At the start, the South had a number of advantages over the North. It was no secret that the Confederate troops retained a significant edge during the early years of the war in terms of horsemanship, a benefit bestowed on them at least in part by climate, specifically the mild winters that allowed them to spend nearly the entire year outside practicing their skills while their adversaries kept warm by the fire. One British observer went so far as to reckon that the Yankee soldiers could "scarcely sit their horses even when trotting."[3]

The South, it must also be remembered, had the home-field advantage. Confederate troops fought a defensive war on their own territory, a land where many soldiers had been born and raised. Fighting on their home turf also allowed the southern forces to conduct maneuvers in places within easy reach of ration and ammunition stockpiles. Union soldiers, in contrast, were forced to carry what they needed with them. Imagine, for a moment, the logistical problems faced by the northern forces. Every 100,000 troops required each day no less than 600 tons of supplies, 2,500 supply wagons, and some 35,000 draft animals, horses and mules that themselves, it bears noting, required feed and forage if they were not to be starved and worn down by the effort of hauling all that matériel.[4]

As the North was soon to learn, the southern rebels also had a secret weapon in store: the environmental conditions that made travel arduous, especially in the winter. Unlike in the North, the ground froze to only a shallow depth south of the Mason-Dixon line. Poorly drained and consisting of soil composed largely of red clay (at least in Virginia, where much of the fighting went on), southern roads turned into quagmires when it rained, leaving Union supply trains to slog through muck that at times buried mules up to their ears.

No one knew better the problems involved in transporting all that Union food and equipment over roads of such questionable integrity than Gen. Ambrose E. Burnside, whose failures are legendary among Civil War buffs. In January 1863, still smarting from the slaughter his troops took at Fredericksburg late the year before, Burnside drew up a plan to cross Virginia's Rappahannock River in an attempt to outflank Lee's army. Dry weather, unusual for that time of year, gave Burnside reason to feel hopeful. On January 20, 1863, Burnside and his men moved out. By dusk, however, it was raining. For the next 30 hours rain pummeled the region, turning the roads to mush. "The mud is not simply on the surface, but penetrates the ground to a great depth," wrote the Union officer Regis de Trobriand. "It appears as though the water, after passing through a first bed of clay, soaked into some kind of earth without any consistency. As soon as the hardened crust on the surface is softened, everything is buried in a sticky paste mixed with liquid mud, in which, with my own eyes, I have seen teams of mules buried." As de Trobriand concluded: "The powers of heaven and earth were against us."[5]

Muck became public enemy number one for the Union forces, causing some to discourse on the particular perils of the mire found in Thomas Jefferson's home state. "Virginia mud," a northern officer pointed out, "is a clay of reddish color and sticky consistency which does not appear to soak water, or mingle with it, but simply to hold it, becoming softer and softer." As they watched the northern forces struggle through the slop that winter day in 1863, Confederate soldiers smirked and held up signs that read "Burnside Stuck in the Mud" and "This Way to Richmond."[6]

Calling attention to the poor weather and soil conditions in the upper reaches of the South, the New York *Evening Post* opined that "operations in a country and climate like Virginia are more destructive and wasteful than advantageous to an invading force."[7] The disaster along the Rappahannock would eventually be dubbed the so-called Mud March. The North had learned a lesson: Never again would the Union launch a major military campaign in Virginia during the wintertime.

Burnside's miscalculation in the Mud March led President Lincoln to remove him from his post. His replacement, Gen. Joseph "Fighting Joe" Hooker, however, proved even less capable of leading the North to victory. In May 1863, Hooker went down to defeat in Chancellorsville, Virginia, giving the Confeder-

UNION WAGON TRAIN

The massive supply trains required by northern forces often fell prey to the South's bad roads and inclement weather conditions. (Chicago Historical Society)

acy one of its greatest victories. But the South's military fortunes would soon change. No longer able to feed his army positioned on the Rappahannock—his men reduced that spring to collecting wild onions and sassafras buds to survive—Lee decided to invade Pennsylvania, where he hoped to find more abundant provisions while delivering a major blow to the Union. On July 3, 1863, however, Lee lost the battle of Gettysburg. The very next day, news spread that Grant and his troops had held out and snatched a victory at Vicksburg, Mississippi.

In the fall of the following year, Gen. William Tecumseh Sherman captured Atlanta and proceeded to make plans for one of the most daring ventures in military history: a 285-mile march to the sea, to Savannah, Georgia, to be exact, a plan designed to deliver a psychological blow to the Confederacy from which, Sherman hoped, it would never be able to recover. Lincoln approved Sherman's march, but deep down he had his doubts. "I know the hole he went in at," he said when the march began, "but I can't tell you what hole he'll come out of."[8] It was a dangerous—some would say suicidal—plan.

Henry Hitchcock, an officer from St. Louis, reported excellent conditions early in the campaign. But by the sixth day out, things turned for the worse. "At last we get off," he wrote on November 21, 1864, "floundered through heavy clay mud, under rain sometimes heavy, sometimes drizzling, threading our way through and by wagons laboring along, up hill and down, or stuck fast. No wonder the weather is such an element in warfare." Hitchcock went on to describe "ruts today fully 18 to 24 inches deep through stiff heavy red clay, some half liquefied, some like wax, or thickened molasses."[9]

Then, the following day, the skies brightened and remained clear for most of the balance of the journey. "As these memoranda show," Hitchcock wrote on December 10 as the troops approached Savannah, "we have been most fortunate in weather—have had but two days of rain, one of cold (not severe) and one or two others only on which the weather was not everything we could wish."[10] Sherman succeeded in presenting Lincoln with Savannah in time for Christmas. But for the weather, however, Sherman's march could have gone down as one of the most insane misadventures in the annals of military history.

FOOD FOR THOUGHT

When the end came for the Confederacy, General Lee and his troops headed for Appomattox, with all but the officers reduced to eating horse feed. Sometimes, however, the men had to make do with leftovers. C. Irvine Walker, a southern officer, claimed that he "frequently saw the hungry Confederate gather up the dirt and corn where a horse had been fed, so that when he reached his bivouac he could wash out the dirt and gather the few grains of corn to satisfy in part at least the cravings of hunger." Other southern military men, desperate to satisfy their hunger, spent time trying to develop a taste for rodents. "We were keen to eat a piece of rat," one soldier wrote. "Our teeth were on edge; yea; even our mouth watered to eat a piece of rat."[11]

Lee himself had wondered as far back as 1862 whether starvation, more than enemy forces, might prove the greater threat. Camped out in northern Virginia, Lee and his troops found the winter of 1862–1863 especially grueling. In 1862, a drought in the South severely depressed the corn supply, compounding the effect of the already meager meat provisions. Over the course of the war, Lee was repeatedly forced to shift his military strategy to make sure that supply lines remained open, at one point warning the Confederacy's secretary of war of the army's impending doom if it could not be furnished with regular and adequate rations. With bacon and other meat in very short supply, the southern forces were reduced to eating mainly cornmeal. Meanwhile, black humor circulated among the troops. Demoralized by the lack of variety in their diet, some Confederate soldiers talked of the "Fed and the Cornfed."[12]

Meanwhile, the horses pressed into military service suffered as much or worse than the men they served. No one regretted this more than General Lee, a man so fond of, as well as dependent on, the animals that he once administered a lecture to his officers on how to adjust a saddle to care properly for a horse's back. Some horses, desperate for food, chewed the bark from trees and ate small scraps of paper strewn about the base camp. Lee did everything he could to find food and save the creatures. He directed that forage in large sections near campaigns be reserved for the army. He forbade farmers from retaining more than six months' worth of corn for use as feed. He even sent cavalry to distant points to save the forage in a given area for the animals pulling the supply train.[13]

By July 1863, as the tide turned militarily against the South, the quartermaster general reported a need for somewhere between 8,000 and 10,000 horses to take the place of those killed or ruined by starvation and other battle threats. When Jefferson Davis, the president of the Confederacy, ordered troops to Georgia, in the wake of the defeat at Gettysburg, Gen. James Longstreet, in command of the mission, had to relinquish some of his artillery units because he lacked the draft animals necessary to haul the equipment. Near the war's end, so little fodder remained near where the Confederate army camped on the Rappahannock that Lee had to send men and horses as far south as the North Carolina border on forage sweeps. "There can be little doubt . . . ," wrote Douglas Freeman, Lee's foremost biographer, that the great general "saw in the prospective failure of the horse supply one of the most serious obstacles to the establishment of Southern independence."[14]

Barely able to feed themselves, much less their mounts, both armies, North and South, dealt with the limited rations by foraging, a euphemism for what we commonly call stealing. Although required to provide compensation to those from whom they took food or animals, in practice soldiers roamed the countryside pillaging whatever they could find. "The government tries to feed us Texains on Poor Beef," wrote one soldier, "but there is too Dam many hogs here for that, these Arkansas hoosiers ask from 25 to 30 cents a pound for there pork, but the Boys generally get it a little cheaper than that I reckon you understand how they get it."[15]

NOTICE.

To the Farmers of Campbell, Franklin, Henry, Patrick, Grayson, Carroll, Floyd, the Western part of Pittsylvania and Halifax, and the Southern part of Bedford Counties :

The surplus Forage in the above district has been set apart for the purpose of feeding the Public Animals not in service.

All the Corn, Rye, Oats, Hay, Fodder and Straw, not required for the use of the people in the above Counties and parts of Counties, will be wanted by the Government for the purpose above stated.

Stables are being erected at suitable stations in the District, at which Farmers will be expected to deliver their surplus Forage, and for which they will be paid the prices fixed by the State Commissioners. The following are the Schedule Prices at present :

Corn unshelled, $3,95 per bushel; Corn shelled, $4,00 per bushel; Rye, $3,20 per bushel; Oats, $2,00 per bushel; Sheaf Oats, $3,70 per 100 lbs.; Hay, per 100 lbs. $3,00; Wheat Straw, $1,30 per 100 lbs; for baling Long Forage, 50 cts. per 100 lbs.; for hauling Long Forage, 8 cents per mile per 100 lbs.; for hauling Corn, 4 cents per bushel per mile.

It is with great difficulty that the necessary transportation for armies in the field can be furnished. The Government, therefore, cannot supply the teams to haul the Forage from the farms to the stations at which it is needed. It will be necessary for the farmers to do the transportation, for which, they will be paid liberal prices.

JAS. G. PAXTON,
Maj. and Q. M.

Fair Grounds, near Lynchburg, Nov. 13th, 1863.

JOHNSON & SCHAFFTER, PRINTERS, LYNCHBURG, VA.

FORAGE CALL

Constantly short of feed for their horses, the Confederacy called on farmers to supply it with whatever surplus forage they had available. (Lamont Buchanan, A Pictorial History of the Confederacy [New York: Crown, 1951])

As early as 1863, Lee worried that the meager rations provided his troops—18 ounces of flour and 4 ounces of bacon—might be weakening morale. One Confederate officer observed that the Union could easily track the movement of the southern forces by simply following "the deposit of dysenteric stool." In the autumn of 1863, when President Jefferson Davis visited the Confederate Army of Tennessee, the troops shouted, "Send us something to eat, Massa Jeff. Give us something to eat, Massa Jeff. I'm hungry! I'm hungry!"[16]

With respect to provisioning its troops, the Union unquestionably had an advantage. Although hardly immune from hunger, northern soldiers received more food per person than any other army in the history of warfare. Bumper yields even allowed the North to earn valuable trade surpluses by doubling the amount of wheat, corn, beef, and pork it exported to Europe. How did the North achieve such a high level of agricultural production with a third of its farm workforce off at the front? Mechanization, in large part, compensated for the shortage of labor. "The severe manual toil of mowing, raking, pitching, and cradling is now performed by machinery," Scientific American reported in 1863. Women, their husbands off at war, embraced the new technology. "Yesterday I saw the wife of one of our parishioners driving the team in a reaper; her husband is at Vicksburg," an Illinois minister wrote. Union forces had not only more food but also a better variety of foodstuffs at their disposal. Items such as canned fruit and condensed milk had existed prior to the outbreak of hostilities, but wartime demands racheted up production. In 1859, Gail Borden opened his first factory for producing condensed milk. By 1863, army contracts boosted Borden's production level to 17,000 quarts per day.[17]

Militarily speaking, the North ate better than the South, with the same imbalance holding true for their respective civilian populations as well. Food shortages and even periodic riots broke out in the Confederacy. Salt, in particular, was in very short supply, especially after the Union naval blockade kept ships, which used it as ballast, from entering southern ports. In December 1862, a group of 20 women cornered a railroad agent yelling "Salt or blood" and ultimately forced him to hand over a bag of the preservative, an absolute necessity in these days before refrigeration. The following year, in Salisbury, North Carolina, 40 to 50 hungry women wielding hatchets sacked several stores and escaped with over 23 barrels of flour plus salt, molasses, and money.[18]

But the most famous food riot occurred on April 2, 1863, in Richmond, Virginia, where Lee's forces stretched the local food supply to its limit. In the latter part of March, a snowstorm dumped a foot of snow on the Confederate capital, rendering roads used by farmers impassable and adding to the food shortage. When the snow melted later in the month, it damaged pumps at the city waterworks and inconvenienced people, mainly from working-class areas, who now had to trudge all the way to an old well in Capitol Square to get water instead of receiving it from a hydrant. The food and water shortage, combined with an explosion on March 13 at an ordnance laboratory that killed 69 people (most of them women), all helped to bring on the bread riot. From all over the city hundreds of women and boys converged on the square screaming "bread or blood." The mob, armed with hatchets, pistols, clubs, bayonets, and "those huge old homemade knives with which our soldiers were wont to load themselves down in the first part of the war," then proceeded to loot bacon, flour, and other items in short supply.[19]

More than simply hunger drove southerners to engage in mob violence. Principles too figured in the decision. The rioters also plundered food in the name of moral reason, refusing to live or, in this case, die by the logic of the market economy. In St. Lucah, Georgia, women food protestors—their husbands off at war—called attention to the storekeepers who stayed "back at home speculating." "Unrelieved suffering," read an editorial published in a soldiers' newspaper on the first anniversary of the Richmond revolt, "asserts an absolute right to what is necessary for its removal."[20] In other words, the rebels rose up to defend an older, and to their minds more just, economic arrangement, a moral economy that entitled everyone to such basic necessities of life as food.

A number of factors lay behind the South's wartime shortage of comestibles. The North's naval blockade, proposed by Lincoln in April 1861, proved extremely effective in cutting off outside trade with the southern states. Equally important, the decisions of the border states of Kentucky, Missouri, and Maryland not to secede from the Union dealt a devastating blow to the southern cause. Loyalty to the republic translated into lost meat and flour in the South, with the three states together representing a third of both the grain and livestock supply present in the slave South.[21]

Food scarcity in the South also had some less obvious sources. Poor weather was one of them. In 1862, drought reduced corn yields throughout large parts of the southern states. "Hundreds of families will not make enough corn to do them and many will make none of consequence," a newspaper based in Greensboro, Alabama, reported. To make matters worse, the heavy rains that preceded the drought created conditions congenial for the development and spread of a rust fungus. The plant parasite devastated the wheat crop, in some places reducing it by a factor of six.[22]

In Mississippi, flooding combined with the 1862 drought to add to the South's woes. High water—higher in places than at any time since 1815—breached levees along the Mississippi, Yazoo, and Ouachita rivers, laying waste to some of the region's most productive land. "There is more to fear from a dearth of food than from all the Federal armies in existence," declared a Jackson, Mississippi, newspaper. Union forces, meanwhile, made their presence felt in the region. Grant geared up for his Vicksburg campaign late in 1862 and by May the following year had seized the city of Jackson in a campaign that Lincoln called "one of the most brilliant in the world." Calls went out by the Confederate army for men to report for duty. Off they went to battle, leaving behind vast stretches of farmland soon to be taken over by weeds, adding to the scarcity of food. When Confederate soldiers capitulated at Vicksburg in the summer of 1863, Union soldiers refused to taunt their captives, knowing full well, in the words of one observer, that they "surrendered to famine, not to them."[23]

Then came the winter of 1863–1864, described by one meteorological expert as "the outstanding weather event of the Civil War." In Clarksville, Tennessee, beginning on New Year's Eve, the temperature plunged a staggering 50 degrees in just 24 hours. In Texas, the Arctic outbreak killed half to perhaps as much as nine-tenths of the cattle found on some farms. Confederate troops went two whole days without any food at all that winter. A soldier forwarded his meat ration to General Lee with a note lamenting that, despite his aristocratic heritage, he had been driven to steal in order to survive.[24]

Apart from bad weather conditions, southerners themselves played a hand in bringing on the chronic shortage of food. No trend contributed more to the dilemma than the move toward cotton monoculture. Cotton specialization would take a giant step forward after the war. But before that, in the 1850s, when the price of the white lint rose dramatically, planters invested heavily in the crop, so heavily that per capita production of such essential foods as corn and sweet potatoes fell over the decade. When the Civil War began, many southern agricultural leaders called upon people to show their support for the Confederacy by abandoning cotton and growing more corn. "Plant Corn and Be Free, or plant cotton and be whipped," one Georgia newspaper declared. Confederate soldiers, the paper went on to explain, "will be powerless against grim hunger and gaunt famine, such as will overwhelm us if we insanely raise Cotton instead of corn." It would not prove easy, however, for the planter elite to give up its money crop and risk the region's monopoly over world cotton production, especially with many believing that foreign dependence on southern cotton would help bring such powers as Britain into the war on their side. Some planters went so far as to grow corn near roads only to sow cotton in more distant reaches where people would be unlikely to detect it.[25]

The reluctance of southern planters to grow food stemmed from more than simply greed and economic self-interest. A major concern involved what to do with their slaves, who would have more time on their hands if they were not out tending cotton. Planting corn exacted much time during the planting and cultivation stages, but came nowhere near matching the long cotton-picking season, which typically lasted four and often five full months. As one Georgia newspaper put it, "No grain crop in this climate needs cultivation more than four months of the year, the remainder of the working season is unemployed. Can the farmer afford to keep his negroes, horses and other capital idle and 'eating their heads off' for the balance of the season?" To deal with this issue, the states of Arkansas and Georgia felt compelled to pass laws aimed at diversifying agriculture, restricting the amount of land planted in the money crop.[26]

Meat also remained a scarce commodity throughout the war, not just on the battlefield but on the plantation as well. The South, as we have seen, had always had more limited livestock prospects than the North, and the corn shortage could not have helped any. Planters took to reducing the amount of pork they provided slaves, instead encouraging them to maintain vegetable gardens. Such gardens, one planter ventured in 1864, would allow blacks to "pass through the year on a small supply of bacon with much less inconvenience and suffering than the peasantry of the balance of the civilized world."[27]

The ineffectiveness of this substitution soon became apparent. As the war progressed, slaves and planters struggled over game in the southern woods. Slaves had long been known to hunt deer, rabbit, and raccoon in order to supplement the diet provided on the plantation. But the reduction in rations may have spurred them to hunt further afield, at times bringing them into conflict with planters who charged them with killing hogs they had set free in the woods to forage. Thus did some planters' pigs meet their sorry fate—dead because of a set of events that began with the opening salvos at Fort Sumter. Although bereft of the glory and theatricality of battle, the struggle to survive biologically in wartime was every bit as important. It figured centrally in the lives of everyone who lived through the era: white and black, soldier and field hand alike.

CONCLUSION

The North did not wage battle in the Civil War to make a moral point about the evils of slavery. Granting that some did oppose slavery passionately, northerners mainly went to war to protect a particular vision of how society should be organized. The freedom to own one's own property and labor power, they believed, stood at the heart of American culture. Only "free soil" and "free labor" could ensure people the economic independence fought for in the earlier American Revolution. The spread of slavery, in other words, threatened the very core of what it meant to be an American. Southerners, for their part, questioned just how humane a society built on wage labor and industrialization could be. As bizarre as it may seem to us today, they strongly felt that the slave system occupied the moral high ground.

These two vastly different conceptions of how a society should be run collided in the years leading up to the Civil War. But more than just politics and ideas were at stake in the two competing ideologies. The emphasis on free soil and labor in the North and plantation-based slavery in the South had implications on the ground itself. Early in the war, the South's commitment to staple agriculture, to the production of cotton, hindered the ability of the Confederacy to feed itself. The more varied agriculture practiced in the North—a region not centered exclusively around one main crop for market—provided both its soldiers and its citizens with a better and more diverse set of dietary options.

A million different reasons might explain the triumph of the North, countless discrete human decisions, a thrust here, a parry there. But natural forces too had a hand in shaping the outcome. Weather influenced the course of combat, a concern with feeding troops and animals shaped major decisions by commanders on both sides, and climate encouraged the growth of staple crops in the South.

Both the North and the South lived and died by the market, by cash-crop farming. The form such agriculture took in the southern states, however, made the region ill equipped to fight a war, especially after the imposition of the Union's naval blockade. As it turned out, the planters played a role in their own demise—King Cotton coming back to bite them in the end.

$$7$$

EXTRACTING THE NEW SOUTH

With the war at an end, one captain in the Confederate army returned home to his father's plantation. He was in for a rude awakening. "Our negroes are living in great comfort," he wrote. "They were delighted to see me with overflowing affection. They waited on me as before, gave me breakfast, splendid dinners, etc. But they firmly and respectfully informed me: 'We own this land now. Put it out of your head that it will ever be yours again.' "[1]

As events unfolded, the captain had less to fear than he thought. The struggle over slavery had ended, only to be replaced by a new conflict over who would control the political and economic destiny of the South, a battle that the former masters and their descendants would decisively win. As far as the land itself was concerned, however, neither the freedmen nor the whites would be completely in charge of their fate.

It is no doubt one of history's great ironies that a culture that once coerced an entire group of people into a state of severe dependency later found itself reduced to semicolonial status, its resources ravaged by outsiders. The South emerged from the war—its fields and livestock plundered, its forests cut down for firewood and barrack timber—as an economically crippled region and persisted that way for at least the next half century. The cotton monoculture, which had gained a strong foothold in the region during the antebellum period, advanced across the landscape at a pace that would have challenged even the most accomplished Confederate cavalryman. In its wake, it left the land scarred, its people, black and white farmers alike, destitute and more dependent on outside sources of food as well as capital. As the region descended into poverty, people from outside the region—northern capitalists, midwestern lumbermen, and British financiers—siphoned off its natural wealth, especially its forests and minerals. The ecological origins of the New South that grew up on the ashes of war centered squarely on the extraction of resources for the benefit of the greater national economy. Blacks were set free in a region enslaved.

FAST FOOD FARMING

King Cotton emerged from the war more imperious and despotic than ever before. As the single most important cash crop in the postbellum South, the staple soared in importance, turning autumn in the stretch from South Carolina to east Texas into a sea of white that drifted off toward the horizon. Like addicts unable to control themselves, Southern farmers grew so much cotton that they continued to undercut their ability to feed themselves. By 1880, per capita corn and hog production in the Deep South plummeted to nearly half of 1860 levels, forcing farmers to import food from the Midwest. Wisconsin flour, Chicago bacon, Indiana hay—all flowed in to shore up the region's food deficit, when in fact, as one observer noted, these items could have been grown in Dixie "at nothing a ton."[2]

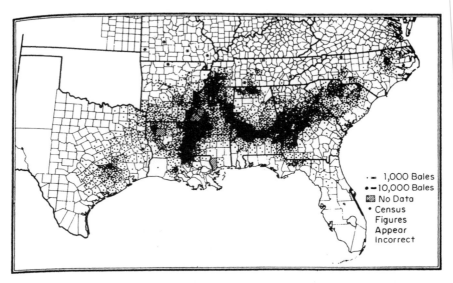

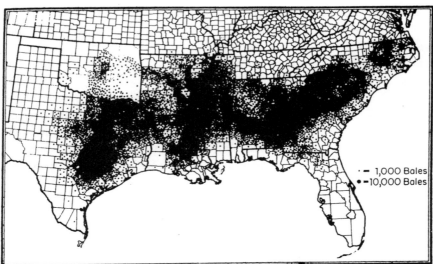

COTTON PRODUCTION, 1859 AND 1899

Although cotton was a major crop in the pre–Civil War South, it was even more widely grown in the post-bellum period. (U.S. Department of Agriculture, Atlas of American Agriculture [*Washington, DC: GPO, 1918*])

At one level, the attraction of cotton is easy to understand. The economic profit from planting was simply far greater than for any other grain crop. With its acid soil conditions and heavy rainfall, the South, unlike the temperate northern states, was not well suited to raising grains and grasses. Add to this the animal parasites that dragged down livestock prospects, and the magnetism of cotton becomes easier to comprehend.

Of course favorable market conditions and this same ecological context had existed in the antebellum South. And yet, despite the extraordinary importance of cotton in the prewar South, it came nowhere near rivaling the crop's incredible dominance in the postbellum era. What happened? Two main factors—the rise of sharecropping and the growing commercialization of farming—explain cotton's eventual chokehold on the region.

Sharecropping developed as blacks were denied the right to own land in the aftermath of the Civil War. By 1868, the same white planter class that controlled the land in the antebellum period continued to retain its title to the region's most valuable resource, only now the slaves had been set free and planters could no longer count on their labor. This proved especially problematic for those who raised cotton because the crop must be picked in a timely way or it can be seriously damaged by rainfall. Freed from their chains, blacks were known to leave planters in the lurch, moving on smack in the middle of the cotton-picking season. Sharecropping helped to resolve this problem by tying laborers to the land for a specified period of time. Planters divided their plantations into 30- to 50-acre farms and rented them out to freedmen, providing tenants with land, seed, and the necessary tools and, in return, taking half the share of the crop at harvest. The arrangement appealed to planters and also to freedmen who, unable to buy land on their own, found that sharecropping at least gave them an opportunity to get out from under the thumb of white supervision. Landlords, however, did reserve the right to dictate the crop mix to tenants; with their own personal fortunes tied to what the sharecropper raised, logic led them to choose cotton because it was more profitable per acre than any other crop.[3]

Sharecropping and the cotton monoculture went hand in hand with the increasing commercialization of farming, spurred by the spread of railroads and merchants. In the 1870s, railroads began laying track in the Georgia Up Country, tying this region more closely to markets in the North. With the railroads in place, merchants, who bought locally grown cotton and sold goods on credit, were not far behind. Under crop lien laws, passed in the 1870s, merchants loaned farmers money with a future crop as collateral. For obvious reasons, they insisted that farmers plant cotton. "If I say 'plant cotton' they plant cotton," one merchant was reputed to have said. With the system stacked in cotton's favor, sharecroppers tripped over each other as they trundled off to their fields to plant more. But the more they planted, the less food they produced on their own. Hence the more they had to turn to stores for supplies, drawing them into a vicious cycle of indebtedness.[4]

Nothing was more critical to cotton growing under the sharecropping system than fertilizer. Landlords and renters alike had little incentive to invest in the long-term health of their land and thus little interest in crop rotation or manuring, practices designed to ward off soil depletion. Current yields were what mattered most to them, with the land simply a vehicle for raising cotton for cash. Such present-mindedness encouraged farmers to mine the soil for all that it was worth, using fertilizer to pump up yields in the short run.[5]

Beginning in 1867, with the establishment of large phosphate mines in South Carolina, commercial fertilizer use boomed. Much of the soil in Georgia and South Carolina suffered from a natural deficiency in phosphorous, a problem the fertilizer addressed with a great deal of initial success. Cotton yields soared as this powerful chemical input bolstered the fertility of the soil. Fertilizer also sped up crop growth, causing cotton to mature more quickly and uniformly. The speedup shortened the cotton harvest to as little as five weeks and lowered the threat posed by rain or frost. Given the virtues of fertilizer and its pivotal role in the cotton monoculture under the sharecropping system, it is perhaps not surprising to find that the South consumed a larger percentage of it (on a per acre basis) than any other region in the nation.[6]

SOIL EROSION
Increasing fertilizer use promoted the constant planting of cotton, which eventually took its toll on the land. The gullies shown here were on a farm in North Carolina. (Library of Congress)

A mix of inorganic chemicals was pumped into ecosystems across the South, ratcheting up what the soil would yield. No longer self-contained entities sustained by their own nutrient cycle, southern farms increasingly became receptacles for various outside inputs in the quest for more cotton. For a time, phosphorous-based fertilizer worked, but what the cotton crop needed most was nitrogen, a chemical not yet incorporated into plant food mixtures. Worse still, as sharecroppers fell further into debt, they bought greater amounts of commercial fertilizer from merchants on credit in an effort to boost output and generate the cash to pay off their loans—a self-defeating process that pushed the soil to its ultimate limit. "Who said fertilizer? Well, that's just it. Every farmer says it, every tenant says it, every merchant says it, and even the bankers must speak of it at times," one observer noted. "The trouble is that in times past the easy purchase and use of fertilizer has seemed to many of our Southern farmers a short cut to prosperity, a royal road to good crops of cotton year after year. The result has been that their lands have been cultivated clean year after year, their fertility has been exhausted." While some areas turned to more ecologically stable crop rotation practices, much of Georgia and South Carolina, as well as portions of Alabama and Mississippi, fell prey to the fertilizer craze. The trend made the late nineteenth century the worst period for soil erosion in the South's entire history.[7]

Single-crop farming is always a perilous enterprise, a point that became apparent when farmers found their soil woes compounded by the arrival of an insect with a taste for cotton. In 1892, the boll weevil, a small insect whose larva fed on the cotton boll, made its way out of Mexico into Texas. Eastward it marched, reaching Louisiana in 1904, crossing the Mississippi five years later, and arriving in South Carolina by 1917. The pest left destruction in its wake, dramatically reducing cotton yields just about everywhere it went. In Greene County, Georgia, farmers picked 11,854 bales of cotton in 1916, the year the boll weevil first arrived. Six years later, the county produced a minuscule 333 bales.[8]

The weevil may well have played a role in the great exodus of blacks to the North that began in 1910—one of the largest migrations in the history of the world. Between 1910 and 1920, it is estimated that as many as 500,000 African Americans left the South for northern cities. Many factors were at work to entice blacks to leave their rural homes, including the higher wages that came with the tightening of the labor market during World War I as well as the South's failure to provide blacks with the social and political equality they deserved. But changes in the land also drove blacks North. In the early 1910s, one woman from Mississippi spoke of a "general belief [among blacks] that God had cursed the land." The boll weevil was especially devastating for black tenant farmers. Under the thumb of creditors who demanded cotton, black tenants had little say over the mix of crops they planted. But more than just the weevil caused blacks to wonder whether God was speaking up. Devastating flooding along the lower Mississippi River in 1912, made worse by the policy of building levees, broke records on nearly all of the river gauges set up to measure water heights between Cairo,

Illinois, and the Gulf of Mexico. It seems fair to say that the pull of higher northern wages combined then with various setbacks on the land and inequality to cause blacks to flee.[9]

Whatever the weevil's role in African American history, it had at least two other consequences. First, it drove farmers to use even more fertilizer to help the cotton crop mature before the weevil attacked it, solidifying the shift away from organic farming. And second, the insect caused cotton yields to decline precipitously. The number of acres devoted to cotton in the Deep South (Louisiana, Mississippi, Alabama, Georgia, and South Carolina) declined an average of 27 percent when figures are compiled for the four years immediately before and after the infestation. The weevil broke cotton's grip on the region, heralding the move to a more diversified form of agriculture centered on corn, peanuts, and hogs. Some farmers even went so far as to thank the weevil for creating a way out of one-crop farming. Citizens in Enterprise, Alabama, actually erected a statue in honor of the bug, one of the more curious national monuments to dot the American landscape, a symbol for what it took—outright calamity—to force southerners to abandon their single-minded and ill-fated relationship with the land.[10]

Blacks too sometimes welcomed the weevil as a way of breaking the grip that cotton and financial dependence on merchants had on their lives. Blues singers immortalized the insect, most famously in this song by Huddie Ledbetter (Ledbelly), who was born in 1888 in Shiloh, Louisiana.

First time I seen the boll weevil, he was sitting on a square.
Next time I seen a boll weevil, he had his whole family there.
He's a looking for a home.
He's a looking for a home.

The old lady said to the old man, "I've been trying my level best
Keep these boll weevils out of my brand new cotton dress.
It's full of holes.
And it's full of holes."

The old man said to the old lady, "What do you think of that?
I got one of the boll weevils out of my brand new Stetson hat,
And it's full of holes.
And it's full of holes."

Now the farmer said to the merchant, "I never made but one bale.
Before I let you have that last one, I will suffer and die in jail.
And I will have a home.
And I will have a home."[11]

OPEN AND SHUT RANGE

If cotton's stranglehold impoverished the ecology of the South, it also helped to drive many people deeper into poverty as well. In the postbellum period, rural population densities, backed by relatively high fertility rates, rose to the point where in 1930 the region was twice as thickly settled as the North. Farm size, meanwhile, continued a relentless downward trend. Rural southerners sunk deeper into poverty as small farm size combined with low production levels to push them to the edge of financial calamity. In 1880, federal census takers described black farmers as "sometimes without bread for their families." "Many are in a worse [economic] condition than they were during slavery." As their diet declined, poor southerners, both black and white, did what they had long been accustomed to doing: They turned to the region's common lands—unenclosed woods and pastures—taking game, fishing, and turning out whatever few hogs and cattle they had to find forage. Only now with pressure on the South's common resources more intense than ever—the product of increased sport and market hunting— many white landlords, merchants, and planters, with the law as their weapon, sought to prohibit the free taking of game by sealing off the range.[12]

In the antebellum period, slaves, especially those on tidewater plantations, headed for rivers and forests to procure food and supplement their rations. "My old daddy," Louisa Adams of North Carolina recollected, "partly raised his chilluns on game. He caught rabbits, coons an' possums. He would work all day and hunt at night." Slaves also hunted and fished for the sport of it, these being among the few recreational activities afforded them. In the woods of the South Carolina Low Country, slaves hunted deer, rabbits, squirrels, opossums, bears, ducks, turkeys, pigeons, and other animals. "Possum and squirrel all we could get," recalled one slave. "Wild turkey, possum. Don't bother with no coon much." In 1831, a visitor from the North observed, "The blacks are never better pleased than when they are hunting in the woods; and it is seldom that they have not in the larder the flesh of a raccoon or opossum." In the Georgia Low Country almost half of the slaves' meat, it is estimated, came from game and fish.[13]

Slaves also counted on the woods as a source of fodder for their livestock. Curious as it may sound, although themselves owned by others, slaves possessed property, including animals like cattle and hogs. One slave, described by a white planter as "more like a free man than any slave," claimed in the mid-nineteenth century to have had 26 pigs, 16 sheep, and 8 cows.[14]

It was to the pine forests and patches of cane commonly found along streams that slaves and whites alike went to run their hogs and cattle. "We raise our hogs by allowing them to range in our woods, where they get fat in the autumn on acorns," explained one resident of the South Carolina Piedmont. Cattle were raised "with so little care, that it would be a shame to charge anything for their keep up to three years old." The open range thrived in the South in large part because the mild winters allowed herders to leave their stock on the range all year round (in the North, farmers had to bring in the animals to prevent them from freezing to death and thus barn size limited the number of animals that could be left free to roam the common lands).[15]

"The citizens of this county have and always have had the legal, moral, and Bible right to let their stock . . . run at large," declared one Georgia Piedmont farmer in the 1880s. Private property in land existed of course in the South from the colonial period forward. But the customary right to use unimproved land for hunting and grazing coexisted with private landownership. The law itself sanctioned the customary practice of grazing livestock in unfenced areas, regardless of who the "owner" of the land might be. So-called fence laws dating from the colonial period put the burden on farmers to enclose their crops with adequate fences, or risk bearing responsibility for any damage roving livestock caused. Early laws prescribing a death sentence for livestock theft were later reduced in severity when lawmakers realized that the customary practice of running cattle and other animals on the commons made it very hard to determine who owned a particular animal. The customary right to use the commons for a variety of subsistence activities persisted in the South until shortly after the Civil War. As the Virginia legislature put it: "Many poor persons have derived advantage from grazing their stock on the commons and unenclosed lands, and to whom the obligation to confine them, or a liability to damages if not confined, would operate as a great hardship."[16]

With emancipation, however, things began to change. Planters wondered how they would ever make a living growing cotton if their labor force continued to roam the countryside exercising their customary right to game. In 1866, one Virginia newspaper bemoaned the fact that planters "suffer great annoyance and serious pecuniary loss from the trespasses of predacious negroes and low pot hunters, who with dogs and guns, live in the fields . . . as if the whole country belonged to them." Slowly, planters called for making private property more private and less open to customary hunting and fishing by commoners. "The right to hunt wild animals is held by the great body of the people, whether landholders or oth-erwise, as one of their franchises," lamented the wealthy South Carolina planter and sportsman William Elliott. One observer who toured the South in the 1870s found that blacks "are fond of the same pleasures which their late masters gave them so freely—hunting, fishing, and lounging; pastimes which the superb forests, the noble streams, the charming climate minister to very strongly."[17]

Planters eventually pushed for the passage of game laws. Beginning in the 1870s, counties in the Black Belt passed statutes that regulated hunting. In 1875, three Georgia counties made it illegal to "kill or destroy" partridges or deer any time between April and October. The new law also prohibited people from using poison to catch fish. In part, planters supported such laws because they sensed, correctly, the depletion of wildlife in the postbellum South. The decline angered planters who enjoyed a good hunt at least as much as their ex-slaves did. But more likely, planters supported the game laws in order to further control the freedmen and get them back to work in the fields. Alabama's passage of a game law in 1876 that only applied to 14 Black Belt counties supports such a view. To some extent the laws may have improved the prospect for game: For example, a fawn who lost its mother in the early fall might be too young to survive the winter. But if the game laws were aimed at improving wildlife populations they also prohibited hunting in exactly the season of the year when planters needed agricultural laborers the most.[18]

Whatever the intentions behind the laws, wildlife in the postbellum South was experiencing a devastating decline. The depletion, however, was not solely the work of freedmen and white farmers. The rise of market and sport hunting also came into play. Wildlife had an incredibly powerful hold on the imagination of late-nineteenth-century Americans. A source of both food and fashion, wild game occupied a place in the hearts of urban consumers and rural folk alike. While trains transported ducks, geese, and pigeons from the Midwest to the tables of New Yorkers, game birds hung from the rafters in such cities as Atlanta, Norfolk, and New Orleans. Women wore feather hats and sometimes even sported entire birds. In the 1880s, the millinery trade spurred on market hunters who brought about the collapse of the heron population south of Tarpon Springs, Florida. In 1896, hunters destroyed 99 percent of the terns nesting on Cape Hatteras.[19]

The meat and feathers came to market courtesy of the railroads. Controlled by northern capitalists by the 1890s, the railroads also encouraged sport hunters to venture into the region "to visit the South and hunt game where it is more plentiful than in any other section of the United States." Access to new weapons such as the breech-loading shotgun and to better ammunition, meanwhile, improved the success of hunters. In North Carolina quail country, residents resented the intrusion of northern hunters and responded by passing county legislation in the 1880s that made it illegal for anyone to transport quail or partridge across state lines.[20]

By the late nineteenth century the southern commons was in turmoil. Market and sport hunters descended in search of game, while cattle and pigs overran it in the quest for forage. Few animals inspired more resentment than the hog, described by one Mississippian, in a fit of anger, as an "old, pirating, fence-breaking, corn-destroying, long-snouted, big boned and leather-bellied" beast. Apart from planters, railroads also suffered from the effects of allowing livestock to roam the range. Under the law, the roads were liable if animals became injured on their tracks. The legal nicety may have driven some stockowners—eager to collect damages—to apply salt to the rails so as to lure the hapless creatures into oncoming trains.[21]

Egged on by the railroads, southern landlords, merchants, and planters took action against the old fence laws in the 1870s. No longer should the farmer be called on to fence his crops, they cried out, while livestock roamed willy-nilly across the landscape. "Why in the name of common sense," one planter asked, "am I compelled to maintain 12 or 13 miles of hideous fence around my plantation at an annual cost of upwards of a thousand dollars, in order to prevent the cattle and hogs which my neighbors turn loose . . . from destroying my crops and robbing my property?" Of course those who favored the open range saw things differently. "Poor man, without a farm of your own; what must become of that cow that gives milk for your prattling babes?" one pro-range advocate from Georgia wondered. "What is to become of the poor widow who is homeless? Freedmen, what is to become of you?"[22]

Although those opposed to the old fence laws objected on the grounds of principle, other more practical matters also influenced their view. The peculiar design of southern fences required a great deal of wood, an increasingly scarce resource in the postbellum years. The most common fence was the so-called Virginia or zigzag fence. It was favored by southerners because it required much less labor than the post-and-hole fence, it could be easily removed to another location if the soil wore out, and it was strong enough to resist marauding bands of swine. The Virginia fence, however, required a great deal of wood in an environment where timber was becoming less available. The shortage resulted from depredations made during the Civil War (soldiers burned fence rails to make fires), from the rise of industrial lumbering, and from feral hogs feeding on the seedlings of such trees as the longleaf pine. Planters thus found that fencing their crops could be a burden. One of the earliest pieces of legislation seeking an end to the open range in Mississippi bore the suggestive title: "An Act to protect citizens in Hinds County in those sections where the fencing and timber has been destroyed by the late war."[23]

Virginia fences, because of their zigzag design, also took up much more land than the straight post-and-hole variety. That was land that could have been used to plant crops, a point not lost on one opponent of the open range. "The old fence rows of Carroll county [Georgia] will make corn enough in three years to pay for

ZIGZAG FENCE

Common throughout the South, this type of fence snaked through the land, taking up more room than the straighter post-and-hole variety. (Library of Congress)

all the crops that will grow in the county for the next ten years." Fencing was clearly no idle matter. Although barbed wire, invented in 1873, could have been substituted for wood as it was in the West, it tended to be expensive and made few inroads, probably because pigs (unlike cattle) were often able to get through it.[24]

For a variety of reasons, including such factors as reasons of principle and the design of fences, those who favored an end to the open range held sway. By the 1890s, a new set of fence laws, often called stock laws, were on the books in counties across the South (although it would take decades, in some places until the 1970s, before the range was fully closed). The laws required farmers and stockmen to pen in their livestock, making them legally responsible if the animals somehow escaped and caused damage to someone's property. The stock laws penalized those—poor whites and blacks—who had formerly relied on the unenclosed stretches of land. People with power and money used the law to preserve the sanctity of their property and make it more private. Those who had once counted on such land had to turn to other means of subsistence.

The stock laws had ecological and biological consequences to match their social ones. Animals formerly allowed to run loose in the woods now became true domesticates. Penned up in barnyards and no longer free to roam the land, the animals were either fattened on feed or forced to graze on self-contained pastures, where overuse, especially on hillsides, may have contributed to the South's already intense erosion problem. The closing of the range also helped to limit the spread of the cattle tick, carrier of the parasitic infection babesiosis (eventually named Texas fever by midwesterners who feared the Lone Star state's infected livestock). In the early twentieth century, the federal government introduced a program for eradicating the tick, now that the animals could no longer roam the landscape and infect one another at will; the move greatly benefited large commercial stock raisers. Tragically, the high capital costs involved in purchasing the technology to eliminate the cattle tick, plus the huge expense of fencing in livestock, combined to further disadvantage southern yeomen who raised just a few cattle for household use. The stock laws, a social development, brought about a biological shift (a less congenial environment for the tick) that led to still more social changes—unfavorable ones, at least from the standpoint of struggling farmers.[25]

The domestication of people and animals, it would seem, went hand in hand, but with one critical difference: The poor people put out by the enclosure of the commons could protest their woes. The fencing controversy, which ultimately worked its way as far west as Texas, figured prominently in the rise of the late-nineteenth-century agrarian protest movement known as Populism. The Populists formed a third political party, the People's party, opposed to the business-dominated organizations run by the Democrats and Republicans. But their critique of American society stemmed in part from changes in the land. For it was there that the yeoman farmer's earlier subsistence lifestyle, resting on corn, some cotton, and the pasturing of hogs in woods and bottomlands, gave way to the single-minded pursuit of cotton alone by the 1880s. Now the logic of distant markets in New York, St. Louis, and Liverpool, not the dietary needs of families, combined with the enclosure of the commons to force such farmers deeper into poverty. Driven from a safer and more ecologically sound form of farming to embrace the monoculture, small farmers became victims of those who sought an end to the open range.[26]

THE INVASIONS

Next to the closing of the range, the rise of industrial lumbering contributed nearly as much to the dispossession of the poor. Lumber production in the South skyrocketed in the 40 years after 1880, as the South overtook the Great Lakes states, which were well on their way to depletion by the turn of the century. The original forest cover in the southern states declined by an astonishing 40 percent, falling from roughly 300 million acres to just 178 million by 1919, as industrial logging, aided by the increasing penetration of the railroad, emerged to clear-cut the countryside. As one lumberman recalled, "You hardly ever left a tree of any size standing and all the little [ones] was torn down." Destruction of the woodlands habitat depressed game and plant populations, further undermining those who turned to the forest to hunt and gather as a means of survival. Of course it was becoming even harder to enter the woods in the first place, as logging and coal companies gobbled up the land. By 1930, industrial enterprises, many serving the interests of those who resided outside the region, controlled nearly two-thirds of all the privately owned land in the southern Appalachians.[27]

The federal government's land policies played a major role in aiding the logging companies' quest for control of the South's timber, much as had happened in the Midwest. In 1866, Congress passed homestead legislation designed to aid the freedmen (as opposed to speculators) that limited the amount of land a person could claim—after settling on it and paying a nominal fee—to 80 acres. But in 1876, southern legislators, emboldened by the end of Reconstruction, obtained repeal of the legislation in an attempt to open up the region's vast supplies of timber and mineral wealth to outside capital. With the southern lands open to unrestricted sales, the great giveaway began. Railroads ran trains for the expressed purpose of aiding so-called land lookers. Boarding in Chicago, those with money to spend headed south to Mississippi and Louisiana in search of prime timberland. Great Lakes states lumber barons, northern capitalists, and British land moguls all rushed south in the 1880s to cash in on the red-hot land boom. Nearly six million acres of land passed out of the federal domain between 1877 and 1888.[28]

But this was nothing compared to the tens of millions of acres of state land sold off, sometimes for as little as 25 cents an acre, during this same period. By 1885, an astounding 32 million acres of state land passed into private hands in

Texas alone. Combined with the assault on common-use rights, the steep decline in public domain further undermined the efforts of yeoman farmers to survive off the land.[29]

Ownership of vast stretches of the southern landscape now rested with a relatively small number of individuals and companies who eyed it mainly for its speculative, timber, or mineral potential. The natural wealth of the countryside, however, was worth little if it could not be transported to markets elsewhere in the nation. To meet this need, railroads crisscrossed the region in a network so vast and all consuming that it almost defies comprehension. The combined amount of track in 13 southern states rose from slightly over 9,000 miles in 1865 to nearly 39,000 miles by 1910. The railroads, one West Virginia historian observed in 1913, "carried into the silence of primeval woods the hum of modern industry." Some lines left no doubt about the purpose of their mission, with one railway dubbing itself "the great lumber route."[30]

The railroads spurred the loggers on as they harvested timber and then turned around and burned what was left. As the southern forests were stripped of their pines (the most commercially valuable stands) and hardwoods, piles of slash sat just waiting for a stray spark from a locomotive to ignite them. According to one estimate, somewhere between 800,000 and 1.2 million acres of North Carolina woodland erupted in flames in 1891. In 1908, a tenth of West Virginia felt the effects of forest fires.[31]

Southerners, however, remained largely unmoved by the smoke and flames. In 1898, when fire raged over some three million acres of North Carolina, the episode rated barely a mention in Raleigh newspapers. The nonchalance derived from the historic role that fire played in the lives of those who raised stock on common lands. Burning the woods was an annual ritual in many parts of the South. It kept down the rough—grasses and saplings—allowing stockmen to drive cattle from one place to another and, most important, encouraged the growth of grasses and other vegetation on which cattle fed. As the lumber industry tried to check the spread of fires, it allowed the rough to flourish and contributed, inadvertently, to the spiraling downward of those raising stock.[32]

Industrial logging contributed more directly to the demise of subsistence practices by altering the habitat. Game such as deer, bears, and turkeys disappeared as the woodlands vanished. Plants such as ginseng, mayapple, and others, which mountaineers had collected and exchanged at stores for cash, met a similar fate.[33]

The forest and its wealth of plants and animals figured centrally in the lives of southern Appalachian mountaineers, which is why they left so much of their land—in some areas as much as 90 percent—unimproved. When the northerner George Vanderbilt, scion of that famed railroad family, bought 100,000 acres of land in North Carolina in order to pursue hunting and forestry, Gifford Pinchot, the conservationist and forester for the estate, said this about those displaced by the purchase: "They regarded this country as their country, their common. And

SHELTON FAMILY

Southerners who depended on chestnut trees like this one for their livelihood were severely affected by the blight. (Great Smoky Mountains National Park)

it was not surprising, for they needed everything usable in it—pasture, fish, game—to supplement the very meager living they were able to scratch from the soil."[34]

The entry of northerners and industrial loggers alike into the southern forests was not the only incursion that the common people had to endure. Compounding their problems was the spread of an alien invader: the chestnut blight. By 1912, the fungus, brought accidentally to the United States in 1904 in a shipment of Asian chestnut trees, had destroyed all of New York City's stock. Then the fungus, which starved the chestnut tree by colonizing the food-storing cortex cells underneath the bark, worked its way south, carried there on the boots and axes of loggers themselves. By 1913, the blight had entered North Carolina. Some experts describe the chestnut tree's near total annihilation in North America as one of the most profound changes in plant life ever recorded in human history.[35]

One of the most important and abundant trees in the eastern forests, the chestnut, once found on some 200 million acres of land, played a far more critical role in the lives of southerners than it did for New Yorkers promenading around Central Park. The poor seeking to survive off of the southern woodlands thus found the blight devastating. Edible chestnuts commonly mounted to a height of four inches on the forest floor, providing a crucial source of food for wild game and grazing livestock both. "The worst thing that ever happened in this country was when the chestnut trees died," lamented one Tennessee resident. "Turkeys disappeared, and the squirrels were not one-tenth as many as there were before." Another mountaineer from Virginia recalled that before the blight it "didn't cost a cent to raise chestnuts or hogs. . . . It was a very inexpensive way to farm. The people had money and had meat on the table too." Children also gathered the nuts, supplementing the diet of mountain families. "The chestnut tree was the most important tree we had," recalled one Kentucky woman. "We needed those chestnuts."[36]

If the blight provided yet another threat to the yeoman farmer's subsistence, it did not stand in the way of the lumber barons. Timber harvesting actually increased in the wake of the epidemic, which eventually infected enough trees to produce some 30 billion board feet of chestnut wood. Meanwhile, the outbreak of World War I only helped to force up lumber production levels, intensifying the pressure on the southern forests. In 1919, one year after the end of the war, the South produced 37 percent of all the nation's lumber, much as the Great Lakes states had done three decades before.[37]

In the 1920s, the South took a page from the history of the American West: Ghost towns appeared in the logged-out areas. The lumber towns that had sprouted as capitalists advanced on the forest shut their doors (with some exceptions of course) just as soon as the last tree hit the ground. In 1923, one observer decried the passing away of the region's pine woods. "Their villages are Nameless Towns, their monuments huge piles of saw dust, their epitaph: 'The mill cut out.'"[38] The great extraction had run its course.

MALTHUS IN APPALACHIA

No place in the South felt the effects of resource extraction more than Appalachia—the mountainous region spanning from western Maryland to northeast Alabama, whose very name is synonymous with poverty and desperation. It was of course not just timber but the vast reserves of coal that lay beneath the earth that attracted investors to this place in the late nineteenth century. The story of coal was much the same as for trees: the invasion of outside capital from the North and abroad, penetration of the railroad, the relentless mining of the resource, sweeping ecological change, and the dispossession of ordinary people. In the eyes of some, the region assumed the status of an internal colony. It is wrong, however, to assume that the descent of Appalachia into poverty was solely the work of outsiders.

The origins of Appalachia's decline and reincarnation as a huge coal pit for supplying energy to the North and Midwest go back to the period just before the Civil War. As population surged between 1850 and 1880—rising 156 percent on the Appalachian Plateau—the eternal struggle to farm the land in an ecologically viable manner became all the more difficult. Farm size plummeted from an average of 350 acres to 173 acres in 1880.[39] The steep hillsides of the plateau were bursting with people, forcing farmers to improve more land. Living standards soon began to fall, making farmers seek wage work.

Into this environment northern and foreign capitalists marched, eager to harvest the natural capital of the mountains, the product of geological forces that had compressed what was once a huge swamp with ferns the size of trees, into one of the world's great sources of energy: bituminous coal. Unlike anthracite coal (a less accessible resource because of the steep pitch of the folds in which it is generally found), Appalachia's bituminous fields, extending over 72,000 square miles from western Pennsylvania to northeastern Alabama, are positioned horizontally, parallel to the surface, and can be mined with relative ease. All that needed to be done was to follow the seams from the surface along the contour of a mountain.

Apart from discovering coal, the mining companies also conveniently encountered people caught in the clutches of a Malthusian dilemma, folks willing to work for low wages and thus make the coal—an expensive item to transport to northern markets—that much more economically competitive. Faced with a decline in living standards, many Appalachians embraced wage labor, while still keeping one foot on the farm. As late as 1923, a report from West Virginia's Raleigh County, in the heart of coal country, found that over 70 percent of miners tended both gardens and livestock to supplement their wages. In this sense, subsistence agriculture underwrote Appalachia's industrial transformation. Coal operators, aware of the subsidy, even encouraged miners to continue to farm on the side.[40]

But it was difficult for Appalachia's workers to lead dual lives as full-time miners and part-time farmers. In the end, the two modes of production came into conflict. As company towns and mining camps colonized the desirable bottomlands, farmers, already beset by more people than available land, were forced to squeeze over. They had little place to go but up, onto the steep hillsides that ran through the region. Farmers had long been accustomed to clearing new land on these steep slopes when their old land wore out. But pressure on the hills mounted for two reasons. First, the lumber boom combined with the demand for mining timbers to further denude these lands. And second, farmers, who were already growing significant amounts of corn to feed their families, were pushed by Prohibition in 1920 to furnish more corn for the burgeoning illegal market in moonshine whiskey. As a result, the hillsides were stripped of their vegetative cover. And without the trees and roots to absorb water, the land became more prone to inundation, a point amply demonstrated on May 30, 1927, when a flash flood in Kentucky's Cumberland Plateau sent nearly 100 mountaineers to their deaths. "This great flood," wrote Harry Caudill, one of Appalachia's staunchest defenders, "marks one of the major milestones which the mountaineers have passed on the road to ruin."[41]

CONCLUSION

Appalachia, like many other parts of the South, had moved by the turn of the century from self-sufficiency in food to economic dependency. A region once made up of people able to feed themselves on their own now became dependent on other places and ecosystems and thoroughly entrenched in market relations. The reasons for this shift are multiple. The steady spread of the cotton monoculture, fueled by the addition of large amounts of phosphorous-based fertilizer, clearly played a role. It drove farmers into debt as they bought more chemicals to speed crop maturation and fight off the boll weevil; they struggled to pay for a product that briefly boosted yields but could never deliver the nitrogen that the cotton plant needed most. Busted yeoman farmers might have looked to the woods to survive, had not planters and merchants been cracking down on the system of common rights to hunt and forage, precisely when the federal government, in league with the states, sold off these very same lands to lumber and mineral companies. The chestnut blight was an additional, perhaps final, blow to those seeking to survive from what little common land remained.

All these trends conspired to leave southern farmers dependent and dispossessed. The compound tragedy affected the poor of both races, but it was especially ruinous for blacks, who had been promised freedom after years of bondage. In addition to a crippling racism, reflected in the rise of rigid segregation laws and of lynchings in the late-nineteenth-century South, blacks found themselves enslaved to a culture that mediated its relations with the land through the institutions of private property and the market. And as we will see, it was an ecological destiny to which their Native American counterparts also succumbed as the nation moved west.

THE UNFORGIVING WEST

In at least one respect, the American West—the vast expanse of land running from the 98th meridian bisecting the Dakotas, Nebraska, Kansas, Oklahoma, and Texas to the Pacific Ocean—was all a big mistake. Following the Civil War a period of unusually wet weather that lasted roughly two decades inspired Americans to head west in droves. Urged on by scientists such as Cyrus Thomas, who pronounced the ample rainfall permanent in nature and "in some way connected to the settlement of the country," Americans forged into the region under the delusion that moisture would increase in proportion to population. As late as 1884, one Chicago reporter wrote, "Kansas was considered a droughty state, but that day is past, and her reputation for sure crops is becoming widely known."[1]

One of the few people urging restraint as settlers rushed across the continent was a man by the name of John Wesley Powell. A Civil War veteran who lost his right arm in the battle of Shiloh, Powell went on in 1869 to successfully navigate the Colorado River. But his greatest contribution to American society stemmed not from his explorations but from his deep understanding of the hard reality that unfolded across the 98th meridian. The West might seem wet and inviting at the moment, Powell argued in the 1870s, but aridity—a fundamental inability to support agriculture without an artificial infusion of water—defined its true character. As the rain charts available at the time made clear, this was a land subject to less than 20 inches of precipitation annually, an expanse amounting to some two-fifths of the nation bereft of the moisture necessary to grow such crops as wheat and corn without a supply of irrigation water. We now know that it is the Rocky Mountains in league with the coastal ranges further west that, by blocking the passage of storm fronts and squeezing water from the clouds, make the West the dry land that it is. But Powell, in his day, understood enough to realize that it was folly to expect the rains to con-

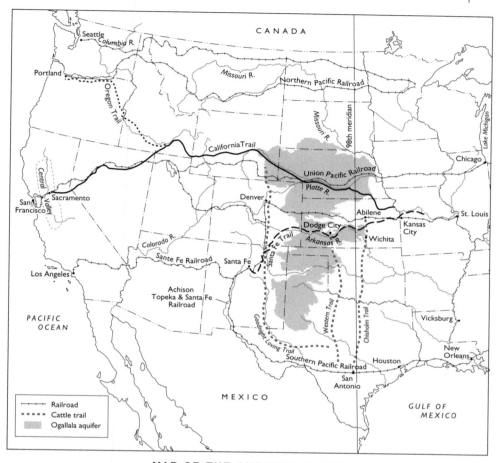

MAP OF THE AMERICAN WEST

tinue forever, that soon the cycle of drought would come around again. As he wrote, we "shall have to expect a speedy return to extreme aridity, in which case a large portion of the agricultural industries of these now growing up would be destroyed."[2]

In this land of little rain, Powell argued, the geometric logic of Jefferson's grid made little sense at all. No settler could expect to succeed on 160 acres—the cadastral survey's magic number—if that land lacked water for farming and ranching. Instead, in 1878, Powell proposed organizing the region into two kinds of land-use arrangements: small, 80-acre farms and large, 2,560-acre livestock ranches, each attached to its respective irrigation and grazing district. Congress and the American people, however, paid no attention to his proposal. Nor did they heed his gloom and doom prediction of drought. But history would vindicate his doom-saying in the end as drought returned in the 1890s. The reasons for this and other such misfortunes arose from the clash of an inherently unforgiving and at times unpredictable land with the dreams and aspirations of a culture not particularly fond of limits.

GOLD!

On January 24, 1848, a carpenter named James Marshall, while building a sawmill on the American River, discovered a small nugget of gold, an event that drove pioneers, brimming with hope, to hitch up their wagons and head for California. Thus began the Gold Rush, one of the earliest and most formative chapters in the history of the West. Or so the textbooks say. But like so many tales of supposed discovery, this one turns out to obscure far more than it reveals about the Anglo-American settlement of the region.

At the very least, officials in Washington, DC, knew about California's gold as early as 1843, when almost 2,000 ounces of the metal arrived in the city from mines in southern California. Perhaps this explains why James Polk, on the day of his inauguration, told his secretary of the navy that the control of California remained one of the main objectives of his presidency. Just a little over a week before the nation declared war on its neighbor to the south, Secretary of State James Buchanan received a letter from Thomas Larkin, the U.S. consul to Mexico, that read, "There are few or no persons in California with sufficient energy and capital to work on mining." Polk was determined to rectify this state of affairs when he addressed Congress on December 5, 1848, hoisting up 14 pounds of the precious metal, recently arrived from California, and adding that the nation was "deeply interested in the speedy development of the country's wealth and resources."[3]

But the problems with the myth of an otherwise obscure carpenter "discovering" gold extend well beyond its implications for fully comprehending the mineral's importance to the nation's expansionist crusade. The Marshall story renders the people who preceded the Anglo-Americans on the land, especially the Indians, all but invisible. It is as if Marshall and his boss were out operating in a virtual wilderness, a place awaiting the arrival of clever and industrious Americans to mine and profit from the landscape. Nothing could be further from the truth. The Indians unquestionably knew about the region's gold. They had to have known about it, busy as they were pruning, transplanting, and burning the landscape, shaping the plant and animal life on which their survival depended. To be fair, it may have seemed to the American pioneers that they were settling in the middle of wilderness. By the time the whites arrived, the Indians—decimated by the arrival of European diseases—no longer preyed on animals and worked the landscape to the extent they once had. Native game populations thus rebounded just in time for the Gold Rush, as did the underbrush in many forested areas. The rising number of deer, antelope, and elk furnished the 49ers with ample food opportunities, but the growth of a tangled understory in the woods hindered travel and increased the risk of fire.[4]

There were some 26 gold mines or discoveries in existence before John Marshall made his so-called historic find. Although Anglos discovered some of these sites, the Spanish and Mexicans played the leading role. These Spanish-speaking residents of California sought placer gold, bits of the mineral that harsh weather had torn from its parent rock and sent tumbling into rivers. The Spanish word "placer" means sandbank, and that is precisely where miners found the gold, a very heavy metal that settled out of the stream along its edges, where the current slows down. When the 49ers arrived they also took up placer mining, using pans, picks, shovels, and sluice boxes to search for dust and nuggets. But the real money was made not by the miners but by merchants (who supplied them) and land speculators.[5]

Placer mining lasted just a short time, as the surface gold slowly ran out. Individual enterprise then rapidly gave way to corporate mining, mainly because it took large amounts of capital to get the earth to yield the precious metal. The companies literally picked up rivers and moved them, diverting the water with dams into wooden chutes so that workers, many of them Chinese, could be sent in to hack at the now dry river beds. The threat of flooding in the winter, a common occurrence in northern California, forced laborers to work with enormous speed, or risk the possibility that the chutes would be washed downstream during a heavy rain. By 1853, nearly 25 miles of the Yuba River had been diverted from its channel. One company on the Feather River built a chute extending 3,200 feet and then sent 260 workers into the abandoned channel to strike it rich.[6]

River mining produced gold, but in nowhere near the amounts to be found in old, dried-up stream channels. Some 70 million years ago, when the Sierra Nevada range was an anemic version of its present monumental splendor, the climate of northern California tended toward the subtropical. For millions of years, the climate subjected the mountains to intense weathering, producing huge quantities of sand, gravel, and gold. In the Eocene period (55 million to 38 million years ago), the mountains began to rise up, and the accumulated mineral wealth along with the rest of the debris slid downstream toward the ocean. Gold was so heavy that it took much longer to make that journey than did gravel or sand. Thus when later volcanic eruptions sent torrents of ash out onto the landscape, rerouting old streams, much of the gold settled into abandoned river channels, where it hardened and remained. Until 1853, that is, when a man named Edward Matteson, a New Englander, discovered that a sufficient source of water delivered by hose could tear apart an ancient hillside, freeing the precious metal in the process. What many miners with picks and shovels took weeks to accomplish was just a day's labor for a few workers who tapped the energy supplied by a large volume of water.

Hydraulic mining, as it soon came to be called, sent miners scrambling for water, a resource unleashed with reckless abandon on the foothills of the Sierra

Nevada. The force of the water amazed onlookers. "Trunks of trees lying in the mine can be made to spin like straws or be hurled away many feet distant," said one. "The amount of soil removed in hydraulic mining must be seen to be believed," another added. Miners along the Feather, Yuba, American, and Bear rivers bombarded the hills with water, eventually producing nearly 1,300 million cubic yards of gravel debris, enough material to bury the city of Washington, DC, to a depth of 19 feet. Hydraulic mining caused more erosion than any other event in the history of the Sierra Nevada, stretching back nearly 600 million years.[7]

Thousands of miles of ditches brought water from the Sierra Nevada to bear on mines located in northern California watersheds. By 1857, some 700 miles of canals crisscrossed the Yuba alone. Billions of gallons of water tore apart the mountains, with the leftover debris coursing into rivers, raising their beds, and destroying salmon spawning grounds as well. In 1869, a tourist from the East noted, "Tornado, flood, earthquake, and volcano combined could hardly make greater havoc, spread wider ruin and wreck, than are to be seen everywhere in the track of the larger gold-washing operations."[8]

The entire hydrological network of northern California received a huge facelift with devastating results. Massive amounts of debris—the excavated remains of the Tertiary period—settled in riverbeds downstream from mines, leaving less room for the water that the rivers had to carry and forcing it to spill out across the flood-

MALAKOFF MINE

Hydraulic mining in the foothills of the Sierra Nevada sent mud, gravel, and sand pouring downstream into California's Yuba River. (Bancroft Library)

plain, killing people and destroying property. Extremely heavy rains in the winter of 1861–1862, with some six feet of water falling between November and January, put much of the Sacramento valley under water so deep that Leland Stanford, the newly elected governor of the state, had to take a rowboat to his inauguration. The heavy rains scoured the mountains, flushing debris downstream, where it buried some of the richest farmland in the state. By 1868, residents of Marysville, California, where the Yuba and Feather rivers intersect, found so much mining sediment in the rivers that their beds rose higher than the streets of the town itself. The town built levees to contain the floodwaters. But in 1874, after a generation of hydraulic mining, the Yuba River's bed had risen an astonishing 16 feet in height.[9]

The debris problem, severe as it was, initially evoked little opposition from those downstream since the economic destiny of these very same towns was bound up with the Gold Rush. But another devastating flood in 1875 helped to change that attitude. The deluge finished off the remaining farms on the fertile Yuba floodplain, a development that angered many in a state fast becoming known for its rich agricultural land. Farmers and others in Yuba and Sutter counties soon banded together to fight the hydraulic mining companies in court, emerging victorious in 1884 when a federal judge closed down one of the area's most powerful com-

"STOPPING A BIG STEAL"

Farmers and townspeople buried by the debris that hydraulic mining sent coursing downstream turned to the law to redress their grievances. In 1884, a federal judge issued an injunction forbidding the Malakoff Mine (renamed North Bloomfield) from discharging any more mining waste into rivers. (The Wasp, October 7, 1881; Bancroft Library)

panies. Hydraulic mining was then exported out of state to Oregon, Idaho, and eventually abroad to Thailand and Colombia, where it continues to this day.[10]

The ecological significance of the Gold Rush, however, was not confined to northern California alone. People had to get to the gold, and to do this they had to traverse the continent. For the first time, ordinary Americans tramped west in large numbers—80,000 just in 1849. They brought in their wake major changes to California. But they also figured centrally in a significant environmental disaster on the Great Plains, a crisis of subsistence for Indians rooted in the expansion of human and animal populations beyond what the land could handle.

Gold seekers took two main trails west across the Great Plains, the vast grassland that occupies the nation's midsection and consisting of parts of the Dakotas, Montana, Wyoming, Nebraska, Kansas, Colorado, New Mexico, Oklahoma, and Texas. The first was the Oregon-California road and the second, the Santa Fe Trail. The traffic along these routes was enormous. Some 300,000 people with more than 1.5 million four-legged creatures—cattle, horses, and oxen—set off along the Oregon road between 1841 and 1859. On the Santa Fe, the wagon traffic alone was impressive, with almost 2,000 vehicles plying the route by the end of the 1850s.

The stream of emigrants—human beings and animals—took their toll on the Platte and Arkansas watersheds. Pioneers cut down timber on the river bottoms to cook with or keep warm. Oxen, cattle, mules, and horses chewed up the region's forage, putting a significant dent in what had once seemed like an almost limitless supply of grass that thrived in the dry environment. The gold seekers even timed their journey west to coincide with the availability of grass. They tried not to leave before it had sprouted enough to support their herds but were wary of setting off too late, when all the forage would have been eaten. All the foot and hoof traffic also trampled a great deal of vegetation. Then there was the damage caused by wagon wheels. Sometimes bunched together in groups 12 abreast, the caravans moved across the region like giant steamrollers.[11]

The central plains environment perhaps would have rebounded from the pioneer invasion had not another mass migration to this very same place been occurring at roughly the same time. While gold seekers were rushing across the plains, Indians, led by the Cheyennes, headed there to capitalize on the large herds of bison and to assume a role as middlemen in a trading network that spanned from New Mexico into Canada. Despite being battered by European diseases, the Native American population grew significantly to perhaps as many as 20,000 people by the 1850s.[12]

The Cheyennes counted on their horses—animals acquired from the Spanish— to track and hunt the mobile buffalo herds. Large numbers of horses, perhaps as many as 5 to 13 for each person, required lots of forage. Forage was especially scarce on the plains in the winter when rainfall tapered off and grama and buffalo grass became less nutritious. That forced the Indians to retreat to river locations where protection from the weather and moister conditions kept grass alive.

Indeed, their very survival on the plains depended on finding adequate forage, fuel, water, and protection from the elements during severe winters. River bottoms such as the Big Timbers, a large stretch of cottonwoods along the Arkansas River in present-day Colorado, served well for a time. But then the pioneers showed up with their horses and oxen in the summer months to exploit this same locale. When white emigrants approached the Big Timbers in the latter part of the 1850s, they found it scalped, prompting the wife of one pioneer to write: "cattle were nearly starved for grass."[13]

A climatic change made matters worse. The central plains experienced uncharacteristically wet weather between 1825 and 1849. A lush, inviting environment resulted, precisely in time to greet both the Indians and whites who passed through the area. But then drought struck, descending across the Arkansas valley in 1849. A more extensive dry spell wracked the central plains in 1855, followed by two even worse droughts in the early 1860s. The Indians turned even more to river locations for water and forage, putting additional pressure on an environment already stretched to its limits.[14]

By the 1850s, the central plains were in ecological turmoil, with more people and animals dependent on a shrinking supply of natural capital. The drought only intensified the suffering, driving Indians to beg whites for food as they passed west. Some Native Americans even stole in order to eat. In 1855, a group of Arapahos made off with more than 2,000 sheep. The following year, Indians reportedly demanded food in return for safe passage along the Santa Fe road.[15]

Then, in 1858, gold was discovered in what became Denver, Colorado, prompting twice as many people to pick up and cross the continent as had done so in 1849. Wagon traffic on the Santa Fe Trail boomed. By the mid-1860s, Denver alone depended on the shipment of tens of thousands of tons of supplies each year from back east. The bottomlands continued their steady ecological descent. The summer of 1859 became known as the "timber clearing sun dance," a name bestowed by the Kiowas who showed up for their yearly ritual on the Smoky Hill River expecting to see a forested grove; instead they found stumps. Whites had normally avoided the area, but now the search for forage and timber to support their overland trek forced them further from the main trail west, bringing them into conflict with Indians.[16]

The number of such conflicts rose and so, in response, did the U.S. military presence. As had happened during the Civil War, the army worried about feeding its horses. It sought out locations at precisely those wintertime haunts so cherished by Indians. Military posts sprouted at the Big Timbers of the Arkansas (Fort Wise) and at other such sheltered sites rich in wood and grass, further undermining the ability of Native Americans to survive.[17]

It would be wrong, of course, to blame the Indians' plight on the quest for gold alone. Indians also contributed to their own demise by keeping far more horses—tens of thousands—than the land could support. Nor did the gold seekers cause the drought.

To move from gold mining to Indians, to horses and mules, and then to drought, forage, and timber seems like helter-skelter history. But this seemingly disconnected chain of topics reminds us of the interdependency of the various aspects of the natural world. This one change in human behavior—the rush to mine gold—had consequences that ramified throughout the continent, in ecosystems far removed from the site of the gold itself.

Plants and animals are not merely a backdrop for history. They are living things that have needs, that make demands on the land. Sometimes the land lives up to the task, and sometimes, because of a variety of factors both human and nonhuman, those needs outstrip the ability of the environment to provide. Such was the anatomy of tragedy on the plains.[18]

LAST OF THE BISON

If few people are aware of the ecological crisis that gripped the Great Plains, virtually everyone knows about the decline of the buffalo, one of the most studied blunders in the nation's environmental past. When the buffalo vanished, so did the hopes and dreams of the Plains Indians, who for more than 150 years had organized their culture around the animal. Sitting Bull put it this way: "A cold wind blew across the prairie when the last buffalo fell—a death-wind for my people."[19]

BISON

The West's most famous animal species, bison survived on the region's shortgrass, which had just the combination of protein and carbohydrates they needed to thrive. (Colorado Historical Society)

As improbable as it may seem, herds of bison could be found in the eastern part of the United States as late as the 1830s. From then on, the buffalo population retreated to the grasslands of the plains. That had been its primary home since the end of the Ice Age, when climatic change spurred the shift from trees to grass in this vast region. Unlike such large animals as mammoths and mastodons, the bison—a prolific reproducer, quick on its feet, and able to subsist on less forage than other megafauna—survived the Pleistocene extinctions. With its other competitors now out of the way, the bison multiplied, gobbling up the aptly named buffalo grass, while fertilizing the soil with its dung, and thus helping to sustain its habitat.

How many bison existed out on the plains has been the subject of much debate. But whatever the actual number it was high, at least before the late nineteenth century. George Catlin in the 1830s found bison so thick that they "literally blacken the prairies for miles together." As late as 1871, one observer witnessed a herd of buffalo in Kansas that reportedly took five full days to venture past. One Indian, asked in the late nineteenth century to recall the glory days of the bison, was blunt about it, signing the words, "The country was one robe."[20]

Estimates of the total bison population have ranged as high as 75 million, but historians and ecologists have recently scaled down that figure considerably, and for good reason. The bison depended on grass to survive; as went the grass, so went the bison. By taking into account the carrying capacity of the grassland, it seems reasonable to assume that the Great Plains supported a population of about 27 million such creatures. Significant threats, however, ranging from drought, perhaps the most important, to predation by wolves (1.5 million may have roamed the plains in the early nineteenth century), affected the buffalo's numbers. The more such threats—and the bison faced many—the more volatile the animal population. Like their human counterparts, the bison also had to face the facts of life in this unforgiving land.[21]

Before the eighteenth century, Native American groups ventured to the plains to hunt buffalo, but the animal remained just one part of their effort to survive in this land. The Indians who came to dominate life on the plains also gathered a variety of plants—roots and berries—and, in some cases, turned to agriculture as well. Like southern yeoman farmers in the years before the Civil War, Native Americans opted for a safety-first strategy, engaging in a diverse set of practices for feeding themselves. And like the South's small farmers, the Plains Indians were eventually driven to specialize—in this case, not in cotton but in buffalo. More than anything else, perhaps, this specialization sealed their fate and set the stage for the decline of both the bison and the cultures that depended on them.

Nothing did more to encourage the Indians to throw their fortunes in with the bison and engage in hunting it all throughout the year than the arrival of the horse. The Spanish brought horses to America in the early sixteenth century, but it took well over 100 years for the Plains Indians to adopt them. Horses greatly expanded the Indians' ability to hunt buffalo, freeing them from the dreary task of chasing after them by foot. Horses were also a huge improvement over the dogs the Indians had formerly depended on for transport. Dogs are carnivores, and during the winter Indians found it difficult to find enough meat to feed them. The horse, however, eats grass, of which there was plenty on the plains. When the Indians discovered the horse they found the key for unlocking the grassland's huge storehouse of energy. The energy allowed the Indians to fortify their mounts and set off to hunt buffalo, to the exclusion of other subsistence activities, save the gathering of berries and roots.[22]

By the eighteenth century, the bison had assumed a place at the center of Plains Indian culture. The Indians roasted and boiled it for food, consuming nearly the entire animal right down to its testicles and marrow. They made bedding, clothing, and rope from it. They used the intestines as containers, the penis for making glue, and the horns for cups. The bison served so many different dietary and cultural needs that one scholar referred to the animal as a "tribal department store."[23]

What impact did the Indians have on the bison population? According to one estimate, Plains Indians killed only about half a million buffalo every year, a sustainable figure in light of the bison's reproductive habits. Indians may have even looked down on those who wasted bison. "Don't kill more meat than you think you can skin and your horse can pack home," one Kiowa told another in 1861 on the occasion of his first buffalo hunt. Other evidence, however, indicates that the Indians' belief system may have encouraged them to overhunt the species. When buffalo disappeared for the year, the Plains Indians believed, they went to underground prairies, reemerging in the spring "like bees from a hive," as one white put it. If they failed to appear in adequate numbers one could still hunt with abandon, safe in knowing that other buffalo were grazing happily in the land down below.[24]

None of this is meant to imply that the Indians engaged in the wanton destruction of the animals. But it would be wrong to assume that a group so deeply dependent on bison was incapable of putting a dent in their numbers. Well before commercial shooters descended in droves on the plains, Indian hunting took its toll. At one time, contested grounds—areas where no single Indian group dominated—sheltered the bison from attack. Indians, fearing for their lives, tended to shy away from those areas. But in 1840, a number of Native American groups on the western plains agreed to peace. No longer looking over their shoulders, Indians waged war against the bison. As a result, by the 1850s the bison began vanishing from the Denver area.[25]

A mere 30 years later, the buffalo would be virtually annihilated. Nothing the Indians did rivaled in importance the role of the market in the animal's demise. Plains Indians had long traded with other Native American groups, often exchanging buffalo for corn. But by the 1830s, the demand for buffalo skins began to rise sharply as European Americans used them to keep warm. In the past, Indians had valued the entirety of the animal. To them, it had use-value, a unique ability to serve a variety of different needs, ranging from food and clothing to much more. The rise of the robe market, however, put a price on the bison, driving the Indians to kill them for their skins alone, leaving the rest of the carcass for wolves to devour. In the 1850s, commercial bison hunting combined with drought—which dried up creeks and stunted the growth of grass—to make life difficult for the buffalo. "The buffalo is becoming scarce and it is more difficult from year to year for the Indians to kill a sufficient number to supply them with food and clothing," one observer along the Platte River reported in 1855.[26]

The real damage to the bison, however, came at the hands of the white market hunters. Beginning in the 1870s, they flooded into the plains to meet the burgeoning demand for leather in industrial America. The growth of industry called for leather belting to power machinery, outstripping the domestic supply of hides. Tanners, hard pressed for skins, were driven to import them from as far away as Latin America. Then in 1870, tanners in Philadelphia discovered a method for turning bison skin into leather. The production of industrial leather required green, unprepared buffalo hides. In the past, Indian women had fleshed the hides, transforming them into buffalo robes for markets in the East. This was a time-consuming process and bottlenecks occurred, a factor that may have inadvertently protected the buffalo against overhunting. Green skins removed the threat of such slowdowns, but there was one hitch: They weighed about five times as much as a robe, possibly as much as 50 pounds each. It would take something far more powerful than the back of a horse to transport the heavy hides to market in the numbers required to satisfy American industry.[27]

That something turned out to be the railroad. The roads pushed through the plains in the years following 1867; the buffalo declined everywhere the trains went. Scarcely a generation later, the bison would be all but gone. At the very minimum, the Santa Fe, Kansas Pacific, and Union Pacific railroads shipped over a million hides in just two years (1872–1874). The bison, recall, had few predators and thus little experience with being attacked. Worse still, from the standpoint of the species, was the animal's tendency to stampede or stand pat when faced with an aggressor. The gun-toting market hunter could not have asked for more cooperative prey. Hunters commonly bagged 2,000 to 3,000 hides in any one season. In 1876, one hunter killed nearly 6,000 bison in just two months, firing his .50-caliber rifle so many times that he went deaf.[28]

Aiding the market hunters was the U.S. Army. It was no secret that military leaders believed that the best way to subjugate the Plains Indians was through the elimination of the buffalo. Lt. Gen. John M. Schofield, in charge of the Department of Missouri from 1869 to 1870, put it this way: "I wanted no other occupation in life than to ward off the savage and kill off his food until there should no longer be an Indian frontier in our beautiful country." Gen. William Tecumseh Sherman, of Civil War fame, wrote in 1868 that "as long as Buffalo are up on the Republican [River] the Indians will go there. I think it would be wise to invite all the sportsmen of England and America there this fall for a Grand Buffalo hunt." Sherman's comrade in arms, Gen. Phil Sheridan, pointed out that market hunters had done more "to settle the vexed Indian question than the entire regular army has done in the last thirty years. They are destroying the Indians' commissary. . . . Send them powder and lead, if you will; but for the sake of lasting peace, let them kill, skin and sell until the buffaloes are exterminated." The army even went so far as to distribute free ammunition to the hide hunters.[29]

With the bison gone from the southern plains by 1878, the hunters moved north. In that locale, the fate of the buffalo rested less on the market hunters and more on the combined forces of ranching and drought. The huge number of cattle imported into the region (Wyoming's cattle population increased from 90,000 to more than 500,000 between 1874 and 1880) competed with the bison for grass, closing off areas where the animal retreated for food and water. When dry spells struck beginning in the 1870s, the bison had nowhere left to turn. In 1882, hunters took the remaining 5,000 survivors present on the northern plains.[30]

Only their bones remained and, fittingly, even these were turned into cash. Dispossessed Indians (and others) collected the skeletal remains of the once vast bison herds, piling them 10 feet high along railroad tracks where bone dealers arranged to ship them east. There they were crushed up and made into phosphate

BISON BONES

In the late nineteenth century, Indians and poor whites collected the remains of dead bison for sale to fertilizer companies. Bones pictured here were at the Michigan Carbon Works in Detroit. (Detroit Public Library)

fertilizer, destined to be spread on the soils of the Cotton South and Corn Belt, providing a nutrient subsidy to distant ecosystems.

In those bones lay a lesson in where economic specialization might lead. When the Plains Indians engaged in the single-minded pursuit of bison, they foreclosed on other avenues for making a living from the land. In a region prone to climatic extremes, this was a risky move that might even have landed them in trouble had the market hunters, soldiers, and railroads never come along.

THE GREAT CATTLE BUST

The death of the bison was the prelude to one of the most stunning transformations ever of a North American biome: the makeover of the Great Plains grasslands into pastures and farms. Cattle drovers and wheat farmers delivered a one-two punch to the grasslands in the post–Civil War years, stripping the region of its original vegetative cover, loosening the soil, and making it far more prone to wind erosion. It was not Malthusian pressures—as in New England or the Chesapeake during the late eighteenth century—that drove the cowboys, cattle companies, and wheat farmers to exploit the plains. No shortage of food compelled them to graze more cattle or plant more wheat. It was, instead, the exchange value of the grass—that is, its ability to turn a profit—that sent them to work rearranging the landscape. By the time they were through, they had set the stage for some of the worst ecological calamities to ever befall the region.

To the rancher, cattle were less a source of food than a means of accumulating wealth. Indeed, the word *cattle* has the same etymological roots as *capital*, the so-called stock of life. As one of the world's earliest mobile assets, cattle was money, but only if the animal could be fed. When it comes to cattle, grass is the currency of accumulation. If the grass is free, as it was on the plains during the postbellum years, then all the better. "Cotton was once crowned king," proclaimed one eastern livestock journal in the 1870s, "but grass is now. . . . If grass is King, the Rocky Mountain region is its throne and fortunate indeed are those who possess it."[31]

Ranching, as it evolved in the American West, originated in the early nineteenth century in southern Texas. It was there that the mixing of Anglo-American cattle from the South and Spanish stock from Mexico produced the breed known as the Texas Longhorn. Hardy and able to thrive on grass, the species, famous for its long horns, reproduced with abandon during the Civil War. The animals roamed the range unsupervised as the men who once raised them went off to fight; others simply gave up tending the creatures as hostilities cut off the market for their meat in southern cities like New Orleans. By 1870, as ranching spread northward in Texas, one county had some 57,000 cattle; another had 159 head for every inhabitant. Closed off from southern markets, ranchers shifted their attentions to the North, where cattle commanded higher prices. After the war, railroads began to work their way across the plains, and towns such as Abilene, Kansas, emerged to unite the southern cattle drover with buyers in the North. Setting off along the Chisholm Trail and other routes, drovers brought their livestock to rail depots, where they were transferred to trains headed east to meet the demand for beef in cities such as St. Louis and Chicago. By 1871, Abilene processed nearly 750,000 longhorns every year, dispatching them to slaughterhouses in cities further east.[32]

Slowly, the Texas ranchers gravitated northward, attracted by the vast stretches of shortgrass they found on the Great Plains. It is estimated that something on the order of five million head of cattle were driven north and west onto the plains between 1866 and 1884. From New Mexico to Montana, the Texas cattle system spread, spurred on by a period of wet weather in the 25 years following 1860. Texas cattle culture evolved in the South's subtropical climate; had not the wet conditions prevailed, the move onto the arid plains would almost certainly have been forestalled.[33]

The Texas longhorn—product of the warm and wet South—was ill adapted to the arid conditions and bitter winters found on the plains. In Kansas, for example, the number of calves surviving to adulthood amounted to only four-fifths what ranchers expected in Texas. The survival rate declined still more the further north one moved. Unlike buffalo, cattle are not well equipped physically to deal with snowy conditions. Bison have gigantic flat heads that they swing from side to side, clearing the ground and allowing them access to the grass below. Not so the longhorn, which stood around and starved when confronted by snow cover. The winter of 1871–1872 was so severe in Kansas and Nebraska that mortality rates for cattle in some areas exceeded 50 percent.[34]

Despite these warning signs the ranchers pushed on, joined in the 1870s and 1880s by investors from overseas, especially from Britain. In nineteenth-century Europe, fatty cuts of beef symbolized power and privilege, but with the pastures of Scotland and Ireland overgrazed, the British turned their attention to the American plains. As early as 1868, cattle were transported live across the Atlantic. The introduction of refrigerated transportation technologies in the following decade helped to solidify the link between the plains grasslands and the British consumer. In 1875, a New York inventor named John Bates employed a large fan and ice to ship 10 cattle carcasses across the Atlantic, with good results. By 1877, one shipping outfit sent some three million pounds of American beef to Britain every month. The beef bonanza was on, as English and Scottish entrepreneurs launched cattle ventures that gobbled up huge swathes of land in the American West. By the early 1880s, foreign investment on the grasslands elicited so much opposition that both the Democratic and Republican parties supported a reduction in alien holdings. "America for Americans," presidential candidate James Blaine trumpeted in 1884, tapping into the anti-British sentiment rife across the West.[35]

Driving the land grab was the ease with which one could arrive on the plains and set up a cattle business. In the early years of ranching, the range was free and open to everyone. If a drover arrived in a valley and discovered cattle, he simply moved elsewhere. The range remained the common property of all those who

COWBOYS

Until fencing, disastrous weather, and other changes put an end to the open range, cowboys of Anglo, Indian, Hispanic, and African American descent tended large herds on the grasslands of the West. (Library of Congress)

wanted to use it. But as American and foreign investors descended on the grasslands, overcrowding soon became a problem. In response, some ranchers purchased barbed wire (invented in 1873), closing off parts of the public domain from intruders. American factories produced 40,000 tons of wire by 1880; much of it was strung across the plains. Between 1881 and 1885, ranchers in the Texas Panhandle laid out 200 miles of fence for preventing cattle from drifting during a storm.[36]

As was true in the South, fencing had some untoward ecological consequences. First, it concentrated cattle in specific locations, a development that led to overgrazing. In the 1880s, one ranch manager from Texas lamented the increase in both cattle and fences. "With this the character of the grass completely changed; where formerly there was long luxuriant grass that would fatten an animal without his having to do too much walking; there is now only short grass at the best of seasons." Second, fences made the already severe winters all the harder for the animals. When the range remained open, cattle caught in a snowstorm would drift across the plains, perhaps escaping the worst conditions. If the animal reached a barrier, however, it remained trapped. As one critic of the fencing mania put it in 1883, "Under the old regime, there was a loose adaptability to the margins of the ranges where now there is a clear-cut line which admits of no argument, and an overstocked range must bleed when the blizzards sit in judgment."[37]

And bleed it did. Huge numbers of cattle died in Utah during the winter of 1879–1880. The same happened in Colorado and Nebraska the following winter. In 1884–1885, cattle die-offs reached as high as 90 percent, as extreme cold plunged south all the way to Texas. Ranchers on the southern plains suffered through another harsh winter the following year. As one observer put it in the spring of 1886, the cattle "died of hunger; they have perished of thirst, when the icy breath of winter closed the streams; they have died of starvation by the tens of thousands during the season when cold storms sweep out of the North and course over the plains, burying the grass under snow."[38]

By the mid-1880s, the western range had been abused for over a decade. The results of that exploitative relationship with the grass were becoming increasingly apparent. Noting the deteriorated state of the pasturelands in 1885, a U.S. government official remarked, "Cattlemen say that the grasses are not what they used to be; that the valuable perennial species are disappearing, and that their place is being taken by less nutritious annuals."[39] Free grass combined with a speculative fever had led ranchers to stock the range with far more cattle than it could reasonably support.

The final blow came in 1886. After a dry summer the year before, fire broke out on the southern plains, reducing the available forage and weakening the animals as winter approached. And what a winter it was. Gale force winds and blinding snow reduced visibility in some areas on the southern plains to 16 feet. The cold extended as far south as Austin, Texas, where below-zero temperatures (Fahrenheit) were reported in January 1886. From Montana all the way to Texas, they died, vast numbers of cattle, too numerous to count, their carcasses piling up in precisely the places one would expect. The cattle drifted south as the blizzards rolled in and they stopped when they came to a fence, pressing in on each other, and scrounging the ground for every last blade of grass they could find. According to a firsthand account of the blizzard by O. P. Beyers, following the right-of-way fence erected by the Union Pacific Railroad, one could walk 400 miles from Ellsworth, Kansas, to Denver, stepping only on carcasses.[40]

Further north in the Badlands of North Dakota, an even worse disaster unfolded. On New Year's Day 1887, the temperature plunged in the southwestern part of the state to minus 41 degrees. Gale force winds and blinding snow arrived on January 28. "For seventy-two hours," one observer wrote, "it seemed as if all the world's ice from Time's beginnings had come on a wind which howled and screamed with the fury of demons."[41]

Spring 1887 arrived with a vengeance. As the land began to thaw, rivers filled with water, a trickle at first that eventually became a torrent. Floods overtook the land, precipitating one of the longest funeral processions in history: tens of thousands of animal carcasses all flowing downstream. On the Little Missouri River, one observer, shocked by what he saw, wrote as follows: "Countless carcasses of

BLIZZARD, 1886

With the range overstocked, a blast of cold weather delivered a punishing blow to western ranching. (Harper's Weekly, February 27, 1886; Library of Congress)

cattle [were] going down with the ice, rolling over and over as they went, so that at times all four of the stiffened legs of a carcass would point skyward, as it turned under the impulsion of the swiftly moving current and the grinding ice-cakes."[42]

It must have been a stomach-turning scene for many a rancher, watching as their investments disappeared downriver in a roar of bankruptcy. In the end, the ranchers fell victim not simply to nature, but to their inability to control their greedy impulses, to the persistent funneling of more stock onto the range. That lack of self-discipline joined with the trail of fences that now gripped the land to deny the Texas cattle—poorly adapted to the cold and dry weather conditions present on the plains in any case—its mobility, its best defense against the weather.

The die-offs of the late nineteenth century offered a textbook lesson on the perils of overstocking the range. No one, however, should see in the disaster an argument for ridding the plains of cattle. Ecologically speaking, the grasslands need cattle or some other herbivore so that the plants and grasses that live there can experience the level of disturbance they need to survive. From the days of the mastodons through the bison, plant life in the grasslands evolved in tandem with creatures that browsed. Too much grazing is a problem, but so also is too much rest for the land.[43]

Sustainable ranching can be conducted on the plains, as the Hidatsas of North Dakota proved in the waning years of the nineteenth century. This Native American group operated small-scale communal ranches, cutting and storing hay to get the animals through the winter. They were not out for big money, but reveled in the freedom and thrill they experienced rounding up cattle, of cowboy life out on the plains. The Hidatsas offer proof that sustainable use of the land does not have to mean forsaking all the pleasures that come with economic development, as long as people can content themselves with small monetary rewards and resist the urge to overstock.[44]

DARK DAYS

As calamities go, the great cattle bust was just one of a number of disasters, big and small, that put an end to the dreams of those who imagined the plains as one vast field of opportunity. The calamities may have appeared natural but were, in fact, the result of a complex interaction between an economic culture unmindful of limits and a volatile physical environment prone to drought, winds, and storms.

Most students of American history are aware of the Dust Bowl, but few learn of the 1890s drought. And yet, in terms of its social consequences, the event may have caused even more suffering and hardship than the well-known 1930s disaster. The groundwork for the calamity was laid between 1878 and 1887, when the same wet weather that gave rise to the beef bonanza also sent farmers from the eastern part of the country out to plains to plant wheat, causing the population in some areas to explode. The population of the western third of Kansas alone rose from 38,000 people in 1885 to 139,000 people in 1887. Optimism ruled the day as railroads and other western boosters, with prevailing scientific theory on their side, promoted the catch phrase "rain follows the plow."

By 1887, the past tense no longer applied with respect to drought. Wheat yields tumbled in response to the dry weather, which extended into the following decade. Widespread reports of drought-induced starvation and malnutrition—relatively minor problems in the 1930s Dust Bowl—began to file in, with some talking of "Anderson fare," a reference to the South's brutal Civil War prison, Andersonville. In Miner County, South Dakota, 2,500 people faced death from starvation, with corn averaging just a meager two to three bushels per acre. Unable to survive, many simply walked off the land. Some areas experienced population losses of half to three-quarters. Suddenly pessimism replaced optimism, with one songwriter telling of "starvin' to death on my government claim." The government, under the provisions of the Homestead Act (1862), sought to open the Great Plains by allowing anyone who settled 160 acres and remained for five years to become its rightful owner. In the late nineteenth century, however, they were more likely to starve first.[45]

To deal with the arid conditions, many farmers tried dryland farming. Centered on the use of drought-resistant grain crops, deep plowing, quick cultivation after a period of rain, and other moisture-conserving measures, the technique succeeded, with the help of high wheat prices, in making the years between 1909 and 1914 a boom period for Great Plains farmers. The good times continued as

SANDSTORM, 1894
Although most people associate blowing dust with the 1930s, severe drought afflicted the Great Plains in the 1890s, leading to dust storms like this one in Midland, Texas. (National Archives)

gasoline-powered machines—tractors, combines, and trucks—dramatically reduced the labor involved in planting wheat. The one-way disk plow, invented in 1926, doubled the amount of sod a farmer could break in a day. While the old moldboard plows (a "moldboard" being a curved plate that forced the soil off to one side) sliced through the sod and turned it over in one unbroken mass, the new disk plows, with their multiple plates, pulverized the soil, increasing water absorption. The huge strides in mechanization eventually gave rise to "suitcase farmers," bankers, teachers, and others who purchased equipment, drove it out to plant wheat, and then returned home before venturing back in the spring to reap their rewards. If their harvests coincided with an uptick in the price of grain, those rewards could be substantial indeed.[46]

When World War I began, the plains farmer was in the perfect position to aid the Allied cause and to plow up millions of acres of grass in the process. Eleven million acres of grass in Kansas, Colorado, Nebraska, Oklahoma, and Texas was destroyed between 1914 and 1919. Wartime demand for wheat drove farmers to plow up more grass, but it also worked to draw the plains farmer ever more closely into the international market economy. Life on the plains became tied to economic imperatives in distant lands, as the soil wealth of the plains was creamed off to feed people across the globe.

But just as important, natural wealth from outside the country was brought to bear on plains agriculture, as U.S. scientists scoured the earth for a species of wheat that would flourish in the arid West. Turning to those parts of Asia that closely resembled the American grasslands, Frank Meyer of the U.S. Department of Agriculture returned with 2,500 new varieties of plants between 1905 and 1918. A Canadian scientist, Charles Saunders, then used some of the Russian wheat species to develop Marquis, one of the two varieties of wheat that account for the bulk of the crop planted on the plains today. It was not just wheat, but Marquis wheat that helped America win the war—a development that, it must be said, also cost the plains its grass.[47]

Gone by 1935 was the native grass that once covered 33 million acres in the heart of what became the Dust Bowl region. When drought conditions—a regular and predictable aspect of life on the plains—emerged once again in the 1930s, the dried-out soil became even more prone to wind erosion. Nineteen thirty-five was the worst year for dust storms; the darkest day in that dark year was April 14, 1935, Black Sunday. From Colorado to Washington, DC, the skies turned black and the sand blew in, blasting the paint from houses, insinuating itself through cracks and keyholes, piling up in front yards. The air came loaded with both dust and rationalization. In Dalhart, Texas, John McCarty, a newspaper editor incensed by the eastern media's efforts to pin the Dust Bowl label on the region, blamed the tragedy on drought and "conditions beyond their [the farmers'] control." Franklin Roosevelt, whose New Deal administration intervened to buttress farming in the disaster-prone plains—offering federal money for relief as well as loans to finance rebuilding—also blamed natural forces beyond anyone's control. Drought was necessary but hardly sufficient to bring on the calamity. It also took an economic culture that viewed the land as capital, a society in which the search for profits guided relations with the earth.[48]

In the last analysis the Dust Bowl amounted to a failure on the part of farmers to adapt to the arid ecological conditions present on the southern plains. When Roosevelt stepped in with federal money for relief and rehabilitation, he caused farmers to think, correctly as it turned out, that the government would intervene in future droughts, giving them an incentive to stay put. Roosevelt thus divided up the potential threat of environmental tragedy in this region and proceeded to share it with taxpayers all across the nation. The risk of drought was divorced from the place in which it occurred, spread out for each and every American to bear, Uncle Sam defusing the harmful effects of natural calamity by shunting their costs elsewhere. It amounted to one huge exercise in risk sharing, one monstrous gift from the North and South to the West. Without it, life on the plains as we know it today would be impossible.

CONCLUSION

What does the history of this unforgiving land have to teach us? First, it provides a new appreciation for the hardships faced by the Indians as they were driven (during the first half of the nineteenth century) across the Mississippi River to make way for cotton plantations. The South's lush landscape assured all human beings relative freedom from hunger; its mild climate virtually guaranteed that no one would freeze to death. When the U.S. government removed the Indians from the South to the West, however, they forced them into an arid region full of volatile weather where survival could no longer be taken for granted.

The second lesson is this: To engage in economic specialization in a place subject to such extreme weather is a risky enterprise. Specializing in cotton farming was one thing in the warm and bountiful South. Pursuing buffaloes or raising wheat in the arid West, where drought could descend at the worst possible moment and where no spring fish runs existed to fall back on, was something yet again. As a general rule, a culture's ability to respond and adapt to environmental change is inversely proportional to the degree to which it specializes. The more single-minded in pursuit of one activity, be it buffalo hunting or wheat farming, the less likely it is to be able to cope with sudden shifts in weather and their consequences on the ground. Only the U.S. government's willingness to absorb and redistribute the risks of life out on the plains has allowed American farmers the liberty to rely solely on wheat. Take away the subsidies and relief aid and let the Kansas farmer bear the full weight of living in this arid land, and suddenly what now seems like rugged individualism becomes revealed as daredevilry in disguise.

CONSERVATION RECONSIDERED

One of the ranchers who watched the blizzard of 1887 wipe out his herd of cattle was Theodore Roosevelt. In the early 1880s, Roosevelt, a New Yorker, built a ranch in North Dakota's Badlands, stocked it with animals, and hired two cowboys to oversee his venture. In the spring of 1887, he headed west to check on the status of his 85,000-dollar investment, arriving in the Little Missouri valley only to find that death had beaten him there. He saw cattle carcasses—23 in just a single little spot—and found his once glorious herd reduced to just "a skinny sorry-looking crew." The ground itself was in no better shape. "The land was a mere barren waste; not a green thing could be seen; the dead grass eaten off till the country looked as if it had been shaved with a razor."[1]

In the fall of 1887, Roosevelt returned once again to the Badlands, this time on a hunting trip. Not much had improved since his last visit. The region's prairie grass had lost the battle with ranchers, ever eager to stock the range with more animals than it could reasonably have been expected to bear. The remaining grass fell victim to desperate cattle seeking whatever little forage they could find in the wake of the death-dealing blizzard of 1887. An eerie silence spread out over the land. Four years earlier, on a visit to this spot, Roosevelt found few, if any, buffalo. In 1885, he lamented the loss of wild sheep and antelope. In 1886, he worried about the disappearance of migratory birds. By 1887, then, the Badlands must have offered a melancholy sight, and Roosevelt proposed to do something about it. He returned to New York to invite 12 of his animal-loving friends over for a meal and in January 1888 they established the Boone & Crockett Club, named in honor of Daniel Boone and Davy Crockett, legendary frontiersmen whom Roosevelt worshipped. The club was one of the first organizations in this country dedicated to saving big-game animals. And it was the work of a man who would go on to become president of the United States, a man whose name has become synonymous with the American conservation movement.[2]

The story generally told about conservation goes something like this. President Roosevelt, an avid outdoor enthusiast, believed the government needed to intervene to save the nation's forests, streams, and other natural resources from rapacious loggers, ranchers, and market hunters alike. To carry out this mission, Roosevelt named Gifford Pinchot to head the newly formed U.S. Forest Service in 1905. Pinchot and his colleagues in the conservation movement, many drawn from fields such as forestry, geology, and hydrology, felt that a rational plan for organizing the nation's use of its natural resources was in order. Business leaders, driven by unrestrained competition for timber, water, and grass, they held, would have to cede authority to expert government planners, with their scientific background, who would see to the most efficient use of the country's natural wealth. Roosevelt, Pinchot, and other conservationists thus were not interested so much in preserving nature untouched as in standing guard to make sure it was used in the wisest, most efficient way possible.[3]

Opposing the "efficient use" brand of conservation, in this story, were the preservationists, the most famous of whom was John Muir. Born in 1838 in Dunbar, Scotland, and brought by his parents to Wisconsin when he was 11, Muir, who experienced a devout upbringing, would go on to found what was by all rights his own religion. It was based on the idea that we are "all God's people"— "we" referring not just to human beings but to foxes, bears, plants, indeed, all elements of the natural world. Humans had no more right to exist than other species of life did. Often touted as the founder of the environmental movement, Muir strongly disagreed with Pinchot and the practical philosophy that informed his view of conservation. He proposed instead that wilderness areas enriched human life, existing as sacred refuges, antidotes to the stresses of modern society. "Climb the mountains and get their good tidings," he once remarked. Muir, who founded the Sierra Club in 1892, felt government had a moral responsibility to preserve nature, not simply to use it wisely in the name of industry. He urged the nation's political leaders to lock away America's wilderness areas and throw the key as far from business as humanly possible, though he came to modify that stance as he was increasingly drawn into the practical world of politics.[4]

In the early years of the twentieth century, these two philosophies—utilitarianism versus preservationism—collided in the beautiful Hetch Hetchy valley in California's Sierra Nevada. In the aftermath of a devastating earthquake and fire in 1906, the city of San Francisco to the south proposed a dam to bring water to the growing metropolis, flooding the valley in the process. Pinchot supported the project on practical grounds. He faced off against the preservation-minded John Muir, who lost the battle. The dam was built and the valley inundated, as human impulse trumped natural beauty.

The problem with this portrayal, as it is rendered, for instance, in most American history textbooks, is that conservation, in both its guises, is primarily viewed as a battle over ideas about nature. Little is said about the effect of conservation measures—such as the establishment of national parks, forests, and wildlife preserves—on the ecosystems that were the target of this important reform impulse. And yet, to consider policies aimed at conserving nature without exploring what happened on the ground—to the natural world (and the people who depended on it for food)—is like teaching the Civil War without mentioning the outcome. Perhaps nature succumbed at Hetch Hetchy, but elsewhere the results of conservation policy were far more complicated. Oftentimes the West's plants, trees, and animals simply thumbed their noses at the supposed experts sent to manage them. Conservationists found themselves unable to fully grasp the complexity of eco-

ROOSEVELT AND MUIR

Shown here posing at Yosemite National Park in 1903, these two key figures in the conservation movement disagreed over the best approach to achieving peace with nature, with Theodore Roosevelt embracing a utilitarian stance and John Muir a more spiritually oriented approach. (Yosemite Museum, Yosemite National Park)

logical forces and erroneously took steps that caused nature to strike back with devastating wildfires and game explosions.

Another problem with the conventional story is that it tends to mask the fact that both strains of conservation thinking—Pinchot's and Muir's—sought to bend nature to conform to the desires of humankind. Both, in other words, contained strong doses of anthropocentrism, not just the utilitarian variety. Even more important, both visions of how to go about conserving nature favored some groups of people over others. As the federal government moved in to try its hand at managing the forests and range in the name of tourism, ranching, and logging, Indians and poor whites, who had depended on such lands for food, found their interests shoved to the side. Conservation for some meant fines and jail time, and empty bellies for others.

TAYLOR-MADE FORESTS

While the conservationists were off dreaming up ways of reining in laissez-faire capitalism, engineer Frederick Taylor was busy inventing a strategy for bringing efficiency to the workplace. Rarely spoken of in the same breath, the two developments ought to be. Taylorism tried to help employers streamline production by eliminating the chaos present on the shop floor, prevailing on workers to use the most efficient set of motions necessary to complete any given task, to yield before the expert and his stopwatch. Conservation, meanwhile, at least in the form that Pinchot espoused, tried to rid not the shop floor but the forests of the very same disorderly tendencies, seeking the most efficient way of producing not steel, but crops of timber and animals. Taylorism controlled workers, conservation controlled nature, and both relied on the principles of scientific management to do so. Frederick Taylor and Gifford Pinchot, in short, were cut from the same mold.

Before Pinchot's view of conservation rose to dominance, an ecologically informed group of foresters had tried to understand the forest on its own terms. Bernard Fernow, for example, one of the early scientific foresters, believed that forests did more than simply serve the economic needs of the American people. As interdependent entities, the woods, if managed properly, could help fend off floods and soil erosion. Forestland, he once wrote, played an important part "in the great economy of nature." Early conservationists, concerned with the overall ecology of federal forestland, evinced an anti-industry stance, opposing the timber companies in their disastrous quest for short-term profits. Conservation, in other words, got off to a promising start.[5]

Eager to please the timber companies, however, Pinchot, who replaced Fernow as chief of the Department of Agriculture's Division of Forestry in 1898, elevated economics over ecology. "The first principle of conservation is development," he wrote in 1910, "the use of the natural resources now existing on this continent for the benefit of the people who live here now." Pinchot felt that his first loyalty was to his own generation of Americans "and afterward the welfare of the generations to follow." Like Fernow, he opposed the unrestrained destruction of the nation's vast forest reserves. But unlike Fernow, he aimed to replace that approach with a scientifically grounded one that emphasized renewal of the resource as a way of serving economic—not ecological—ends.[6]

Pinchot had no intention then of simply putting the woods off limits to loggers. He was far too practical-minded for that. The forests existed to serve the economic demands of the nation, he believed, and to do that the lumber industry needed to cede authority to the experts at the Forest Service, who would tell them when it was time to cut a tree down. "The job," as Pinchot put it, "was not to stop the axe, but to regulate its use." Trees, in this view, were just like any other resource, human or natural. Frederick Taylor studied the behavior of workers in order to find the most efficient path to more production; Pinchot and his colleagues studied trees with the same end in mind. The woods could yield a constant source of timber if its trees were harvested at the proper time and then replanted, creating a second-growth forest even more manageable and in tune with the needs of the American economy than the original stands it replaced.[7]

At the outset, Pinchot galvanized the American public behind his forest initiative by calling their attention to an impending resource scarcity. By the turn of the century, the nation's timber frontier was coming to a close, as lumbermen ventured to the Pacific Northwest, having already cleared vast portions of the Great Lakes states and South. In 1906, lumber consumption reached 46 billion board feet, a record that has yet to be broken. With prices rising, Pinchot and Roosevelt both raised the prospect of a wood shortage. "A timber famine in the future is inevitable," Roosevelt declared in 1905. Clearly the nation's original forest cover had decreased, from 850 million acres in the early seventeenth century to roughly 500 million acres by the dawn of the twentieth century. Famine or not, the context was ripe for intervention, a point Pinchot clearly sensed.[8]

"Forestry is handling trees so that one crop follows another," Pinchot was fond of saying. What he meant, reduced to its essence, was that left to its own devices, nature was far too inefficient to serve the demands of a modern, industrial economy. Nothing irritated Pinchot and his fellow foresters more than the sight of an old-growth forest, filled with mature, dead, and diseased trees. Those old and disorderly forests needed to come down to make room for a new crop of timber. "To the extent to which the overripe timber on the national forests can not be cut and used while merchantable, public property is wasted," intoned Henry Graves, who followed Pinchot as chief of the Forest Service. Like a worker prone to loafing and distraction, the forest too became the target of the efficiency experts.[9]

Anything that got in the way of a speedup in forest production—old growth, disease, insects, and fire—had to be extinguished. But what Pinchot and his disciples either failed to fully comprehend or chose to ignore was the complexity and, above all, the interdependency of the forest. The various elements that made up the woods—trees, plants, insects, and animals—functioned as a unit. Small changes could have enormous impact. A change to one element in the mix—

removing a dead tree or ridding the forest of an insect—had consequences that ramified throughout an ecosystem, at times, ironically, even interfering with the business-oriented goals of the conservationists to boot. A species of moth, for instance, fed on the needles of Oregon's Douglas fir trees, a sight that drove the Forest Service wild. But behind the scenes hundreds of different species of wasps, flies, spiders, and birds were eating the moths, providing the agency with a free extermination treatment. When federal foresters in Oregon's Blue Mountains tried to eliminate the moths early in the twentieth century, the insect's predators lost out and died too. The moths then bounced back with a vengeance to devour the trees once again.[10]

A dead tree, an obstruction in the eyes of an efficiency-minded forester, was a viable habitat from the perspective of an insect. Thus removing fallen trees eliminated a food source for thousands of carpenter ants, preventing them from carrying out their duties on the forest floor: decomposing dead wood and returning it to the soil. The Forest Service eventually wound up interfering with the cycle of death and decomposition on which the future health of the woods rested.[11]

Pinchot's brand of conservation did even more damage when it came to the issue of fire. Fire had of course long been a major component of the West's, indeed of North America's, ecological mosaic, and early foresters remained fully aware of this fact. In much of the South as well as large parts of California, people set fire to the woods to reduce brush and encourage the growth of pasturage. In 1910, one timber man went so far as to call on the government to make burning mandatory in the Golden State. But it was not an auspicious year for incendiarism, not with fires in the northern Rockies raging out of control. The spring of 1910 was the driest month on record in the northwestern United States. That fact, combined with the buildup of slash, as logging increased and Indian burning of the land declined, led to one of the greatest wildfire disasters in American history. Conflagrations raged across the states of Idaho, Montana, Washington, and Oregon, sending smoke as far east as New England.

The fires left a legacy on government policy as enduring as the effect they had on the ground. Specifically, the 1910 fires worked to elevate the policy of fire suppression into a veritable religion at the Forest Service. Pinchot laid the intellectual groundwork for such a policy change. "I recall very well indeed," he wrote in 1910, "how, in the early days of forest fires, they were considered simply and solely as acts of God, against which any opposition was hopeless and any attempt to control them not merely hopeless but childish. It was assumed that they came in the natural order of things, as inevitably as the seasons or the rising and setting of the sun. To-day we understand that forest fires are wholly within the control of men."[12]

In 1910, at precisely the same time that Pinchot argued for suppression, the eminent ecologist Frederic Clements confirmed the views of foresters like Fernow, who viewed fire as a creative and positive environmental force. But Pinchot and those who came after him in the Forest Service remained unimpressed with such thinking. In keeping with the guiding spirit of efficiency and control at the heart of his brand of conservation, Pinchot feared the disorder and chaos that fire produced, especially if the conflagration in question was set on purpose. In 1898, he wrote, "forest fires encourage a spirit of lawlessness and a disregard of property rights." Those who burned the forest, for whatever reason, were no better than criminals, outlaws engaged in what federal foresters would soon call "incendiarism" or "woods arson."[13]

In the year following the 1910 calamity, Congress passed the Weeks Act, which allowed the federal government to purchase as much as 75 million acres of land and led to a consensus among federal and state officials on the need for fire suppression. Suppressing forest fires—a major preoccupation of the Forest Service for the bulk of the twentieth century—proved in the end both misguided and self-defeating. Fires aid the decomposition of forest litter and help recycle nutrients through an ecosystem. Without them growth slows down. Worse still, by suppressing fires, the Forest Service allowed fuels to build up, increasing the possibility for catastrophic conflagrations. Once again, nature had the last laugh, as Pinchot's brand of conservation centered on economic imperatives and anxiety over lawless behavior trumped an earlier, more broadminded concern with the forest's noneconomic functions.[14]

REVENGE OF THE VARMINTS

There is a dark side to conservation, although one would never know it from reading a U.S. history textbook. Roosevelt and Pinchot swooping in to rescue the wanton destruction being carried out across the landscape, planting trees and giving birth to a new and improved forest—none of this smacks of anything cold-blooded in the least. Left out of this rosy scenario, however, is the fact that conservation, because it was founded on the most productive use of the land, sometimes ventured into the realm of death and destruction. It is no coincidence that the most destructive period in the nation's wildlife history—replete with the ruthless and systematic annihilation of some entire animal species—coincided with the decades when conservation gripped the nation's political imagination. Efficiency and extermination went hand in hand.

Taking their cue from Pinchot's philosophy of making trees over into harvestable crops, game managers in the early twentieth century tried to do the same for animals, cultivating those species favored by sport hunters and tourists such as elk, bison, waterfowl, and especially deer. By the 1880s, overhunting and habitat loss had caused the populations of these animal groups to plummet. To revitalize them, federal and state wildlife managers pushed for laws regulating hunting and setting up refuges. In 1903, Roosevelt designated Pelican Island in Florida as the first such federal wildlife preserve. Five years later came the National Bison Range in Montana on an old Indian reservation. Tourists queued up to see what amounted to the pathetic remnants of the once abundant and glorious species.

PINCHOT WITH SCOUTS

A man concerned with law and order, Gifford Pinchot aggressively pursued the policy of total fire suppression. By interfering with the natural fire cycle, this approach increased the risk of calamitous conflagrations and, ironically, led to more loss of life. (Library of Congress)

Conserving some species, however, meant killing others. In 1915, Congress set up a new division within the Department of Agriculture's Bureau of Biological Survey, the arm of the government (founded in 1905) responsible for game management. It had an ominous title: Predatory Animal and Rodent Control Service. Its mission was to exterminate those creatures that preyed on the rancher's cattle and sheep and the sport hunter's elk and deer. In the eyes of the conservation-

minded, mountain lions, wolves, coyotes, and bobcats, among other species, became the Satans of the animal kingdom. "Large predatory mammals destructive to
livestock and game no longer have a place in our advancing civilization," was how
one biologist at the bureau put it.[15]

There were 40 million sheep in the West by the last decade of the nineteenth
century, in addition to vast numbers of cattle. All were defenseless before the predators that roamed the plains looking for some substitute fare now that the buffalo
had been driven off the land. Wolves proved especially destructive to livestock;
indeed, it would be hard to overestimate the hatred ranchers had for the species.
Cowboys commonly strung a captured wolf between two horses to tear it apart.
But poison, mainly strychnine, was the preferred method of dispatching them.[16]

Bounties, established by a number of western states during the late nineteenth
century, spurred hunters to kill predatory animals. But it took the intervention of
the federal government with its extermination program to put an end to the predator problem. The ruthlessness of the campaign—steel traps, guns, and strychnine
in hand—is hard to fathom. An astonishing 40,000 animals were killed in
Wyoming alone between 1916 and 1928—coyotes, wolves, bears, bobcats, lynxes,
and mountain lions, plus prairie dogs, gophers, squirrels, and jack rabbits, which
had the annoying habit of eating the settlers' crops. "Bring Them in Regardless of
How," went the slogan coined by one hunters' newsletter. It was all-out war and
when it was over—by 1926, no wolves existed in Arizona—the West's ranchers,
farmers, and sport hunters could rest easier at night.[17]

Life in western America seemed to be moving along swimmingly in the post-
predatory age until it began to dawn on some people that such species as wolves,
coyotes, and mountain lions actually served a purpose in life. An object lesson
on the importance of predators unfolded on Arizona's Kaibab Plateau. In 1906,
Roosevelt set aside a portion of the area as a wildlife refuge known as the Grand
Canyon National Game Preserve. Roughly 4,000 deer lived in the refuge in the
year it was founded. Enter the federal hunters, who between 1916 and 1931 took
4,889 coyotes, 781 mountain lions, and 554 bobcats. Victory, went the shout, as
the deer proliferated, swelling to perhaps as many as 100,000 by 1924, a gain in
productivity to end all gains. But two winters later, the deer population crashed,
reduced by some 60 percent, as the animals starved for lack of forage. When such
predators as coyotes and mountain lions are not around to hold down their numbers, deer will reproduce almost endlessly, populating their habitat beyond what
it can bear and dying in classic Malthusian style.[18]

While deer overran the Kaibab Plateau, hordes of mice were marching on the
town of Taft, California. In 1924, the Bureau of Biological Survey had launched,
to the glee of farmers, an all-out effort to eradicate coyotes, hawks, and other
predators from Kern County. Two years later, the rodents, their numbers now
unchecked, descended in droves. "The mice," one report had it, "invaded beds
and nibbled the hair of horrified sleepers, chewed through the sides of wooden
storehouses to get at food supplies, and crawled boldly into children's desks at

OF MICE AND MEN
Efforts to exterminate predators sometimes had perverse consequences. Here federal government forces repel an invasion of mice in California. (California Historical Society)

Conley School." Passing cars crushed the mice that littered the road, making some highways too slick for safe travel. Farmers resorted to mechanical harvesters to fend off the rodents. Eventually the Bureau of Biological Survey was called in to exterminate the varmints it had poisoned into existence in the first place. Conservation had more than a few such ironic moments.[19]

PARK RULES

Managing game was one thing, but administering it to attract thousands of big game–loving tourists was something yet again. The setting aside of national parks in the late nineteenth century raised a host of problems for the nation's conservationists. Chief among these was how to rationalize game in the interests of tourism—that is, to create and preserve a wilderness experience where visitors could be sure to find elk, bison, and other large animals. In carrying out their mission, the managers of wildlife ran up against a number of obstacles. Native Americans and rural whites—inclined to view the creatures more as a food source than as curiosities—did not appreciate the restrictions the managers imposed on hunting. Complicating matters further, delineating an arbitrary park boundary and using it to contain wild species with biological needs for food that sent them outside the park left government officials forever playing the role of traffic cop.

The national park movement stemmed, in part, from a change in American attitudes toward wilderness. Back in the colonial period, the word referred to desolate, wild places untouched, as yet, by civilization. There was little, if anything, positive about wilderness areas in the minds of the first settlers, who diligently set about improving—fencing and farming—the raw material of nature. By the late nineteenth century, however, the meaning of the word had undergone a sea change. Wilderness areas were no longer thought to be worthless; in fact, just the reverse was the case: They were increasingly viewed as places of virginal natural beauty in need of the most zealous care.

Not that the economic impulse that informed the early idea of wilderness disappeared completely. In setting aside the first national parks, Congress made a point of looking for worthless lands—regions with limited agricultural and ranching prospects and no sign of valuable minerals—possessed of monumental grandeur. Unlike European countries, the United States, a much younger nation by comparison, had few cultural icons to match the castles and cathedrals that gave Old World states unique national identities. With the country emerging from the divisive Civil War, its status as a unified nation still quite fragile, congressmen searched the landscape for awe-inspiring physical features—stunning mountain scenery, vast and colorful canyons, spectacular geysers—for its citizens to rally around.[20]

In 1872, Congress settled on a rectangular piece of land some two million acres in extent where Wyoming, Idaho, and Montana come together, an improbable place for agriculture, averaging some 6,000 feet in altitude and prone to frost, but containing hundreds of geysers, mud pots, and other geothermal wonders. Here was a picture-perfect spot to knit together the fledgling nation, North and South, East and West, a place so majestic and so capable of uniting the country under God that Congress purchased a painting of the area done by artist Thomas Moran to hang in the Capitol. "This will be the grandest park in the world—the grand, instructive museum of the grandest Government on Earth," proclaimed the *Nevada Territorial Enterprise*. To congressmen such as Henry Dawes of Massachusetts, who worked to establish the park, Yellowstone represented nature in its most pristine state, a beautiful but harsh wilderness environment so formidable that not even Indians, he asserted, could live there, a place seemingly without history.[21]

It would be wrong, however, to see the establishment of Yellowstone, the nation's first national park, as simply the work of Congress. The railroads played a major role as well—financiers such as Jay Cooke and Frederick Billings and their Northern Pacific company, a corporation that stood to gain immensely from the passenger traffic that the park would bring. As Billings once remarked, "commerce could serve the cause of conservation by bringing visitors to a site worthy of preservation." In 1883, the Northern Pacific completed its route across the country, the second transcontinental railroad in the nation's history, putting Yellowstone within reach of tourists nationwide. That same year the nation went on standard time to accommodate railroad travel, a key development in the streamlining of modern life that perhaps also explains the fascination tourists had with the scheduled eruptions of Yellowstone's most famous geyser, Old Faithful, which as one observer remarked, "played by the clock."[22]

YELLOWSTONE PARK ROUTE

Major supporters of national parks, railroads like the Northern Pacific drummed up riders by capitalizing on Yellowstone's spectacular natural phenomena. (Library of Congress)

Advocates for Yellowstone may have thought they were preserving a wilderness area. But it is more accurate to say that they were inventing it. In Yellowstone's case, creating wilderness meant rendering the Native Americans, who laid claim to the area, invisible when, in fact, they had long used it for hunting, fishing, and other means of survival. Preservation of the country's national parks and Indian removal proceeded in lock-step motion. Treaties and executive orders signed between 1855 and 1875 effectively consigned the Bannock, Shoshone, Blackfeet, and Crow Indians to reservations, where they would be less likely to interfere with tourists headed for Yellowstone. Park supporters rationalized the removal of Indians by relying on a time-tested strategy first used in the colonial period. The Indians, they pointed out, made no agricultural improvements to the area; use it or lose it, went the boosters' logic. The rugged physical environment of the park, inhospitable to farming and other economic uses, helped support this supposition, as did the view of park officials such as Philetus Norris, who explained that Indians avoided the Yellowstone area because they held its geothermal features in "superstitious awe."[23]

As late as 1962, one historian observed that only "deteriorating, half-miserable-animal, half-miserable-man" types inhabited the park prior to its creation. This was little more than park and railroad propaganda masquerading as facts. Park officials were quite aware of the Native American presence in Yellowstone and its potential to frighten tourists. As Superintendent Moses Harris explained in 1888, "the mere rumor of the presence of Indians in the park is sufficient to cause much excitement and anxiety." The Northern Pacific Railroad, meanwhile, did what it could to allay such fears. It recommended that tourists visit the Little Big Horn (where George Armstrong Custer and his troops went down to defeat in 1876) on their way to Yellowstone, safe in knowing that the Plains Indians no longer posed any threat.[24]

The year following Custer's defeat, the U.S. Army waged war against the Nez Perce Indians, at one point chasing them straight through Yellowstone National Park. The Nez Perce, according to accounts written at the time, were lost and frightened by the park's geothermal sites. But as Yellow Wolf recalled years after the battle, the Indians "knew that country well before passing through there in 1877. The hot smoking springs and high-shooting water were nothing new to us."[25]

In fact, a number of Native American groups were intimately familiar with the park and its offerings. The Shoshones, for example, hunted buffalo, fished, and gathered various plants, activities that depending on the season could lead them into the area eventually designated as parkland. Aided by horses, even more distant Indian groups descended on the park to trap beaver and hunt elk. Perhaps not surprisingly, the decline of the buffalo beginning in the 1870s only made Indians more dependent on the park's wildlife for food. And in an ironic turn of events, the displacement of Native Americans onto reservations may actually have increased their visits to the park. Denied adequate rations in the government camps, such groups as the Crows and Shoshones made up the balance by setting off to hunt on unoccupied public lands, a right granted to them in an 1868 treaty. As the agent for Idaho's Fort Hall Reservation explained, "Being short-rationed and far from self-supporting according to the white man's methods, they [Bannocks and Shoshones] simply follow their custom and hunt for the purpose of obtaining sustenance."[26]

The prospect of Indians taking game found within the confines of Yellowstone was long a bone of contention between native groups and park officials. In 1889, Superintendent Moses Harris called Indian hunting an "unmitigated evil" and lamented that it would be impossible to protect the park's remaining game if Yellowstone continued "to afford summer amusement and winter sustenance to a band of savage Indians." Locals who acted as guides to well-off hunters from the East also resented Indian poaching of game because it instilled fear in their clients while decreasing the likelihood of a successful outing.[27]

In 1896, the U.S. Supreme Court in the leading case of *Ward* v. *Race Horse* overturned the protection the 1868 treaty granted Indians to hunt on unoccupied government land in a seven-to-one decision. Even though it was common knowledge that the Shoshone and Bannock Indians hunted game to feed themselves and, moreover, that insufficient rations on the Fort Hall Reservation left many malnourished and more inclined to hunt on their own, Justice Edward White asserted that hunting was a privilege "given" to the tribes by the U.S. government, one that could be revoked when called for by "the necessities of civilization." In his dissenting opinion, Justice Henry Brown pointed out that "the right to hunt on the unoccupied lands of the United States was a matter of supreme importance to them [the Indians]. . . . It is now proposed to take it away from them, not because they have violated a treaty, but because the State of Wyoming desires to preserve its game." The case effectively upheld a 1895 Wyoming law regulating the taking of wildlife, making it illegal for Indians to hunt on public land during seasons closed to hunting and undermining the centuries-old subsistence practices of the Yellowstone area's Native American groups. But unlike the well-known *Plessy* v. *Ferguson* case decided in the same year (establishing "separate but equal" segregation), *Ward*, although heavily criticized then and since, has not been systematically overturned, remaining to this day a legally influential opinion.[28]

The only thing as annoying to park officials as an Indian taking down one of Yellowstone's grand four-legged creatures was the sight of a rural white doing so. The founding of Gardiner, Montana, in 1883, on Yellowstone's northern border gave whites seeking game a base from which to launch their forays into the park. "In the town of Gardiner there are a number of men, armed with rifles, who toward game have the gray-wolf quality of mercy," wrote the eminent conservationist William Hornaday.[29] Whites also gathered wood from the park and grazed cattle, creating a situation so chaotic that the U.S. government was forced to call on the military to restore order in the wilderness. In 1886, the cavalry moved in and stayed more than 30 years, until 1916 when the National Park Service took over the administration of Yellowstone.

The military put the park in order, gratifying those like John Muir, interested in safeguarding the nation's natural wonders. "Uncle Sam's soldiers," exclaimed Muir, were "the most effective forest police." The military restricted entry into the park, forcing visitors to use one of four main entrances instead of entering willy-nilly along the many surreptitious trails that Indians and rural whites had bushwhacked. It suppressed fires, which Indians in the area had long been accustomed to setting intentionally to kill game and manage the landscape to their liking. It erected fences to prevent cattle and other stray animals owned by whites from venturing within park boundaries. And it sought to prevent the poaching of game, which Congress, in 1894, had elevated into a federal offense. Conservation, as it played out in the national parks, essentially transformed such ingrained and acceptable behaviors as hunting, collecting, and fire setting into crimes like trespassing, poaching, and arson.[30]

The motivation behind this strand of conservation thinking again stemmed, in part, from a concern with lawless behavior. Just as Gifford Pinchot feared the chaos and threat to property rights posed by fire setting, wildlife advocates like William Hornaday voiced a similar concern over the perils of poaching. Hornaday, who was born in Plainfield, Indiana, in 1854, moved with his family to Wapello County, Iowa, as a young child. Living on the edge of an extensive and sparsely settled stretch of prairie, Hornaday often saw huge flocks of passenger pigeons and other birds, which evidently made quite an impression on him. He later went on to become a taxidermist and, in 1896, was chosen to head the New York Zoological Park, familiarly known as the Bronx Zoo. As director of the zoo, he spoke out in favor of wildlife conservation and against the reckless slaughter of game. He was particularly rankled by those, mainly immigrants and blacks, who killed wildlife for food. "The Italian is a born pot-hunter, and he has grown up in the fixed belief that killing song-birds for food is right!" he wrote in 1913. In the West especially, he noted, violators of game laws were often set free by sympathetic juries on the pretext that the suspect needed the meat to survive. Hornaday could not have disagreed more with such reasoning. "Any community which tolerates contempt for law, and law-defying judges, is in a degenerate state, bordering on barbarism; and in the United States there are literally thousands of such communities!" Whatever his love for animals, there is no denying Hornaday's abiding concern with law and order, or his anti-immigrant rhetoric, both of which probably derived from the flood of foreigners to America's shores at the turn of the century.[31]

For their part, rural whites took game within the park for several reasons. First, the market in elk teeth boomed after the founding in 1868 of the Elks Club, a New York City fraternal order, which used them for everything from rings to cuff links. Whites also sold hides for cash or traded in return for items such as coffee and sugar that were not easily obtained in the Yellowstone area. Second, these locals depended on game as a source of food, especially during economic downturns. One unemployed worker arrested in 1914 for poaching game in the park claimed it was the fact that he was "broke all the time" that drove him to crime. As one park official noted in 1912, elk wandering out of Yellowstone were often killed by "families that otherwise might have had a slim meat ration for the winter due to dull times for workingmen in this section of country." And third, poaching offered an alternative to the discipline of wage work. As one newspaper put it, "Some men would rather spend a month or more time in trapping a beaver or two, or killing an elk at the risk of fine and imprisonment, than earn a few honest dollars by manual labor."[32]

If it was hard to get rural whites to obey the law, it was even harder to force the park's animals to cooperate with the authorities. The source of the problem was severalfold. To begin with, the boundaries of the park did not conform to a discrete ecosystem. The park was huge, to be sure, but not big enough to support and protect all the species of wildlife that roamed it, a fact recognized by none other than Gen. Philip Sheridan. Surprisingly, after years spent trying to annihilate the buffalo (and the Indians who depended on it), Sheridan had a second career as a conservationist. Following a tour of Yellowstone in 1881, he suggested that the park be doubled in size in order to encompass the full range of migrating species of wildlife. That never happened, mainly because much of the land Sheridan had in mind wound up as part of a national forest instead.

As it turned out, the arbitrary confines of the park proved considerably troublesome when it came to preserving the tourist-friendly elk. Elk stayed in the park's higher elevations during the summer and early fall, but when winter hit, with its snow and severe cold, the animals drifted into the lower elevation river valleys further north, their so-called winter range. There was only one problem: Much of that range lay outside of Yellowstone's boundaries. But when the erection of fences and the establishment of communities north of Yellowstone forced the elk to winter inside the park, the animals gobbled up much of the available plant cover and caused the park's habitat to decline.

Climate also shaped the prospects for the park managers' beloved big game. A sharp plunge in winter temperatures occurred between 1885 and 1900. The years from 1877 to 1890, meanwhile, proved the greatest in terms of winter precipitation. Thus the harshest winters on record in Yellowstone occurred during the latter part of the 1880s, with snow and cold limiting the access of such large herbivores as elk to forage. Climate combined with unregulated hunting depressed wildlife populations and may have spurred the calls for military intervention in the park's affairs.[33]

In the century following 1900, winters in Yellowstone grew increasingly mild, expanding forage prospects and creating more favorable conditions for herbivore populations to expand. This trend toward more mild weather coincided, as it happened, with the advent of predator control in the park. Federal hunters were sent to the park in 1915 after an official from the Bureau of Biological Survey visited and recommended the extermination of all coyotes and wolves before they devoured all of Yellowstone's elk. A huge debate has swirled over the number of elk present in the park, but one estimate placed 1,500 animals there in the late 1870s, rising to 20,000 to 30,000 by 1919. In the latter year, drought gripped the area in the summer, followed by a severe winter. By early in 1920, very little forage remained and, according to park service estimates, 6,000 animals starved to death. "The range was in deplorable condition when we first saw it," reported biologists who visited in 1929, "and its deterioration has been progressing steadily since then."[34]

If a debate rages over the exact elk count, changes in vegetation seem indisputable. Communities of willow shrubs once graced Yellowstone's northern range. Over the course of the twentieth century, however, the willows vanished. The available evidence suggests strongly that the elk were to blame, although climate change and fire suppression may also have played a role. However the willow disappeared, the change had effects that extended up and down the food chain. Beavers relied on willow for building dams and for food. Thought to be common in the park in the early nineteenth century, beavers were vanishing by the 1930s. Change rippled through Yellowstone. Wetland habitat declined with the beavers no longer around to maintain it, making the park drier overall. As river habitats dried up, white-tailed deer, a species that depended on these environments, disappeared, becoming extinct in the park by 1930. Birds and even grizzly bears may have suffered as well.[35]

Despite Yellowstone's vast expanse of land, separating the region from the larger ecosystem and packaging it for sale to tourists—chiefly by encouraging the proliferation of big-game species—had unintended consequences. Elk and bisons came to rule this world at the expense of beavers, deer, and other animals, as well as the wolves and coyotes that were killed off intentionally. We have here conservation of the few at the expense of the many.

CONCLUSION

"The natural resources of the Nation," Gifford Pinchot wrote in 1910, "exist not for any small group, not for any individual, but for all the people."[36] Pinchot called attention to one of the conservation movement's greatest legacies. For most of the nineteenth century, the federal government occupied itself with disposing of the nation's natural wealth, often to railroad, mining, and timber groups, which then claimed the land as private property and exploited it for all it was worth. With the birth of conservation, however, the federal government shifted roles from gift giver to expert overseer, assuming control over large sections of the continent and seeking to manage them, as Pinchot noted, in the interests of the American public.

That was an important achievement, especially in a nation wedded from birth to the concept of private ownership of land. Yet it must be borne in mind that conservation—whatever its merits over the government attempt to stimulate development at any cost—did not function in the interests of all Americans. At the core of the movement stood the clash over class and racial politics.

"The national parks must be maintained in absolutely unimpaired form for the use of future generations," said Secretary of the Interior Franklin Lane in 1918.[37] What he really meant was that national parks and their animal populations had to be administered to suit the needs of the middle-class tourists streaming into them. Compared to other unprotected lands, the parks were certainly less subject to human intervention. But to view them as untouched or "unimpaired" is to deny all the many attempts by government officials to shape what went on there, especially the efforts by game managers to conserve those animals that appealed to the parks' mainly better-off white tourist clientele.

It is impossible not to be struck by the incredible number of contradictions that surround the history of the conservation movement. In getting back to nature in the national parks, to take one glaring example, tourists were actually bearing witness to an engineered environment, and a fragile one at that. By the late nineteenth century, Yellowstone was one of two places in North America where small numbers of buffalo existed (the other was Canada's Wood Buffalo National Park). Market hunters, however, decimated this remaining herd between 1889 and 1894. A concessionaire by the name of E. C. Waters then imported a handful of bison from ranching magnate Charles Goodnight and shipped them off to Dot Island in Yellowstone Lake, where a steamboat shuttled tourists out to see them. Meanwhile, the U.S. military launched its own effort to restore bison, setting up an enclosure and dragging in bales of hay to lure the animals in for a dose of domestication. The buffalo failed to show. The hay the military cut destroyed bison habitat in the Hayden valley, spurring them to move on rather than accept the cavalry's offer.[38]

Far more lasting success was obtained beginning in 1902, when President Roosevelt hired Charles "Buffalo" Jones, a bison expert, to maintain Yellowstone's herd. Jones purchased animals from private ranchers and set up a corral near one of the park's main entrances, although it was later moved to the Lamar valley, where it flourished for half a century. The bison gave the tourists something to see and the railroads a new selling angle. A 1904 advertisement trumpeted: "BISON once roamed the country now traversed by the North Pacific. The remnant of these Noble Beasts is now found in Yellowstone Park reached directly only by this line."[39]

If park boosters were shameless in using bison to lure tourists, they bordered on deceitful when it came to employing Indians to entice people into the park. In his Dot Island venture, E. C. Waters tried to find a few Native Americans to complement the imported bison in the exhibit. But the Crow Indians he asked refused his offer. That did not stop the Northern Pacific, however, from using a small group of Blackfeet Indians to advertise the scenic beauty of Glacier National Park, another destination serviced by the line. In 1912, the railroad's president, Louis Hill, arranged to have 10 Indians set up tepees on the roof of a New York City hotel to attract publicity for this new western attraction. The national parks were virgin territory, devoid of Indians, congressmen had said when setting up the parks. Now the railroads wanted the Native Americans back.[40]

Bison and Indians were the two icons that, more than anything else, symbolized the destruction of both nature and culture in the American West. Employing them to sell the American people on the need to visit the newly conserved and "unspoiled" parks amounted to one huge exercise in cultural self-deception. Could anything be more paradoxical than using contrived groups of animals and people, annihilated in the so-called winning of the West, to lure tourists to supposedly "untouched" wilderness? If conservation broke the pattern of unrestrained, economic development of the natural world, it substituted in its place a subtler political agenda shot through with irony.

10

DEATH OF THE ORGANIC CITY

Before 1880 it was not the least bit unusual to walk out into the streets of Atlanta and find cows. In 1881, however, the city's political leaders decided that bovines were no longer welcome. The cows could come home, as the saying goes, but not to the streets of Atlanta—not after the city council passed a law making it illegal for cattle to roam the town. Apparently a large number of working people, who depended on the animals as a source of milk and meat, objected to the ordinance. A man named J. D. Garrison denounced the law as little more than a thinly veiled attempt at class warfare. "I speak the feelings of every man when I say this is the dictation of a codfish aristocracy," he said. "It is an issue between flowers and milk—between the front yard of the rich man and the sustenance of the poor family."[1]

The large animals that once wandered the streets of urban America are of course long gone. Finding out how and why they disappeared means taking a journey back to the late nineteenth century, to the Progressive Era, when cities across the nation underwent a major cleanup.

While conservationists put the countryside in order, another group of reformers trained their sights on urban areas. In 1869, only nine cities had populations exceeding 100,000; in 1890, 28 had reached that mark. A third of all Americans now lived in such places. New York, Chicago, Philadelphia, St. Louis, Boston, and Baltimore, in that order, were the nation's largest population centers, filled with immigrants who worked producing apparel, forging steel, and packing meat. Crammed with people and factories, in addition to the pigs, horses, mules, cattle, and goats used for food and transport, the city emerged by the late nineteenth century as a dark and filthy place. Muckraker Upton Sinclair, in his novel The Jungle, captured the enormity of the problem, describing the "strange, pungent odor" people smelled as they approached Chicago's stockyards—a stench "you could literally taste"—and the chimneys belching out smoke that was "thick, oily, and black as night."[2]

Enter such Progressive Era reformers as Jane Addams, Robert Woods, and Florence Kelley, people who fervently felt that the creation of a clean and healthful environment, not genetic predisposition as had formerly been believed, could defend against ignorance and criminality. Taking their cue from the British, they formed settlement houses, most famously Hull House, established by Addams in Chicago in 1889—the model for some 400 such community institutions nationwide. The settlement houses engaged in a host of efforts to improve the lives of slum dwellers, setting up kindergartens and sponsoring everything from health

MORTON STREET, NEW YORK CITY

Progressive Era reformers such as New York's street-cleaning commissioner George E. Waring, Jr., modernized sanitation services. Waring increased both pay and morale among the city's street-cleaning crew with excellent results, as demonstrated in these two photographs, one taken in 1893, the other in 1895, after Waring assumed his post. (George Waring, Street-Cleaning and the Disposal of a City's Wastes [New York: Doubleday and McClure, 1897])

clinics to music studios to playgrounds. In 1894, Addams herself, in an effort to lower the mortality rate in one ward, led a group of immigrant women from Hull House on a nightly inspection designed to check up on the work of the city's garbage collectors.

As important as the sanitary reforms were—especially the improved water and sewer systems that led to a decline in disease—they came at a cost. All dirt is not equally bad; cleaner cities are not necessarily better for everyone. Indeed, there were some virtues to the filth. Life in the "organic city," a place swarming with pigs and horses and steeped in mountains of manure, was dirty, but it also had a certain social and environmental logic.

Today we rarely associate big animals with urban areas, with the possible exception of the horse-and-buggy tour. In the nineteenth century, however, it would be impossible to imagine such places without the creatures that roamed the streets, not to mention the stinking piles of excrement they left behind. In these days before municipal trash collection, working-class women fed their families with pigs that fattened on city garbage. Horses carried people and goods, hauled pumps to help put out fires, and even produced power for manufacturing such things as bricks and lumber. Horse manure, meanwhile, did not go to waste. It streamed into surrounding vegetable farms, where it bolstered soil fertility. Even a good deal of human waste, which piled up in privies and cesspools in the days before sanitary sewers, found its way to the rural hinterlands. City dwellers and their animals were largely integrated into the regional soil cycle, supplying it with the nutrients for growing food that was then trucked back into town. Thus did life proceed in the organic city, with vegetables and hay flowing one way and waste the other.

In the late nineteenth century, reformers bent on sanitation put an end to the city in its down-to-earth form. They drove the pigs out, forcing the working class to rely more on the cash economy for food, and substituted municipal garbage collectors for the hogs. They replaced horses with electric streetcars, ending the city's role as a manure factory and stimulating nearby vegetable farmers to turn to artificial fertilizers. They built sewerage systems that carried waste off into lakes, rivers, and harbors, eliminating the privies and the "night soil" men who had delivered the excrement to the countryside—distancing urbanites from the land they had once helped to enrich. Overall, public health improved. But the poor were left to fend for themselves in the wage economy as the urban commons—akin to the open range in the South and West— vanished. Public health indeed had its virtues, but it also had some important social and ecological tradeoffs.

WALKING SEWERS

When Europeans visualized America in the nineteenth century, they thought of Native Americans, a strange new group of people unknown on their continent.

But when they pictured American cities, it was not Indians and buffaloes but pigs that came to mind. No animal loomed larger in their image of U.S. urban areas. "I have not yet found any city, county, or town where I have not seen these lovable animals wandering about peacefully in huge herds," wrote Ole Munch Ræder, a Norwegian lawyer on a visit to America in 1847. Swine, he observed, kept the streets clean by "eating up all kinds of refuse. And then, when these walking sewers are properly filled up they are butchered and provide a real treat for the dinner-table."[3]

Working-class women, who depended on pigs to supply food for the table, allowed them to scavenge the urban commons for garbage. While rural hogs fed on the forest's acorns, city pigs fed on the waste people threw away, converting it into protein for the working poor. But a food source to some proved a nuisance to others. So many pigs wandered the streets of Little Rock, Arkansas, at mid-century that, according to one newspaper report, they had come "to dispute the side walks with *other persons*."[4] These creatures were not the sedate porkers one encounters today at the zoo; they were wild animals that injured and occasionally killed children. A nasty and brutish lot, the urban pigs copulated in public and had the annoying habit of defecating on people.

The authorities in New York City had sought to ban swine from the streets as early as the 1810s. But public outcry led to the prohibition's repeal. In 1818, however, a grand jury indicted two men for the misdemeanor of "keeping and permitting to run hogs at large in the city of New York." The first of the accused was convicted, after failing to mount a defense of his actions, and forced to pay a small fee. The second man, a butcher named Christian Harriet, decided to fight the charge. "The dandies, who are too delicate to endure the sight, or even the idea of so odious a creature," might welcome a conviction, Harriet's lawyers argued. "But many poor families might experience far different sensations, and be driven to beggary or the Alms House for a portion of that subsistence of which a conviction in this case would deprive them." Closing the urban commons, in other words, would take food out of the mouths of the poor.[5]

"It is said, that if we restrain swine from running in the street, we shall injure the poor," Mayor Cadwallader Colden observed. "Why, gentlemen! must we feed the poor at the expense of human flesh," he asked? Eliminate the commons and the poor would be forced to find jobs to pay for food, instead of taking their meals at the expense of the city's more refined residents. As for the fact that swine played a useful part in cleaning up the city's streets, Colden intoned, "I think our corporation will not employ brutal agency for that object when men can be got to do it."[6]

In the end, Harriet was convicted. As of 1819, setting pigs free became a crime, but that did not deter people. In 1821, city authorities went to war against the pigs, taking many into custody as Irish and black women banded together to defend the animals. Other significant pig-related conflicts erupted in 1825, 1826, 1830, and 1832. Pigs played a central role in the lives of the poor, who were willing to do what they could to save them.[7]

PIG ROUND-UP

On August 13, 1859, Frank Leslie's Illustrated Newspaper published this picture of police pursuing hogs. The animals were banished from the area below 86th Street in Manhattan by the following decade. (Kelvin Smith Library, Case Western Reserve University)

In 1849, however, the urban commons experienced a fatal blow. Cholera broke out in New York, and health officials linked the outbreak to the city's filthy conditions. No animal symbolized dirt more clearly than the pig. Police, armed with clubs, drove thousands of swine out of cellars and garrets, banishing them uptown. By 1860, the area below 86th Street had been secured as a pig-free zone. But in the uptown wards, the pigs still ruled. So many hogs roamed the area around 125th Street in Harlem at mid-century that the area came to be known as Pig's Alley. City authorities in New York and other urban areas, meanwhile, continued to tolerate pigsties as late as the 1870s, with some tenement residents even boarding them in their rooms, demonstrating the importance the poor attached to the animal.[8]

By the last decades of the nineteenth century, the urban commons drew to a close not just in New York, but in cities throughout America. Mayor Colden's wish for a pig-free city, one where women could walk the streets "without encountering the most disgusting spectacles of these animals indulging the propensities of nature," seemed well within reach.[9] The urban pig was ultimately exiled to the farmyard, where, to this day, it perpetuates for people the division between the country and the city.

CITY AS MANURE FACTORY

Like the pig, the horse also played an important, if somewhat hidden, role in urban ecology, one overshadowed by its far more obvious place at the heart of economic life. No animal, with the possible exception of the mule (important only in the South), did more to serve the transportation needs of urban areas.

In the early days of cities, horse-drawn buses (omnibuses) operated on cobblestone streets at speeds hardly faster than a walking pace. In the period just before the Civil War, however, the horse car spread to cities across the nation. Faster and more efficient than the older omnibuses, teams of horses hitched to passenger cars transported people and goods up and down iron tracks. By 1890, more than 32 million passengers climbed aboard New York City's horse car lines.

The number of urban horses nearly doubled to a little under three million over the course of the last third of the nineteenth century. The adoption of the horse car contributed to the rise, as did the expansion of railroad transportation. As trains shipped more goods from point to point, horses were needed to haul the freight from terminals to the ultimate destination.

The horses' importance to urban life was made amply apparent in 1872 when a fire scorched Boston's business district. Normally used to pull fire equipment, the horses, struck down by a flulike disease, were either dead or ill and thus unable to answer the call for help. The fire charred over 700 buildings as a result. Equines in other cities ultimately felt the effect of the outbreak (in Detroit, delivery companies made do with hand carts), which killed somewhere on the order of five percent of all the urban horses in the Northeast and Canada.[10]

Horses generated power for transportation (and manufacturing too), but they also produced staggering amounts of manure, somewhere between 15 and 30 pounds per animal every day. In Milwaukee, this translated daily into 133 tons of horse droppings. In 1900, one health officer in Rochester, New York (apparently with nothing better to do), calculated that the city's 15,000 horses contributed enough dung each year to completely cover an acre to a height of 175 feet. Worse still, the stinking piles bred countless numbers of flies, which harbored disease, including typhoid fever. Then there was the dust to contend with. Horse turds dried up in the heat, only to be pulverized by the creatures themselves as their hoofs made contact with the pavement. Ground horse excrement was the nineteenth-century equivalent of auto pollution—and was just as irritating to people's respiratory systems.[11]

The problems created by horse dung would have been even worse were it not for an ingenious ecological move on the part of farmers living on the outskirts of cities. They purchased the horse manure and used it to fertilize their hay and vegetable crops. The hay then went to feed the urban horse population and the vegetables to enhance the dinner tables of the city's better-off residents. As a truck farmer from New Jersey explained: "In our large commercial and manufacturing cities where wealth has concentrated, and where abound families who live regardless of expenditures, fabulous prices are freely paid for vegetables and fruits to please the palate or adorn the table." By the mid-nineteenth century, a reciprocal system, with manure passing one way and vegetables and hay the other, had grown up in New York, Baltimore, Philadelphia, and Boston.[12]

New Yorkers perfected the system. The opening of the Erie Canal in 1825 propelled the city's rise to commercial dominance and spurred farmers near the waterway to give up grain production in favor of potatoes, cucumbers, cabbages, onions, and sweet corn, all of which commanded good prices in the city's market. In 1879, Brooklyn and Queens, New York, now the very essence of urbanity, even led the nation in market gardening. Brooklyn was described by one source as an "immense garden" serving the "vast and increasing demand of the city of New York for vegetables and fruits of a perishable nature."[13]

The soil in Brooklyn and Queens is shallow, limiting the ability of roots to spread, and is not particularly adapted to storing moisture. Normally a farmer would need to keep plenty of hay on hand to feed the livestock that produced the soil-fortifying manure. But with Manhattan dairies and stables located nearby, it made economic sense for farmers to sell their hay and purchase horse manure in return. Manure from all over the New York City area formed the ecological lifeblood of Brooklyn and Queens farming. Brooklynites, one newspaper noted, "are, no doubt, glad to get rid of their filth (and the Board of Health will compel them to do so) [but] our farmers are glad to obtain means with which to enrich their lands, and to pay a fair price for such materials." Horse manure was so critical to farming that one King's County landowner even made a provision in his will that his son receive "all manure on the farm at the time of my decease."[14]

This ingenious early effort at recycling, however, proved short-lived. By the end of the nineteenth century, improvements in refrigeration and railroad transportation allowed farms in the South and California to outcompete Brooklyn and Queens for New York City's booming vegetable and fruit trade. Meanwhile, in the late 1880s, the advent of electrified streetcars drove the horse and its manure out of cities all across the nation. In 1912, a traffic count revealed, for the first time, more cars than horses in New York. By the following year, so little evidence remained of the manure-based truck farms that the Brooklyn Botanic Garden found itself weighing the educational potential of putting vegetables on exhibit. It was the museum's sense that "innumerable children and young people . . . have never seen . . . beans and peas growing on the plants that produce them."[15] Vegetables and horse manure now joined pigs on distant farms, further reinforcing the division between urban and rural life and contributing to the illusion of the city as somehow existing outside of nature.

FLUSH AND FORGET

Before the rise of the "flush and forget" mentality, human waste actually served a purpose in life. But to understand its role we must put aside all squeamishness and, as it were, follow the shit. Generally speaking, mid-nineteenth-century city dwellers relieved themselves in outhouses or privies. From that point, the excrement found its way into privy vaults and cesspools, which were little more than holes in the ground. Some waste seeped into the surrounding soil. Some of it in-

PRIVY

Night soil from privies such as this one on Thompson Street in New York City was often shipped to the countryside for use on farms or sold to dealers who made it into fertilizer. (Library of Congress)

variably drained into the street when the vaults backed up and overflowed. And some fell to so-called necessary tubmen (a "necessary" being another name for a privy) to deal with. The tubmen—a job often filled by African Americans—used buckets, casks, and ultimately carts to haul away the night soil, referred to as such because the men did their dirty work after people had gone to sleep. Predictably, some of the slop wound up spilled in the streets. Some was dumped into nearby rivers and lakes. But a good deal of it, at least by the late nineteenth century (when reliable figures are available), journeyed in good biblical fashion back onto the earth.

In 1880, nearly half of the more than 200 U.S. cities surveyed deposited night soil on the land or sold it to dealers who made it into fertilizer. As late as 1912, tubmen in Baltimore, still without a sewer system, cleaned out roughly 70,000 privy vaults and cesspools. Barges then shipped the waste to the outskirts of town, where it was sold in 1,000-gallon quantities to farmers. They used it to grow tomatoes, cabbages, and other vegetables for urban consumption.[16]

Of course the vast majority of human excrement produced in cities did not resurface on farms. But that said, a viable system for recycling human waste existed in nineteenth-century America. What forces combined to cause its downfall? How did urban populations across the nation find themselves cut off from the soil and bereft of the role they once played in maintaining it?

The story begins with water. In the early nineteenth century, most urbanites depended on cisterns and wells; those who could afford to purchased water from petty proprietors who went from door to door. As urban populations surged, and

CREATIVE DESTRUCTION

East Main Street, West Boylston, Massachusetts, pictured here in 1896, was flooded and destroyed to make way for the Wachusett Reservoir, which supplied the city of Boston with water. (Metropolitan District Commission Archives, Boston, MA)

leaking privies contaminated the underground supply, however, the demand for fresh water rose. In response, cities established public water systems. Philadelphia led the way, and New York, Boston, Detroit, and Cincinnati soon fell into step. On the eve of the Civil War, the nation's 16 largest cities all had municipal waterworks in operation. By 1880, nearly 600 public water systems were in use across the country, complex networks that often brought water from lakes, at times miles and miles away, to serve the needs of urban areas.[17]

In 1842, New York City, for instance, opened its Croton Aqueduct, which transported water over 40 miles from Westchester County. The city would eventually draw on the Catskill watershed, some 100 miles north. In 1848, Boston tapped Lake Cochituate, 15 miles to the west, and early the following century went even further afield to dam the waters of the Nashua River to create the Wachusett Reservoir. The water brought life to the city, but death to parts of the rural towns of West Boylston and Clinton, Massachusetts, which were inundated, its residents sent packing, to support population growth in a faraway urban land. Meanwhile, clear across the continent, Los Angeles was concocting its own imperial plan for draining off the natural wealth of the countryside. In 1906, the city obtained the necessary rights of way from the federal government to build a 235-mile aqueduct that would bring water from the Owens River directly into the metropolis. In perfecting their plan, city officials secured the help of the nation's foremost conservationist, President Theodore Roosevelt. "It is a hundred or thousandfold more important to the State and more valuable to the people as a whole," he remarked, "if [this water is] used by the city than if used by the people of the Owens Valley."[18]

As supply increased, demand boomed in cities across the nation, especially as the rich installed water closets, the forerunner of the modern toilet. A mere seven years after completion of the Cochituate Aqueduct in 1848, some 18,000 Boston households had water connections. Further west, Cleveland commandeered Lake Erie in 1856. One year later, Clevelanders used eight gallons of water per person each day; in 1872 they were using 55. There was only one problem: The cesspools and privy vaults could not handle all the waste. Although an alternative existed in the earth closet (a device consisting of a seat placed over a container of dirt, which "flushed" dirt over the excrement and thereby produced fertilizer), waste removal by water eventually ruled the day. Persuaded by the convenience of water, residents in some cities lobbied their governments to allow them to hook their drains up directly to existing sewers. But these sewers were designed with a grade steep enough only to handle free-flowing rainwater, and broke down when used to transport glutinous torrents of human waste. As sewers backed up and cesspools oozed, cities across the nation began to drown in their own filth.

To deal with the problem, engineers, city officials, and sanitary experts rallied around the idea of more underground plumbing. Eventually, thousands of miles of sewer pipe were laid, as human waste went flushing into rivers, lakes, and harbors. Common wisdom at the time held that running water purified itself, which is true as long as the amount of waste does not exceed the ability of bacteria in the water to break it down into harmless substances. Unaware of the fine points involved in wastewater disposal but attracted to its convenience, major cities built nearly 25,000 miles of sewer lines by 1909. But whereas water supplies tended to be paid for out of public monies, sewers went in only at the request of property owners, who were assessed accordingly. In other words, only those who could afford better public health received it. In 1857, New York City had installed just 138 miles of sewers along its 500 miles of paved streets, circumnavigating the city's poorest sections. One New York landlord, desperate to hold down his expenses, protested having to pay a sewer assessment. Sewers, he remarked, "are an unhealthy arrangement and should be avoided at all times if possible."[19]

Others, however, seemed less driven by mercenary motives than by practicality in opposing the transformation of the underground into a huge wastewater superhighway. In 1853, one farmer from Ulster County, situated along the Hudson River, lamented that New York City was annually wasting enough human excrement to grow 180 million pounds of wheat. Engineer and sewer expert George Waring, Jr., believed New Yorkers were flushing away some five million dollars' worth of valuable fertilizer each year. Prominent New Yorker and journalist Horace Greeley, meanwhile, labeled the city's wasteful practice an "inexplicable stupidity" and observed that ancient societies had been undermined by "the exhaustion of the soil through the loss of such manures in their capitals." It was ridiculous, he wrote in 1871, to pay for guano when New York "annually poisons its own atmosphere and adjacent waters with excretions which science and capital might combine to utilize at less than half the cost."[20]

Although a number of efforts were made beginning in the late nineteenth century to use urban sewage on farms, especially in the West, a region desperate for water no matter what its source, U.S. cities had by the 1920s severed the connection between human waste and the soil. Seduced by the convenience of water, urban areas, packed with people and water closets, unwittingly launched one of the largest aquatic experiments in the nation's history.[21]

In 1933, the western end of Lake Erie, one observer remarked, "looked as if it were coated with green paint." That paint was algae—an algae bloom, to be more precise. Algae are microscopic plants normally present in lakes. In Lake Erie's healthier days algae existed in sparse numbers, in part because the lake's limited supply of phosphorous kept them from flourishing. But when the cities around the lake—Buffalo, Cleveland, and Toledo—started discharging untreated sewage into it, the algae had a field day. Human waste contains large amounts of phosphorous and with city dwellers flushing away in their water closets, more of it wound up lake bound, where it made the algae thrive. Eventually, the algae died and the green slime sank to the bottom, where bacteria set to work decomposing it—using lots of oxygen to carry out the job. Beginning in the late nineteenth century, the oxygen decline (in conjunction with overfishing) changed the species make-up of Lake Erie and the rest of the Great Lakes. Whitefish, herring, trout, and sturgeon, the major commercial fish, depend on clear, oxygen-rich water. With the decline in lake conditions, however, species more adapted to the new aquatic environment, such as yellow perch, catfish, and pickerel, replaced them.[22]

Urban sewage had an even more devastating effect on fish in the lower part of the Delaware River. As late as the 1890s, the Delaware watershed's shad fishery was the nation's largest, supplying urbanites as far away as Cleveland, Chicago, and areas further west with a fish that was enormously popular in the Gilded Age. A catch of 16.5 million pounds in 1899, however, plummeted to just 210,000 pounds in 1921. A number of factors probably contributed to the decline, including overfishing and changes in precipitation. But the primary blame rested with Philadelphia's burgeoning population and the enormous amount of waste-laden water it flushed out into the Delaware. Water use in the city skyrocketed, increasing from 58 million gallons per day in 1880 to an astounding 319 million 30 years later. All that water, of course, once used, had to go somewhere. The sewage entering the river was so foul-smelling that by the early twentieth century sailors were known to jump ship rather than spend the night breathing in the noxious fumes. By the decade of the 1910s, dissolved oxygen in the river near Philadelphia registered just two to zero parts per million. With shad requiring at least five parts per million to survive, the fish—headed upstream to spawning grounds—suffocated and died.[23]

One could point to other examples of the harmful effects of sewage on aquatic life, such as oyster contamination in San Francisco Bay, Newark Bay, or Staten Island Sound. But the point is that installing sewers, although hailed as a victory for public health, also had some sorry ecological consequences. Human waste was discharged into lakes and streams, at times polluting the water supplies of towns downstream. Instead of having social value in maintaining a region's agroecology, it became just plain shit. By the turn of the century, city dwellers knew little about where their food came from and perhaps even less about where their bodily waste went, as sewers helped obscure from view the very real ecological impact of biological necessity.

THE GARBAGE PROBLEM

In the period before the 1870s, urbanites took it upon themselves to dispose of their own garbage. Some people just left it outside for pigs to devour. Others gave it to "swill children," who collected it in carts and sold it to farmers to use as fertilizer or hog feed. It would be wrong to romanticize this system of waste removal. In Milwaukee, one account from the 1870s describes the "little garbage gatherers" leaving the alleys "reeking with filth, smelling to heaven."[24] But this approach did have the virtue of giving social value to garbage, recycling it for human good, as well as providing a much-needed source of income for working-class families struggling to survive in the city's Dickensian economy.

Whatever the virtues of this ad hoc approach to disposal, it broke down in the face of the mountain of garbage created by the teeming masses who populated U.S. cities by the late nineteenth century. Consider the problem of dead horses. In 1880, New York City carted away some 15,000 of them, with an average weight of 1,300 pounds each. In 1912, when cars began to dominate the city, Chicago still had to send scavengers out to take care of 10,000 horse carcasses.[25]

Surveys conducted between 1903 and 1918 showed that a single city dweller produced a half ton to a ton of refuse each year. Ashes from the burning of wood and coal remained the single largest refuse item, at least in the colder climates of the Midwest and North. In the South, the warmer weather and longer growing season meant more organic waste, which had to be taken care of quickly before it rotted. Watermelon rinds alone made up 20 percent of Savannah, Georgia's, summer garbage in 1915. But with the nation's economy becoming increasingly organized around consumer spending, generating a vast array of new packaged items, the amount of garbage increased dramatically. Between 1903 and 1907, trash collected in Cincinnati rose from 21,600 to 31,255 tons, an increase of nearly a third, a trend apparent in most American cities.[26]

CAROLINE BARTLETT CRANE
Known nationally for her work in the municipal housekeeping movement, Crane is shown here inspecting a Seattle garbage incinerator. (Western Michigan University)

In the 1880s, along came the sanitary reformers to tackle the stinking piles of refuse. Women, especially, championed the cause. In New York, 15 women from the wealthy Beekman Hill area, incensed by the dirt and dust that soiled clothing and ruined homes, complained to the city board of health about a pile of manure they claimed was roughly 25 feet in height. The owner of the pile, Martin Kane, employed approximately 100 men to remove manure from stables that held on the order of 12,000 to 13,000 horses, selling the dung as fertilizer to nearby farmers—often stockpiling it until prices rose to his satisfaction. Kane was eventually ordered to remove the nuisance, but he was later allowed to reopen his operation as long as he promised to keep the pile of horse droppings at a minimum.[27]

Freed by servants from many of the chores associated with taking care of their homes, middle-class women took to the streets to join the municipal housekeeping movement. In 1884, the women banded together to form the Ladies' Health Protective Association, an organization dedicated to street-cleaning and municipal garbage reform. There followed the Women's Health Protective Association of Brooklyn, the Municipal Order League in Chicago, the Women's Civic Association in Louisville, and the Neighborhood Union in Atlanta, a group of African American women who prevailed on the city to provide black residents with trash collection. Entering the traditionally male domain of civic life, women activists, led by the legendary Jane Addams and other Progressive reformers, succeeded in expanding their public authority, but ultimately had only limited success in improving sanitary conditions.[28]

Municipal garbage collection of course put the swill children out of work, although it took some time. In Milwaukee, aldermen let each ward decide whether it wanted contractors, hired by the city, to pick up its trash. But the new service failed when residents, still loyal to the swill children, refused to turn over their garbage. "Most of the garbage . . . is removed by boys and girls and women, mostly of Polish nationality, who use the material collected to feed hogs," a health department report noted. In 1878, a new health commissioner finally convinced officials to establish one garbage contract for the entire city. New restrictions on both children and pigs accompanied the contract. As one working-class newspaper put it, "it is a great pity if [our] stomachs must suffer to save the noses of the rich."[29]

Once collected, where did city garbage go? In part it depended on the kind of garbage a place produced. Incinerators, a technology invented by the British, proved popular in the southern states, where the warm climate and large quantities of organic waste made immediate disposal imperative. Northern cities, in contrast, had more ash, which accumulated in piles and then was generally dumped on the land or at sea. The city of New York was notorious for dumping garbage in the Atlantic Ocean—some 760,000 cubic yards of refuse in 1896 alone. Chicago unloaded its refuse in Lake Michigan. St. Louis and New Orleans both turned to the Mississippi River. In 1886, New York's garbage scows pitched 80 percent of the city's 1.3 million cartloads of refuse into the sea. From there it drifted south to New Jersey, where swimmers commonly encountered it—as old mattresses and shoes bobbing along in the waves.[30]

Smaller cities often sold their garbage as hog feed or set up pig farms. (The quantity of refuse in large cities prevented them from doing the same because it would have required costly additional collections to keep the refuse from rotting.) City-owned piggeries flourished, especially in New England, where temperatures cooperated in keeping the garbage edible. In the early twentieth century, 61 cities and towns in Massachusetts operated some kind of swine-feeding program. Grand Rapids, St. Paul, Denver, and Los Angeles also used pigs as garbage disposals. During World War I, the U.S. government, anxious to conserve food, encouraged more cities to feed their refuse to hogs. The practice, however, called for the careful separation of the edible organic matter from the glass and other items hazardous to such creatures. "Surely very few phonograph needles would find their way into the garbage pail," one government report opined, "if the householders could imagine the tortures suffered by the unfortunate animals."[31]

Feeding refuse to pigs, which could be slaughtered and turned into pork, gave garbage a role in the food cycle. Still, by the turn of the century, the vast majority of urban refuse was either buried, dumped at sea, or burned—in short, wasted. Before the rise of a consumption-oriented economy in the late nineteenth century, Americans as a whole generated little in the way of trash. Swill children salvaged scattered pieces of food, which their mothers incorporated into meals, and sold metal, bones, and bottles to junk dealers. Ragmen scoured city streets for old clothes for making paper. Women fed leftover food scraps to chickens and pigs. The recycling of waste, in other words, played a role in producing goods and bolstering living standards. Then municipal trash collection eliminated the swill children. The invention of wood pulp did away with the need for ragmen. The recycling networks that had arisen earlier disappeared and a social system dedicated to clean homes and cities superseded them. Ironically, that move simply shifted waste outside the immediate food and soil cycles to downstream and downwind regions, where it did far more harm.[32]

CONCLUSION

The great cleanup, which spelled death for the organic city, had many virtues: a decline in diseases, especially water-borne ones like typhoid fever, and an improved and more aesthetically pleasing urban environment, plus no more pigs to contend with on the streets. But tidying up the metropolis meant compromising life in other quarters. A whiter and brighter life came at the cost of fish kills, algae blooms, and garbage-strewn beaches. The cleaning compulsion also hurt the poor, who once put filth to work in the service of the family economy. Meanwhile, the rise of mass production and distribution—packaged foods, thick newspapers, products planned, on purpose, to become obsolete—made it even more difficult for American cities to keep pace with what its citizens no longer wanted. How did this new consumer culture go about feeding itself? What did it do with its trash? How did people get from place to place? To such questions we now turn.

PART THREE

CONSUMING NATURE

11

MOVEABLE FEAST

Had Thomas Jefferson, drafter of the Declaration of Independence, been alive at the time, he no doubt would have been delighted to see the "Liberty Bell" created for the 1893 Columbian Exposition in Chicago. It was quite a sight—6,500 oranges meticulously piled into a monument to freedom and democracy, courtesy of some deft souls from California.

Jefferson not only played an important role in the birth of the nation but was also an avid horticulturalist who cherished a good apple or pear. And although he never made it to California, he left his mark on the American West by securing the Louisiana Purchase and masterminding the rectangular survey that divided the region up into manageable boxes. How profoundly happy he would have been to find that, clear across the continent, his efforts were literally bearing fruit.

By the turn of the century, huge changes were afoot in daily life. Self-sufficiency at home gave way to mass production. Many of the items that Americans had come to depend on—from food and clothing to cars and cigarettes—now came from distant factories. A new and radically different system of distribution emerged to market these products, centered on brand names and advertising. By 1910, this new consumer economy catapulted the United States into the greatest industrial power on the face of the earth.

From an environmental perspective, consumerism involved equally radical changes. Its most important legacy stemmed from the separation in space of production from consumption. The growth of specialized, one-crop industrial agriculture in places such as California brought the commercialization of farming to a new level. Just as oranges traveled to the Midwest for the exposition, by the turn of the century California factory farms routinely sent trainloads of fruit—enough to build millions of orange, pear, plum, and cherry bells—across the nation to the tables of American consumers.

Meanwhile, the farms that once dominated the outskirts of New York City, until the turn of the century the nation's most important produce-growing center, lost ground to competitors in California and the South. In California especially, orchardists operated free from the worry of frost, which periodically buffeted New York growers. Capitalizing on a more favorable climate, on cheap labor from Asia and later Mexico, and on the virtues of speedy, refrigerated train travel, California's fruit and vegetable growers went on to become the richest farmers in the nation. As early as 1927, two-thirds of all canned fruit purchased in the United States originated in the Golden State. By 1980, two-fifths of all the nation's fresh produce was grown there. The rise of this moveable feast, however, exacted a high social and ecological price.

CITRUS LIBERTY BELL

Composed of 6,500 oranges, this replica of the famous Liberty Bell was displayed at the 1893 Columbian Exposition, organized to celebrate the 400th anniversary of Columbus's voyage to America. (Final Report of the California World's Fair Commission . . . [Sacramento, CA: State Office, 1894])

LAND OF SUNSHINE

In the late nineteenth century, boosters tried to lure people to the Golden State by selling them on the climate. And no one did more to market the image of California as a sun-drenched oasis than the journalist Charles Fletcher Lummis. In 1885, Lummis, recovering from a bout of malaria, decided that the best route to recovery was to journey, by foot, from his home in Cincinnati, Ohio, some 3,000 miles to Los Angeles. After 143 days of walking, Lummis arrived in southern California, tan, fit, and eager to testify to the virtues of the west coast's magnificent climate. In 1895, Lummis became the editor of a magazine aptly named Land of Sunshine. In it he argued that California's sunny climate made people healthier and fostered intellectual and creative talents. It was no coincidence that some of the world's greatest minds, from Jesus to Plato to Michelangelo, came from lands blessed with a great deal of sun. In the United States, he deduced, all roads led to Los Angeles.[1]

Much of what Lummis told his readers was hype. But there is little question that California's cloudless skies—putting aside for the moment the agricultural implications of too little rain—gave it an edge over the East when it came to growing food. Indeed, California is one of only five places on the planet blessed with such a sun-rich climate (the others are central Chile, southern Africa, southern Australia, and the Mediterranean basin). In Fresno, California, the heart of raisin country, for instance, average precipitation in May is just a third of an inch. Barely a tenth of an inch of rain falls in June, and essentially none in July and August. Virtually all of the area's 10 inches of precipitation occurs between November and April. The rest of the year it is sunny, amazingly so, with sunshine favoring the city an average of more than 90 percent of the time in the summer months.

Californians have something known as the Pacific High to thank for all the sunny weather. This zone of high pressure lies stationed off the coast of the central part of the state, deflecting all precipitation north to the Pacific Northwest. From late March until October the high pressure stands watch over the Golden State's sunny skies, before drifting south to Mexico in the fall and allowing rain to slip in. As regular as clockwork, the Pacific High returns north in the spring, and with it sunshine beats down on the land, creating perfect conditions for photosynthesis.

With respect to solar radiation, California has struck it rich. But the state's good fortune does not end there. It extends into the realm of geology as well. One of the largest river valleys on earth, the Central Valley, an area nearly the size of England, stretches more than 400 miles through the center of the state. Drained by the Sacramento River in the north and the San Joaquin in the south, the valley is, in the words of one environmental scientist, "the richest agricultural region in the history of the world."[2]

In the 1860s, wheat rose to dominance in this valley. Hundreds of square miles of land were planted in the crop, fields so colossal that it was not uncommon for a team of plows to work their way across an expanse, then camp out for the night before rising the following day and forging back across the farm. A generation later, California emerged as the nation's leader in wheat production. The bulk of the crop, produced with the help of horse-drawn plows and huge steam combines, was exported across the world. But wheat's reign was brief. As early as 1883, wheat prices began to decline, bottoming out in 1894 as Argentina, Russia, Canada, India, and Australia began growing large quantities of grain and flooding the market. Meanwhile, California wheat growers, eager to cash in on the bonanza, began to deplete the fertility of the soil. When they sought new land to exploit, however, they found that prices were high, especially relative to such places as Kansas and elsewhere on the Great Plains, where land could be bought for little more than a filing fee. Hemmed in by the ocean and with nowhere else to turn, California wheat farmers would have to find higher-paying crops to grow if they wanted to prosper.[3]

This is where fruit and transportation came in. As long as farmers depended on local markets in the West to sell their fruit crop, overproduction and low prices for oranges, plums, grapes, and peaches would prevail. But if a way could be found to ship the produce—which unlike wheat was bulky and perishable—to markets in the Midwest and East, then California farmers might realize great wealth. Although a transcontinental rail link had been built by 1869, it was not until the 1880s, when competition brought down rates, that orchards turned to the railroads for shipping fresh produce. But they were only able to capitalize on the roads if they could ship the fruit east without its spoiling. It took the meat industry's perfection of the refrigerated railroad car in the 1880s truly to launch the transcontinental shipment of fruit. In 1888, cherries and apricots left the Golden State aboard a train using the new refrigerated technology for shipping produce for the very first time. Firms such as Armour and Swift sent meat to California and loaded up their cars with fruit for the return trip. By the turn of the century, consumers in New York City and other urban areas could now buy fruits and vegetables out of season.[4]

Apart from being more perishable and bulkier than wheat, fruit also required more water. Especially in California's drier southern reaches, that was a hard-to-come-by commodity. Irrigation offered an answer. Early on, some grape growers believed that irrigating led to a reduction in quality. However, California's passage of the Wright Act in 1887—sanctioning the creation of government units to oversee the collective control of irrigation—coupled with droughts in 1889, 1890, and 1893, helped to convert the skeptical. By 1890, California had emerged as the nation's leader in irrigated acreage. "But for irrigation," one orchard owner explained in 1893, "much of our best fruit lands necessarily would be still a desert waste, and some of the special productions of the irrigated regions would be almost unknown in the great markets of the East."[5]

Instead of expanding onto fresh soil—the basis for most agriculture in land-rich America up until this time—California fruit growers increased their yields by turning to such capital-intensive technologies as railroads and irrigation works. Instead of moving the frontier, they poured money and technology into the land in an effort to maximize output. This new industrial form of agriculture focused exclusively on the efficient production of crops for national and international markets, using large amounts of capital and wage labor.[6]

By the turn of the century, a sweeping 800-mile fruit belt stretched down the length of the state. Apple, pear, cherry, plum, and apricot orchards dominated in coastal areas. Inland in the Santa Clara valley—known today as Silicon Valley—plum trees yielding hundreds of pounds of fruit each spread out across the landscape long before anyone had even heard of high technology. By 1886, the state as a whole produced 40 million pounds of prunes, the bulk of which wound up shipped to the East. In the Central Valley, peaches and pears flourished, crops that ripened before the onset of the long, hot summer weather. Raisins, meanwhile, became the signature fruit of Fresno County, with growers availing themselves of the hot August sun to dry out the grapes.

New York area farmers lost significant ground to the California factory farms, especially during the winter season, when the climate made agriculture impossible. But when the weather turned warmer, New Yorkers still bought fresh locally

BROOKLYN FARMS

Now a byword for urban life, the Flatbush section of Brooklyn, New York, shown here in the 1870s, once hosted some of the most productive vegetable farms in the nation. (Brooklyn Collection, Brooklyn Public Library)

grown produce, as they had done for generations. The farms that once spread out across Brooklyn and Queens succumbed by the 1920s, but not because the California growers undersold them. Instead, it was the superior marketing ability of their competitors across the continent that put them out of business.[7]

SUN KISSED

Before the late nineteenth century, few Americans believed, as many commonly do today, in the value of a diet rich in fruits and vegetables. In fact, many urbanites worried that eating fresh produce might actually worsen their health, bringing on such dread diseases as cholera or dysentery. Aside from the nuts and raisins consumed once or twice a year at holiday time, the diet of most Americans centered on foods full of fat, starch, and salt.[8]

Although truck farms had sprung up outside of major cities, introducing residents to a variety of fresh produce, it took a self-conscious effort on the part of California orchards to sell consumers on the idea that fruits and vegetables ought to play a part in everyone's daily fare. By the turn of the century, the campaign appeared to be paying off. "The old prejudices against fruit are fast passing away," observed one grower in 1893. "Fruit has become a necessity rather than a luxury." In 1910, a housewife put it this way: "When I first began to keep house, ten years ago, we ate cereal, eggs and coffee for breakfast, with fruit occasionally instead of cereal; but now we must have grapefruit every morning. . . . [T]hen, when I go to market and see fresh beans, cucumbers and spinach, I buy them without really stopping to think; so easily tempted are we." As the reference to fresh produce suggests, marketing on the part of California growers initially helped to increase the demand for locally grown produce.[9]

At one time, fruit passed into eastern markets with little concern for quality. But in an effort to stimulate national demand, California orchards set out to standardize their products. Growers and shippers joined in establishing formal sets of rules for packing fruit, specifying uniform box sizes and shapes. The fruit itself was classified into various grades—fancy, choice, and standard. "We must be guided by the experience and adopt the practices of other successful manufacturers, and so arrange and classify our products that each purchaser may secure the identical commodity he orders in the most convenient form," explained one grower. The state government in California, spurred on by a freeze in 1912 that left many growers with little choice but to ship damaged fruit east, also stepped in and passed the Fresh Fruit, Nut, and Vegetable Standardization Act of 1917 to regulate quality.[10]

Growers themselves chose to specialize in those species of fruit that best met market imperatives. Some 60 different varieties of pears—Bosc, Giffard, Joan of Arc, Vicar, Wilder Early, among others—once grew on this continent. But California farmers eventually zeroed in on one main variety, the Bartlett, a pear that was easy to grow, can, and ship, and thus suitable for commercial harvesting. By the early twentieth century, Bartletts made up roughly 80 to 90 percent of the pears raised in California.[11]

Standardization helped orchards sell fruit in eastern markets, but to transform crops such as raisins and oranges into year-round staples, growers had to become more aggressive. New marketing organizations formed to oversee the harvesting, processing, and shipping of fruit, while engaging in brand name advertising. California raisin growers, centered in sunny Fresno County, produced record-setting yields in the 1890s, but found that demand did not keep up with supply, forcing down prices. To solve the problem of underconsumption, the growers founded a cooperative organization, but it soon failed. Then, in 1912, the California Associated Raisin Company was formed, a group uniting over 1,000 orchards. In one of the new company's very first moves, it created the "Sun-Maid" brand name to market its product. Using one part feminine mystique and one part raw natural power, the company tried to sell Americans on the idea that they could get back in touch with nature and improve their health by buying the product. The Sun-Maid label, showing a girl in a red bonnet with the sun in the background, became one of the most successful trademarks in food history. Then the growers launched an advertising campaign, pitching the raisins in newspapers and women's magazines. Sales agents went from grocer to grocer in major cities hawking the product. In the 1920s, the growers marketed raisins in little nickel packages, the perfect size to fit into a school lunch sack. In six months' time, the company sold 17,000 tons of five-cent boxes valued at 18 million dollars. As consumption boomed, raisins went from being a luxury item eaten only on holidays to an expected and ordinary part of daily fare.[12]

As late as the early 1880s, oranges too remained a luxury item, more a Christmas stocking stuffer than a dietary staple. Since the end of the Civil War, growers in Florida had shipped oranges north by boat during the holiday season. By the mid-1880s, improved railroad transportation allowed Florida orchards to outcompete their counterparts in California for the eastern market. One New Jersey vegetable farmer marveled at the way that farmers in Florida "with their evergreen productiveness, have been able to revolutionize the old conditions, by sending to the northern cities, even when snow clad and ice bound, the fruits of balmy summer." Then, in 1895, a freeze pummeled the Sunshine State. The year before the cold, Florida outstripped California by roughly a million boxes. The onset of the freeze, however, caused Florida production to plummet. By 1909, nearly three-quarters of all the citrus consumed in the United States came from California.[13]

But more than just a cold spell accounted for California's lock on the national orange market. In 1885, Americans consumed almost no citrus fruit; in 1914, they were eating roughly 40 oranges per year. Credit for that change must go to the California Fruit Growers Exchange, founded in 1893 (eight years after Florida established a similar organization). The exchange united some 15,000 growers and 200 packing associations around the processing and marketing of citrus. At one time, some 200 different brand name oranges existed. The fruit exchange, however, sought to streamline marketing by creating the Sunkist (originally Sun Kissed) trademark and stamping it on each and every orange grown. During the early decades of the twentieth century, Sunkist's marketers blanketed the nation with images of its product. It created picturesque labels for use on the tens of millions of citrus crates it shipped every year. It advertised in newspapers and magazines, set up billboards, helped grocers and especially chain stores to create elaborate window displays, and ran promotional spots on the radio. By the early 1930s, the organization had over 1,000 billboards in 11 metropolitan markets, including one in New York's Times Square that reached, it is estimated, one million people each day.[14]

The invention of the electric juicer and the discovery that ascorbic acid (vitamin C) prevented scurvy bolstered Sunkist's marketing prospects. By the middle of the 1930s, a fifth of all Sunkist oranges were being consumed in juice form. In the early years of the twentieth century, middle-class Americans commonly worried that the advent of modern, urban life had cut them off from the natural world, especially the sunlight that had formerly fostered good mental and physical health. Advertisers capitalized on this yearning for nature by warning mothers to make sure that their children received food in its natural form. And what could be more wholesome than a sun-kissed orange? Oranges soon became an essential part of a normal, healthy diet. Per capita consumption shot up during the first two decades of the twentieth century. "The public may remember the slo-

SUNKIST DISPLAY

Before the early twentieth century, Americans purchased food from neighborhood grocers, who stood behind counters and took their orders. The Piggly Wiggly chain, first opened in 1916, pioneered self-service grocery shopping, allowing customers to choose fruit, often artfully displayed, and other items for themselves. (Library of Congress)

gan, 'An apple a day keeps the doctor away,'" wrote one observer in 1928, "but it possesses much more specific and convincing information concerning the health value of oranges." Hailed as an antidote to the ills of modern living, the orange surpassed the apple as the key to health, a means of putting a little sun into everyone's day.[15]

Not wanting to be left behind, prune and apricot growers also adopted the solar motif, forming the Sunsweet brand in 1917. Growers tapped the sun's energy and then turned around and marketed the fruit by convincing consumers of the wholesomeness of their product. It was a perfect strategy for reaching sun-starved city dwellers. Advertisements of women proffering the fruits of the land conveyed the impression that what consumers bought came straight from nature to their kitchen table. But such an image obscured the role played by both the growers and the workers they hired. Flawless oranges and plump raisins could be bought in urban groceries and chain stores with nary a thought given to the incredible amount of human energy that went into making them.[16]

COPING WITH PESTS

The first step in producing perfect-looking plums and oranges was to find the right species for a particular growing environment. Luther Burbank, a Massachusetts-born plant breeder, probably had more impact in this regard than any other individual. In the 1870s, Burbank, seeking to improve the vegetable varieties available in New England, invented a potato well adapted to the region's stony soil. He then headed west to the Golden State, where he continued to cross-fertilize and graft plants with an eye toward their commercial value. "Only by growing the most perfect fruit possible could a profit be made," he told a group gathered in Sacramento in 1899. "The fruit grower of to-day is strictly a manufacturer, and should have the latest and best improvements." By this he meant fruit engineered to grow rapidly, such as the plums—large, rich in sugar, and easy to ship—he introduced into California in the 1880s.[17]

Although one newspaper once called him "the Edison of horticultural mysteries," Burbank is scarcely remembered today. In part, his obscurity stems from the fact that he never received legal recognition for his work. Edison had over 1,000 patents to his name; Burbank had not a single one. The originator of Idaho's now famous Russet Burbank potato, a crop valued at 17 million dollars in 1906, he garnered just 150 dollars for his efforts. "A man can patent a mouse trap or copyright a nasty song," he once wrote, "but if he gives to the world a new fruit that will add millions to the value of earth's annual harvests he will be fortunate if he is rewarded by so much as having his name connected with the result." Not until the passage of the Plant Patent Act in 1930 was it possible for plant breeders to transform living things such as fruit trees into intellectual property.[18]

Growing species tailor-made for sale on the national market was one thing. But orchards had to overcome a number of other obstacles if they were going to profit by providing consumers with perfect-looking fruit. Chief among these was the threat posed by a variety of agricultural pests. When California's growers replaced the region's natural vegetation—its sweeping expanses of tules, a grass much like a bulrush, and its perennial species of bunchgrass—with domesticated plants, they opened themselves up to insect infestation, like all farmers who simplify an ecosystem. The problem was made considerably worse by the huge number of plant species imported into the state in the 60 years after 1860: exotic varieties of apple, plum, and cherry trees, plus hundreds of other shrubs and vines. With the new plants came insects, buried in the fruit and hidden under the bark.[19]

Numerous such pests existed, including the pear slug, the apricot shot hole, peach blight, red scale, purple scale, citrus mealy-bug, red spider mite, and on and on. Perhaps the most troublesome insect was the cottony cushion scale, a bug that attacked California's orange groves beginning in the 1880s. It is hard to say how the scale arrived. One theory is that it first appeared back in 1868, when a shipment of Australian lemon trees arrived in San Mateo County. The scale then worked its way south. Growers first tried oil soaps, liquid sprays, and hydrocyanic gas. But none of the remedies worked. Eventually, it dawned on some Americans that since growers in Australia did not suffer from the scale, a predator must have existed there that kept the insect in check. On a visit to Australia in 1888, an American delegation returned with a species of ladybug that they hoped would rid California of the problem. Miraculously, the strategy worked. The beetle was able to fly, flitting from tree to tree and preying on the immobile scale fixed on leaves and branches. Liberated from the pest, California's citrus industry boomed in the last decade of the nineteenth century.[20]

It was a novel solution to an intractable problem, but using bugs to fight bugs—known as biological control—proved a short-lived solution. It was impossible to find predators to deal with all the insects that threatened California's fruit and vegetable crops. And not all predators survived when transported out of their original habitat. Chemicals, however, offered what many growers saw as a more workable solution. Orchards eventually turned to new synthetic poisons such as arsenate of lead. Supported by the research of scientists at the University of California at Berkeley, fruit growers sprayed and fumigated their way to success, as yields per acre marched upward by early in the twentieth century.[21]

California eventually went on to lead the nation in pesticide use. The quest to deliver delicate fruit to market in pristine condition in part explains the state's obsession with insecticides. But like a drunk addicted to alcohol, farmers found it hard, once a decision to spray had been made, to stop. As pests developed resistance to one poison, another had to be found in the ceaseless effort to keep California's landscape from reverting back to its ecologically complex and diverse ancestry. Apart from its harmful environmental effects, increasing pesticide use also severely compromised the health of farm workers, who handled the chemicals directly.[22]

With the pests out of the way, growers still had to make sure the crops were picked and packed in a timely and efficient manner. Fruit farming remained, even in the age of the tractor and combine, a very labor-intensive enterprise. One acre of tomatoes alone demanded roughly 1,000 hours of work to bring it to maturity. Growers thus yearned for a cheap labor force, especially given the already high expense of pesticide- and irrigation-based farming.[23]

Growers needed lots of field hands to bring in the summer harvest, but during the rest of the year the demand for labor remained relatively low. Work on a diversified farm, like the ones in early New England, which planted a variety of different crops, employed family members year-round. One-crop farming, however, was a seasonal enterprise. In other words, the orchards wanted temporary and cheap workers, laborers who would arrive just in time to pick the crops before they rotted and then disappear down the road, relieving growers of any additional financial burden.

The make-up of the migrant labor force changed over time. A large pool of Chinese workers tended the fields beginning in the 1870s. By 1880, Chinese workers composed a third of California's agricultural labor force. As it turned out, the Chinese had a great deal of experience raising fruit. During the Gold Rush, they often tended produce on truck farms near mining areas. Many of the Chinese also hailed from Guongdong province, a center for citrus growing in their homeland. In 1882, however, Congress, responding to the racist fears of white workers who viewed the Chinese as a threat to their own job prospects, passed legislation suspending immigration for 10 years.[24]

The Chinese Exclusion Act of 1882, as it was called, forced California growers to turn more to Japanese workers, who had considerably less experience raising fruit. Some 80,000 Japanese immigrated to the United States between 1898 and 1907, mostly young men who wound up working in California. More problematic than their lack of experience with fruit culture, however, was that as a group, they expressed considerable interest in owning property of their own. They had no intention of toiling away forever in the fields of white fruit growers. Instead, they saved money and later went off to buy farms of their own.[25]

California orchards eventually would come to rely on immigrants from Mexico, not Asia, to do the tedious stooping and heavy hauling. When the Mexican government, after a revolution in 1911, failed to live up to the expectations of workers, many headed north in search of wage labor. Nothing could have made California growers happier than a cheap and docile labor force willing to disappear back across the border when work became scarce. By 1930, some 368,000 Mexicans lived in California. Although working conditions in the fields were brutal, growers rationalized exploiting laborers by arguing that Mexicans were naturally suited to work in the blistering hot weather. The Mexican, explained one apologist, "is fitted by natural environment to withstand our climatic conditions . . . and able to perform work which demands hard physical exertion."[26]

No matter what their ethnicity, the workers were tuned in to the natural world. Guidelines established by the California fruit standardization act required boxed fruit to have a certain sugar content. That meant that fruit had to be picked when it was ripe and not a moment before. Workers, for instance, knew to glean the southward facing sides of trees first, where more sunlight struck, ripening the fruit most rapidly.

Bruised and otherwise mishandled fruit, of course, ate into a grower's profits. At the turn of the century, orange growers struggled to deal with a troubling blue mold. The mold seemed to strike injured oranges especially. This knowledge led managers to institute "careful handling" procedures to ward off the natural process of decomposition. By the 1920s, borax (and later other chemicals) was used to kill the mold. As always, the goal was to produce uniform, eye-appealing fruit that advertisers could sell to consumers—shiny oranges, seemingly untouched by human hands, that shoppers could pluck from the shelves unmindful of all the human labor that went into producing them.

But the goodness of nature had its price. In 1939, Carey McWilliams, a lawyer and labor sympathizer, published *Factories in the Field*, a muckraking piece that highlighted the abuses and poverty of migratory work in California. The book turned on its head the advertisers' image of fruit descending magically from some garden paradise. Considered by some to be the nonfiction equivalent of John Steinbeck's Pulitzer Prize–winning *Grapes of Wrath* (published in the same year), McWilliams uncovered the grim tale of routinized labor and rank exploitation behind the brightly colored fruit. In the wake of labor unrest, growers organized in the 1930s to put workers in their place, a process boldly described as "farm fascism" by McWilliams, who wrote of "Gunkist" oranges and the plight of the worker under industrial farming. The growers eventually branded McWilliams "agricultural pest no. 1." The smiling woman on the raisin label betrayed not a trace of the blood and sweat that went into the transformation of California into a stripped-down ecosystem catering to markets back east.[27]

WATER AND POWER

By the 1920s, California overtook Iowa as the nation's leading agricultural state. Roughly nine million orange trees and 73 million grapevines spread out across the landscape, amid other crops such as alfalfa, rice, peaches, lemons, plums, prunes, beans, walnuts, cotton, beets, and apricots. These were just some of the more than 200 commercially grown crops produced in the Golden State. Most were plants that had no business being grown on arid lands and would never have survived but for irrigation.[28]

At the outset, California farmers relied on surface water. But in the 1890s, the perfection of the centrifugal pump brought a vast reserve of underground water— perhaps as much as 750 million acre-feet (an acre-foot is equal to 326,000 gallons)—within reach. The pump, in other words, put growers in touch with enough water to flood the entire state of California to a depth of seven feet. In 1910, Tulare County, a major agricultural center, had 739 pumps; in 1919, it had 3,758.[29]

Beginning in 1918 and lasting until early the next decade, droughts caused growers to run their pumps with abandon. The result was predictable. In the upper San Joaquin valley, the average ground water level plummeted nearly 40 feet between 1921 and 1939. As the water table dropped, great numbers of ancient oak trees and other native plants died, and thousands of acres of farmland, dependent on the stored underground water wealth, went out of production. By the 1930s, vast expanses of some of the richest agricultural land in the nation were in jeopardy.[30]

Growers could have limited their water use and submitted to government control over pumping. But they felt it would interfere too much with profitability. Thus a new source of water had to be found if California was going to retain its position as the fruit basket of the nation. It had long been known that the northern reaches of the long Central Valley had two-thirds of the water but only one-third of the land fit for cultivation. Bringing the water south to where it was needed most would take, according to a state plan broached in 1933, a massive plumbing project. But with the nation mired in a depression, insufficient private money existed to finance such an ambitious scheme. So the state of California turned instead to the federal government for support.

In 1937, Congress authorized the engineers and planners at the U.S. Bureau of Reclamation to begin work on the Central Valley Project, a monumental scheme that, after nearly two decades of work, resulted in four major dams, four elaborate canal systems, and a lot of federally subsidized water for California's growers. The bureau had been created earlier in the century subsequent to the passage of the National Reclamation Act of 1902. Established to fight monopolies and encourage the family farm, the legislation set up a system whereby money from the sale of public lands would be used to reclaim patches of soil from the clutches of the desert. Under the law, a landowner was entitled to only enough federal water to irrigate 160 acres—Jefferson's magic number and a figure pushed by the railroads, who worried that anything smaller would discourage settlers from taking up farming in the West. When the Central Valley Project came under federal control, it too had to live up to this requirement, meaning that big-time growers with land above the 160-acre limit would have to divest.[31]

California's great Central Valley was certainly a place ripe for land redistribution, which, on the surface at least, is what the new federal water project would mean. Sixty percent of all the landholdings in the southern part of the valley were over the federal limit. Just three percent of the region's growers controlled 40 percent of the cropland. "This degree of concentration of land ownership," wrote the authors of one 1940s study, "is rarely encountered in the United States." In 1946, the Standard Oil Company alone owned nearly 80,000 acres in the area slated to receive federal water.[32]

But what should have been a means of redistributing land more fairly instead wound up becoming a huge federal giveaway. First, a group of liberal economists in the Franklin Roosevelt administration argued that the 160-acre figure was a minimum, not a ceiling. They proposed a maximum farm size of 640 acres instead. Then, after the New Deal liberals caved into the big growers, the Truman administration and its new Bureau of Reclamation chief, Michael Straus, came into office calling for "technical compliance" with the reclamation law. As far as they

were concerned, giant corporate growers could sign land away to their employees and then lease it back, giving them the right to receive subsidized federal water in the process. By requiring growers to comply with only the letter and not
the spirit of the law, the bureau reinforced the valley's unequal land distribution
pattern.[33]

Did the completion of the giant Central Valley Project alleviate California's water woes, the intent of the plan? In fact, the project actually accelerated depletion
of the aquifers. Indeed, the federal government's generosity even led farmers to
plant more acreage. The inexpensive government water, in other words, spawned
agricultural expansion. The federal irrigation projects, however, could never keep
up with the demand, leaving farmers with no choice but to dig deeper wells. In
the 1940s, for instance, Kern County farmers ventured down 275 feet to tap underground water. In 1965, they had to travel nearly 200 feet deeper to reach the
much-depleted supply.[34]

On the one hand, the Central Valley Project spelled more ecological trouble for
California. On the other, it left agriculture largely in the hands of the corporate
growers—the main beneficiaries of federal intervention. But now of course the
growers had to contend with the Bureau of Reclamation, which compromised
somewhat their jealously guarded autonomy. By the 1940s, California and the
American West more generally had become a "hydraulic society," a culture organized around the domination of its most precious resource—water—by growers and federal engineers. Whatever democratic pretensions remained from the
1902 reclamation act had dried up like an old irrigation ditch.[35]

No scheme better suggests the sheer arrogance and imperial ambitions of the
modern hydraulic West than the North American Water and Power Alliance
(NAWAPA). Dreamed up in the early 1960s, NAWAPA was the brainchild of the
giant Ralph Parsons engineering firm of Pasadena, California. The company set its
sights on the Canadian province of British Columbia, one of the most water-rich
places on the face of the earth and heir to some 4–10 percent of all the freshwater
available in the world. Not one to think small, the engineering firm proposed shipping that water through a complex system of tunnels, reservoirs, and pump stations
south to the arid West at a cost of billions of dollars. Had the plan been carried
out—inflation and the rise of the environmental movement in the 1970s put the
brakes on it—it would have led to the forced relocation of the 150,000 people living in Prince George, British Columbia, plus untold damage to tens of millions of
acres of wilderness. "The environmental damage that would be caused by that
damned thing can't even be described," remarked hydrologist Luna Leopold. It is
hard to imagine a more grandiose plan for dominating the natural world.[36]

CONCLUSION

By the turn of the century, California, like the Cotton South, had emerged as a region founded on agricultural specialization—first wheat, then fruit, and by the

1920s, cotton, referred to in the San Joaquin valley as "white gold."[37] But the California growers took monoculture several steps further down the road of industry. Southern planters specialized in cotton, but they also produced corn and other foods for their own consumption. The fruit farmers of California, however, used virtually every acre of land to grow fruit for national and international markets. And where the southern planter tended to expand onto new soil to increase production, the west coast farmers plowed more capital and technology into what available land they had. It would be hard to overemphasize the importance of the changes that took place in California agriculture between 1890 and 1925. Large-scale operations wedded to just a handful of plant species and to irrigation, pesticides, and cheap labor—these were the hallmarks of the revolution in farming pioneered in the Golden State.

Together such changes formed the basis of modern agribusiness. Thanks to these shifts, urbanites across the nation no longer worried where their next meal would come from. California agriculture solved the demographic dilemma posed by a culture rapidly shifting from a rural to an urban base, a society where fewer and fewer people grew food for the metropolis. In the short stretch between 1917 and 1926, four million people left farming and some 19 million acres of land went into retirement. And yet, agricultural production increased by a stunning 25 percent. Ironically, instead of a food shortage, Americans soon had a crisis of abundance on their hands.[38]

Industrial farming boomed in California, accounting by 1930 for more than a third of all such farms in the nation. But if Golden State agriculture solved the problem of feeding urbanites, it also exacted a price in the process. Increasing amounts of water and pesticides kept these large-scale farms viable and protected them from the falling prices that accompanied an abundance of food. Genetic diversity declined as growers streamlined crop production, planting only those plant varieties best suited to market imperatives—species, like squarish tomatoes, that shipped well and looked good in the stores. Ecology suffered and so too did direct democracy, as corporate enterprises with large amounts of capital, and a yen for cheap labor, came to lord over the agricultural social structure. Ironically, even nutrition paid a price. Although California marketers championed the health benefits of eating more fruits and vegetables, the long distances the produce had to travel to market reduced its nutritional value. And what of the old farms outside of New York City that grew more nourishing food? These once vibrant enterprises would soon be replaced by apartments, highways, and sprawl—populated with new residents largely unmindful that the streets they traversed on the way to work once grew cabbages and other vegetables.

THE SECRET HISTORY OF MEAT

In 1954, a 52-year-old struggling salesman named Ray Kroc, who had sold everything from paper cups to Florida real estate, traveled to San Bernadino, California, to hawk his latest item, the Multimixer milkshake machine. He headed for a restaurant owned by two brothers named Mac and Dick McDonald. Kroc sat outside the octagonal building, transfixed by the sight of customers, queuing up, one after another, to buy sacks and sacks of hamburgers. The restaurant appealed to him on a number of levels. He liked the stripped-down, simple menu centered around the hamburger. He admired the preparation process, which resembled a kind of assembly line for food. Even the building with its arches impressed him. And the name McDonald's seemed to have a nice ring to it. "I had a feeling," he later wrote, "that it would be one of those promotable names that would catch the public fancy."[1]

No food is more closely associated with American consumer culture than the hamburger. Only the invention of the automobile rivals the rise of fast food meat eating in terms of its consequences for both nature and social relations. What Henry Ford did for the car, Ray Kroc did for the hamburger, mass producing them in accordance with the strictest of standards and placing them within easy reach of the vast majority of the American population.

Behind the Golden Arches and the other ways in which modern Americans go about feeding themselves, however, lay a set of profound changes in our relationship with the land, more specifically, in agriculture itself. To support the masses of new consumers eager for beef, raising livestock evolved into a factory enterprise. Beef led the way, but in the years after World War II poultry and pork production perfected the industrial form. Thousands of animals were confined to feedlots and were fed corn, soybeans, and fishmeal, plus vitamins, hormones, and antibiotics. Such a diet used massive amounts of water and energy—to grow the feed; water the cattle, pigs, and chickens; and produce the fertilizers that farmers depended on more than ever before. With crops and animals raised in separate places, manure lost its role as a vehicle for transporting solar energy and nutrients back to the soil and instead became a major source of water pollution. Munching a hamburger may seem innocent enough, but the nation's love affair with meat has had enormous consequences for people and ecosystems across the continent, impacts of which most consumers were (and are) only dimly aware.

THE DEBUT OF BEEF

Before the late nineteenth century, pork, not beef, dominated the national palate. The popularity of pork is not surprising in light of all the advantages there were to raising pigs. To begin with, swine are terrific reproducers. Their litters tend to be large, in contrast to cows, which take more than twice as long (nine months versus a little less than five) to give birth to just one calf. In 1539, when the explorer Hernando De Soto came to Florida, he brought 13 pigs with him; a mere three years later he had 700. Pigs are also extremely versatile. They will eat just about anything, from acorns in the forest to garbage in the city. Not to mention that when it comes to converting plant matter into animal protein, they are more than three times as efficient as cattle. Pigs also love corn, a crop that American farmers were particularly fond of raising. And finally, in the days before refrigeration staved off decomposition, pig meat took much better than beef to salting and smoking. For all these reasons, pork played a far larger role than beef in the American diet up until the end of the nineteenth century.[2]

Despite all these virtues, however, the pig did have one main disadvantage that limited its commercial prospects: Unlike cattle, swine are hard, if not impossible, to drive for long distances. Hogs were thus slaughtered in many small-scale packinghouses scattered across mid-nineteenth-century America. The plants in Cincinnati were the only exception. Situated near where several rivers join the Ohio and benefiting from the Miami and Erie Canal, opened in 1827, Cincinnati emerged by the 1830s as the nation's leader in pork packing. The city managed to tap the rich agricultural resources of the Ohio valley so successfully that it eventually became known as Porkopolis.[3]

Cincinnati's pork packers took the first steps in streamlining meat production. Long before Henry Ford employed the assembly line for mass-producing cars, Porkopolis packers pioneered a method for slaughtering animals in large numbers. By hanging pigs from a rotating wheel, workers were able to efficiently gut the animal before sending it on to the chopping table, where butchers would finish the job of cutting the meat and packing it off to market. "No iron cog-wheels could work with more regular motion," wrote landscape architect Frederick Law Olmsted on a visit to the city in the 1850s. "Plump falls the hog upon the table, chop, chop; chop chop; chop, chop, fall the cleavers. All is over." Thus was born the "disassembly line" for the mass slaughtering of livestock.[4]

Exactly how much pork Americans produced in the nineteenth century is difficult to say. But a conservative estimate places production in 1849 at 139 pounds per capita, declining to 119 pounds 40 years later. By that time, the grasslands of the Great Plains had been opened for settlement, and beef had begun to take on a larger role in the American diet.[5]

In the 1850s, the area west of the Mississippi River, save for eastern Texas and the very western extreme of California, was largely a cattle-free zone. Over the next 50 years, however, bovines increased dramatically; they rose from 15 million in 1870 to 35 million in 1900. Once the buffalo had been driven to the brink of extinction, cattle filed into their former eco-niches. There was only one problem. Population growth in the West did not keep pace with cattle's rise to dominance. In 1880, more than half the nation's cattle resided west of the Mississippi, in an area with less than a quarter of the American population. How to get the cattle protein into the stomachs of people in the populous East became a problem in desperate need of a solution.[6]

Cattle drovers and later the railroad emerged to help resolve this dilemma. But the perishability of beef, which, unlike pork, did not lend itself as well to salting or smoking, meant that the animals had to be slaughtered near where they would be consumed. Before the end of the nineteenth century, beef packing remained in the hands of local butchers, who ran small-scale operations to serve their communities.[7]

The advent of refrigeration, however, revolutionized the beef-packing industry. Efforts to develop a refrigerated railroad car began in the 1850s, but only late the following decade was a car with enough cold air circulation developed to carry a load of dressed beef (cleaned animal carcasses) between Chicago and Boston. The legendary Gustavus F. Swift later hired an engineer to improve the refrigerated railroad car, enhancements that would soon make his cars the most popular among the nation's major beef producers.[8]

By the 1880s, the slaughter and marketing of beef evolved from a local business handled by neighborhood butchers into a national industry dominated by major meatpacking centers such as Chicago, Kansas City, and St. Louis. A handful of companies, Swift and Armour the most prominent, emerged to capture the newly industrialized meatpacking trade. In the 1880s, these companies began building branch houses across the nation, cold-storage facilities that received the dressed beef from packinghouses and distributed it to grocers, who marketed it to consumers. In 1887, the five largest packinghouses had just a few branch houses in operation. Ten years later, however, the companies had 20 plants and roughly 600 branch houses for distributing their product. Meat now traveled in refrigerated railroad cars from the Midwest as far as California.[9]

The national trade in dressed beef, however, did have its critics. Railroads, which had previously invested large sums of money in building stock cars for transporting animals, were among the first to object. The railroad companies also believed they would lose money as the lighter dressed beef replaced the considerably heavier live cattle. Butchers, meanwhile, feared for their jobs, as the new meatpacking industry took over the role of slaughtering, improving on the disassembly line originally developed for pork. In 1886, the meat cutters assembled to form the Butcher's National Protective Association, an organization that tried to undermine consumer confidence in dressed beef by warning that it was unsanitary.[10]

The most famous critic of meatpacking was journalist Upton Sinclair, whose 1906 novel, The Jungle, included vivid descriptions of the horrific conditions found in meatpacking plants. "It was too dark in these storage places to see well, but a man could run his hand over these piles of meat and sweep off handfuls of the dried dung of rats. These rats were nuisances, and the packers would put poisoned bread out for them; they would die, and then rats, bread, and meat would go into

MARKET ROOM

Cattle carcasses, also known as dressed beef, were stored in large rooms cooled with ice, like the one shown in this late-nineteenth-century Chicago packinghouse. The meat was then shipped to butchers, who cut it up for sale to consumers. (Chicago Historical Society)

the hoppers together." President Theodore Roosevelt read the book and wasted no time in dispatching federal investigators to Chicago to learn more about the industry's filthy conditions, information that was then used to pressure Congress into passing legislation (the 1906 Meat Inspection Act) mandating sanitary workplace conditions for those companies engaged in the interstate meat trade.[11]

Sinclair's book proved upsetting to people accustomed to purchasing meat from trusted local butchers. But if they were disgusted by conditions at the faraway packinghouses, consumers also must have found it hard to resist the lower prices that the meat-packers offered. When a steer was slaughtered, only a little more than half of its live weight could be cut up into usable meat for sale. The other 45 percent of the steer was wasted, as was the cost of shipping it. With dressed meat, however, packers transported a far higher percentage of usable beef, lowering their transportation costs and allowing them to pass some of the savings on to consumers. Meat-packers also encouraged their distributors to slice the dressed beef up into a variety of cuts and to do everything possible to enhance its appearance, in order to lure consumers into buying more on impulse.[12]

By World War I, meatpacking had diffused across the Great Plains. Chicago still led the nation in production, followed by Kansas City, Omaha, and St. Louis. The so-called Big Five meat-packers accounted for roughly half of all red meat produced in the United States. The giants controlled about 90 percent of all the branch houses, assuming almost complete dominance in some markets. Nearly all the beef distributed in New York City, for example, came from the Big Five.[13]

Ironically, Sinclair's novel, by drawing attention to the unsanitary environment in the factories and sparking a legislative initiative, helped to restore the public's confidence in meat, and thus laid the groundwork for the industry's eventual success. And yet, Sinclair actually set out not to indict meat but to alert people to the brutal labor conditions present in the plants. What mainly concerned him was the plight of immigrant laborers, who worked at high speeds and had to contend with new production technologies that he compared to "the thumbscrew of the medieval torture chamber." The new corporate slaughterhouses dehumanized workers and made them indifferent to the fast-paced killing of living creatures. "It was like some horrible crime committed in a dungeon, all unseen and unheeded, buried out of sight and of memory."[14]

FAT IS KING

Before a steer made its trip from the plains grasslands to the stockyard for slaughter, it made one last stop. After cattle had been allowed to graze on the western range for a period of years, they journeyed to Iowa or Illinois. There a stock feeder purchased them and briefly fattened the animals on corn before shipping them off to the meat-packers. A symbiotic relationship emerged between the grasslands and the Corn Belt. The former reared cattle; the latter fattened them in preparation for slaughter. Grasslands and feedlots combined to produce the fat-laced beef that meat-packers found easiest to sell to consumers.[15]

Prior to the Civil War, stock feeders waited until steers were five or six years old before finishing them on grain and shipping them to market. But by the latter part of the nineteenth century, they could no longer be bothered with the five-year wait. Land was expensive in Iowa, Indiana, and Illinois, where the feedlot grew to dominance, and to make the land pay, stock feeders felt pressured to purchase young steers—two years old—and to fatten them quickly on corn. The speedup allowed for a far more intensive and profitable use of their property.[16]

By the late nineteenth century, feedlots gained in popularity in the Midwest and, in the process, allowed the meatpacking industry to further indulge consumers with fat-laden beef. When slaughtered, cattle finished on feedlot corn were fatter than animals raised on grass alone. But it took large amounts of grain to produce relatively small amounts of protein.

When the U.S. Department of Agriculture (USDA; established in 1862 under Lincoln) created its beef grading system in 1927, it further solidified the grip that fatty meat had over the American diet. Under the USDA guidelines, the higher the fat content, the better the beef quality. By giving marbled beef its stamp of approval, the government increased pressure on stockmen to feed cattle as much grain as possible to yield the most profitable product. The new quality grades also helped to institutionalize the feedlot and made raising livestock a more factory-oriented enterprise.

Feedlots became even more central to animal agriculture after World War II, when the development of aluminum irrigation pipe and hybrid varieties of sorghum transformed the southern plains into the nation's major feed grain region. The genetic enhancement of sorghum, a major source of animal feed, allowed the crop to tolerate the closely spaced plantings found on irrigated farms. It also helped the crop adapt nicely to the high doses of nitrogen-based fertilizer widely employed after the war. Using knowledge gained from the wartime production of explosives, manufacturers made an inexpensive new breed of fertilizers that freed farmers from the task of growing clover and alfalfa hay. In the past, cattle and sheep were fed these grasses and their manure was spread over fields to supply it with the nitrogen that corn, wheat, and other crops took from the soil. With the advent of artificially produced fertilizers, however, farmers had even more freedom to specialize in either the crop or the animal end of the business.[17]

Cattle once played a role in a diversified farming regime that integrated animals and crops. Stock produced the manure for carrying nutrients back to soils depleted by raising corn or wheat. But as occurred earlier in the city, the feedlot broke the manure and crop cycle and instead transformed cattle into virtual machines for channeling grain into fat. Cattle went from being valuable carriers of nutrients and solar energy, the lifeblood of the farm system, into half-ton fat factories.

SPEEDUP

Despite these innovations at the packing plant and feedlot, it took time for beef to outdistance pork for dominance over the national palate. As late as 1950, pork still had the edge, with Americans consuming about six pounds more pig than cow per person. What happened to make beef the centerpiece of the U.S. diet?[18]

To begin with, a number of important changes on feedlots further streamlined beef production. In 1935, only about five percent of the nation's more than 40 million beef cattle were fed grain. But after World War II, giant feedlots sprung up to capitalize on the demand for high-quality cuts of meat. Grocery chains, such as Safeway Stores, sought prime cuts of beef to cater to more affluent and discriminating consumers. Since cattle fed only on grass could not make the grade, massive feedlots stepped in to serve this emerging market. Some of these operations, such as the Texas County Feedlot, built in Oklahoma in 1965, handled as many as 50,000 animals a year. Many of the feedlots made the Great Plains their home, eventually drawing the meat-packers with them.[19]

By the postwar period, the calves sent to feedlots were more likely to have been raised on planted pasture than allowed to roam freely over the public range as in the past. After reaching a weight of 400 pounds, the animals were then sold to feedlots, where they doubled in weight in as little as four months—a big improvement over the time it once took to finish cattle for slaughter. A number of factors helped to shorten the fattening process. First, beginning in the 1950s, stock raisers began using feeds laced with antibiotics. The steady dose of medicine promoted growth and also gave farmers the ability to confine massive numbers of animals—not just cattle, but pigs and chickens as well—together without the worry of contagious diseases. The use of antibiotic feed additives skyrocketed, increasing from 490,000 pounds in 1954 to some 1.2 million pounds in 1960 to roughly 9 million pounds in the mid-1980s. By the 1990s, animals consumed 30 times the amount of antibiotics used by human beings.[20]

A second factor that helped to propel weight gain was the development of the synthetic hormone DES (diethylstilbestrol). Discovered in the 1930s, DES, an artificial form of estrogen, promoted growth, increasing the weight of steers from 15 to 19 percent. By the 1950s, DES was commonly employed on feedlots. Feedlot managers had grown so attached to the drug that when its use was finally banned in 1979 because of the dangers it posed to human health, they ignored the prohibition and continued to implant animals—some 427,275 cattle alone—with it.[21]

While antibiotics and hormone therapy shortened the time cattle spent on the feedlot, another set of changes hastened the slaughtering process. Technologically speaking, there had been relatively little change on the killing floors of packing plants between 1930 and 1960. Then, in the 1960s, a host of new instruments—stunners, hide skinners, electric knives, and power saws—increased productivity in meatpacking by nearly 50 percent.[22]

A new generation of firms arose—the old Big Five had been hobbled by federal antitrust actions—to take advantage of the technological changes revolutionizing beef production. Chicago, Kansas City, and St. Louis, once the major packing centers, gave way to new plants built in Denison, Iowa; Dakota City, Nebraska; Holcomb, Kansas; and elsewhere on the Great Plains near the giant feedlots—cutting down on transportation costs. Iowa Beef Packers (IBP), founded in 1960, emerged as the most innovative of the new generation of firms. Over the course of the next 20 years, the company constructed factories in Iowa, Nebraska, Minnesota, Texas, and Kansas. In 1981, it built a 14-acre meat plant in Holcomb, a state-of-the-art facility that then ranked as the largest slaughterhouse in the world.[23]

But the company's greatest innovation was the "boxed beef" concept. In 1967, the company took the earlier dressed beef idea one step further: It began wrapping beef in individual packages instead of shipping entire carcasses. If it was more efficient to ship sides of beef, as opposed to live animals, it was even more profitable to load trucks and railroad cars with tightly fitting boxes. "A side of beef has an awkward shape—it can't be neatly packed, and a side has a lot of bone and trim that will never go into the meat case," explained one IBP executive. "It was logical to move to boxed beef." It was not long before the operators of feedlots insisted on buying cattle with a uniform size, weight, and genetic stock so that when cut they would fit nicely into a box. Boxed beef saved on transportation costs and also allowed supermarkets to rid themselves of many highly paid butchers, with IBP shipping a product cut specifically for the retail trade.[24]

In 1970, the company changed its name from Iowa Beef Packers to Iowa Beef Processors to reflect the streamlining of its slaughtering operation. By using capital-intensive technology to simplify and speed up the killing and cutting of animals, IBP was able to employ cheap, immigrant labor, often people of Mexican or Laotian descent. As IBP's chief executive officer put it in 1980, "We're proud of our workers, but basically we can teach anybody to do a job in our plant in 30 days or less—they don't need the skills of an old-time butcher who had to know how to cut up a whole carcass." The disassembly line, with its chutes, chains, and conveyor belts, moved so quickly that in one IBP plant workers were reportedly denied bathroom breaks. Others resorted to taking methamphetamines. The pace of the line has made meatpacking today one of America's most dangerous trades, with approximately 43,000 workers reported injured or ill every year. Working conditions at U.S. slaughterhouses, one food expert recently observed, are "now clearly more dangerous and debilitating than at any time since Upton Sinclair wrote The Jungle" in 1906. Conveniently, the states hosting the nation's largest feedlots were also ones that tended to be solidly anti-union.[25]

By 1980, IBP had become the leading boxed beef processor in the nation, slaughtering 5.7 million cattle in its 10 plants. Behind it were other giants, Cargill and ConAgra, who also championed the new, neater trend in packaging. In 1976, Americans were consuming nearly 130 pounds of beef per person, more than double the amount they ate in 1950. The sudden and enormous rise in beef-eating, however, was not simply the result of developments in feedlots and packinghouses. Cultural changes in how and where Americans went about eating that beef also played an important role.[26]

TWO ALL-BEEF PATTIES

More than anything else, it was the rise in popularity of the fast food hamburger that launched Americans on a bovine extravaganza. The origins of the hamburger are obscure. As far back as the 1830s, something called a hamburg steak was evidently served at Delmonico's restaurant in New York City. But in all likelihood, the hamburger, as we know it today, emerged in the early twentieth century. White Castle, founded in 1921 in Wichita, Kansas, was the first company to promote the hamburger as a form of fast food. Spreading from Kansas to cities across the Midwest and then to markets in the East, White Castle sold its burgers for five cents apiece and catered mainly to a working-class clientele, often building locations near factories. In one banner week in 1925, the company sold over 84,000 burgers, stuffed into insulated bags printed with the slogan "Buy 'em by the Sack" printed across it.[27]

It was not until the 1950s, however, that fast food restaurants assumed their dominant role in American culture, in large part because of the work of McDonald's founder, Ray Kroc. After his visit to the famed San Bernardino hamburger bar, Kroc bought the franchise rights from the two McDonald brothers. In 1955, Kroc opened his first restaurant in a suburb of Chicago.

Kroc realized that if he made his hamburgers bland enough, holding off on seasonings and spicy sauces, he could sell them to a wide segment of the American population, even to children. Indeed, Kroc self-consciously made children, with their unsophisticated palates, the principal target of his advertising, creating the Ronald McDonald clown as a way of pitching his burgers. According to one poll conducted in 1986, 96 percent of children surveyed were able to identify Ronald, with only Santa Claus scoring higher.[28]

Kroc also seemed to have a knack when it came to locating his restaurants. In 1959, having opened 100 stores to date, Kroc hired an airplane to help him identify the best sites for future stores. He singled out shopping centers and large intersections as he sought to capitalize on the nation's suburban, highway-oriented culture. Clever placement near housing developments helped him attract overworked mothers. "You Deserve a Break Today," the company sloganeered. As one foreign observer marveled, "A family of four can save Mother two hours in the kitchen, eat and drink for about $5 and get back into their station wagon in fifteen minutes flat." On less hectic days, a family might choose to linger at one of the playgrounds that soon became fixtures at McDonald's and other fast food restaurants, allowing the chains to capitalize on the decline in open space endemic to heavily developed suburban areas.[29]

Everything in McDonald's was (and is) planned, right down to the size of the hamburger patty itself: 3.785 inches across, weighing 1.6 ounces and containing no more than 19 percent fat. Kroc put earlier efficiency experts such as Frederick Taylor to shame. He sought total control, taking apart each and every step in food preparation and service and detailing exactly how it was to be accomplished in a company operations manual. The first such manual was 75 pages in length, spelling out such trivial details as the order in which to flip rows of hamburgers (third row first). Over the years, the manual has grown to the point where today it fills over 600 pages.[30]

The assembly-line production of hamburgers was the retail counterpart to the equally efficient cattle disassembly line. In both cases, the introduction of machines and precise instructions allowed employers to hire cheap labor. McDonald's now trains more people than the entire U.S. Army, primarily young adults, ages 15 to 19. Like the new generation of meat-packers, McDonald's has been fiercely anti-union. In the 1970s, the company staved off more than 400 unionization efforts, using lie detector tests in at least one instance to intimidate employees.[31]

McDonald's has experienced extraordinary success. In 1972, the company became the largest meal-serving organization in the nation. In 1976, when beef eating in the United States peaked (it has since declined because of worries about its health effects), McDonald's was selling more than six million hamburgers a day. By the late 1990s, one in seven visits out to eat found the American consumer headed for its Golden Arches. The orgy of hamburger-eating has helped make McDonald's the world's largest beef buyer, relying on the slaughter of three million cattle each year in the United States alone.[32]

"OVER 17 BILLION SERVED"

Drawn in 1974, near the peak in American beef consumption, this sketch of Americans eating hamburgers inside the Statue of Liberty pictures a small "M" for McDonald's on the crown. (Library of Congress)

The rise in hamburger-eating was of course good news for America's beef industry. Clever marketing by fast food companies helped their market share, but so did initiatives that had gone on earlier in Washington. In 1946, the USDA legally defined what a hamburger could be and, under its definition, a "hamburger" could contain nothing but ground beef and beef fat. Although any kind of fat would do the job of binding together a burger to keep it from falling apart on the grill, the agency, by decreeing that only cattle fat could be used, gave the beef industry a veritable patent on perhaps the only food product more American than apple pie. Because cattle set free on open pastures and fed on grass alone do not have enough fat, the fast food companies turned to the sedentary, feedlot cattle, which had a thick layer of fat carved off at slaughter. In the end, the fast food companies received the ingredients for making inexpensive hamburgers, while the beef industry received a monopoly on the nation's most popular food item.[33]

The beef industry has continued to exert tremendous clout in Washington. Beginning in the mid-1950s, at precisely the time that Americans sat poised to go on a beef-eating splurge, scientists uncovered a relationship between diets high in fat and heart disease. With evidence of fat's harmful effects mounting, liberal Senator George McGovern opened hearings in 1977 on the relationship between food and chronic diseases. His committee's report recommended that Americans "decrease consumption of meat." The National Cattlemen's Association, however, objected to the government's advice. Shying away from doing battle with the powerful beef lobby, McGovern's committee revised its recommendation. Instead of a blanket statement advising citizens to eat less meat, the committee weakened its position, counseling consumers to decrease the consumption of "animal fat, and [to] choose meats, poultry, and fish which will reduce saturated fat intake."[34]

In the early 1990s, when the USDA determined that American consumers needed more guidance in choosing healthy food, the beef industry again intervened. This time the agency came up with a food pyramid. Grains and cereals occupied the longest band at the base, vegetables and fruits occupied the layer above, and meat and dairy products were the next layer up, with fats and sugary items capping off the chart. The National Cattlemen's Association cried out that the guide unfairly stigmatized beef. That caused the USDA to backpedal and ultimately to postpone publication of the pyramid. When it finally released the guide, the USDA revised its accompanying recommendations and urged consumers to eat two to three portions of meat and dairy each day, the same advice it had been giving Americans since as far back as 1958. But what really pleased the industry was the agency's modification of its stance on the upper limits of meat eating. In 1990, it had advised Americans to consume on a daily basis no more than six ounces of meat per day. Under the revised food pyramid provision, however, the upper limit was bumped up to seven ounces—yet another triumph for the beef lobby.[35]

OIL, WATER, GRASS

The problems with beef extend well beyond the threat that it poses (at least if consumed in large amounts) to human health. Raising cattle on feedlots is an immensely energy-intensive enterprise. Where some of the energy goes is readily apparent, as in the fuel needed to run farm equipment. But it also takes a tremendous amount of energy to produce the fertilizer that farmers use to produce corn, which in the United States is grown largely to fatten livestock. In 1990, America's cornfields used roughly 40 percent of the nitrogen fertilizer consumed in the nation. One study (from 1980) demonstrated that it took 17,000 kilocalories of energy to produce a kilogram of beef. That is the energy in about a half-gallon of gasoline, all for just 2.2 pounds of meat.[36]

Apart from being a heavy drain on the nation's energy supply, beef producers are also gluttons when it comes to water. When you add together all the water it takes to produce a pound of beef—to irrigate grain, water the stock, and process the cattle—the total comes to 360 gallons. This demand for water is especially problematic on the Great Plains, home to the nation's feedlots and beef processors. At IBP's Holcomb, Kansas, plant, 400 gallons of water are needed to slaughter and process just one animal. That translates into 600 million gallons of water every year to process one million head of cattle. The water comes from the Ogallala aquifer, a 174,000 square mile underground reservoir that once contained nearly 10 trillion gallons. More than half of that magnificent supply is now gone, and if present levels of consumption continue it is quite conceivable that the Ogallala will be tapped out in just a few more decades.[37]

Beyond these ecological impacts is the effect that cattle-raising has had on the vast landholdings of the federal government, both in national forests and in other prime pasture areas. In 1934, Congress enacted the Taylor Grazing Act to bring some semblance of order to the public domain. The act set up a system for leasing the land to ranchers and established a National Grazing Service (which later became the U.S. Bureau of Land Management) to supervise the cowboys. Although explicitly set up as a rental arrangement, the system has led permit holders to treat the leases as a form of private property. In other words, ranchers have at times sold something that was not theirs to sell, the right to use government-owned land to graze cattle.[38]

The low price charged ranchers for grazing permits has long been a bone of contention. The price has often been just a fraction of what the land would lease for if it were privately owned. And since the government's price is calculated per animal unit month—the forage it would take to feed a cow and her calf for 30 days—ranchers have had an economic incentive to overstock the public range. To some, the grazing program amounts to little more than a government handout, or "cowboy welfare" in the words of the radical environmentalist Edward Abbey.[39]

The predictable result has been rampant overgrazing, especially along streams, where cattle congregate to access water and forage on level ground. A 1990 study by the Bureau of Land Management and the U.S. Forest Service (the other organization that oversees public grazing lands) revealed that only a third of its nearly 58 million acres of holdings were in either good or excellent ecological condition.[40]

In the intermountain West—the area between the Rockies and the Sierras and Cascades—cattle have had some unforeseen consequences. Cattle are heavy, exerting on the order of 24 pounds per square inch of land. Their sheer weight, combined with their constant grazing of the native bunchgrasses, has severely disrupted the soil in vast stretches of the public range. Into this environment in the

1890s came an Old World plant that westerners called cheatgrass, a species so pernicious that it robbed farmers of their livelihood. Stockmen initially welcomed the
nonnative plant, which thrives in disturbed soils. It soon became clear, however,
that cheatgrass had limited value as forage. It dies quickly, and the dead grass has
little nutritional content. Worse still, the plant, in part because it does not stay
green for long, promotes the spread of wildfires. Cheatgrass is now the single
most common plant species in this region.[41]

If all these impacts were not enough, there is one final irony. Although cattle
ranchers in the intermountain West make use of some 300 million acres of federal land, roughly 16 percent of the entire continental United States, they produce
a mere fraction (three percent in the early 1980s) of the beef consumed in this
country. The rest is either raised on private lands by stockmen in eastern states or
imported.[42]

THE CONFINEMENT

Despite all the changes outlined here, there is one aspect of the steer's existence
that has not changed all that much: They still spend nearly all their lives outside
grazing, save for the last three months spent on feedlots. The lives of chickens and
pigs, however, have changed far more dramatically. Since the 1950s, the industrial paradigm has been applied even more thoroughly to U.S. poultry and hog
farming. The quaint image of Old MacDonald's farm, a peaceful scene where roosters followed cows around the barnyard, has given way to large-scale operations
founded on the confinement of huge numbers of chickens and hogs in indoor
quarters. The animals' lives are closely monitored and controlled, from birth to
death. And with hog and poultry production concentrated in the hands of just a
few large corporations, modern animal agriculture has emerged as one of the nation's most formidable environmental challenges.

Back before the 1930s, chicken was considerably less popular than it is today.
The meat, which was dry and unappetizing, came primarily from sterile old hens.
But the development of the broiler industry in the Delmarva Peninsula (where
Delaware, Maryland, and Virginia come together) introduced Americans to modern chicken-eating as we know it. Broilers were tender, young roosters, suitable,
as the name suggests, for broiling (the old chickens were normally fried). The
market for broilers boomed during World War II as the government's "Food for
Freedom" program urged Americans to eat more chicken and leave the beef and
pork for the troops.[43]

In the 1950s, when antibiotics became widely available, farmers began moving
chickens from the barnyard into indoor facilities. By early the following decade,
large, vertically integrated firms controlled all aspects of chicken production—
hatching, feeding, and ultimately slaughtering the animals. Instead of thousands
of small farmers and poultry processors, large corporations emerged by the 1960s
to control all phases of broiler production, marketing individualized brands sold

directly to consumers. In 1968, Frank Perdue, whose father entered the Delmarva broiler business during the 1930s, went on television himself to attest to the quality of his birds. The Perdue company fed its birds xanthophyll, derived from marigold petals, to turn their skins from white to yellow, making them better looking and tastier. By 1970, Perdue controlled more than 15 percent of New York City's broiler market.[44]

Perdue started out processing about 18 birds per minute. The birds were hung by their feet and stunned before having their throats slit, heads and feet severed, and lungs vacuumed out. After that, they were cut up, wrapped in plastic, and ready to ship. In 1979, production had increased to some 300 birds per minute. For the disassembly line to run efficiently, all the birds had to have the same body shape, making it necessary for Perdue and the other major poultry companies to control all aspects of the growth and production process, beginning with the bird's genetic stock. The broilers were genetically engineered to grow larger thighs and breasts than the wild chickens from which they descended. They were also programmed to grow quickly, reaching a weight ripe for slaughter in half the time (just seven weeks) it had once taken the birds to mature.[45]

Broiler companies concentrated in the South, where the warm climate cut down on barn-heating costs. In Arkansas, packing plants sprouted near where farmers raised the birds (under contract with the companies) in large confinement barns. By locating in anti-union states such as Arkansas, the companies also held down their labor costs. The rise of large-scale broiler companies has almost completely eliminated the small chicken farmer. Between 1974 and 1992, the percentage of sales by broiler producers selling 100,000 birds had increased from 70 to 97 percent of the national total. Today, the chicken has taken the place of the passenger pigeon as the most populous bird in the nation.[46]

Virtually the same set of changes unfolded in the pork industry. Antibiotic use allowed farmers to confine the animals in football-field size buildings containing concrete and steel pens. The creatures were genetically identical and programmed to produce a leaner meat to compete with chicken in both fat and cholesterol content. Once a breeding sow delivered piglets (about every five months), they were shipped off to a nursery farm and eventually to a finishing farm, reaching a marketable weight of 250 pounds in only six months.

The man generally credited with industrializing hog farming is a North Carolinian named Wendell Murphy. Beginning in 1969, after an epidemic of cholera caused state officials to quarantine his pig herd, Murphy convinced his neighbors to take over the risk of raising hogs. He provided the pigs and feed; the farmers put up the land and labor. Murphy agreed to pay the farmers a specified price for each pig they raised to market weight. If hog prices shot up, Murphy gained; if they went down, he took a loss. But by only paying for live pigs—it was too bad for the farmers if the pigs died—Murphy shifted the risk of hog raising to others. To contract with Murphy, farmers had to build large confinement barns, structures that have become more automated and expensive over the years. Predictably, the number of hog farms nationwide has declined precipitously (from 600,000 to 157,000 between 1984 and 1999) as the animals are concentrated in fewer, larger indoor settings.[47]

In the year 2000, Smithfield Foods acquired Murphy Family Farms and became the largest hog raiser and pork producer in the world. Taking its cue from the giant chicken firms, Perdue and Tyson, Smithfield employs vertical integration, controlling all aspects of pork production from the pig's birth to its conversion into bacon and other products. "There's only one way to get consistency—that's to have common genetics, feed the animals the same way and process them the same way," remarked Smithfield's chief executive officer Joseph Luter.[48]

Smithfield operates a nearly one-million-square-foot plant in Tar Heel, North Carolina. The factory can dispatch 32,000 hogs into pork in just a single day. The concentration of hog farms and meatpacking plants in North Carolina over the last 20 years is no accident. Anti-union sentiment, low wages, and lax environmental regulations, some of which were advanced by none other than Wendell Murphy himself (who served as a state senator in the 1980s and early 1990s) account for the trend. By the 1990s, North Carolina was home to almost twice as many hogs as people, with 10 million creatures crammed into the state.[49]

Huge confinement barns stocking thousands and thousands of animals have posed a new and formidable set of environmental problems. Chief among these is the question of what to do with the millions of tons of animal waste. By some estimates, in the United States today there is something approaching 130 times more animal waste than human waste produced each year. That amounts to approximately five tons of manure for every citizen.[50]

Back in the days when manure was integrated into the crop and nutrient cycle, animal waste posed few problems. All that changed with the advent of megafarms and feedlots for producing livestock. As one environmentalist has explained, "The problem is that nature never intended for 80,000 hogs to shit in the same place."[51]

To save on labor costs, pig manure is simply flushed away with hoses into holes in the floor. From there it is channeled into giant lagoons. In 1995, approximately 25 million gallons of hog waste from a 12,000-animal "barn" in North Carolina—more than twice the amount of oil involved in the notorious 1989 Exxon Valdez incident—spilled out of one such lagoon. The waste eventually flowed into the New River, where it annihilated virtually all aquatic life in a 17-mile stretch, in effect forcing the public to bear the high ecological costs associated with factory-style animal farms.[52]

Together vast amounts of hog and chicken waste, laden with such nutrients as nitrogen and phosphorous, have wended their way into coastal waters. In 1991, North Carolina's Pamlico Sound was the scene of a fish kill so massive that bulldozers had to be called in to bury the dead creatures. Although the exact cause of this massive die-off and other more limited fish kills in Chesapeake Bay is not known, some scientists suspect that hog and chicken manure is the culprit. The animal waste, they surmise, sets off algae blooms that deplete oxygen from the water and put stress on fish populations. The algae also help to feed a microscopic organism named pfiesteria—dubbed "the cell from hell"—which can release a toxin lethal to fish. Manure, once a vital and integral aspect of farm life, has disappeared from the barnyard into the nation's waters, where it has become one of the most serious environmental dilemmas of our time.[53]

CONCLUSION

This chapter should not be taken as an anti-meat manifesto but as a plea for understanding the historical roots of modern beef-eating and its ecological and social impacts. Once farm cattle fed on grass and hay; pigs ate garbage, including waste produced in some of America's largest cities; and chickens trailed cattle around the barnyard pecking grass seeds out of the dung they left behind. The animals converted matter unsuitable for human consumption into a much-valued source of protein. The rise of factory-style livestock production, especially in the decades after World War II, transformed these farm animals into eating machines requiring large quantities of corn and soybeans. Livestock guzzled energy and water, shedding their old role as garbage collectors and assuming a new one as waste producers—ironically, usurping industrial enterprises as the nation's leading source of water pollution. Old MacDonald is turning over in his grave.

AMERICA IN BLACK AND GREEN

Compared to Henry Ford, Thomas Edison, and the other heroes of American consumerism, the name Thomas Midgley rings few, if any, bells. And yet despite his relative obscurity, Midgley, a research chemist born in 1889 who died, according to one obituary, by accidentally strangling himself with "a self-devised harness for getting in and out of bed," played a fundamental role in some of the consumer age's most celebrated products.[1]

Over his career, Midgley made two discoveries that profoundly influenced both the course of American consumer culture and the make-up of the atmosphere. In 1921, while working for General Motors (GM), he uncovered that lead, when added to gasoline, eliminated engine knock, a breakthrough that allowed automakers to boost engine performance and sell faster, racier cars. The advance, however, came at the expense of releasing a known poison into the environment. Later, Midgley went on to invent Freon, the first chlorofluorocarbon. Americans received better air conditioners, deodorants, and hair sprays, but future generations would pay the price for them with skin cancer as the compounds damaged the ozone layer, which shields the earth from the harmful effects of ultraviolet radiation. Midgley, in the words of historian J. R. McNeill, "had more impact on the atmosphere than any other single organism in earth history."[2]

In the automobile-oriented suburbs sprouting up all over the nation after World War II, land that had once yielded food was paved over with asphalt and converted into sprawling subdivisions and lawns. Forced to hit the road to fill their stomachs, Americans piled into cars and headed for supermarkets and restaurants, especially after Congress created more time for leisure by passing legislation (in 1938) making the 40-hour, five-day work week the national standard. Fast food hamburger outfits remained so centered around the automobile that it took over a decade after opening in the 1950s before McDonald's even bothered to install seats and tables in its restaurants.

Car culture ushered in a vast and sweeping network of roads and interstate highways for knitting together metropolitan centers and outlying suburbs. In a sense, the freeway took the place of manure in uniting the ecological fortunes of the country and the city. Gone were the animals, hay, and potato fields, and instead tract housing arose and the lawn was born, grass that was grown mainly for its aesthetic appeal. Cut off from any direct relationship with their food supply, Americans now had the luxury of planting turf grass (originally imported from northern Europe) and dousing it with tons of water, fertilizer, and pesticides— rendering the land from coast to coast into a verdant sea. With 30 million acres under cultivation, the lawn is now the nation's number one "crop." Needless to say, the new national landscape, painted in black and green, left behind a trail of social, ecological, and biological consequences.

LIVE FREE AND DRIVE

The rise of the automobile is a well-known chapter in the American past. First built in the 1890s as a luxury item for the well-to-do, the car eventually became a mass-produced commodity. The man chiefly responsible for this momentous change was Henry Ford, who pioneered the use of the assembly line in auto production. In 1914, concerned that the market for cars would remain limited as long as even autoworkers themselves could not afford them, Ford began paying some of his employees five dollars per day, at the time a relatively high wage. By 1929, nearly 50 percent of all U.S. families owned automobiles, a milestone not reached in England until four decades later.

Although some opposed the automobile—early in the century, a group of Minnesota farmers, for instance, plowed up roads and strung barbed wire between trees—most Americans embraced the car with enormous enthusiasm. The automobile succeeded because it met the real, legitimate needs of people for a means of transportation. Consumerism, in part, had reorganized people's relationship with the land in the way that transformed the car from a luxury to a necessity. Food and clothing once produced in the home, especially by women, were by the 1920s bought in towns and villages. By the 1930s, 66 percent of rural families and 90 percent of urban families purchased store-bought bread instead of making it on their own. More shopping meant that people spent more time in cars on their way to stores. People's priorities quickly changed. In the 1920s, an inspector from the USDA asked a farmwoman why she bought a Model T before installing indoor plumbing. "Why you can't go to town in a bathtub!" she exclaimed.[3]

The impact of the car went far beyond its ability to provide consumers with a convenient means of doing their marketing. It also helped to stimulate suburbanization. The suburbs began as far back as the 1840s with the advent of railroad travel, proliferating after the Civil War with the development of streetcar lines. By the late nineteenth century, cities such as New York, Chicago, and Philadelphia became increasingly wedded to factory production and, somewhat later, to financial activity. With real estate developers following World War I far more interested in constructing office buildings than new housing, many middle-class residents left the city for the suburbs, relying on cars to shuttle them back and forth to work. By 1940, 13 million Americans lived in auto-centered communities not serviced by public transportation.[4]

If the automobile met the genuine need for transportation, especially in the more decentralized suburban environment, it also brought with it a vast amount of social baggage. Tellingly, the French term *automobile* and not the British phrase *motorcar* came to predominate. *Motorcar* focused attention on the engine, the driving force behind the new form of transportation. But *automobile* suggested something far more complex, literally, self-movement. The idea that cars could free people from train and streetcar schedules, instead propelling them on their own through space, conformed to American ideals of freedom, individuality, and democracy.[5]

Automobiles were sold to Americans with precisely this notion of freedom and liberation in mind. An advertisement by the Ford Motor Company shows a woman persevering in the face of inclement weather. Snuggled in behind the wheel of her Ford's heated cabin, the woman sets off free from the worry that snow or rain might in some way impede her trip into town. Complete independence from the forces of nature is the message being conveyed.

But the freedom of movement that the automobile made possible came at a price, although advertisers often distracted Americans from confronting it. Far better, at least from the auto industry's perspective, if people remained walled off from the social and environmental costs of car ownership, much as the woman driver in the Ford advertisement is seen insulated from the elements at large. It would be wrong, however, to conclude that no one at the time recognized the problems presented by the automobile. "Our streets smell badly enough without the addition to the atmosphere of vast quantities of unburned gasoline," declared one observer in a 1910 issue of the magazine *Horseless Age*. Gasoline not only caused pollution. Its status as a nonrenewable resource even led some engineers and industry analysts to worry about whether an adequate supply would always remain available. As early as 1905, engineer Thomas J. Fay foresaw that "One of the great problems of the near future in connection with the popularization of the automobile will be that of an adequate and suitable fuel supply."[6]

Alternative fuels such as grain alcohol existed. But relative to gasoline, alcohol was more expensive, about double the price per gallon at the turn of the century. And that price did not include a federal excise tax placed on alcohol beginning in 1862 to help defray the Union's costs in the Civil War. In 1907, the tax was repealed. But the process of denaturing alcohol, to render it undrinkable in an effort to preserve the sobriety of the American republic, added to its price and gave gasoline the edge. Compounding gasoline's advantage was the fact that it took more alcohol than gas to cover the same distance. Added to this was the political muscle of the petroleum interests. Together these factors combined with the nation's long-standing concern with temperance to produce a terrible dependency of another kind.[7]

GET THE LEAD IN

Henry Ford pioneered mass production, but it was Alfred P. Sloan, Jr., the president of General Motors, who figured out a way of selling everyone on the need for all these new cars. In 1927, Sloan introduced the annual model change as a way to "keep the consumer dissatisfied." He reasoned that if people saw their neighbors driving around in a new car with features their own vehicle did not have, they too would soon be heading off to the showroom. Under Sloan's leadership, GM surpassed Ford as the nation's number one auto producer. The company succeeded not by offering consumers a basic means of transportation—Ford's stock in trade—but by holding out the prospect of faster cars that grew more stylish and larger with every passing year. It was a stroke of genius that set the stage for GM's decades-long dominance within the industry.[8]

Leaded gasoline was the key to fulfilling Sloan's ambitions for GM, at least in the realm of auto performance. Early on, cars had to be cranked by hand to start. But in 1911, the invention of the self-starter eliminated the laborious task of hand cranking, allowing women especially to take to the roads. Automakers could now produce cars with larger, easy-to-start engines. The electrical breakthrough, however, had one drawback: Customers noted a knocking sound coming from the engine. If cars were going to be larger, faster, and easier to use, then a way had to be found to eliminate potential engine damage from "knock."[9]

Not long after the invention of the self-starter, the staff at Dayton Engineering Laboratories Company (DELCO) discovered that ethanol or grain alcohol, when burned in a car's engine, helped to remedy knock. The problem with grain alcohol, however, at least as the oil companies saw it, was that anyone, even ordinary people, could make it. Thus in 1921, when Thomas Midgley, who was working at the DELCO lab, now owned by GM, discovered that tetraethyl lead also functioned as an excellent antiknock agent, the oil and lead interests rejoiced.[10]

In early 1923, the first gallon of leaded gas was pumped in Dayton, Ohio. The following year, GM, the Du Pont Chemical Company (which controlled roughly a third of GM's stock), and Standard Oil of New Jersey, combining their various patents, manufactured leaded gasoline under the "Ethyl" brand name. There was only one problem. A few months before Ethyl went on sale, William Mansfield Clark at the U.S. Public Health Service came forward to explain that tetraethyl lead was exceedingly poisonous and had the potential (through the lead oxide it produced when burned) to endanger public health in heavily traveled areas.[11]

In 1922, U.S. Surgeon General H. S. Cumming wrote a letter to Pierre du Pont, chairman of the board at the chemical company, inquiring about the health hazard posed by leaded gasoline. Midgley responded on the company's and GM's behalf. The public health effect of leaded gasoline received "serious consideration," he wrote, but "no actual experimental data has been taken." Despite the lack of evidence, Midgley believed that "the average street will probably be so free from lead that it will be impossible to detect it or its absorption." With no studies to draw on, how could Midgley be so sure of its safety? That remains a mystery, and a doubly curious one given that shortly before responding to Cumming, Midgley had come down with lead poisoning.[12]

In 1923, General Motors, reasoning that any in-house scientific study it did would be viewed skeptically, agreed to finance a study by the U.S. Bureau of Mines into the safety of tetraethyl lead. The following year, the newly formed Ethyl Gasoline Corporation negotiated a new research contract with the bureau that required the government agency to submit its results to the company for "comment, criticism, and approval." This was not going to be a disinterested piece of research. The bureau soon issued a report downplaying leaded gasoline's potential adverse impact on public health. The report prompted one rival car manufacturer to ask whether the bureau existed "for the benefit of Ford and the GM Corporation and the Standard Oil Co. of New Jersey, . . . or is the Bureau supposed to be for the public benefit and in protection of life and health?"[13]

The bureau's biased approach caused some in the scientific community to object. Alice Hamilton, a physician who studied the industrial use of lead and its medical effects (and the first woman faculty member of Harvard Medical School), doubted the safety of leaded gasoline, especially if its use became widespread. In 1925, Yandell Henderson, a physiologist from Yale University, predicted that if the industry had its way, lead poisoning would emerge slowly but "insidiously . . . before the public and the government awaken to the situation."[14] He turned out to be right. With the burning of huge quantities of gasoline (especially in the three decades after 1950), lead was deposited on the soil and, unknowingly, tracked into houses across the nation. Infants crawling on the floor then picked it up on their fingers and ingested it, interfering with the development of their nervous systems and contributing to hyperactivity and hearing loss, among other effects, although it would be decades, as Henderson surmised, before the full scope of the problem became evident.

In 1926, another federal study again found "no good grounds for prohibiting the use of ethyl gasoline." The authors did note, however, that widespread use of leaded gasoline at some point might present a health hazard and urged additional follow-up studies, but none were ever done. Instead, the manufacturers of the product financed all the research into leaded gasoline's safety. Although Midgley and others in the auto, oil, and chemical industry knew about other more benign alternative additives (ethyl alcohol blends, for example), they pushed lead, probably because of the huge profits they stood to make from its sale.[15]

Leaded gasoline allowed Detroit to boost performance and sell more automobiles, but at a high biological price. Even something as pernicious as radioactive waste breaks down over the long run, but not lead. In the United States alone, seven million tons of lead were released between the 1920s and 1986, when it was phased out as automakers switched over to catalytic converters. Ethyl is gone, but the lead remains, having insinuated itself into the land, water, and air, as well as the bodies of all life forms.[16]

MASS TRANSIT MELTDOWN

As it turned out, it would take more than speed and style to ensure the auto's dominance over mass transit. Rising numbers of automobiles in the 1910s and

RAIN STORMS will play tricks on you. And so will an old motor—unless it has Ethyl.

But stop beside the pump that bears the Ethyl emblem every time you need gas and then you *know* what your car will do.

It will run its best all the time!

You don't always want top speed—or flashing pick-up—or the extra power it takes to zoom over hills in high. But when you do, you *want 'em!* And when you're driving at moderate speed, Ethyl makes the difference between real pleasure and just going somewhere. It brings back the *fun* you used to get from your car.

Stop at an Ethyl pump and discover what millions of others know today: *The next best thing to a brand-new car is your present car with Ethyl.* With oil companies selling Ethyl at only 2c a gallon over the price of regular, you can't afford not to use it. The savings Ethyl makes in repairs and upkeep more than offset this new low premium. Ethyl Gasoline Corporation, New York City.

NOW
SOLD BY OIL COMPANIES AT
only **2**c PER GALLON
over "regular"

Ethyl contains lead. © E. G. C. 1933

NEXT TIME STOP AT THE ETHYL PUMP

"THIS CAR NEEDS ETHYL"

The makers of Ethyl gasoline touted the power and pickup that came with the use of its product but chose not to highlight the lead that was one of its main ingredients. (Time, November 20, 1933)

1920s did not directly spell the end of public transportation. In fact, if the figures on mass transit use are broken down, some cities—St. Louis, New York, and Chicago, for example—actually showed an increase in ridership between 1918 and 1927. GM's effort to spur consumption through model changes and faster, more stylish cars was partly a response to the continued vitality of public transportation. But even these changes failed to give the industry the boost in sales it longed for. Stronger measures, the automakers concluded, were in order.[17]

Not that public transportation was without problems. Streetcar companies throughout the nation were buckling under from debt. They were saddled with municipal regulations that forced them to keep fares low and often prevented the elimination of unprofitable routes. In addition, unionized transit workers compelled the companies to pay high wages. The combined effect of all these trends placed the industry in jeopardy before 1920, but they alone did not lead to its demise. It would also take the collective actions of the auto, truck, tire, and oil companies, in league with the federal government, to help accomplish that.[18]

In 1932, GM launched a plan to buy up urban transit systems throughout the nation and replace the trolleys with buses, another one of its product lines. One theory has it that the company did this not so much to destroy mass transit as to create a market for its diesel buses. Joining forces through a complex interlocking directorate with a group of jitney companies—the streetcar's competition—GM spent 18 months in the mid-1930s putting New York City's trolley system, one of the world's largest, out of business, substituting buses in the process.[19]

In 1936, GM formed National City Lines, a consortium made up of Firestone Tire and Rubber, Phillips Petroleum, Standard Oil of California, and Mack Manufacturing, the truck company. Over the course of the next decade, the group took control of almost 40 transit companies located in 14 states. It also acquired a controlling interest in a number of other companies located in four additional states.[20]

Eventually the federal government caught on to the National City scheme and in 1947 a grand jury indicted the company and its affiliates—GM, Firestone, and the others. Prosecutors brought suit against the consortium for violating the Sherman Antitrust Act (1890), which prohibits companies from conspiring to restrain trade. The government argued that the National City group required the streetcar companies to pledge never to use electric trolleys and forced them to buy supplies—buses, tires, and so on—exclusively from the consortium. The case dragged on for eight years; in the end the government triumphed. Although acquitted of the more serious charge of conspiring to restrain trade, the court did find that the group had entered into a "collusive agreement" to monopolize the transit market. It was, however, a hollow victory. GM alone sold buses to National City worth roughly 25 million dollars, and yet it and the other guilty companies walked away with fines of 5,000 dollars each, the convicted executives with just a one-dollar penalty.[21]

Franklin Roosevelt's New Deal, meanwhile, was funneling huge amounts of money into building roads but little into mass transit. As far back as 1916, the

Federal Road Act made funds available to states to establish highway departments. Legislation passed in 1921 set up the Bureau of Public Roads and outlined a plan for a network of highways linking cities with more than 50,000 people. But it was under the New Deal that road-building in America began in earnest. Nearly half of the two million people employed in New Deal programs worked constructing roads and highways. During the decade of the 1930s, the total amount of surfaced roads doubled, to more than 1.3 million miles, while mass transportation languished. Public transit commanded just a tenth of the funds that the Works Progress Administration expended on pavement.[22]

America was well on its way to becoming what one critic has termed an "asphalt nation," as a variety of forces—serious weaknesses in the streetcar industry, GM's quest to sell buses, and the state-sponsored building of roads during the Depression—limited the choices available to consumers. No outright conspiracy worked to defraud the American public; people had a certain measure of control over the autocentric decisions they made. Indeed, many no doubt enjoyed the pleasures that came with driving a car. But that said, for all the freedoms that accompanied automobile culture, it was (and is still) the case that they often distracted people from the larger economic forces shaping their lives.

TO BUILD IS HUMAN?

Were it not for World War II, the automobile's rise to power no doubt would have continued unabated. The war, however, put a dent in American auto culture. The production of cars for civilian use ended, temporarily, and gas rationing began. Posted highway signs read "Victory Speed 35 Miles Per Hour" in a further attempt to save both oil and rubber to aid the Allied cause. Mass transit ridership increased, while the number of miles Americans traveled in cars fell from 334 billion to 213 billion between 1941 and 1944.[23]

Indeed, the war years emerged as a moment of ecological and social possibility, a brief period of innovation that bucked the trend toward more automobiles and roads. In the Los Angeles area, a place now known for its love affair with the car, arose a housing development that shunted the automobile to the periphery. Completed in 1942, Baldwin Hills Village consisted of garden apartments built around inviting expanses of open space. Planners and architects created a pedestrian-friendly community that turned out to be one of the city's most vibrant neighborhoods.[24]

But once the war was over, the nation's romance with the car reemerged to take command of the American landscape. On July 3, 1945, the Ford Motor Company, which had suspended civilian production in 1942, built its first new sedan for domestic use. It took just a month for the assembly lines to gear up to raise production to 25,000 cars per day. Soon thereafter the nation's roads and streets became choked with traffic. "AVENUE TRAFFIC IS TIED UP BY CROSS-STREET CONGESTION," proclaimed one New York newspaper, a headline that would seem silly today.[25]

"RIDE TOGETHER, WORK TOGETHER"

In 1942, the Japanese blocked American access to Asian rubber, stimulating a call for carpooling to conserve this precious resource. (Library of Congress)

Even before the war, some city planners had discovered that building more roads to solve traffic problems did not always work. In fact, under some circumstances adding a new road to relieve congestion actually made the traffic move even more slowly, a condition known as Braess's paradox after the German mathematician—Dietrich Braess—who first explained the problem in 1968. Although the theory behind the paradox was still unformulated in the 1940s, New York

City planners watched firsthand as new bridges and roads went in only to find that they worsened traffic, as motorists jammed both the new and the old routes.[26]

Such complexities, however, were lost on Robert Moses, a road builder to match any in history. Born in 1888 and raised amidst great wealth, Moses went on to hold a long list of public appointments, including stints as the head of New York City's Park Commission and the Triborough Bridge and Tunnel Authority. For four decades, Moses wielded power in one capacity or another in New York, using his influence to help reshape the city and the surrounding areas into the megalopolis that it is today. His achievements were colossal. Just about every major highway that exists in the New York City area was a Moses creation: the Van Wyck, the Bruckner, the Major Deegan, the Whitestone, the Clearview, the Cross-Bronx, the Staten Island, the Brooklyn-Queens, and the Long Island expressways. He also was responsible for building 416 miles of parkways, roads that barred trucks and that stretched out into the surrounding Long Island suburbs, plus major bridges such as the Triborough, the Verrazano, the Bronx-Whitestone, and the Throgs Neck, among others.

Before Moses came along, rarely was a highway built within the confines of an American city. There were roads, to be sure, that connected one city with another, roads that existed on the outskirts of urban areas, but few roads barreled straight through the heart of a metropolis. The expressway, however, was Moses's stock in trade. To the question of what to do with the people and buildings in the way, Moses had a simple answer. In his own words: "You can draw any kind of picture you like on a clean slate and indulge your every whim in the wilderness . . . but when you operate in an overbuilt metropolis, you have to hack your way with a meat ax." Moses, an expert ax wielder, dislocated an estimated 250,000 people from their homes to build the roads he said the city needed. "You can't make an omelet without breaking eggs," he was fond of saying.[27]

But Moses did more than just uproot a quarter-million people. His environmental legacy has been even more profound. The roads he built, with nary a thought given to mass transit, brought suburbanization, following furiously, in its wake. And because the suburbs had fewer people per given unit of space than higher-density cities, they were unable, until far into the future, to support a mass transportation system. This made roads a self-fulfilling prophecy. As a result, places such as Long Island became giant parking lots, with commuters inching back and forth between suburban homes and jobs in New York City.

The road that did more than any other to transform Long Island into a huge stretch of suburban auto-centered sprawl was the Long Island Expressway (LIE). In 1955, the year workers fired up their bulldozers to make way for the LIE, approximately 90,000 drivers made the commute from the island into the city. In the next 30 years, went the prediction, population growth would double the number of commuters. The LIE was originally designed as a six-lane road—three lanes in each direction. A single lane could handle roughly 1,500 automobiles per hour, giving the road a capacity of 4,500 cars in each direction. The road, in other words, would be able to handle just five percent of the island's 1955 commuter population.[28]

Recognizing that the numbers did not add up, some foresighted planners advised setting aside the center of the expressway for mass transit. Such a rapid transit system would be able to accommodate 40,000 people each hour, nearly 10 times what the road would accomplish. One study estimated the cost of the mass transit option at approximately 21 million dollars, a minuscule amount compared to the 500 million dollars earmarked for the expressway. Moses, however, would hear none of it. He forged ahead with the expressway before the mass transit study was even completed, making it impossible to add the track without spoiling the work already accomplished. Moreover, by failing to acquire the rights of way (the space necessary to build such a mass transit system), Moses foreclosed it as a future option. Whenever planners returned to study the feasibility of increasing public transportation, they discovered that acquiring the land on either side of the expressway—now densely packed with homes and businesses—was prohibitively expensive. Moses built his road, and commuters to this day are paying the price. (Although the Long Island Rail Road predated Moses, by the time he left office in 1968, it had become dilapidated and so thoroughly trounced by competition from the new highways—which, once built, had nowhere near the labor costs involved in hiring railway conductors and engineers—that one reporter described it as "the kind of train that, if smaller, would make your little boy cry if he found it under his Christmas tree.")[29]

Moses—who, ironically, never learned to drive—was surely an extreme example of where the obsession with automobile travel could lead. But what happened in New York was hardly unique. Beginning in the 1950s, planners throughout the country began ramming highways through cities, linking urban centers with surrounding suburbs and shortchanging mass transit in the process. The driving force behind all the road-building and suburban expansion was a set of federal programs that had one thing in common: They conceived of cities as primarily dinosaurs and sought to help residents escape them.[30]

Nothing worked to encourage the flight to the suburbs more than the Interstate Highway Act of 1956. By the 1950s, a number of special interest groups lined up to support federal funding of more roads—the automobile industry, truckers, bus operators, oil companies, the asphalt and construction industries, plus various labor unions. And if this coalition of powerful lobbying groups was not enough, the Cold War gave legislators another reason to support an elaborate road network. The reasoning went as follows. The threat of a nuclear attack made it imperative for the nation's population not to congregate in large urban agglomerations. Small-scale cities and low-density suburban communities connected by a vast network of superhighways would thus help ward off the Red Menace.[31]

In 1954, President Dwight Eisenhower formed a committee to explore the nation's need for roads. Its chairman was Lucius Clay, who held a seat on the General Motors board of directors. The committee recommended—no doubt much to Clay's delight—what ranks as the most formidable public works project in the nation's history. It consisted of a massive road-building program that became the basis for nearly all the suburban sprawl that has come to define the geography of modern America. The passage of the Interstate Highway Act provided 50 billion dollars over 10 years—figures suggested by Robert Moses, who played a major role in designing the legislation—to build 41,000 miles worth of interstate highways. The government would assume 90 percent of the cost, with individual states making up the balance.[32]

"What's good for General Motors is good for the country, and vice versa," Charles Wilson, GM's president, announced the year following the passage of the act. Such self-serving comments aside, there is no question that the federal highway legislation boosted the bottom lines of America's automakers and the other special interests, from oil to asphalt, that lobbied for its passage. Mass transit continued on its relentless downward spiral, while expressways stretched out toward the horizon. Not only did the 1956 legislation earmark billions for roads, but it also set up the Highway Trust Fund, which allowed the government to tax gasoline and tires for use in building more roads. Just one percent of the money in the fund has gone to support mass transit. Is it any wonder that, as early as 1970, an automobile-centered city like Los Angeles managed to devote a third of its total land surface to roads, parking lots, and driveways?[33]

Never did the prospects for suburban expansion look brighter than in the postwar period. Not only did the federal government provide funds for roads, but it also established an entire host of programs and policies that inspired the building of homes in auto-dependent suburbs. The impetus for this move was the postwar baby boom, which strained the housing supply. To deal with the shortage, the U.S. government, prompted by builders, guaranteed low-interest Veterans Administration and Federal Housing Administration mortgages. Just as important, the federal tax code was changed in the 1940s to allow homeowners to deduct both mortgage interest and property taxes. Renters—and the vast majority of big-city dwellers were renters—were given no such deduction. The tax break amounted to a huge federal giveaway that fostered suburban homeownership at the expense of low-income renters in urban areas.[34]

In 1950, America's suburban population stood at 36 million. Twenty years later, the number had doubled to 74 million. In 1970, there were more suburbanites than city dwellers or rural folk. The rush to the suburbs came largely as a result of the U.S. government and its road-building and house-building programs. The price of suburban life has been amortized to taxpayers across the nation, with the benefits going mainly to those affluent enough to buy cars and to live amidst the sprawl, not the poor and minority residents left behind. Urban decay and suburban sprawl remain two sides of the same coin.[35]

THE PERILS OF SPRAWL

In 1946, the Levitt family, whose name has since become synonymous with suburban growth, purchased 4,000 acres of what had once been potato farms on Long Island and turned it into a town with over 17,000 houses. They named their

> Dear Mr. President
> we Have no Place
> to go when we
> want to go out
> in the canyon
> Because there
> ar going to Build
> houses So could you
> Set aside some
> land, where we could
> Play? thank you four listening
> love SCOTT

BACKYARD BLUES

Suburbanization led to a major decline in open space, a trend that especially affected children. In 1962, Scott Turner, age seven, sent this letter to President John F. Kennedy. (U.S. Department of the Interior, The Race for Inner Space [Washington, DC: Division of Information, 1964])

creation Levittown. The Levitts did for housing what Henry Ford did for cars. They figured out how to mass-produce homes and bring them within reach of the multitudes, especially working-class and newly married couples. Time magazine dubbed Levitt and Sons "the General Motors" of housing.[36]

First they brought in bulldozers, a technology developed during World War

II, to level the landscape and remove whatever tree cover remained. Then the Levitts divvied up the production process into 27 separate steps, from concrete foundation to landscaped home. From their start on Long Island, the Levitts branched out to colonize old spinach and broccoli farms outside of Philadelphia. They also constructed tract housing in Willingboro, New Jersey. Their success transcended the bounds of these individual communities and ultimately inspired similar residential developments across the nation, in cities such as Boston, Portland, Los Angeles, and Houston, to name but a few.

During each year of the 1950s, developers encroached on an area one million acres in extent—larger than the size of Rhode Island. As they attempted to maximize profits, builders left very little open space. In the New York metropolitan area, subdivisions built after World War II had just a tenth the amount of space reserved for parks that communities developed prior to the war possessed. As early as the 1960s, planners predicted that Los Angeles County would confront a shortage of recreational open space on the order of 100,000 acres by 1975.[37]

Eager for more fresh land, developers entertained the idea of building on marshlands, floodplains, and even hillsides. "With level land near cities getting scarce and costly," *House and Home* magazine disclosed in 1953, "many builders are taking to the hills. Big islands of rolling land left high and dry in the first waves of expansion are getting a second look for development. New earth-moving equipment and techniques are making hill building possible as never before." Split-level homes, developed in the 1950s to accommodate steep grades, proliferated. In the foothills and more mountainous areas of Los Angeles County, for instance, bulldozers made way for more than 60,000 homes. Suburban expansion in places such as southern California, however, entailed significant risks. As Los Angeles developers pressed ever harder against the San Gabriel Mountains, residents paid the price. In 1969 and 1978, for example, the geologically active mountain chain released a torrent of debris—tons and tons of mud and boulders, some the size of cars—that turned quiet suburban life into a nightmare.[38]

Wildfire posed an even more persistent menace. The foothills of the San Gabriels are covered with chaparral, a dense thicket of evergreen shrubs that flourish in a climate defined by hot, dry summers and moist, cool winters. Chaparral is extremely prone to fire; indeed, the flames actually help nurture the growth of the various small trees and shrubs. When developers descended on the foothills of Los Angeles, they were building in the midst of one of North America's most flammable environments.

In a sense, suburbanites and developers conspired to bring disaster upon themselves. Wealthy residents in such places as Malibu enjoyed the privacy and beauty of the brush, although it significantly increased the risk of fire, a point borne out in the devastating blaze that torched the area in 1956. More important, the proliferation of fire-prone wooden roofs in the postwar period boosted that hazard even further. Tragically, fashionable southern California homeowners opposed the one strategy that experts believed could have helped ward off disaster: prescrip-

MALIBU FIRE, 1956

Firefighters, who once focused their efforts on controlling outbreaks in wilderness areas, found that the Malibu disaster marked the start of a new breed of conflagration that occurred on the border between backcountry and built-up suburban developments. (Regional History Collection, University of Southern California)

tive burning. Setting fire to the land every five years or so reduces both the fuel load and the possibility of more serious conflagrations. Their own worst enemies, residents of toney neighborhoods objected that such a strategy would blacken the countryside and reduce property values. Instead, they relied on the state and federal governments, with their firefighters and disaster relief, to bail them out when self-inflicted calamity hit. The scale of the subsidy given suburban development was simply staggering, especially when one considers that in the 1980s alone, 10,000 wildfires struck the Golden State.[39]

HOME AND GARDEN

Just about everything we associate with the suburban home—the car, the lawn, the very house itself—guzzles nonrenewable fossil fuels. For 25 years following the end of World War II, American homes consumed rising amounts of energy. In the 1960s alone, energy use per house rose an unprecedented 30 percent.[40]

But the high-energy home was not the inevitable outcome of suburban expansion. It might surprise some to learn, for instance, that in the 1940s even such mainstream magazines as *Newsweek* touted the virtues of solar design. These innovative homes were oriented toward the south to capitalize on the sun's heat in the winter and had overhangs to shield them from the scorching summer sun. They saved on precious natural resources and appealed to America's wartime conservation mentality. Even into the late 1940s and early 1950s, solar homes commanded serious attention from architects, builders, and the popular press. Once again, the World War II era represented a moment of ecological possibility. As the 1950s unfolded, however, the availability of cheap heating fuels like oil and natural gas dimmed the attraction of the sun. Before too long, the federal government retreated from investing in solar research. "Our descendants 1,000 years hence may curse us for using coal, oil, and gas to heat our homes, when we might as well have used the sun," declared one solar researcher in 1954.[41]

With solar design waning in popularity, the stage was set for an orgy of suburban home energy use. In 1945, very few American homes had air conditioning, even though the technology was available as far back as the 1930s. But as air conditioning units became cheaper and more compact in the late 1940s, sales began to rise. Even more important was that once the wartime housing shortage ended in the mid-1950s, builders had to figure out how to continue to stimulate demand for new homes. Air conditioning proved the answer to their prayers. In effect, builders found themselves in the same position as the auto industry in the 1920s, after the need for basic transportation had been met by Ford's Model T. Air conditioning became the equivalent of GM's annual model change. The addition of air conditioning to new homes tempted buyers to trade up. Women who stayed at home while their husbands left for air-conditioned offices helped fuel the market for central air. Not only that, the National Weather Bureau also worked to further sensitize people to the perils of heat. In 1959, the bureau put forth a "Discomfort Index," a composite measure of both heat and humidity. The air conditioning industry seized on the index as the perfect way to know when it was time to crank the machine to "Hi Cool."[42]

Between 1960 and 1970, the number of air-conditioned houses went from one million to almost eight million. The energy-intensive machines added comfort to the home and it unquestionably made life more bearable in the South. It also helped to lengthen the lives of those suffering from heart or respiratory disease. It is worth noting, however, that properly designed solar houses could have achieved at least some of the same ends, and at a far lower environmental cost.[43]

The suburban home's drain on energy resources also had some less obvious causes. When such large-scale builders as the Levitts cleared the land of trees, they exposed the new homes to both more heat and more cold, increasing the energy that had to be expended to keep the temperature comfortable inside. With the trees gone, developers then planted grass to cover up the scarred earth left behind in the building process. A quick and simple means of sprucing up the terrain, however, soon turned into a major-league obsession. Whatever complexity existed in the agricultural ecosystems that preceded suburbia gave way to a homogenous sea of green, a mass-produced landscape to accompany the mass-produced homes. Homeowners broke out lawnmowers, pesticides, fertilizers, and sprinklers as they set about furiously transforming the landscape into a lush green carpet. Oil and natural gas, it turns out, are the chief components in the production of nitrogen-based fertilizer. Power mowers, of course, also use fossil fuels and, not only that, contribute far more than one might expect to air pollution. One hour spent mowing grass is the equivalent in terms of emissions produced to driving a car 350 miles. Suburban homes guzzled energy, both inside and out.[44]

Landscape architect Frederick Law Olmsted pioneered the lawn in its suburban incarnation. In the 1860s, Olmsted designed a suburban community outside of Chicago, with houses set back enough from the street to allow homeowners to plant a nice swath of grass. "A smooth, closely shaven surface of grass is by far the most essential element of beauty on the grounds of a suburban house," wrote lawn advocate Frank J. Scott in 1870. Fittingly, standardization maven Frederick W. Taylor played a role in American lawn history, experimenting with grass that he hoped could be "made in much the same way that an article is manufactured in a machine shop or factory."[45]

In the 1920s, as the economy evolved into its present consumption-oriented mode, companies specializing in lawn-care products preyed on the fear that failing to keep grass neatly manicured reflected badly on homeowners themselves. "Many a lawn that looks passable at a distance shows up very poorly when close by," read a brochure for one lawnmower company in 1928.[46] At a time when advertisers urged women to scrutinize the inside of homes for all traces of dirt and sold them new products to eliminate it, companies peddling lawn-related items urged the man of the house to assume his civic duty and make sure the grounds appeared well trimmed and orderly.

During World War II companies such as O. M. Scott & Sons turned the lawn into a means of national unity and moral uplift. "Your lawn is the symbol of peace at home and its proper maintenance a vital factor in keeping up morale," read a 1942 advertisement for the seed company.[47] Tending lawns evolved into a patriotic duty, no less important than fighting the nation's enemies.

When the war ended, the lawn truly began to swallow the landscape. Gardeners threw down grass seed with each new subdivision. Meanwhile, the game of golf, with its fairways and putting greens, became a national pastime. Earlier in the century, the U.S. Golf Association and the USDA joined forces to find new species of turf grass suited to America's diverse physical environment. When, following World War II, golf became a multibillion-dollar business, champions such as Sam Snead, Arnold Palmer, and Jack Nicklaus were recruited to advertise mowers and other lawn supplies.

Good-looking lawns brought happy families in their wake, or so advertisements and television shows told viewers. The TV show *Father Knows Best*, first aired in 1954, opened with a shot of a meticulously kept lawn before zooming in on the family itself. The Vigaro Lawn Food company ran a similar spot. Maintain your lawn well, went the message, and you too could look forward to domestic harmony, or at least convince neighbors that life was as perfect indoors as out.[48]

Of course the perfect lawn, like the ideal family or body, was nearly impossible to achieve. Four out of five Americans, according to a 1981 poll, expressed dissatisfaction with the state of their lawn. A simple ecological fact explains why the quest for the gold medal lawn ended so often in failure: Turf grass is not native to North America. Most of the grass species come from northern Europe and evolved under moister, cooler conditions than those largely present on the U.S. mainland. Such species flourish in a wet northern climate like Newfoundland's, but to grow turf grass in the continental United States, one must be prepared to water, fertilize, and mow constantly. In Europe, grasses adapted themselves to being grazed by livestock, meaning that they grew and flowered regularly to meet the dietary needs of animals such as cattle. Were it not for this fact, cutting the lawn would never have become the suburban weekend ritual that it is today.[49]

It was difficult enough to grow turf grass in America, but the relentless quest for perfection—a neat, bright green expanse free of weeds and insects—has increased the stakes and costs of lawn care. Keeping lawns green requires a huge amount of fertilizer. As late as the 1920s, suburbanites spread manure on their lawns come the fall. But the decline of the horse in urban life led homeowners to turn to commercial fertilizers—increasingly so after World War II, when they became readily available in an artificial form. Prior to 1940, one pound of nitrogen fertilizer per 1,000 square feet of lawn was all the experts recommended; by the 1970s, the figure had risen to eight pounds for the same area. In the early 1980s, Americans spread more chemical fertilizer on their lawns than the entire nation of India used to grow food for its people. Excessive use of nitrogen fertilizer fosters algae blooms, as the nutrients run off into rivers, only to emerge in coastal waters where they harm aquatic life. Fertilizer also contaminates ground water supplies and may play a role in causing cancer, birth defects, and "blue baby syndrome," where an infant's blood is deprived of oxygen.[50]

Were homeowners willing to tolerate a little disorder, they could have forgone the fertilizer. Clover, once a common species in grass seed mixtures, provides a free fertilizer treatment. It absorbs air-borne nitrogen and, when it dies, returns the nutrient to the soil, where it helps nurture the grass. But after World War II, clover, like other "weed" species, came under attack. "It's time to take up arms against the weeds," read one 1955 article extolling the virtues of a flawless lawn. "From now on, when man and nature meet on the lawn, it's dog eat dog."[51] It was as if when the battles overseas ended, Americans, deprived of an outside threat, declared war on the unseen enemies lurking in their yards.

As went the weeds, so went the bugs. By applying the metaphors of war to insects, Americans elevated the killing of bugs into a battle for the nation's very existence. Insects played an important role in World War II. At one point in the early part of the war, Gen. Douglas MacArthur estimated that mosquitoes had caused two-thirds of his troops in the South Pacific to come down with malaria. Although considered a dangerous insecticide today, DDT (dichlorodiphenyltrichloroethane), first tested in the United States in 1942, saved the lives of countless U.S. soldiers and millions of others across the globe at risk of malaria. In light of its success abroad, when the war ended, DDT was deployed at home on American soil.[52]

In 1944, *Life* magazine contemplated waging war against the Japanese beetle, a turf grass pest especially troublesome in the Northeast. "Japanese beetles, unlike the Japanese, are without guile," the article explained. "There are, however, many parallels between the two. Both are small but very numerous and prolific, as well as voracious, greedy, and devouring." The deeply ingrained racism of wartime rhetoric was adapted to the postwar insecticide mania, as the civilian use of DDT—proclaimed "the atomic bomb of the insect world"—and other poisons snow-balled.[53]

Aside from the dangers pesticides posed to human health, they also killed organisms helpful in decomposing grass clippings. That left homeowners little choice but to throw out the clippings as "waste"—losing yet another opportunity for a free fertilizer treatment. If they wanted healthy and green yards, it was off to the store to purchase more fertilizer, in a never-ending cycle of ecological catch-up.

The lawn has become a perfect vehicle for promoting economic growth under consumerism, luring Americans into a war they cannot win. Much of the nation's climate and geography stands in the way of triumph. But from the standpoint of those in the lawn-care industry, the fact that total victory remains elusive is, of course, a source of great profits. The unattainable quest for perfection has allowed suppliers to sell Americans on the need for an arsenal of high-energy pesticides, herbicides, and lawn tools in a battle that is essentially over before it starts. What Alfred Sloan accomplished with his yearly model change and postwar builders did by promoting air conditioning, the nation's lawn-care industry arrived at by virtue of ecological misfortune. Turf grass species developed in colder European climes simply cannot flourish easily in this country. Consumer capitalism, a system of social relations predicated on people's inability to satisfy their insatiable needs, easily took root in the American lawn.

CONCLUSION

Suburban sprawl has had a profound effect on ecosystems across the United States. Taken together, lawns and automobiles have redefined the American landscape— knitting the nation together in swaths of green and ribbons of black. But sadly, by locking into auto-centered suburbanization, our culture may well have imperiled its ability to respond to future environmental challenges.

The reduction of meadow, prairie, desert, and forest habitats—with their complex vegetative complexes—into a lawn monoculture is one of the singular ecological inventions of modern American history, a shift that affected not just plant life, but various birds, insects, butterflies, and small mammals. Simplified lawn ecosystems attract large numbers of birds, it is true. But whereas the native vegetation allowed for a range of avian life, the lawn has drawn only those species—house sparrows and starlings, for example—that feed on the seeds and insects commonly found on the streamlined green expanses. From the loss of species diversity to fertilizer-induced ground water contamination, the American lawn continues to exact a high environmental toll.

The lawn even has the force of law behind it. Many communities forbid homeowners (and have in places for 100 years) from letting "weeds"—that is, undomesticated vegetation—take over their front yards. Nor is grass allowed to grow over a certain specified height. Some jurisdictions have even mandated jail time for such offenses. In the late 1980s, one Maryland couple refused to mow their foot-high grass, a protest that eventually helped galvanize resistance to lawn totalitarianism. Although the couple eventually won their case—prevailing on the county to change its law—the suburban meadow movement faces an uphill battle against the thoroughly entrenched ruling lawn culture.[54]

Compared to the lawn, the ecological impact of the car seems far more glaring and obvious. The tendency to evaluate technology in terms of physical objects has focused attention on the automobile's obvious by-products, its role in generating petroleum dependence, air pollution, toxic waste, and global warming—all major effects of the nation's shift to cars as the primary means of transportation. But if we consider not just the car but the system of highways that has arisen, a fuller and less recognized understanding of auto culture's impact on nature emerges. The creation of a national interstate highway system, like the making of a national lawnscape, has had significant effects on local habitats. When Interstate 75 slashed through Florida's Big Cypress Swamp, it split the habitat of the Sunshine State's panther population and caused its numbers to decline. Meanwhile, in the Northeast, the salt spread on roads during the winter has caused some tree species like oaks to dwindle and other, such salt-tolerant ones as sycamores to grow instead. And anyone wondering why ragweed dominates the edges of such roads might care to know that the species thrives on salt.[55]

Ecological conditions in modern America have changed, and they will continue to evolve. Unfortunately, however, decisions made by large corporate interests such as the auto and oil lobbies (and their government supporters) have narrowed our culture's range of options in responding to change. What is good for GM or some other large and powerful institution or interest, as anthropologist Roy Rappaport once observed, cannot be good for the country. By forcing us so thoroughly down one single path, conformity limits our ability to respond in the face of an unforeseen turn of events. Whether we have mortgaged the future by committing ourselves to auto-centered suburban expansion is debatable. But there is no question that we have foreclosed, to a major extent, on our ability to adapt to the ecological changes ahead.[56]

THROWAWAY SOCIETY

The garbage wars began in the 1990s when New York City found that it was running out of room to store its trash. At first it may have seemed like a simple problem, nothing that could not be solved by a fleet of tractor-trailers carrying garbage to open spaces further south and west. If only Virginia's Gov. James S. Gilmore had not spoken up. "The home state of Washington, Jefferson and Madison has no intention of becoming New York's dumping grounds," he declared.[1] New York City Mayor Rudolph W. Giuliani responded that accepting some trash was a small price to pay for the enormous cultural benefits that tourists from all across the nation experienced when they came to town on vacation.

Culture in exchange for garbage seemed like a reasonable deal, unless you found yourself living in one of the unlucky places now playing host to what the city no longer wanted. "It may be out of sight, out of mind," for New Yorkers, remarked one resident of Old Forge, Pennsylvania, home to a landfill that receives trash originating in Brooklyn and Queens. "But in our neck of the woods, we are the ones feeling the impact, we have the hundreds of tractor trailers every day with the New York license plates and a landfill that is tearing apart the side of a mountain." Not everyone is so negative, of course. Charles City County, Virginia, received some 3.4 million dollars in 2000 from Waste Management, Inc., for the privilege of operating a 1,000-acre landfill, the ultimate destination of waste produced in a large part of Brooklyn. "Our elementary, middle and high schools are all new and they were built from landfill dollars," the chairman of the county's board of supervisors recently explained. "That is a very concrete benefit." Indeed, the trash-financed schools certainly gave the term *recycling* new meaning.[2]

Show me your trash and I'll tell you who you are. A consumer culture eager for the newest and latest gadgets was a society destined to confront the avalanche of items it no longer needed. Indeed, the very concept of planned obsolescence, introduced by GM in the 1920s, presupposed increasing amounts of waste. Before World War II, GM made small model changes each year, with a major revision once every four to five years. After the war, significant stylistic changes—a new set of tail fins or lights—occurred more frequently. Quality also declined, to the point where, by 1956, Americans were junking their cars roughly three years earlier than in the 1940s. It is little wonder that in 1969, New York City alone faced the problem of dealing with 57,000 abandoned automobiles.[3]

Derelict cars made up just one small part of the solid waste stream produced by the culture of consumption, a stream that turned into more of a torrent as the baby boomers came of age during the 1960s and 1970s. Before the war, plastic played a very limited role in material life, incorporated mainly into radios and some furniture. After the war, as oil became the driving force behind the American economy, plastics, which are made from petroleum, became ubiquitous, used in everything from dry cleaning bags and disposable pens to Styrofoam and shrink-wrap. Packaging also exploded in importance. By 1964, every American consumed a staggering 2,000 packages on average per year. An array of disposable products from plastic silverware to paper cups, meanwhile, enshrined convenience as the dominant selling point of postwar consumerism. Even the advent of computers, initially hailed as a step toward the paperless office, has resulted in more wasted reams as Americans run off multiple drafts of documents formerly produced just once on a typewriter. "People said paper would shrink with the computer—just the opposite is happening," explained the vice president of a Canadian paper mill. "Office paper is the fastest growing segment. People print out everything they see—Web sites, e-mail."[4]

As New York City's garbage woes suggest, the nation's landfills began experiencing a space crunch starting in the early 1980s. Between 1982 and 1987, 3,000 landfills, filled to capacity, had to be shut down. In the densely populated Northeast, the space shortage became especially severe, compelling cities to ship trash out of state, where it often wound up on the doorsteps of the poor. Garbage, driven out of sight and out of mind, now circulates the country just like any other commodity, before being dumped wherever the free market system dictates.

PAPER MOUNTAIN

Of all the many products associated with the culture of consumption, from disposable diapers to fast food containers, it is paper that remains the nation's number one solid waste, accounting since 1960 for more than a third of all the trash in landfills. How did this come to be?

The roots of the current paper profusion go back to the nineteenth century and the development of newsprint, arguably the first mass-produced throwaway product. Before the 1880s, newspapers were printed on paper made from old rags collected from households across the country and processed in mills. But with the development of a machine for grinding wood into pulp (invented in Germany in the 1840s), the production of newsprint in the United States skyrocketed from 130 tons per day in the 1870s to 1.9 million tons in 1900. Newsprint was cheap and not particularly durable, qualities that made it ideal for conveying information about ephemeral events. By the turn of the century, logging companies turned the nation's once vast forest reserves into pulp on an unheard-of scale, as Americans consumed nearly 60 pounds of paper and paperboard per person. "Satan came walking up and down and he devised methods of making paper from wood pulp," the famed clergyman and author Edward Everett Hale wrote in 1906. "What follows is that you enter your forest with your axes in summer as you once did in winter, and you cut down virtually everything." The vast majority of the paper made from these trees was destined for the garbage heap. Today, a year's subscription to the *New York Times* takes up roughly 1.5 cubic yards of landfill space and weighs more than 500 pounds.[5]

Newspapers, depending on market conditions, can be recycled, but not the omnipresent merchandise catalogue, another product presently clogging up the nation's landfills. Montgomery Ward and Company established the first mail order company in the 1870s. In 1874, it put out a 72-page catalogue. In the 1880s, the catalogue grew to over 500 pages and, by the turn of the century, had ballooned to 1,200 pages. Like newspapers, catalogues had a very limited shelf life and eventually went into the trash to make room for another thick book advertising a new seasonal product line.[6]

Paper, of course, also plays a major role in packaging. We take it for granted today that purchased products come in packages. But in the nineteenth century, everything from pickles to flour to toothbrushes was sold in bulk. The move toward packaging consumer items began in the late nineteenth century. In 1899, the National Biscuit Company patented a cardboard and wax paper carton for selling crackers, once sold out of a barrel. The new In-Er-Seal carton, the company informed consumers, shielded the biscuits from moisture, keeping them fresh. Companies such as Prophylactic Tooth Brushes even went so far as to sell buyers on the very package itself—not simply what it contained. Packages, went the sales pitch, worked to protect consumers from germs, once easily picked up as buyers rummaged through piles of loose brushes.[7]

Cleanliness and convenience also figured prominently in the increasing sale of a long line of paper products—from napkins and cups to towels and tissues. Paper towel use, for example, boomed between 1947 and 1963, increasing from 183,000 tons to over 629,000 tons, as consumers were sold on the product's multiple uses—from draining meat to wiping up spills. "Wastebaskets—Do You Have Enough?" read the title of a 1957 article in *Better Homes and Gardens*. "Trend today is to larger wastebaskets—to take care of the increasing use of paper napkins, plates, towels, place mats, tissue, wrappings." Although accounting by the 1970s for just a small fraction of the solid waste stream, the rise of disposable paper products embodied the postwar trend toward convenience and made throwing things away into a veritable national obsession.[8]

Far more important in terms of the mountain of paper created have been corrugated boxes and newspapers, which by the 1960s were the number one and two solid waste items. Newspapers are especially problematic because paper and other organic materials break down very slowly in landfills. Mummification, not biodegradation, more aptly sums up life at the dump. This fact is especially alarming with respect to newsprint because, until recently, a good deal of lead went into the ink used.[9]

Between 1956 and 1967, the amount of paper disposed of as trash increased by nearly 60 percent, from 22 million tons to 35 million tons. Meanwhile, recycling trended downward. Some 27 percent of the paper consumed in the United

States was recycled in 1950, declining to 23 percent in 1960 and only 18 percent in 1969. In paper recycling, everything hinges on the market. Without a demand for recycled paper—often used to make fresh newsprint, wallboard, and insulation—collection is pointless and potentially even counterproductive. By the early 1990s, a glut developed in the United States—too many old newspapers and not enough demand—leading some companies to dump it abroad. As a result, surplus paper upset recycling programs in both Asia and Europe.[10]

Recycling is a questionable solution to the waste problem for another reason. In principle, tying up newspapers and leaving them at the curb makes a great deal of sense, but it is, nonetheless, a retail-level solution to what is a wholesale systemic problem. Instead of confronting the trash dilemma at its source—the paper factories—recycling shifts responsibility to ordinary people who had little say or role in creating the predicament in the first place. In the 1970s, a coalition of paper, plastic, aluminum, and glass companies ran magazine and TV spots showing an American Indian crying at the sight of litter tossed onto the road (see p. 12). "People start pollution," the advertisement declared. "People can stop it." What the advertisement failed to mention was corporate America's own stake in the nation's solid waste woes. The commercial located responsibility at the individual level, drawing attention away from the major role that industry itself played—through its relentless efforts at increasing consumption—in perpetuating waste.

DOWN THE DRAIN

The postwar increase in paper and plastic packaging, especially for food items, did have some redeeming ecological value. As the market in processed products boomed, the amount of food that consumers actually threw away declined. Manufacturers removed the leaves and shells from food at the factory and thus landfills received more paper, plastic, and metal and less in the way of foul smelling organic matter. But packaging still did not liberate Americans from coping with kitchen waste.

"Waste" that had once served a useful purpose literally became garbage, something with so little value it could be safely flushed down the drain. The electric garbage disposer was invented in the 1930s, but it was only after World War II that the rage for convenience made a serious inroad into the American kitchen. Only a single company, General Electric, manufactured the appliance before the war; by 1948, however, 17 companies had jumped into the market. In the wake of a cholera outbreak at area pig farms, the town of Jasper, Indiana, required all homeowners to install disposers in 1950. "Jasper is the first town in the world to banish that unsavory, unhealthy relic of the dark ages—the garbage can," trumpeted *McCall's* magazine. Although such cities as Boston and New York prohibited them, fearing that the ground food waste would clog their antiquated sewer systems, by 1960 other urban areas (Denver, Detroit, and many places in California)

HOG PEN

This 1939 hog pen was located next door to the Oklahoma City dump, where its owner rented the right to allow his animals to feed on garbage. Such swine-feeding operations persisted in some places until the early 1960s. A decade later, a mere four percent of the nation's food waste wound up as pork, with the remainder sent to landfills or flushed down the drain. (Library of Congress)

required them in all new homes. In 1959, disposers could be found in four million American households.[11]

Paralleling the trend toward flushing away kitchen scraps occurred a similar devaluation of organic matter outside the house. The quest for the perfectly green lawn, as we have seen, led homeowners to substitute nitrogen-based fertilizer for grass clippings. The result was a profusion of yard waste, clippings, leaves, and other organic material that otherwise marred the velvety green carpet yearned for by suburbanites. Since at least 1960, yard waste (by weight) has constituted the second largest component of the nation's solid waste stream, surpassed only by the king of the dump, paper. Over the last four decades, however, the quantity of yard waste has been slowly declining. In 1989, the Environmental Protection Agency, grappling with the mountain of solid waste produced nationwide, urged communities to ban it from landfills. Many communities have established municipal plants for turning it into compost, used to improve soil fertility on farms and golf courses. Still, large-scale composting—as opposed to, say, simply mulching grass clippings and leaving them on the lawn—is subject to economic constraints. Some of the earlier facilities, lacking adequate financing, ran out of money before the composting process had been completed, effectively turning the site into an exceedingly smelly landfill. In any case, Americans have had nowhere near the success with large-scale composting—nor have they demonstrated anything like the political commitment—that European countries have.[12]

In postwar America, food and yard waste was something to dispose of as readily as possible. Suburbanites, instead of reusing organic material, burdened the land with what was now seen as simply garbage. In this sense, the lack of landfill space, apparent by the 1980s, was at least partly a function of suburban development itself and unquestionably an avoidable disaster.

SOME THINGS ARE FOREVER

Twentieth-century consumerism has rested on convenience and disposability, but durability too has been an important ecological issue. On the one hand, modern consumer culture has broken the local recycling systems of the past and, on the other, has turned to products so durable that they threaten never to go away.

The proliferation of plastic products in the postwar years—everything from trash bags to Christmas trees—has in many ways come to symbolize the nation's materialistic impulse. In the famous scene from the 1968 movie The Graduate, a family friend tells Dustin Hoffman: "I just want to say one word to you. Just one word . . . Plastics. . . . There's a great future in plastics." As far as business advice was concerned, it was reasonably sound: Americans have used more plastic with each passing year. In 1976, more plastic was manufactured, in terms of cubic volume, than all steel, copper, and aluminum combined. In part the proliferation of plastics stemmed from the idiosyncrasies of production. Relative to other products, plastics are expensive to manufacture in small quantities because of the high fixed costs involved in making the molds and production equipment. Companies must thus produce huge quantities to recoup their investment.[13]

Measured by weight, plastics have gone from composing a mere 0.5 percent of total solid waste in 1960 to 8.5 percent in 1990, a steady, although hardly explosive, increase. These figures, however, are by weight, which is why they are commonly cited by the plastics industry itself. In terms of volume, the impact is far greater, with the substance making up anywhere from 16 to 25 percent of the waste stream.[14]

In recent years, plastics have been "light-weighted," somewhat reducing their impact. Plastic grocery bags, for example, were 40 percent thinner in the early 1990s than they were in the mid-1970s. While plastics take up less room in landfills, they can take hundreds of years to degrade. Although it is possible to make the substance break down more quickly, it requires a novel and expensive production process. The "greener" plastic also takes up as much if not more room than the nonbiodegradable kind. Indeed, the entire idea of biodegradable plastic may be little more than a scheme to allow corporations to falsely market their products as being green. "Degradability is just a marketing tool," a representative of the Mobil Chemical Corporation once said. "We're talking out of both sides of our mouths because we want to sell bags. I don't think the average consumer even knows what degradability means. Customers don't care if it solves the solid waste problem. It makes them feel good." And besides, most manufacturers choose plastic precisely because it is so durable and resistant to decay.[15]

Plastics may well represent a greater ecological threat at sea than on land. In the 1980s an estimated 52 million pounds of packaging were dumped from commercial fleets into the ocean every year, in addition to 300 million pounds of plastic fishing nets. Tens of thousands of sea mammals, birds, and fish died as a result of the plastic tidal wave. One estimate placed the amount of fish with plastic lodged in their stomachs, interfering with digestion, at 30 percent.[16]

For many environmentalists, plastic has come to symbolize all that is wrong with America. There is no question that in terms of the toxic waste produced in making it, a synthetic product like plastic is cause for concern. But with respect to disposal, it is rubber, a material every bit as important to the culture of consumption, that has posed an even greater environmental challenge.

The problems with rubber derive from the nation's love affair with the road. Early in the century, when the automobile was just getting its start, rubber came from Brazil, where workers went from tree to tree making cuts and capturing the

TIRE DUMP

Piles of discarded tires, like these in Kilgore, Texas, littered the American landscape as early as the 1930s. (Library of Congress)

latex, in order to meet the rising demand for tires. By the end of World War I, however, Asia, where major plantations were built on the Malay Peninsula, had eclipsed the Amazon as the world's leading rubber source.

In the years after World War II, as the automobile rose to dominance, America's stockpile of used tires began to grow. But the increase was slow since it was possible to harvest the discarded rubber and reuse it for making new tires. Beginning in the 1960s, however, tire manufacturers began to reject such recycled rubber. The advent of the steel-belted radial, increasing concern with tire safety, and a surplus of synthetic rubber all contributed to the downfall of tire reprocessing. Nor did it help that the new generation of steel-belted radial tires were harder to recycle.[17]

The result was predictable: a massive buildup of used tires. By the 1980s, Americans threw away roughly one tire for every man, woman, and child, some 200 to 250 million each year. Of that amount, an estimated 168 million eventually entered either landfills or junkyards.[18]

The problem with tires is that like old ghosts they have a way of returning to haunt. Bury them with a bulldozer and they will eventually resurface as they expand back to their original shape. So the operators of dumps routinely collected them and put them in piles. Soon the piles became literally mountains. By 1990, somewhere between two and three billion scrap tires existed nationwide. Not surprisingly, California, with its affinity for auto transport, led the country in the 1990s with roughly 28 million tires located at 140 sites.[19]

What harm is there in tire mountains? Unexpected biological consequences have been one result. Beginning in the 1970s, a market arose in the United States for used tires imported from Japan and other Asian countries. (Japanese drivers are apparently more finicky than Americans, who are untroubled with buying slightly worn tires.) The tires made the trip overseas and so, evidently, did the Asian tiger mosquito (*Aedes albopictus*), which can transmit a number of diseases to humans, including malaria and some forms of encephalitis. Because of their ability to retain water, tires provide ideal breeding environments for mosquitoes. In 1984, the Asian mosquito surfaced in several Houston area tire dumps. By 1997, the insect, hitching a ride as the tires were hauled around the nation's vast interstate system, had expanded into 25 states, although, as yet, no evidence has linked the mosquito to the onset of disease in this country.[20]

Of more concern is the fire threat that tires pose. Since the 1980s, a number of blazes have broken out at tire dumps around the country (and in Canada) as lightning, arson, and spontaneous combustion have ignited the huge stockpiles of rubber. In 1983, a fire at a Virginia tire dump burned for a full nine months. Somewhere between five million and seven million tires went up in the blaze, producing 250,000 million gallons of toxic sludge. "You don't know what Hell's going to look like," said one volunteer firefighter, "but you had that feeling about it."[21] A 1998 California tire fire smoldered for more than a year because officials feared that suppressing it might contaminate ground water. And in 1999, what has been described as the West's largest tire pile, near Westley, California, went up in smoke after a lightning strike, igniting a blaze so fierce it required the state to hire a crew of professional firefighters from Texas to extinguish the inferno.

The fire threat has helped to spur recycling efforts, which increased markedly in the 1990s. Scrap tires have been used to make roadways, cover landfills, and in place of rock as a substitute drainage material. They are also burned to make cement. But once again market imperatives undercut such efforts. The demand for recycled rubber simply cannot keep pace with the millions of tires Americans heave each year. As one scrap tire expert put it, "tires, like diamonds, are forever."[22]

DUMPED ON

Between 1940 and 1968, Americans doubled the amount of solid waste, per capita, they produced each day, from two to four pounds. Today, the United States leads the industrialized world in waste generation, producing twice the amount of trash per capita as such countries as France, Britain, and Japan.[23]

To deal with the garbage, cities in postwar America built sanitary landfills. Earlier in the century, municipalities had relied on incinerators. But they were expensive to build, and burning garbage severely compromised air quality. In the years following World War II, the number of municipal incinerators fell from some 300 to just 67 in 1979. Landfills took up the slack. Unlike a dump, where garbage was scattered willy-nilly across an area, a landfill, thought to be a concept invented by the British in the 1920s, involved burying the garbage with dirt on a daily basis, a practice designed to eliminate the foul smell from decomposing organic matter. The idea left open the possibility that the area might again become productive—landscaped and transformed into real estate—when its capacity for garbage had been exhausted. Although landfills may have appeared in America early in the twentieth century, they arose in great numbers after 1945. There were roughly 100 landfills when the war ended and 1,400 a decade and a half later.[24]

The notorious Fresh Kills landfill in Staten Island, New York, had its start in 1948. Robert Moses planned to fill the area with garbage for about two decades and then turn the site into viable real estate suitable for homes, parks, and light industry. That has yet to happen, although it remains a possibility. Before its reinvention as a dumping ground for New York City's trash, the Fresh Kills area was essentially a swamp. Indeed, the word kill is Dutch for creek. In the 1940s, scientists had yet to realize that wetlands (a term ecologists only first employed in the 1950s to replace the pejorative swamp) served an important ecological role. We now know that wetlands absorb and filter water and thus help prevent floods, while preserving water quality. Unaware of this information, planners believed that wetlands made perfect landfill sites. In fact, moist environments, where trash and soil are in direct contact, aid biodegradation, causing the surrounding water and soil to be contaminated with toxins. (Today landfills are commonly lined with plastic to prevent this problem.)[25]

In the booming postwar years, a number of other landfills went up in the New York metropolitan area. But given the high water table throughout much of the region, especially Long Island, it was not long before people discovered the dangers involved. Slowly the brimming landfills, indicted as nuisances, began to close down, but Fresh Kills, the largest in the city, indeed, in the nation, hung on. At its peak in 1986, the landfill received a stunning 21,000 tons of garbage each day. When the Edgemere landfill in Queens shut down in 1991, Fresh Kills became the city's last remaining solid waste disposal site. As monuments go, Fresh Kills is nearly unrivaled. It is the second largest man-made structure in the world, only lagging behind the Great Wall of China.[26]

Staten Islanders, unsurprisingly, are not impressed with what the city has built them. "You ask yourself what it would smell like if you had a huge piece of rotting meat in your back yard," one local business owner complained in 1996.[27] The stench, however, is only the beginning of the problem. Millions of gallons of leachate, a toxic, sludgelike substance that oozes from landfills, have flowed straight into New York Harbor. In addition, tons of methane gas emanating from the pile pollute the air every day. Perhaps most sobering of all is this: As of the late 1990s, the Fresh Kills facility was disposing of just 0.02 percent of all the solid waste produced in the United States.

Whatever the problems of Fresh Kills, it has for decades met the city's needs for waste disposal. It is worth remembering that as a culture we need to do some-thing with our trash. The only question is who will bear the costs. In 1996, Republican Guy Molinari, Staten Island's borough president, decided that the time was right to ask the city of New York to close down Fresh Kills. For generations Molinari and his family had fought the dump; now with Republicans occupying both city hall (Rudy Giuliani) and the governor's mansion (George Pataki), Molinari prevailed on New York City to let Fresh Kills rest in peace. The decision was made despite the knowledge that the landfill still contained some 20 years' worth of unused capacity. Although the details surrounding the move remain shrouded in secrecy, this much is clear: City leaders gave virtually no consideration to what closing the site might mean for public health and environmental quality such as the increasing truck traffic that would come as trash was shipped to transfer stations located outside the city.[28]

Now the landfill is closed. That, of course, is the fate of all landfills. The 1980s witnessed a series of such closings. In the period between 1979 and 1986, some 3,500 landfills shut down either for lack of space or because of their failure to comply with tougher federal safety standards. Meanwhile, new landfills did not open to replace the defunct ones. During the mid-1970s, the state of Texas licensed about 250 landfills per year; in 1988, it licensed fewer than 50.[29]

To pick up some of the slack, northeastern cities, where the space crunch has been particularly acute, have started shipping their garbage out of state. Traveling trash itself is nothing new. During the 1960s, large numbers of so-called transfer stations came on line. These facilities, common in urban areas with limited dis-

THE FINAL BURIAL

The last load of New York City garbage destined for the notorious Fresh Kills site on Staten Island arrived on March 22, 2001. The landfill, now closed, was at points as high as the Statue of Liberty. (Mary Chapman)

posal sites, were essentially garbage terminals where collection trucks came to unload trash before it went, often by barge, to a more distant resting place. The interstate movement of trash increased in the 1980s, with New York, New Jersey, and Pennsylvania exporting eight million tons, mostly to the Midwest. By 1995, every single state, even Alaska and Hawaii, either imported or exported garbage. More than 17 million tons circulated throughout the nation in an intricate web of movements.[30]

In the summer of 1992, 80 boxcars worth of New York City trash left the South Bronx headed for a landfill in Libory, Illinois. There was only one problem: The landfill's permit had expired by the time the trash train arrived. The load of putrefying waste changed course and made stops in Sauget and Fairmont City, Illinois; Kansas City, Kansas; Medille, Missouri; Fort Madison, Iowa; and Streator, Illinois. No one seemed to want it. Eventually the entire smelly mess had to be hauled back east—the sides of the cars buckling as the heat swelled the size of the load—and buried in the Fresh Kills landfill.[31]

That same summer, another trainload of trash pulled out of New York and again chugged west toward Sauget, Illinois. This time residents protested the dumping of out-of-state garbage in their community by organizing a sit-in. "The people here have dictated they don't want any part of it," the town's mayor remarked. "If it was from Illinois, it might not be near as bad. But being from New York, they frown on that."[32]

The "poo-poo choo choos," as the media dubbed them, were just one symptom of the dilemmas raised by the free market in trash. Over the course of the 1980s and 1990s, increasing numbers of landfills were taken over by the private sector. By 1998, nearly two-thirds of all waste destined for a landfill went to a private facility. Many of these installations are now owned by large, multinational corporations such as Waste Management, which operates over 300 landfills and serves approximately 19 million residential customers nationwide.[33]

None other than the U.S. Supreme Court helped sanction the move toward the privatization of waste. In a string of cases dating back to 1978, the court has held that state laws attempting to bar interstate trash shipments violate the Commerce Clause of the Constitution, which gives Congress the right to oversee trade among the states. Prior to 1978, the court had commonly allowed states the right to regulate imported goods that compromised human health. In a landmark decision involving the city of Philadelphia and the state of New Jersey, the court overturned that precedent and has upheld its new position for more than two decades. As a result, garbage has become a commodity that moves, unfettered by state laws, according to the market's invisible hand.[34]

The court's decision might well impress many economists, but its social ramifications have proved more dubious. One recent study of garbage movement has uncovered three important trends. First, trash seems to move from states with high population densities to those with lower ones. Second, the waste gravitates from states with high per capita incomes to poorer ones. And third, the trash apparently flows from states confronting fewer air and water pollution problems to those with more such dilemmas. Are the rich dumping on the poor? Perhaps. The commodification of anything—whether it is land, water, beaver, bison, or even garbage—it is best remembered, has always produced both winners and losers.[35]

CONCLUSION

Garbage thus met very much the same fate that meat and fruit did earlier in the century. By the postwar period, Americans had become largely unaware of where their food came from and of where their trash went to. In this sense, garbage had become an abstract entity, a "solid waste stream" that went flowing to either local landfills or wherever the calculus of the market took it.

The solid waste problem is a creation of the American consumer economy and its incredible penchant for producing seemingly endless numbers of things made to break down or to go obsolete, a culture in love with beautiful cars and lawns while oblivious to the full consequences of those desires. Locally sited landfills, where things went to die, at least served as a reminder of what it meant to produce and consume. But with the increasing trend toward a national free market in garbage, with New York City's sanitation fleet headed for the state line, trash has become lost in space in one of the world's largest nations.

SHADES OF GREEN

Spontaneous combustion is not something that is supposed to happen to a river, unless it happens to be the Cuyahoga, an 80-mile long stream that cuts through the center of Cleveland, Ohio, before debouching into Lake Erie. The worst fire on the Cuyahoga raged through a shipyard, seriously burned three tugboats, and resulted in excess of 500,000 dollars in damage. Exactly what caused the river to ignite that day is not totally clear. What is clear is that water was not the only substance flowing in the river that day. "We have photographs that show nearly six inches of oil on the river," Bernard Mulcahy, a fire prevention expert, said after the blaze.[1]

It was 1952. American soldiers were battling in Korea and Dwight D. Eisenhower was poised to win the presidency in a landslide victory. The Cuyahoga, meanwhile, was merely repeating itself. A half-century earlier, on December 31, 1899, two men operating a Cleveland railroad bridge were minding their own business when one of them noticed, in the words of a newspaper account, "a great volume of smoke intermingled with flame rising from the river." The fire, however, caused no significant damage.[2]

So when fire broke out yet again on the river on June 22, 1969, no one in Cleveland was probably all that surprised. Although a picture appeared on the front page of the city's main newspaper, the actual story detailing the fire lay buried deep inside. "It was strictly a run of the mill fire," said Chief William Barry of the Cleveland Fire Department. To this day, Clevelanders must wonder why the 1969 fire, which did merely one-tenth the damage of the 1952 conflagration, became such a focus of national attention, solidifying, it might be added, the city's reputation as the "Mistake by the Lake." Later that summer, the Cleveland disaster became a poster child for the ills of modern America when Time magazine unveiled a new "Environment" section with a report on the sorry state of the Cuyahoga. "Chocolate-brown, oily, bubbling with sub-surface gases, it oozes rather than flows." What changed to make a routine event in the local history of a gritty industrial city into an environmental cause célèbre?[3]

As the story of the Cuyahoga suggests, the culture of consumption with its predilection for oil left a giant footprint on the nation's landscape. It brought about everything from the devastation of rivers and draining of wetlands to declines in biodiversity, ground water, public grazing lands, and air quality to the degradation of manure from a farm asset into a major pollution headache to the transformation of the very landscape itself into a dichromatic expanse of black and green.

CUYAHOGA FIRE, 1952

Although most people recall only the 1969 fire that helped marshal support for the environmental move-ment, Cleveland's Cuyahoga River, home to a large number of oil refineries by the latter part of the nine-teenth century, often ignited, as it did here in 1952. (Special Collections, Cleveland State University Library)

How could such a sweeping set of ecological changes not sow seeds of protest in its wake? As early as the 1930s, wilderness advocates introduced Americans to the idea that making an area off-limits to development could actually enrich society more—in the benefits it conferred on the soul—than allowing timber, oil, and mining interests to profit from such areas. But by the 1960s, environmentalism began to evolve in a different direction, away from its wilderness roots and more toward a broader concern with ecology itself. In a decade known for its political activism, be it demonstrations against the Vietnam War or protests for civil rights, environmentalism took on the trappings of a mass movement organized around cleaner air and water for all, not just in wilderness areas.

By the following decade, ecology-based environmentalism grew to be one of the most dramatic and significant reform movements in American history. The movement questioned corporate capitalism's tendency to view nature solely as an instrument in the service of economic gain. It helped inspire the push for a vast set of new environmental regulations. It even brought a whole new field of law into existence. Within the space of just two decades, it created a concern for nature that penetrated the fabric of everyday life. A 1990 Gallup poll found that an incredible three-quarters of those Americans surveyed fashioned themselves environmentalists.[4] Environmentalism has evolved into a diverse, multifaceted phenomenon—broad enough to include within its spectrum everyone from conservative Washington lobbyists in suits to renegade ecowarriors in jeans and plaid shirts.

SAVING THE WILD KINGDOM

The automobile brought rising numbers of Americans to the doorstep of wilderness. By the early 1920s, perhaps as many as 10 million to 15 million people were piling into their cars and heading off on summer vacations away from the hectic pace of urban life. Millions more set off on Sunday afternoon trips to nearby lakes and woods now within easy reach. Under the leadership of Stephen Mather, the National Park Service reorganized itself to accommodate automobile tourism. In 1913, Mather arranged to open Yosemite National Park to cars. Four years later, Yellowstone did the same. The number of visitors leapt from 356,000 to 1.3 million in just seven years (1916–1923), as the National Park Service engaged in a

AUTO CAMP

The period between the two world wars witnessed a boom in outdoor recreation. Companies selling everything from tents to packaged food sprung up to cater to the American passion for auto camping. This camp, photographed in 1923, was located near or in Yellowstone National Park. (Library of Congress)

massive publicity campaign, replete with photographs, postcards, and magazine articles. As the parks became tourist attractions, nature came to be seen as a separate and faraway locale packaged up for human consumption. "Yellowstone is like an aquarium," observed writer E. B. White on a visit in 1922, "all sorts of queer specimens, with thousands of people pressing in to get a glimpse. . . . [I]t is so obviously 'on exhibition' all the time."[5]

This commercialized approach to nature triggered the first calls for wilderness preservation. After World War I, a preservation movement arose that lobbied for the setting aside of undeveloped "wilderness areas." A wildlife biologist named Aldo Leopold played a leading role in the effort. Born in 1887 in Burlington, Iowa, Leopold went on to study at Yale University's School of Forestry, which existed courtesy of a gift made by none other than Gifford Pinchot. After receiving his master's degree in 1909, Leopold took a job with the Forest Service and, in the 1920s, succeeded in getting it to establish wilderness locales within its holdings, places off-limits to automobiles, roads, and other forms of development. Leopold is far better known, however, for writing A Sand County Almanac, published in 1949, a year after he collapsed and died while fighting a fire that broke out near his home in central Wisconsin. "We abuse land because we regard it as a commodity belonging to us," he wrote. "When we see land as a community to which we belong, we may begin to use it with love and respect." In the book he argued that planners must transcend narrow economic considerations in decisions over land use and instead adopt a broader ethical interest in preserving trees, insects, and other living organisms for their own sake. Adopting such a "land ethic," he believed, meant resisting the temptation of preserving individual wildlife species— the focus of most conservation efforts to that point—for the sake of the health of the larger ecosystem. "A thing is right," he concluded, "when it tends to preserve the integrity, stability, and beauty of the biotic community. It is wrong when it tends otherwise."[6]

Critical of the trend toward transforming nature into a commodity and selling it to would-be tourists, Leopold and other early wilderness advocates were some of the culture of consumption's most ardent foes. During the 1930s, the packaging of the natural world as a recreational resource gained momentum, as the New Deal, through organizations such as the Civilian Conservation Corps, added roads and campgrounds to the country's national parks and forests. In 1935, plans to build a parkway across a part of the Appalachian Mountains galvanized preservation advocates and led Leopold, forester Robert Marshall, and several others to form the Wilderness Society, a group opposed to the commercialization of nature represented by auto-centered tourism.[7]

Whatever the threat that tourism posed to wilderness, it was far outweighed in the postwar period by the pressure placed on the nation's forests and rivers by suburban development and economic growth. By the 1940s, private forest holdings in the Pacific Northwest, the country's last lumber frontier (with the Midwest and South already logged out), were edging toward exhaustion. This trend, combined with the postwar suburban building boom, drove the timber industry to call on Washington to open up the federal forests to logging. Logging required roads, and the Forest Service dutifully complied. Between 1940 and 1960, road mileage in national forests doubled from 80,000 to 160,000, or more than three times the extent of the present-day interstate highway system. The amount of timber harvested from the national forests between 1950 and 1966 amounted to twice what had been cut in the prior four and a half decades. And as road-building and timber-cutting mounted, wilderness areas became increasingly fragmented and open to abuse.[8]

In the mid-1950s, the Wilderness Society pressed Congress to protect the nation's forests in the face of this mounting assault. Eight years later, Congress complied, passing the Wilderness Act, legislation that gave the Forest Service the power to sequester some nine million acres of land from development. The act made the preservation of wilderness into national policy and, in this respect at least, represented a signal achievement. The legislation also had some significant flaws. It set aside just 9 million of the 14 million acres that the Forest Service had designated as wilderness and allowed mining in such areas until 1983—a move that sped up development in the places Congress sought to "preserve."[9]

Simultaneously with the assault on forests, more than four decades' worth of efforts to tame western rivers were about to reach their zenith. In 1911, the first major dam went up across the Colorado River. Twenty-five years later, Hoover Dam, a colossal 700-foot structure, rose up in the Colorado valley. By 1964, there were 19 large dams impeding this one river's journey to the sea.

Leading the charge for dams was the U.S. Bureau of Reclamation. In the 1940s, the bureau began building what it called "cash register" dams, profit-making structures for generating valuable electricity. The proceeds went to subsidize the bureau's irrigation projects, which sold water cheaply—and at taxpayer expense—to agribusiness. An early such dam was to go up on the Colorado in Echo Park, one of Utah's most scenic canyons and a part of the Dinosaur National Monument.[10]

Wilderness advocates, however, cried out, and no one more so than David Brower. As a child growing up in Berkeley, California, Brower had heard about the famed controversy over the Hetch Hetchy valley, dammed in 1913, despite the efforts of the preservationist John Muir, to serve the imperial dreams of San Francisco's business community. Brower was determined not to let history repeat itself. As executive director of the Sierra Club, he joined with other wilderness advocates to mount a massive publicity effort. They launched a direct mail campaign that asked such questions as, "Will You DAM the Scenic Wildlands of Our National Park System?" They produced a color movie; New York publisher Alfred Knopf put out a slick book of photographs titled This Is Dinosaur. All the attention created such a stir that tourists descended in droves on the canyon, some 45,000 in the summer of 1955 alone. In the end, Brower and the conservationists prevailed. There would be no Echo Park Dam. But to save Dinosaur, the wilderness advo-

HOOVER DAM

Completed in 1936, Hoover Dam, which rises to a height of 726 feet, took five years to build and claimed the lives of over 100 workers. It was the first in a long line of dams built along the powerful Colorado River by the U.S. Bureau of Reclamation. (U.S. Bureau of Reclamation)

cates agreed to plans for a dam at Glen Canyon, also on the Colorado. Brower considered the Glen Canyon Dam, completed in 1963, one of the biggest mistakes of his life; as the dam filled, some of his friends worried that he might even commit suicide.[11]

Never again, Brower said to himself. In 1966, the Bureau of Reclamation announced that it would build two dams and flood the Grand Canyon. Brower and the Sierra Club flew into action. When the bureau suggested that the dams might actually afford tourists a better opportunity (because of the lake they would create) to see the area in question, the wilderness advocates took out full-page advertisements that blared: "SHOULD WE ALSO FLOOD THE SISTINE CHAPEL SO TOURISTS CAN GET NEARER THE CEILING?"[12] Their efforts paid off; no dams went up along that stretch of the Colorado.

To Brower goes the credit for transforming environmental issues into the focus of a national campaign. Not surprisingly, Sierra Club membership grew from 7,000 in 1952 to over 77,000 in 1969. He succeeded in large part because of his media savvy. But he also prevailed because his brand of pull-out-all-the-plugs environmentalism struck a chord among those Americans fed up with life in an affluent, materialistic society where economic logic trumped everything else. "Objectivity," Brower once said, "is the greatest threat to the United States today." Brower opposed objectivity because he was for moral absolutes, for the position that being reasonable about building dams and other environmental issues was simply another way of saying, "Let's compromise for the sake of the greater economic good."[13]

And yet, despite such high-mindedness, it is surely ironic that Brower and his colleagues saved Dinosaur by transforming it into a tourist attraction, packaging and selling its virtues in print and on film. Glen Canyon, meanwhile, a place un-

SIERRA CLUB FLOAT TRIP

Wilderness advocates flocked to remote and previously unknown sections of the Colorado River in the mid-1950s as conflict erupted over plans to build the Echo Park Dam. (National Park Service, Harpers Ferry, West Virginia)

known to most, took on water because no such sales job ensued. Brower was for moral reason, but to garner support he felt compelled to engage in the same sales techniques employed by Madison Avenue. The success of his publicity campaign attracted flocks of tourists, placing stress on the very wilderness—Dinosaur National Monument—that he was trying to save.

Brower also succeeded because he was able to tap into some fertile cultural terrain. Postwar America was a world where nature had increasingly come to be seen as an amenity, an object of leisure-time pursuit, as much as something employed in the service of production. Nature films are a case in point. In the 1950s, Walt Disney Studios produced a series of films shot in open prairies and ancient forests, perceived by many as pristine wilderness areas removed from both urban and suburban life. *The Vanishing Prairie* (1954), for instance, was set "before civilization left its mark upon the land." In such films and others, Disney packaged nature for mass audiences, transforming wilderness into a commodity that anyone able to afford the price of a movie ticket could enjoy. Wilderness advocates, in turn, capitalized on the public's evident fascination with unsullied nature. In 1955, the Audubon Society went so far as to award Walt Disney a medal for his role as a conservationist.[14]

Disney's version of the wilderness experience resonated in the thoroughly contrived suburban developments that had sprung up in the postwar years, where the homogeneity of the lawn replaced indigenous plant life. With the advent of television—more than 40 million sets were sold between 1946 and 1955 alone—nature shows such as *Wild Kingdom* (premiering in 1963) offered suburbanites an avenue of escape from the tedious landscape outside their picture windows. Hollywood reinforced the sense that nature existed somewhere far away, out beyond the reach of land developers and real estate agents. From such a perspective, it was all too easy to justify more development in urban and suburban locales, where untouched nature no longer seemed to exist. If nature shows aided Brower and his cause, they implicitly said that nonwilderness areas were unimportant, legitimating further economic growth in those terrains.[15]

DECLARATION OF INTERDEPENDENCE

It took the work of a marine biologist named Rachel Carson to change the terms of the debate over environmental reform. Wilderness was at the heart of Leopold's and Brower's environmentalism. Carson, however, took ecology as her main point of departure.

Carson resurrected and breathed new life into a very old intellectual tradition dating back at least to John Muir (1838–1914). Muir believed that the natural world existed in a complex, interdependent harmony. Any disturbance by human beings to this smooth functioning relationship threatened to send out dangerous ripple effects, potentially undermining all semblance of natural order. In the 1950s, the influential ecologist Eugene Odum provided a scientific defense of much the same view. Odum held that ecosystems—all plant and animal organisms together with their habitat—always evolved toward, if they had not already achieved, a state of order or "homeostasis." Interfere with the ecosystem in some fundamental way, and this intricate interrelation of species and habitat might begin to unravel.

Carson's genius was to take these views and effectively popularize them in her 1962 book *Silent Spring*, a stinging critique of America's chemical dependency. She embraced the idea that all of nature was bound up in an interdependent web of life, which humankind had the potential to destroy. She then took this concern and tapped into the Cold War political climate, arguing, in effect, that the threat from pesticide use, her main concern in the book, was no different than the danger that radioactive fallout posed to human life. Touted by industry as nothing short of miraculous, pesticides boomed, their use increasing an astounding 168 percent per year between 1949 and 1968. And yet, very little scientific information existed on their possible ecological and health effects. It was this lack of knowledge that Carson sought to address in her book, calling attention to the ways in which pesticides upset nature's balance. "We spray our elms and the following springs are silent of robin song," she wrote, "not because we sprayed the robins directly but because the poison traveled, step by step, through the now familiar elm leaf-earthworm-robin cycle." Such a sequence of events reflected "the web of life—or death—that scientists know as ecology."[16]

Although she used the word sparingly in her book, Carson helped to transform *ecology* into the rallying cry of the environmental movement. Unlike *wilderness*, conceived as a world apart, the word *ecology* suggested, in a sense, the reverse—that all life was bound up in an intricate, interconnected web. Human beings, she believed, were thus part of the balance of nature, not divorced from it in the way that some wilderness advocates implied.

Needless to say, the pesticide industry mounted a massive attack against Carson and her book, at one point threatening to sue her publisher. They dismissed her as just another hysterical woman with a "mystical attachment to the balance of nature," even going so far as to brand her a Communist. But the assault did little to undermine the popularity of the book, which remained on the *New York Times* best-seller list for 31 weeks. In fact, the book, in the opinion of some, did more to galvanize the modern environmental movement than any other single publication. One historian has even called the work "the *Uncle Tom's Cabin* of modern environmentalism."[17]

In the mid-1960s, Americans received an object lesson in the meaning of ecological interdependence. A drought began in the year Carson published her book, the worst dry spell since the 1930s. This time, the precipitation deficit battered not the Southern Plains but the northeastern part of the country, from Maine south to Virginia and west to Ohio and Michigan. The drought lasted four years, focusing increasing public attention on the nation's supply of water, especially in the Great Lakes, the largest body of freshwater in the world. Lake Erie alone contains nearly 10,000 square miles of water—more than six times the size of Rhode Island. It is a vast lake, a body of water so large that it must have seemed as if nothing humankind could do would affect it in any profound way.[18]

But with the lake level falling because of the lack of precipitation, the true cost of the culture of consumption became readily apparent. Residents living in the area near Lake Erie learned that they drew their water from what amounted to one huge cesspool. Cities such as Detroit and Buffalo allowed tens of thousands of tons of untreated sewage to drain into the body of water. But it was soapsuds—skeins of foam 300 feet in places, clinging to the shore like so much cotton on Santa Claus's cheeks—that really captured the public's attention. The use of synthetic detergent ballooned over the course of the 1950s and early 1960s as more households installed automatic washing machines. The suds that washed up on the shores of Lake Erie, that had turned the lake into what *Time* magazine called "a North American Dead Sea," came from something as simple as doing the laundry.[19]

In truth, the suds were just a symptom of a far more serious problem. Detergents contained phosphates, a nutrient that, as we have already noted, caused algae to bloom like mad on the lake, only to die, decay, and drain oxygen from the water, oxygen that other life forms needed to live. By the 1960s, Lake Erie was indeed on its way to the funeral parlor and people could not help but notice.

David Blaushild, the owner of a Cleveland auto dealership, started a petition drive; when it was over about one million people lent support to his Save Lake Erie campaign. He passed the pages and pages of signatures on to Ohio Governor James Rhodes, who himself sent the package to the federal government, calling on the Department of Health, Education, and Welfare to intervene immediately. "We want action, and we want it now!" he wrote. Public outrage over the degradation of Lake Erie was boiling over. In 1969, one scientist involved in assessing the lake's ecology probably spoke for many Americans when he said: "In this day and age, in a society which is so affluent—to have to paddle in its own sewage is just disgusting."[20]

The flames that lapped the banks of the Cuyahoga River that same year confirmed for many that the nation's environmental problems had gone so far as to turn a body of water into a fire hazard. Even California, once looked on as the land of hopes, dreams, and untrammeled natural beauty, was feeling the impact of modern petroleum-based life. Several months before the Cuyahoga went up in flames, an oil spill off the coast of Santa Barbara, California, combined with strong winds to defile about 20 miles of white sand beach in this affluent community. One year after the disaster, Roderick Nash, a professor of history at the University of California at Santa Barbara, appeared on television to lecture on the ecological ills of life in modern America, calling his message a "declaration of interdependence."[21]

The tumultuous political context of the late 1960s drew even more attention to the ecological concerns raised by Carson and others. As the Vietnam War escalated, widespread suspicion of government and established, corporations like Dow Chemical, makers of napalm, dovetailed with Carson's warnings about pesticides. The feminist press, meanwhile, took to criticizing the "male-feasance" of American agribusiness, focusing on the perils of DDT, a chemical Carson singled out as especially troubling. One feminist publication lampooned the high levels of DDT found in the bodies of new mothers with a cartoon showing a woman squirting a fly with breast milk. In 1969, the *Rat*, a radical underground newspaper, observed that "the word 'ecology' had been lifted from the dusty academic shelves of abstract scientific definition." It was now "a powerful breathing consciousness . . . that no radical could avoid." In 1970, economist Robert Heilbroner declared simply, "Ecology has become the Thing."[22]

Across the country, neighborhood activism surged in response to the radical political climate and the growing media attention devoted to ecological problems. In Santa Barbara, environmental activists formed GOO, Get Oil Out, in an attempt to put an end to the drilling going on off the coast of their community. In Chicago, Paul Booth, a founder of the radical New Left organization Students for a Democratic Society, helped to form CAP, Citizens Action Program, to protest the pollution spewed by the coal-hungry Commonwealth Edison electricity company. "Think Globally, Act Locally" went the cry of these activists as they protested everything from air pollution to the building of new superhighways.[23]

Thinking in global terms became easier as people's very concept of the planet earth contracted. Just as detergents and other pollutants worked to shrink the size of the Great Lakes, once thought to be so large that no human activity could harm them, the U.S. space program accomplished a similar feat for the earth itself. In the summer of 1969, a month after the Cuyahoga ignited, Neil Armstrong became the first human being to walk on the moon. Americans began to get a clear picture of just how small and potentially vulnerable their planet was as astronauts beamed back images of the earth as seen from outer space. In 1972, the Apollo 17 astronauts took a picture of the earth, an image that astronomer Carl Sagan once called an "icon of our age." Later in the 1970s, then President Jimmy Carter remarked, "From the perspective of space our planet has no national boundaries. It is very beautiful, but it is also very fragile. And it is the special responsibility of the human race to preserve it."[24]

We may never know exactly what caused the birth of the modern environmental movement. But it might be speculated that, together, Carson's eloquent book combined with an extraordinary dry spell, a superheated political climate, a series of made-for-TV ecological disasters, plus an arresting image of the earth as seen from outer space all dramatized the elemental interdependence of life on the planet. The social and ecological underpinnings of modern consumer society, often masked by distance or suppressed by corporations, briefly made themselves seen. Many no doubt realized the impact turning on the washer could have for a distant lake. A sharpening of the links between everyday life under consumerism and its ecological consequences laid the groundwork for the emergence of a new

VULNERABLE EARTH

Four years before this 1972 picture was taken by the Apollo 17 crew, another group of U.S. astronauts orbited the moon. Their trip inspired poet Archibald MacLeish to write, "To see the earth as it truly is, small and blue and beautiful in that eternal silence where it floats, is to see ourselves as riders on the earth together." (NASA)

moral framework, one that urged Americans to take responsibility for their actions with respect to nonhuman nature. Call it the environmental movement.

THE MAINSTREAM

Although his motives were far from pure, Richard Nixon was arguably one of the greenest presidents ever to occupy the White House. In the tumultuous political atmosphere of the 1960s, it was far safer for establishment politicians to support the environment as opposed to the more threatening antiwar agenda being served up by campus radicals. No one recognized this better than Nixon. Some of the most important pieces of environmental legislation ever passed became law under his signature, beginning with the National Environmental Policy Act, which he signed—live on television—on January 1, 1970. Discussion of major federal undertakings, whether it was building a dam or constructing a highway, would no longer take place behind closed doors, but in public where everyone from environmental activists to corporations could debate the potential ecological fallout.[25]

The act marked the start of a veritable torrent of federal legislation, transforming such issues as air and water pollution, in the past dealt with, if at all, on the state and local level, into matters of national policy, creating more than a dozen important new pieces of environmental legislation. They included the Clean Air Act (1970); the Water Pollution Control Act (1972); the Federal Insecticide, Rodenticide, and Fungicide Act (1972); the Coastal Zone Management Act (1972); the Marine Mammals Protection Act (1972); the Endangered Species Act (1973); and the Energy Policy and Conservation Act (1975), which for the first time set federal fuel economy standards. To deal with industrial wastes, Congress passed the Toxic Substances Control Act (1976), the Resource Conservation and Recovery Act (1976), and the Comprehensive Environmental Response, Compensation, and Liability Act (1980), better known as the Superfund law. The Environmental Protection Agency (EPA; established in 1970) became the government's watchdog on pollution issues, eventually becoming one of the nation's largest federal agencies.

The massive legislative arsenal read like a gigantic handbook on how to counter the ills of a modern, consumption-oriented society. It dealt with everything from industrial pollutants to protecting endangered species to cleaning up the synthetic detergent problem. Although none of the legislation interfered, to any major extent, with corporate America's hold over the environment, the gains were real nonetheless.

The Clean Air Act of 1970, for example, set air quality standards for pollutants such as carbon monoxide, ozone, and lead—standards based not on what they would cost industry to attain but on a scientific determination of the risk they posed to human health. The result has been unquestionably positive for the lungs of many Americans. By the 1990s, smoke pollution fell nearly 80 percent from where it was in the 1970s, while lead emissions plummeted by 98 percent. Still, the legislation had some significant flaws. New air pollution sources received vigorous policing, but preexisting sources were "grandfathered" in under the law. Monitoring took place close to the factories producing the pollution, leading business to opt for tall smokestacks so emissions would miss the sensors and instead drift off somewhere else downwind. Nor did the initial legislation place any cap on the total amount of emissions, although later legislation regulating lead and sulfur did so.[26]

The Water Pollution Control Act of 1972 was a tougher measure, mandating permits for all businesses discharging pollutants—no grandfathering allowed. It unquestionably led to major improvements in the quality of the nation's waters. According to one 1982 estimate, the required pollution control devices had been installed on 96 percent of the industrial sources of wastewater. But because the EPA, charged with overseeing the legislation, had no authority to regulate pollution coming from such sources as hog farms and storm water runoff, some bodies of water actually experienced declines in water quality.[27]

In putting forth such environmental reforms, Congress took its cue from the American public. Never before had the citizens of this nation shown such over-

BAD AIR

Scenes like this one from 1953, showing New York City's Chrysler Building obscured by smog, were common in U.S. cities before the beginning of clean-air regulations in 1970. (Library of Congress)

whelming concern for the planet as they did in the 1970s. The decade opened with Earth Day, the brainchild of Gaylord Nelson, a Wisconsin senator, who proposed a teach-in on the environment modeled on the antiwar protests popular in the 1960s. He hired some graduate students from Harvard University to pursue the project. On April 22, 1970, an estimated 20 million people turned out for a series of demonstrations, parades, and rallies in support of ecological issues, the clearest evidence to date of environmentalism's status as a mass movement. Students at the University of Minnesota staged a mock funeral for the automobile by burying an internal combustion engine. In New York City, author Kurt Vonnegut told a crowd assembled in Bryant Park, "If we don't get our President's attention, this planet may soon die. . . . I'm sorry he's a lawyer; I wish to God that he was a biologist."[28]

Although they had little or nothing to do with Earth Day, mainstream environmental organizations benefited immensely from the upsurge of concern it symbolized. Audubon Society membership, for instance, rose from 120,000 in 1970 to 400,000 in 1980. Sierra Club membership swelled more than 46 percent over the same period. In the 15 years after 1970, participation in environmental organizations went from 500,000 to 2.5 million—powerful evidence of the public's growing interest in the environment.[29]

To advance their various causes, the groups found themselves turning increasingly to the law, especially now that the entire environmental regulatory system was open to public scrutiny. The new legislation passed in the 1970s gave these environmental organizations the opportunity to affect the debate over matters of wide-ranging ecological importance. Now the federal government had such organizations as the Environmental Defense Fund and the Natural Resources Defense Council looking over its shoulders, making sure it enforced what Congress intended.

Although aggressive litigation led to some important triumphs, the mainstream environmental groups were often beholden to corporate sponsors. Ford Foundation support for the Environmental Defense Fund and other groups, for instance, required them to present all lawsuits to a committee, chosen by the foundation, for review. A 1990 study of seven major environmental groups revealed that their boards were well stocked with executives from such notorious polluters as Exxon, Monsanto, Union Carbide, and other major corporations. And as these organizations became more corporate indentured, they became more persuaded by the logic of "win-win" solutions to environmental problems, an approach that employed market incentives, as opposed to new regulations, to compel corporate compliance. Such talk was of course a long way from the ideals and no-holds-barred approach of such early environmentalists as David Brower.[30]

GRASSROOTS

While the mainstream environmental movement has made law and legislation its focus, grassroots community groups have carved out a far more ambitious agenda, seeking both ecological justice and social empowerment. Unlike the largely white, male-dominated big green organizations, these activist groups are far more diverse, with working-class women and people of color playing the leading role.

They also have been far less compromising and less interested in wilderness, which cultivates an image of nature at some distance from the experiences of ordinary people. Instead, the groups have sought to build decent places to live by liberating their communities from the grip of corporations.

Working-class environmental concerns first began to emerge in the late 1970s with the Love Canal disaster. Located in Niagara Falls, New York, the Love Canal community was built during the 1950s on a landfill once used by the Hooker Chemical and Plastics Corporation. Some 100,000 drums of chemical contaminants lay buried at the site. In the early 1970s, a woman named Lois Gibbs moved to a bungalow in the development, thinking she was buying the American dream. She soon learned that what she had bought was a whole lot of misery. Her children fell ill with epilepsy, asthma, and blood disorders.

In 1978, a reporter did a story on the buried chemicals and their potential dangers for the people of Love Canal. It turned out that Gibbs was not alone in her troubles; other residents suffered from chronic illnesses, birth defects, and miscarriages. Banding together, Gibbs and other afflicted residents organized the Love Canal Homeowners Association to deal with the problem. But state and federal officials responded slowly to their plight, so slowly that at one point Gibbs and 500 others took two EPA officials hostage for five hours to call attention to their dilemma. Jimmy Carter eventually declared Love Canal a disaster area, and the government paid for its evacuation. Gibbs moved to Virginia and went on to found the Citizens Clearing House for Hazardous Wastes (now the Center for Health, Environment, and Justice), an organization that by the late 1980s provided support to more than 5,000 grassroots groups concerned with the effects of toxic waste on their communities.[31]

Love Canal evolved into a symbol of reckless corporate behavior, but even more importantly, it worked to galvanize women around the issue of environmental justice. One of the most successful Love Canal protests was a Mother's Day Die-In, in which women called attention to the relationship between corporate-generated toxins and reproductive health. In the wake of the New York disaster, other groups led by women arose, including Mothers of East Los Angeles and Mother's Air Watch of Texarkana, Arkansas. These activists have tended to forgo litigation for the sake of aggressive protests and publicity campaigns. The mainstream environmental organizations, Gibbs explained, ask: " 'What can we support to achieve a legislative victory?' Our approach is to ask: 'What is morally correct?' "[32]

That approach, however, has led many to brand them "overemotional" women. Cathy Hinds, from a small rural community in Maine, became concerned, correctly as it turned out, that her well water might be contaminated. When she reported her suspicions to her physician, he downplayed them and instead prescribed a tranquilizer.[33]

LOVE CANAL

Members of the Love Canal Homeowners Association protested Hooker Chemical's dumping of toxic chemicals in their neighborhood. (Buffalo Courier-Express Collection, E. H. Butler Library Archives, Buffalo State College)

To brand women environmental activists as "hysterical housewives" and deny their claims is to embrace a very narrow and unsophisticated understanding of how we learn about the natural world around us. In this view, it is absurd to think that one could learn anything about the relationship between ecology and health from housework. Yet it turns out that Hinds first suspected her water was contaminated after observing dark stains on her clothes and fainting spells among family members. One does not need to reject scientific knowledge to recognize that there are also simple ways, outside the laboratory, of gaining insight into nature.

Race was largely absent from the debate over Love Canal because the victims were primarily white working-class people. But in 1982, when an EPA-sponsored toxic waste dump was slated for Warren County, North Carolina, a poor and largely African American area, residents rose up in protest. With dump trucks loaded with contaminated soil set to roll, protesters, including many women and children, threw their bodies in the way. More than 500 people were arrested, including several civil rights leaders.

The protest resulted in a number of inquiries into the relationship between race and hazardous waste siting. Were African Americans and other people of color literally being dumped on? The evidence, generated through both government and other studies, strongly suggested that they were. One 1987 study found that three out of five blacks lived in places with abandoned toxic waste dumps.[34]

Although people of color have borne the greatest burden for toxic waste, it remains unclear as to whether such groups were explicitly targeted for abuse. It would be surprising, however, if some racism did not come into play. It is also likely that toxic waste landfills, once sited, lowered surrounding land values, drawing those who lacked the means to live elsewhere to these areas. In any case, a 1992 study pointed out that fines imposed on polluters in white areas were, on average, more than five times the fines leveled on outlaws operating in minority communities.[35]

American Indian communities also had to confront toxic waste problems. Although not directly targeted for dumping, Indian reservations often sat atop rich uranium deposits—a fact that often made them repositories of the nation's industrial poisons. Uranium mining in the Southwest began in the 1940s with the advent of nuclear energy. By 1960, some six million tons of uranium ore had been mined on Navajo lands, generating serious problems with both water and soil contamination. Perhaps not surprisingly, teenage reproductive organ cancer rates in Navajo quarry areas are 17 times the national average. In 1979, shortly after the well-known nuclear reactor disaster at Three Mile Island in Pennsylvania, a dam at the Church Rock mine in New Mexico ruptured, sending radioactive tailings spilling into the Rio Puerco River. To this day, radiation levels in the area around the spill remain high. Although at times offering resources, the mainstream environmental organizations have largely ignored the uranium issue, leaving it to small grassroots groups such as the Eastern Navajo Diné Against Uranium Mining to wage the battle.[36]

William Ruckelshaus, the EPA's first administrator, who later became the head of Browning-Ferris, a major solid waste hauling firm, once called the grassroots movement one of "the most radicalized groups I've seen since Vietnam." But the larger question is whether the efforts of the grassroots groups are effective in taming the behavior of American corporations. The available evidence suggests that they have been. In 1990, an EPA report noted that public opposition to hazardous waste sites was creating a landfill capacity problem. That no doubt encourages Lois Gibbs, who once said that her organization's goal with respect to toxic waste was "basically like plugging up the toilet." Whether fewer disposal options will translate into actual waste reduction, however, remains to be seen.[37]

JOBS VERSUS NATURE

While the grassroots groups were demanding environmental justice for the dispossessed, a radical group named Earth First! came to the defense of the plant and animal kingdom. Taking a page out of the work of Norwegian philosopher Arne Naess, members of Earth First! rejected the view that human needs should form the basis of our relationship with nature. Casting aside this shallow ecological framework, they opted instead for what Naess called "deep ecology," the view that all living organisms, both human and nonhuman, had equal claims on the earth. Philosophically speaking, they argued, human beings are no more important or valuable to life on the planet than lichens, trees, grizzly bears, or wolves are. It was, by most accounts, an extreme view. And one that eventually caused cracks to open in the Earth First! organization, as those concerned with the plight of workers worried that the focus on preserving wilderness at all costs had backfired, driving people who made a living in the woods directly into the arms of their corporate employers.

Earth First! endured its harshest test—one that cut to the core of the group's commitment, or lack thereof, to both social justice and ecological reform—in the old-growth forests of the Pacific Northwest. Located between the Pacific Ocean and the Cascade mountains and reaching from California north into Canada, these ancient, undisturbed woodlands offer a storybook picture of wilderness (perhaps explaining why the Disney company used them as the setting for many of its nature films). These majestic forests contain within them tremendous diversity—not simply trees with large diameters, but also dead and rotting trees, in addition to more than 600 different species of organisms, everything from northern spotted owls to mycorrhizal fungi. Prior to human settlement, the old growth may have covered 15 million to 24 million acres in the Pacific Northwest.[38]

As previously noted, the privately owned forestland in this region came under increasing pressure after World War II, with the suburban housing boom driving up the demand for wood. By the 1960s, the stepped-up cutting led to the inevitable exhaustion of the private forest reserves. Nor did timber companies bother with replanting before this time. A decade later, the decline led the timber industry, in league with homebuilders, to lobby the government to sell more timber rights in the national forests.

The 1980s were a pivotal decade for the old-growth regions. First, mainstream and more radical environmental groups seized on a slowly developing body of new ecological knowledge that revealed, more clearly than ever before, the perils of timber harvests for various animal species. And second, the election of Ronald Reagan in 1980 led to the appointment of federal officials who did everything in their power to increase timber cutting on national forestlands. Reagan also galvanized the environmental movement when he pushed through such long-standing critics of federal regulatory efforts as Anne Gorsuch and James Watt to take control, respectively, of environmental agencies like the EPA and the Department of Interior.

The man who had the largest say in the fate of old growth, however, was John Crowell, Jr. Reagan named Crowell, a lawyer for the Louisiana Pacific Corporation, a giant timber company, as assistant secretary of agriculture for natural resources and the environment, a position that gave him control over the Forest Service. He had barely unpacked his boxes before he called on the service to double the amount of timber it allowed companies to cut. With the U.S. economy in a recession and housing starts falling, the wood was destined for export overseas to Asia. The timber industry trained its sights on the old growth, in other words, not to meet domestic needs, but because it could make large profits by shipping unprocessed logs to foreign markets. In 1987, a record-breaking 5.6 billion board feet of timber was cut in the old growth of Washington and Oregon.[39]

It would be wrong to place all the blame for the liquidation on the Reagan administration alone. At the Forest Service, built-in incentives kept timber sales high. Under a law passed in 1930, for instance, the agency was allowed to keep nearly all of the money it made on timber sales for use in building roads and buying equipment. Meanwhile, counties made up entirely or in part of national forestland also found their financial destiny tied to the sale of federal trees. They received 25 percent of the receipts from timber sales, making them equally active proponents of cutting.

Even before the Reagan years, some members of the mainstream environmental movement had become disillusioned with the Forest Service's commercial orientation and the greens' response to it. In 1980, Dave Foreman, an ex-Marine and Wilderness Society staffer, along with several others, founded Earth First! on the premise that "in *any* decision consideration for the health of the earth must come first." Three years later, the organization—fed up with the discreet legalisms of the major environmental groups—began driving nails into trees in Oregon's Siskiyou Mountains. They reasoned that the practice of tree spiking, as it came to be called, would pose such a threat to safety—given the risk of serious injury when a saw blade struck a nail—that timber companies would place the affected areas off-limits to cutting. But since the people making the decision to proceed were not the ones who would bear the safety risk, the cutting continued. In 1987, George Alexander, a worker at the Louisiana Pacific company's mill in Cloverdale, California, used a band saw to cut into a spiked log. Shrapnel sliced through his protective facemask, breaking his jaw and knocking out his teeth. No evidence surfaced linking Earth First! to the accident, but the group's indifferent response angered many of its critics.[40]

The following year (1988), with timber cutting on federal lands booming, controversy erupted over the fate of the spotted owl. The logic behind the quest to save the owl, which makes its home in the Pacific Northwest's old growth, was as follows. Environmentalists believed, based on scientific information, that the species served as an indicator of the general health of the forest ecosystem. Save the owl and the old trees would be preserved in the process. With the U.S. Fish and Wildlife Service refusing to list the owl as endangered, 23 environmental groups filed a lawsuit arguing that the agency's actions violated the Endangered Species Act of 1973.

Initially, the environmentalists triumphed on a number of fronts. In 1988, a federal court ruled that by not adding the owl to its protected species list, the Fish and Wildlife Service failed to comply with the law. Two years later the agency listed the owl. That same year, a Forest Service report recommended that the government protect the owl by banning logging on eight million acres of Pacific Northwest land. Finally, in 1991, a federal court barred the service from selling any more timber until it came up with a plan for managing the owl and its habitat.

These developments sent shock waves through the timber industry. In a sense, however, the owl controversy gave the logging companies just the issue they were looking for to help marshal support for greater access to federal timberland. Environmentalists, they argued, were stifling economic growth and snuffing out jobs. The owl was thus the perfect scapegoat for drawing public attention away from the problematic nature of the industry itself, in particular, its tendency to overcut, eliminate jobs (either through automation or by moving its operations out of the Northwest), and export whole logs overseas. Instead the industry made it seem as if environmentalists, eager to use the fate of a measly owl to send the nation back to the Stone Age, were at the root of the region's social problems. In fact, their very own business practices, not the environmental movement, were to blame.

Beginning in the late 1980s, the timber industry set out to advance its cause by joining forces with the Wise Use movement. Founded by direct-mail fundraiser Alan Gottlieb and ex–public relations consultant Ron Arnold, who was fed up with environmentalism's assault on industry, the movement was made up of grassroots organizations dedicated to supporting economic development, preserving private property, and opposing federal interference in land-use decisions. In the tradition of the Progressive Era conservationist Gifford Pinchot, the Wise Use people stood for the responsible stewardship of the nation's resources, or so they said. Mainstream and radical groups wanted to unduly compromise the economy through wilderness preservation, but not the Wise Users, who claimed they would deftly balance nature's needs with economic imperatives.

In the Pacific Northwest, the industry backed groups such as TREES, Timber

Resource Equals Economic Stability. One timber company invited a representative from the group to address disgruntled workers in 1990. "If we let these damn preservationists have their way with our National Forests," he told the crowd, "we'll be wiping our ass with recycled toilet paper." Workers took the message to heart: Soon dead owls were found nailed to trees. One bumper sticker sold in logging towns read: "Are You an Environmentalist or Do You Work for a Living?" capturing the either-or quality (jobs versus nature) of the debate.[41]

As a result of the environmental movement's focus on wilderness, with little thought given to those living near the sacred gems, Wise Use groups were able to cast the problem in dualistic terms: One was either for saving jobs or for saving nature. It was that simple. The timber industry thus convinced many workers that their problems lay with the environmentalists—not with the corporations. Never mind that for over a decade starting in 1980, the firms had been cutting wages, shifting operations to non-union areas in the South, or moving mills to Mexico.[42]

By the early 1990s, Earth First!, detested by loggers and corporations both, was itself beginning to fracture under the stress placed on the organization by its extreme nature-centered views. Dave Foreman left the group as some members questioned whether the philosophy of deep ecology made any sense in a capitalist system riven with class conflict, where the real stakes were not whether nature would be used to advance economic growth, but how it would be used and to whose benefit. Could social justice for workers and ecological balance in the forest be made to work together? Judi Bari, the daughter of two socialists and herself a former union organizer, was one Earth First! member—opposed to tree spiking and the more general indifference to the rights of workers—who thought that they could. In the wake of the George Alexander tragedy, Bari tried to interest women and workers in the group by focusing on workplace concerns such as mill closings and safety. To advance her cause, she helped organize Redwood Summer, which took place in northern California in 1990, a nonviolent protest for both ecological and social justice modeled on Martin Luther King's civil rights demonstrations.

Bari, who died of cancer in 1997, stood up for workers and correctly discerned the limitations of environmental reform. By focusing too exclusively on preserving pristine nature and ignoring the economic implications for workers of restricting access to federal timber lands—"they can get jobs in shopping malls," one activist said coldly—these groups have forced loggers to embrace the corporate line, forfeiting on an opportunity to recruit labor to their cause.[43] And yet, loggers too have been known to hunt, fish, and hike the woods. No doubt some of them have a love for wilderness that equals the passion of any card-carrying member of Earth First! Many like nature just as much as the next environmentalist. But what they do not like, it seems safe to say, is seeing their economic interests ignored. Far less willing to strike a bargain than the mainstream groups and far more interested in melding ecological issues with social justice, activists such as Bari have at least tried to widen the focus of environmentalism to move beyond a single-minded concern with wilderness and ask what saving nature means for those who make a living in such areas.

CONCLUSION

"There is hardly a political question in the United States which does not sooner or later turn into a judicial one," Alexis de Tocqueville, the famous nineteenth-century French visitor to America, once observed. Many reform groups, of course, most notably those involved in the civil rights movement, have turned to the law to advance their respective causes. But in invoking the law in its fight for national ecological well-being, the environmental movement has taken this trend to a new level. Environmental issues have been wrapped in multiple layers of legislative and legal doctrine, as nature has been literally legalized in a way that would have been unimaginable before the 1960s. Statutes with ecological significance filled just 30 pages of the *Environmental Law Reporter* in 1970; by 1989, the number of pages had ballooned to over 800. Those laws and rules have improved air and water quality and, more generally, have worked to restrain the aggressive impulses of corporations and developers eager to put profit over ecology.[44]

Even without the long-standing history of recourse to law, it is perhaps not surprising that a movement founded on a growing awareness of the ecological interdependence of modern consumerism would turn to it to sort out responsibility when things went wrong. Under the present free enterprise system, where the real environmental costs of an activity are often shunted from the producer to a local community (as in the case of factory-style pig farming) or to the public at large, the legal arena is perhaps the only place for righting a corporation's conventional arithmetic. One of the truly seminal achievements of environmentalism has been its power to unmask the ecological consequences of human actions, a process that has at the very least brought various economic interests—from Montana mining companies to Texas oil men—face to face with the on-the-ground consequences of their decisions, whether they are willing to be held accountable for them or not.

16

PLANET U.S.A.

In 1925, automobiles rolled off the Ford Motor Company's Highland Park assembly line, outside of Detroit, at the rapid-fire pace of one every 10 seconds. Without rubber for tires, not one of them was going anywhere. The demand for rubber skyrocketed in the 1920s, the product of increasing numbers of cars and the Goodyear company's introduction of the balloon tire, an innovation that offered Americans a more comfortable ride at the cost of 30 percent more rubber than the high-pressure tires used earlier. U.S. automakers faced just one problem: Southeast Asian plantations, controlled by the British and Dutch, had virtually cornered the rubber market.

In 1927, Henry Ford set out to break the Asia rubber monopoly by purchasing, for a miniscule sum, rights to land greater than the size of the state of Delaware in the Brazilian Amazon. Rubber had long been grown here; indeed, the *Hevea* species first evolved in this region before Europeans commandeered it for use on their Asian plantations. Ford and his associates named the massive new rubber plantation—what else?—Fordlandia. Workers set to work building roads, railroads, a port, schools, churches, tennis courts, even a golf course sculpted right into the middle of the jungle. By 1929, nearly 1,500 acres of rainforest had been cleared and planted with rubber trees. Trouble, however, broke out almost immediately. Malaria, yellow fever, hookworm, and labor riots plagued the Ford complex. The most serious threat came from leaf blight, a fungal menace that the rubber trees had once adapted to by growing in a scattered fashion across the forest floor. But the imperatives of capitalist production demanded the concentration of rubber trees, allowing laborers to tap the latex without having to travel much as they went from tree to tree. Five years into the project leaf blight traumatized Fordlandia. Ford and his associates moved to a new site, but again things went wrong. Drought struck in 1938 and in 1942 swarms of caterpillars descended on the trees. In 1945, Ford, a legend in American business history, bailed out of the project, stopped in his tracks by bugs and fungi.[1]

Ford failed in his foray into the Amazon. But for every such disaster there were hundreds of success stories, projects that together have transformed the ecology of the planet. It seems safe to say that when it comes to global ecological change no country has had more far-reaching impact than the United States. Yet as Ford's travails suggest, there was nothing predestined about the success of American companies abroad. It was the product of a set of conditions that crystallized in the aftermath of World War II, a massive global economic restructuring that created an environment extremely congenial to U.S. companies wishing to do business overseas.

When one considers the environmental impact of multinational companies of American origin and adds in the effects of explicit foreign policy and banking initiatives designed to spread free markets, private property, industrial agriculture, and consumerism—not to mention the impact that domestic energy trends have had on global ecology—the term "superpower," coined to describe the postwar United States, could not be more apt.

ARMS RACE ECOLOGY

When World War II ended, another battle began, the so-called Cold War. The conflict pitted the United States and its allies in the capitalist world against the Soviet Union and other Communist states. It lasted from 1945 until the toppling of the Berlin Wall in 1989 and the later disintegration of the USSR. Often viewed as a watershed in American diplomatic history, the Cold War is rarely considered from an ecological perspective. But the events and policies that grew out of it helped to reshape global ecology all the same.

Perhaps the most direct and long-lasting environmental impact stemmed from the nuclear arms race waged by the two states. Atomic bomb making requires the

HANFORD ATOMIC RESERVATION
The Hanford nuclear weapons facility located on the Columbia River in the state of Washington irradiated Americans downwind of the site, both accidentally and on purpose. (Library of Congress)

production of plutonium, described by the man who discovered it in 1940 as "fiendishly toxic." For nearly 50 years, such U.S. weapons facilities as the sprawling Hanford Atomic Reservation in the state of Washington produced a toxic brew in the quest to defend against the Red menace. But ultimately, the main victims of atomic diplomacy turned out to be the American people themselves. The Hanford facility released into the surrounding air, water, and soil a host of deadly radionuclides, including uranium, americium, cesium, and plutonium. Between 1944 and 1947, the Hanford facility intentionally spewed into the air 417,000 curies of radioactive iodine 131, a cancer-causing agent—more than 27,000 times the amount of iodine involved in the notorious Three Mile Island disaster. What officials at Hanford were seeking to find out with this catastrophic human experiment remains, to this day, unclear.[2]

A far more extensive series of experiments occurred at the U.S. government's infamous Nevada Test Site outside of Las Vegas. Between 1951 and 1963, 126 atomic bombs were detonated, above ground, at the 1,350-square-mile complex. In 1953, a third of the 14,000 sheep located east of the site died, killed off by radiation exposure. The results were positively macabre, with some lambs born without ears or tails or with hearts positioned outside their bodies. The human toll is impossible to calculate. In the 1950s, one Atomic Energy Commission memo described those living downwind from the site as "a low-use segment of the population." The downwinders the government had in mind here were of course real, flesh and blood civilians—car salesmen, ranchers, housewives, in addition to many Native Americans dependent on deer, rabbits, and other animals and plants contaminated in the testing—human beings who lost hair, skin, teeth, lungs, and, in some cases, their lives.[3]

The biological consequences of the nuclear arms race were (and are) simply staggering. It seems hopelessly inadequate and crude to put a price tag on such far-reaching destruction. But according to one estimate, in the United States alone, it will take three-quarters of a century to achieve just a partial cleanup of defense-related contamination at a cost ranging anywhere from 100 billion to 1 trillion dollars.[4] Globally, the fact that U.S. military installations remained, for the most part, exempt from environmental regulations has left many parts of the world profoundly contaminated and with little prospect of remediation. In a sense, we are all—Americans and non-Americans alike—downwinders.

BANKING ON NATURE

As extensive and serious as this toxic legacy is, it pales when compared with the ecological consequences that have flowed from bringing as much of the planet as possible into the orbit of the free market. The first step in making the world safe for the production and consumption of commodities occurred in 1944 in the little town of Bretton Woods, New Hampshire. World leaders gathered there to form the World Bank and the International Monetary Fund (IMF), each capitalized with more than 7 billion dollars in funds. Led by the United States, which as the largest financial contributor has played the leading role in shaping these institutions, the banks were charged with helping to make the world safe for free trade.

U.S. Secretary of the Treasury Henry Morgenthau, who presided over the Bretton Woods meeting, nicely summed up the assumptions behind this new global economic order. In his view, as spelled out at the conference, limitless economic expansion was the key to world peace and stability. He urged the Bretton Woods delegates to seize the opportunity for increasing "material progress on an earth infinitely blessed with natural riches."[5] If Morgenthau had any doubts about whether the planet itself could support billions of people all driving automobiles and embracing American consumerism, he evidently held them in check. In any case, his main concern was with preserving the short-term interests of American industry through world economic integration.

Morgenthau went on to lead the World Bank, which, along with the IMF, for more than 50 years has used its financial clout to shape global economic development. Lending money at various times to more than 100 nations, the bank has funded everything from massive dams for irrigation and hydroelectric power to sweeping road systems designed to open up vast stretches of forest to economic growth. The point was to encourage poor nations to organize their economies around the export of timber, minerals, livestock, and other valuable commodities to industrialized countries.

The model for many of these projects could be found right in the United States. In 1933, the federal government embarked on an immense plan for rescuing the Tennessee River valley, an expanse of flood- and erosion-prone land mired in poverty in the heart of Appalachia. A federal agency, the Tennessee Valley Authority (TVA), oversaw an elaborate scheme, centered on flood control and generating inexpensive electricity, for breathing new life into this embattled region. The authority built more than 20 dams and later went on to construct massive coal-fired power plants designed to provide electricity to poor rural areas. Never before in American history had a federal agency been formed to manage the economic prospects of such a vast region, making it the perfect model for the new international order symbolized by the World Bank. Critics of the TVA have shown that, although the undertaking had some positive economic implications for the valley, its ecological and social costs were immense. The building of dams flooded many areas and forced thousands of people to relocate. All told, 15,000 people were displaced in Tennessee's Norris River basin alone. Meanwhile, the strip mining of coal ransacked the landscape and led to serious pollution and erosion.[6]

Similar kinds of problems emerged across the globe as developing nations constructed massive public works projects along the same lines. Thailand is a case in point. Since 1957, 26 large-scale irrigation and hydroelectric projects have been built, the majority with support from the World Bank or other outside financial institutions. The bank-sponsored Bhumibol hydroelectric dam, built in the 1960s, was typical. It generated energy, but at the expense of the forced relocation of 3,000 people.[7]

Until recently, the bank also spent years helping the Thai government focus its economy around the export of timber, rubber, palm oil, and sugar cane. Loans subsidized the creation of large-scale plantations dedicated to such export-oriented

BUILDING TVA'S DOUGLAS DAM

As the first major effort at federally sponsored regional development, the Tennessee Valley Authority built 21 dams and promoted modern agriculture based on fertilizer and pesticides. It has served as a model for the large-scale river basin development carried out in Brazil, India, and other developing countries. (Library of Congress)

agriculture. Breakneck economic development had at least two important consequences. First, as more land was cleared for agriculture, forests declined dramatically—from 53 percent to 28 percent of the nation's total land area between 1961 and the late 1980s. Deforestation, in turn, played a role in the massive floods that tore through the nation in 1988. Second, the transformation of the countryside into large-scale agricultural enterprises left millions of people with no land at all. Evicted in the name of more efficient, U.S.-style economic development, landless farmers and their families flooded into cities. The vast majority of Bangkok's prostitutes, one recent study has shown, came from such poor rural areas.[8]

The wrenching social and ecological consequences of World Bank–sponsored development stand in marked contrast to the small-scale irrigation agriculture that once dominated the countryside. Rice farmers had long been accustomed to banding together to build simple irrigation systems using mud, bamboo, and logs to channel the water. This method prevented sediment from building up, a problem caused by large-scale dams, which often completely seal off a river. These local committees also saw to it that upland forest areas were protected to ensure that the watershed would function in an ecologically sustainable way.[9]

Apart from funding major water projects, the World Bank, in league with the U.S. Agency for International Development, also pushed livestock programs. Between 1963 and 1985, the World Bank poured 1.5 billion dollars into Latin America for precisely this purpose, with much of the money channeled into raising beef for export. Feeding livestock necessitated a reorganization of the agricultural landscape. In Mexico, land that had once been planted with corn, rice, and beans for feeding people increasingly produced sorghum and other fodder crops. Such livestock programs not only compromised Mexico's food security—eventually forcing the country to import corn from Canada and the United States—but also threatened the subsistence farmers' very existence. Since it is cheaper to raise animals commercially on large farms than on small ones, the livestock industry became concentrated in fewer hands.[10]

By the 1980s, the untoward consequences of the U.S. development model had become glaringly apparent. Environmental groups in America cried out for reform. Congress passed legislation designed to rein in the World Bank and other multilateral banking institutions. It threatened to hold up their funding until they agreed to tread more lightly on the developing world. The banks were forced to hold meetings to consider their environmental performance and to include indigenous people in the planning of future projects.[11]

Reform is one thing, but an escape from the economic calculus that leads such banking institutions to treat developing nations as little more than tools of the global capitalist system is something yet again. In 1991 the World Bank's chief economist, Lawrence Summers, observed (in an internal memo leaked to the press) that Africa was "vastly underpolluted," pointing out as well that "the economic logic behind dumping a load of toxic waste in the lowest-wage country is impeccable." The World Bank claimed the memo was meant to "provoke debate" within the bank. "Your reasoning is perfectly logical but totally insane," Brazil's secretary of the environment later told Summers. In reality, most economists measure human life in terms of its ability to produce present and future wages. Dumping toxic waste where life is cheap, whether it be the barrios of Los Angeles or some poor Third World nation, remains, in the minds of many economists at least, a justifiable and economically efficient way of handling the disposal problem. No reform that Congress is likely to impose on the World Bank, or any other institution involved in global development, is likely to change the economic philosophy at the heart of the free enterprise system.[12]

THE GREEN REVOLUTION

The actions of the World Bank, the IMF, and other such U.S.-dominated global financial institutions went hand in hand with a more formal attempt to transform Third World agriculture. Beginning in the 1940s and accelerating in the 1960s and 1970s, the "Green Revolution" swept across the developing world, transforming much of it into a mirror image of U.S. industrialized farming. The transfer of high-yielding strains of various crops—especially wheat, rice, and maize—developed by U.S. plant geneticists to poor nations was at the center of this initiative. Postwar American policymakers concerned with issues of overpopulation, hunger, and the potential for political unrest that might ensue, especially in nations in close proximity to Communist states, saw in the Green Revolution a way out of these dilemmas. Solving the world's food problems was of course a worthy cause. And all the better if it could contribute to national security by making the planet safe for democracy.[13]

The United States itself had effectively gone through its own Green Revolution beginning in the 1930s. Before this point, farmers growing corn, for example, depended on the natural process of pollination to produce seeds, which in this case were the actual corn kernels themselves. When the wind blew, pollen from different varieties of corn plants became airborne and fertilized the same or other corn plants. A diverse gene pool was the result. Then, in the early part of the twentieth century, scientists took the seed from two hybrid varieties of corn—each bringing with it different genetic stock—to produce a "double-cross" hybrid. The move led to a dramatic increase in corn yields. In the 1930s, companies sold the new and improved seeds to farmers throughout the Midwest's Corn Belt. World War II, which siphoned manpower from American farms, made high crop yields increasingly important and further aided the sale of hybrid seeds. By the 1960s, the new generation of corn almost completely dominated America's fields.[14]

These varieties were a boon yield-wise, but they also narrowed the gene pool of corn (as company-bred seed eclipsed pollination) and led to the further intrusion of corporate enterprise into agriculture. The nonhybrid corn seeds could be replanted from one year to the next without diminishing yields. This was not true, however, of the hybrid varieties. Replanting culminated in a reduced harvest. Each year, farmers had to buy more from seed companies, who coveted the parent stock and breeding sequence for the double-cross, hybrid corn. Instead of producing their own corn seed or trading for it with a neighbor, farmers now found themselves more dependent than ever on outside companies for agricultural germ plasm. Seeds, like many other aspects of the natural world—land, water, and animals—had made the leap from a public good to a sheer commodity.

With the advent of commercially available hybrid corn seeds, yields, which had been declining, increased dramatically. One of the first people to realize the commercial value of the new seeds was Henry Wallace, a prominent Iowa farmer who went on to become secretary of agriculture in the Franklin Roosevelt administration. In the 1940s, Wallace convinced the Rockefeller Foundation—a private organization that believed increased food production would ward off the Communist threat and contribute to global stability—to set up an agricultural research center in Mexico. The Mexican government, faced with a floundering economy and increasing population growth, had earlier asked the United States for help with its farming sector. The Rockefeller Foundation recruited plant scientist Norman Borlaug to work on developing a new, more productive breed of wheat to boost Mexican harvests. Eventually, Borlaug, who in 1970 won the Nobel Peace Prize for his work, succeeded in breeding a set of high-yielding semi-dwarf wheat varieties. The new strains of wheat were bred to require heavy doses of nitrogen and to focus photosynthetic activity into the production of grain, as opposed to the stem of the plant. Shorter stalks also kept the wheat heads—now much larger—from toppling over.[15]

From its origins in Mexico, the Green Revolution—with the aid of the Rockefeller and Ford foundations, the United Nations, and the U.S. Agency for International Development—spread around the globe. In the context of the Cold War there was much concern in U.S. government circles that India would, like China before it, turn to Communism. But the new technical advances in plant breeding were not simply foisted on an unwilling nation; like their Mexican counterparts, the Indian government, faced with difficulties providing enough food for its growing population, welcomed the initiative. By the 1960s, Borlaug's new wheat seeds had made their way to the subcontinent, with the country becoming self-sufficient in grain by the end of the decade. In the 1970s, the Philippines, another Green Revolution convert, had achieved self-sufficiency. Across the globe, in countries such as Turkey, Iran, Iraq, Brazil, Indonesia, Kenya, Egypt, and others, new high-yielding varieties of wheat and rice were boosting food prospects. In the space of little more than a generation, the new hybridized varieties came to dominate global agriculture by the early 1990s, making up three-quarters of all the wheat and rice grown in Third World nations. A major event in the history of biological exchange had taken place.[16]

The Green Revolution unquestionably succeeded in increasing the world's supply of food. Worldwide, harvests tripled between 1950 and 1990. Malthusian concerns that population would outstrip the available food supply were proved wrong.

But in the last decade, the new breeds have had a diminished effect on world grain harvests. The Green Revolution has also had some troubling side effects.[17]

In effect, the Green Revolution took American industrialized agriculture and exported it abroad. Just as had happened to U.S. farmers beginning in the 1930s, those who worked the soil in foreign lands found that they had lost control over the agricultural gene pool, as seeds went from being a free good to a commodity that had to be purchased. Farmers who had once saved seeds and exchanged them freely among themselves now had to figure out how to pay for the expensive new varieties.[18]

The new generation of higher yielding seeds also undermined the nutrient cycle. In India, for instance, rice was once raised for food but also to produce fodder, which, when fed to livestock, resulted in valuable manure for maintaining soil fertility. The new Green Revolution varieties—which had less stalk and more grain—broke up this endless cycle of nutrient transmission and substituted a more costly and ecologically destructive one-way production system. Basic agricultural inputs like seeds, fertilizer, and pesticides now had to be purchased to produce a single, commercially viable product: grain. Nitrogen-based fertilizer was especially crucial to the success of the new dwarf species. "If I were a member of your parliament," Nobel laureate Borlaug told Indian politicians in 1967, "I would leap from my seat every fifteen minutes and yell at the top of my voice, 'Fertilizers! . . . Give the farmers more fertilizers!'" By 1980, India was importing 600 percent more fertilizer than in the late 1960s. As fertilizer use boomed, lakes and rivers suffered increased pollution, as some of the chemicals missed their mark.[19]

Ultimately, the Green Revolution dramatically reduced genetic diversity. Countless ecologically adapted, locally grown species of wheat and rice were replaced with just a handful of varieties. By the mid-1980s, the thousands of different kinds of rice once grown in the Philippines gave way to just two Green Revolution species.[20]

The Green Revolution, in conjunction with the increased mechanization of farming, also encouraged monoculture. This trend led, as single-crop farming almost always does, to increased problems with pests. Beginning in the late 1960s, a bacterial blight followed by the tungro virus struck the new dwarf rice in Southeast Asia. Infestation led, predictably, to greater reliance on pesticides. In the Philippines, pesticide imports quadrupled between 1972 and 1978 alone. Ultimately, the Green Revolution forced Third World nations down the path of chemical dependency, producing the same energy-intensive agriculture that had come to reign in modern America.[21]

Increased grain yields, many have argued, were worth the ecological costs. By the 1970s, for example, peasants in Malaysia, who for centuries had lived under the specter of famine, had enough rice to last the entire year. In the Philippines, grain harvests improved so much that by the late 1970s the country was actually exporting rice. The benefits of the increased yields, however, seem to have bypassed the Philippine people, who remained one of the most poorly fed groups in all of Asia. Similarly, in India, wheat yields in the Punjab boomed in the 1960s while, at the same time, the number of people living in poverty actually increased. Even in Malaysia, a supposed success story, the results of the revolution, upon further investigation, proved far more mixed. The greatest profits from the revolution went to those with the means to afford large amounts of land and capital, contributing to increased social inequality.[22]

DEAD WOOD

Private enterprise also took its toll on the Third World, especially in tropical environments where rainforest capitulated to the rising demands of American consumer culture. In the 70 years following U.S. victory in the Spanish-American War—a struggle that gave the nation its first overseas empire—American business poured into Latin America, various Pacific islands, and, to a lesser extent, Africa.

To Hawaii and the Philippines went U.S. sugar corporations to carve out plantations—driven by the doubling in per capita consumption of the sweetener between 1880 and 1915—transforming diverse ecosystems into giant agricultural empires founded on the harvesting of just a single crop. In Costa Rica, Ecuador, Guatemala, and other Latin American counties, companies such as United Fruit and Standard Fruit created "banana republics" to satisfy the cravings of American consumers (some 95 percent of whose households purchased bananas by the 1970s). In the 1950s, the firms introduced a more disease-resistant species of banana, one that also required increasing amounts of pesticides and fertilizer to be productive.[23]

Meanwhile, earlier in the century rubber and tire magnate Harvey Firestone trained his sights on Liberia. He succeeded where Henry Ford had failed. By 1960, he had amassed the largest rubber plantation on the face of the earth, a 74,000-acre enterprise that came at the expense of hardwood forest, as well as the Africans from whom the Liberian government appropriated land for the project.[24]

And then there was the demand for beef so that all those American baby boomers could have their hamburgers, TV dinners, and luncheon meat—meals that resulted in an assault on the rainforests of Central America. In the 1960s and 1970s, U.S. multinationals opened nearly 30 new meatpacking plants in such countries as Honduras, Costa Rica, Guatemala, and Nicaragua, a move that encouraged local oligarchs to acquire more cattle and plant more pasture. Between 1950 and the early 1980s, the amount of land devoted to cattle increased from just an eighth to more than a third in Costa Rica alone. Tropical forest equivalent to roughly the size of the entire nation of India disappeared in the period between 1960 and 1990. That tremendous change in the planet's land cover came mainly as a result of the voracious American appetite for consumer goods, from instant coffee to tires and banana splits.[25]

Compounding the ecological effects of direct U.S. economic intervention abroad were the indirect consequences of global economic integration that came with the lending of money to "improve" life overseas. Loans for building dams, roads, and acquiring American-produced goods may have raised the standard of living of some in the Third World, but the money also had to be paid back. As those loans increased, developing countries felt compelled to liquidate whatever natural capital they had to earn the money needed to service all their debt.

In the 1960s, American companies, selling everything from construction equipment to pesticides, found that U.S. banks, both big and small, were eager to lend money to developing countries to facilitate these transactions. Then, in 1973, war broke out between Egypt and Israel, and, in just a few months, oil prices increased fourfold as Arab petroleum producers sought to retaliate against the United States for siding with the Israelis. Money flooded into the Organization of Petroleum Exporting Countries, funds that developing nations, now faced with higher prices for oil and consumer goods, desperately needed. U.S. and other Western banks, acting as intermediaries, lent Third World countries money like there was no tomorrow (especially after 1979 when oil prices doubled again)—money that would be repaid by the sale of natural resources.[26]

But there was a tomorrow. The easy money could not and would not last forever. A global recession in the 1980s dampened demand for such commodities as wood and minerals that the struggling nations were counting on to generate the exchange to pay back their debt. The Third World debt problem soon assumed crisis proportions. Between 1982 and 1990, developing countries paid a staggering 1.3 trillion dollars to creditor nations. To help these nations meet their financial obligations, the World Bank and the IMF did what came naturally: They lent them more money. In exchange, the banks forced the debtor nations to reform their economies, to remove barriers to trade and government subsidies, bringing them more into line with the free market ideals so dear to the industrialized world. Stuck on a debt treadmill, developing countries became even more dependent on the export of commodities—timber, fish, minerals—to pay back their loans.[27]

It would be wrong to simply assume that increasing debt meant decreasing environmental quality. The relationship is not quite so clear-cut. But with respect to deforestation at least, a relatively strong correlation does seem to exist. One study of the 24 largest debtor nations found that two-thirds of them experienced major deforestation in the 1980s. Brazil, for example, the largest debtor nation, had to come up with 12 billion to 14 billion dollars in interest payments each year by the late 1980s. To raise that kind of money the country turned to soybeans, a cash crop in demand worldwide. But to grow soybeans on that scale, a significant amount of land in the agriculturally rich southern part of the country had to be dedicated to large-scale commercial farming. And before that could happen, the peasants living there had to be relocated. Thus the Brazilian government, with loans from the World Bank for a road-building project, urged farmers in the south to migrate north to the Amazon, where land was plentiful. There was only one problem: The land was covered with trees. By the mid-1980s, the forests of the

Brazilian Amazon were under attack. The burning done to clear them was so extensive and intense that it could be seen from outer space.[28]

Brazil was not alone in its debt and deforestation woes. Nations such as Costa Rica, Ghana, and the Philippines also liquidated woodlands to generate greater foreign exchange earnings in the decades after 1960. Tropical forests, one of the most biologically diverse areas on the planet, declined by a third between 1960 and 1990. As we have seen, not all the clearing can be blamed on the Third World debt crisis. But one study has estimated that reducing a nation's debt by 1 billion dollars could decrease deforestation by anywhere from 20 to 385 square miles.[29]

CARBON ACCOUNTING

It would be unfair to blame the United States alone for bringing on debt-driven deforestation or the other ecological problems that have stemmed from spreading economic development to the far reaches of the globe. Other industrialized nations—Japan, Britain, Germany, and France, among others—must shoulder some of the responsibility as well. But with respect to one aspect of global environmental change, America stands alone. By the end of the twentieth century, the United States used more energy per capita than any other nation in the world, twice the rate of Sweden, roughly three times that of Japan or Italy. As of 1988, the United States, with just five percent of the earth's population, consumed 25 percent of all the world's oil and released roughly a quarter of all the world's atmospheric carbon. That last fact made America the carbon capital of the planet.[30]

Back about 4.5 billion years ago, when the earth was formed, roughly 95 percent of the atmosphere consisted of carbon dioxide. The emergence of plant life, however, changed the planet's atmospheric composition. Plants, through the process of photosynthesis, absorbed carbon dioxide. Carbon was drawn out of the atmosphere and settled in the earth's vegetation, which eventually died, decomposed, and formed coal and oil. Meanwhile, the atmosphere's carbon dioxide load declined dramatically to the point where it composed less than one percent of the planet's total.

With the onset of industrialization and the burning of fossil fuels, the earth's previous atmospheric history was sent into reverse. Instead of being drawn out of the air, carbon was now extracted from the ground and launched into the sky once again. In the United States, the largest surge in energy consumption occurred between the late 1930s and the 1970s, ballooning by some 350 percent. Americans began using more oil and natural gas to meet their industrial, agricultural, and everyday needs for transportation and housing. Oil and natural gas contain less carbon than coal or wood, but this small piece of good news was more than outweighed by the huge increase in demand for electricity and fuel as the nation's economy became more consumption-oriented. In 1950, Americans drove three-quarters of all the world's automobiles. They lived increasingly, as we have seen, in high-energy suburban homes, with inefficient electric heaters and air conditioners. A 1970s color television, left on for the four hours a day that a household on average watched, was the energy equivalent of a week's worth of work for a team of horses. U.S. energy consumption slowed in the 1970s and 1980s, as manufacturers introduced more efficient appliances. Still, by the late 1980s, Americans consumed more petroleum than Germany, Japan, France, Italy, Canada, and the United Kingdom did *together*.[31]

Burgeoning fossil fuel use in the twentieth century left its mark on the carbon history of the earth. But deforestation also added to the atmosphere's carbon load. Forests normally serve as vast "carbon sinks," producing oxygen while keeping carbon dioxide in check. The massive clearing of forests in the United States early in the century, however, combined with the huge increase in postwar tropical deforestation (in which much of the wood was burned, releasing carbon dioxide in the process), has helped to reshape atmospheric conditions. In 1900, carbon dioxide levels measured about 295 parts per million (ppm). By 1950, that figure had increased to 310 to 315 ppm, rising to roughly 360 ppm by 1995, courtesy of the double punch provided by both fossil fuel consumption and deforestation.[32]

Carbon dioxide, in combination with other greenhouse gases such as methane and ozone, traps the sun's heat. In the course of a century (1890 to 1990), the average surface temperature of the earth increased by 0.3 to 0.6 degrees Celsius. That temperature rise, which has lengthened the growing season in parts of the northern hemisphere, could have happened naturally, although it bears pointing out that such a change is unheard of in the last 600 years of human history.[33]

What is perhaps most remarkable about the global warming issue is how quickly it has become the focus of national concern. It was not all that long ago that global cooling occupied the attention of U.S. political leaders. As recently as the 1970s, a number of extreme weather events, including freezing conditions in Florida, produced anxiety over a temperature decline. A spate of publications with such titles as The Cooling (1976) and Forests, Famines and Freezes (1977) filled the bookstores. In 1974, the CIA even issued a report that assessed how a decrease in temperature would affect America's geopolitical prospects.[34]

During the 1980s, however, the advantage shifted to the global warming theorists, partly as a result of the extraordinary drought and heat wave of 1988, a year, President George Bush later said, when "the earth spoke back." In June of that year, climate scientist James Hansen went before Congress to say that he was "99 percent confident" that the greenhouse effect was contributing to global warming. Almost overnight, anxiety about rising temperatures captured the attention of the American public.[35]

From the outset, environmentalists seized on the postulated human role in global warming as a means of advancing a variety of goals, from protecting air quality to preserving forestland. Although evidence showing humankind's part in the problem continues to mount (and a recent study reported that human influence accounted for 75 percent of the increase in average global temperature over the last century), scientists still cannot say definitively what accounts for the warming trend. Changes in global ocean currents or in the amount of energy emitted by the sun could also be at work.[36]

By focusing almost exclusively on the suspected, but until recently not fully verified, human role in the warming, the environmental movement has allowed industry—oil, gas, coal, and auto companies, primarily—to cast the entire problem as a theory in need of more research. More studies, not serious action to reduce fossil fuel use, goes their cry. But scientists are not debating whether global warming has occurred; that is accepted. It is the cause of the warming and future projections about how much the earth will heat up that divides them. U.S. industrial interests have papered over the areas of scientific agreement and instead engaged in a concerted campaign to mislead the American public. In the early 1990s, the Information Council on the Environment, a group made up of coal and utility companies, hired a public relations firm to, in its own words, "reposition global warming as theory rather than fact."[37]

The U.S. auto industry has also played a role in this whitewash, financing lobbying groups set up to dismiss global climate change and staging an aggressive campaign to hold the line on what is probably the single most important factor in carbon emissions: fuel economy. In the 1980s, U.S. carmakers succeeded in getting the federal government to relax fuel economy standards by arguing that they would have to close down factories to meet stricter requirements. In 1973, when the energy crisis began, American automobiles averaged about 13 miles per gallon of gasoline (MPG). By the early 1990s, that number had increased to almost 27 MPG. That seems like a significant increase, yet it works out to a less than one mile to the gallon improvement per year. Moreover, since the number of vehicle miles traveled doubled between 1970 and 1990 to 2.2 trillion miles, the gain in fuel efficiency has been entirely wiped out. The improvement in efficiency, in any case, was largely the result of legislation passed in 1975 that established "corporate average fuel economy" or CAFE rules, allowing automakers to produce any kind of car as long as the vehicles when averaged met the MPG standards set by the federal government.[38]

In 1992, Bill Clinton campaigned for president on the promise that he would increase the CAFE standard to 45 MPG. His commitment to a fuel economy increase grew out of his concern with the question of global warming. While Clinton campaigned, then President Bush signed a global warming treaty at the 1992 Earth Summit in Rio de Janeiro, Brazil. Under the treaty, industrialized nations agreed by the year 2000 to voluntarily cut back their carbon dioxide emissions to the level they were at in 1990. To meet this goal, U.S. vehicles would need to be three to four times more efficient than they were, averaging something on the order of 80 to 90 MPG.[39]

The auto industry was not willing to seek a dramatic increase. Indeed, it even balked at Clinton's more modest 45 MPG goal. But when elected, rather than stand up to Detroit, Clinton caved in. In 1993, the administration announced that the federal government would team up with American automakers to produce a new, super-efficient car. Instead of raising fuel economy standards—the quickest way to reduce carbon dioxide—there would be more research and development. "This is the sensible approach to global warming," declared Robert Eaton, Chrysler's chairman, "not an international treaty based on inconclusive science that would have no chance of solving the problem (if we have one)."[40]

The new clean car initiative has thus far done nothing to aid in the global warming dilemma, although it may have helped appease a few environmentalists. It also, according to one former auto official, diverted attention from what has become the most important development in automotive history in the last 20 years: the sport utility vehicle or SUV. In 1997, when the parties to the earlier Rio treaty sat down in Kyoto, Japan, to work out binding carbon emission standards for industrialized nations, the New York Times ran an article attacking SUVs and other light trucks as the epitome of American excess. These vehicles guzzled gas, coughed pollution, and made the typical sedan look like a wondrous green machine by comparison.[41]

The SUV pollution problem stemmed from a simple fact: Light trucks were excluded from the 1975 fuel economy legislation because, it was argued, farmers and construction workers used them for business purposes. In fact, the trucks have long functioned in the same capacity as cars. When Chrysler rolled out its first minivan in the 1980s, it took advantage of this loophole to evade fuel economy standards.[42]

By the 1990s, U.S. carbon emissions were on the rise. Not only were Americans spending more time on the road, they were traveling increasingly in the least fuel-efficient vehicles. Minivans, SUVs, and pickup trucks constituted some 40 percent of all vehicles sold in the United States. In 1999, when Ford unveiled a gigantic new SUV, the Excursion, a more than 18-foot-long behemoth that, depending on engine size, gets between 10 and 18 MPG, it advertised the truck as "a low-emission vehicle." Not to be outdone, the aptly named Freightliner company, a division of Daimler-Chrysler, recently announced plans for the biggest SUV ever, a truck that will get a meager 10 miles to the gallon. The Unimog, as it is called, stands nearly as tall as a basketballhoop and weighs a whopping 12,500 pounds, roughly the equivalent of four Toyota Camrys. Bigger may be better, as Detroit claims, but rarely is it cleaner. Today, the average fuel economy of all new cars and trucks sold in the United States during the 2001 model year remains at its lowest level in two decades.[43]

In a nation where driving and the freedom to pollute have become virtual inalienable rights, it is no surprise to find significant resistance to a global accord that would force the nation to conserve. In 1997, the U.S. Senate voted 95–0 against ratifying any global warming treaty that did not require developing nations themselves to reduce carbon emissions, even though Americans consumed on average somewhere between 50 and 100 times the energy of someone from Bangladesh.[44]

Another blow to the carbon cycle occurred in the year 2000 at a meeting in the Netherlands, when an attempt to put the finishing touches on a global warming treaty collapsed. U.S. and European negotiators reached a stalemate as the talks broke down over carbon accounting. The United States sought to use its expansive forests as a way of offsetting its enormous carbon emissions. In other words, rather than cut fossil fuel use through fuel economy increases, the Americans wanted credit for the nation's tree cover. The trading of carbon rights was precisely the type of win-win approach that mainstream environmental groups in the United States had long advocated in an attempt to give business an incentive to conserve. In Europe, however, where environmentalists have taken a more uncompromising stance with industry, no such bargains exist. To the Europeans, what the Americans proposed looked like little more than a scheme for evading responsibility for cleaning up the global atmospheric commons. "We have strong interest groups in German society," said one conference negotiator. "What shall I tell them if the United States makes a fire road in a forest and flies airplanes over it and says that it is an emissions project? They'd say you're ridiculous."[45]

PIRATES, PATENTS, AND PLANTS

Global warming is hardly the only environmental issue around which the United States has run afoul of its counterparts in Europe and the Third World. Another major recent source of conflict has centered on the emerging field of biotechnology.

In 1973, two U.S. biologists, Stanley Cohen and Herbert Boyer, combined genetic material from two different species of living organisms that, on their own, would not normally reproduce with each other. The new biotechnology, as it was called, allowed scientists to manipulate genes and to introduce new and potentially valuable traits into plants and animals.

It was not until the 1980s, however, that the commercial value of biotechnology—which some have compared to the discovery of fire—began to be realized. Investor interest awaited the development of a brave new legal world, one where living organisms could be patented and owned, giving corporations an incentive to finance research and development in this promising field. At the time Cohen and Boyer made their discovery, a patent could be secured for plants such as fruit trees and strawberries (under federal legislation passed in 1930) and for crops bred with seeds such as wheat and soybeans (under the 1970 Plant Variety Protection Act). Then in 1972, a scientist from General Electric tried to expand the reach of the law by patenting a microscopic organism, a type of bacteria that broke down crude oil and mopped up tanker spills. The U.S. Patent and Trademark Office turned down his request. In 1980, however, the U.S. Supreme Court, in a five-to-four decision, ruled that the oil-eating bacterium was "patentable subject matter." Wall Street was elated. New public offerings of biotechnology stocks surged.[46]

The Supreme Court's decision was among the more far-reaching attempts to commodify nature in American history. The decision marked the culmination of several hundred years spent forcing the natural world into the straitjacket of private property, a process that began as far back as the seventeenth century when the colonists arrived and put up fences in an attempt to exclusively own the land.

Armed with the legal tools necessary to fully capitalize on their investment, biotechnology firms set about researching and developing new plant and animal species. They justified such endeavors as part of the long-standing effort to feed a hungry world. With the Green Revolution having run its course, they argued, an opportunity existed to boost agricultural yields and help impoverished children worldwide. "Worrying about starving future generations won't feed them. Food biotechnology will," read one advertisement by Monsanto, a leader in the field.[47]

But, in truth, feeding the malnourished has never been the driving force behind biotechnology. Profits, more than people, motivated this bold new science. Giant multinational corporations such as Monsanto and Du Pont have tried to cater to consumption-driven economic imperatives, while hooking farmers on pesticides and other chemicals sold by these very same companies. Early efforts focused on products that would ship well and appeal to consumers, such as tomatoes genetically programmed to ripen more slowly and taste better. More profitable has been the effort to develop genetically modified crops such as soybeans, which are mainly fed, not to people, but to livestock. The soybeans are engineered to survive in the face of large pesticide applications. (In the United States, pesticide use on animal feed is not as strictly regulated as it is on crops meant for direct human consumption.)

Monsanto introduced an entire line of crops designed to tolerate heavy doses of the company's most popular pesticide product. Farmers can funnel the pesticide into sprinkler systems and spray far and wide, killing weeds without worrying about harming the crops. In return, the company requires customers to sign an agreement forbidding them from saving any genetically modified seeds produced for replanting, from sharing the company's patented seeds with neighbors, and from using any pesticide except the one sold by the company itself. It has even hired Pinkerton detectives in the United States and retired Canadian Mounted Police across the border to handle those who break the rules.[48]

In the United States, biotechnology's ecological impact has been limited, mainly because the Ice Age deprived much of the continent of biodiversity already. But history shows that introducing new, nonnative species, while potentially highly advantageous from an economic perspective, can also have unpredictable, at times devastating, results. The chestnut blight, gypsy moths, and other problematic fungi and insects have demonstrated the risks associated with introducing new plants and animals into nonnative U.S. habitats.

To date, nearly all of the newly patented biotech crops have been planted in the United States, Canada, and Argentina. But developing countries, many of which are far more biologically diverse than the industrialized nations, are also feeling the effects. Realizing the genetic gold mine still to be found in Third World countries, "bioprospectors" from the United States have set off to strike it rich abroad.

Consider, for example, the neem tree found in India. Various parts of the tree have long been used there to treat a variety of medical ailments, as well as to fend off locusts, boll weevils, and other pests. In the early 1970s, a U.S. citizen imported neem seeds in an attempt to use them to develop a pesticide. He eventually sold his patents on the tree to W. R. Grace, the multinational corporation, which went on to patent a number of solutions derived from the tree's seeds. Although Indian farmers have long been aware of the tree's valuable uses, one Grace executive characterized such local, nonscientific efforts as an exercise in "folk medicine."[49]

From corporate America's perspective, Third World genetic material is often thought of as part of the "common heritage of mankind," a gift of nature. In reality, the thousands of plant species once found in these nations (prior to the Green Revolution's narrowing of seed stock) did not evolve on their own; they were the product of countless hours of labor, much of it conducted by peasant women who used kitchen gardens to breed and manage plant and animal life for domestic uses. "God didn't give us 'rice' or 'wheat' or 'potato,'" Suman Sahai, an Indian opponent of bioprospecting, has observed. Peasants did, working diligently over thousands of years to develop domesticated species from wild ones.[50]

Unwilling to credit such labors, U.S. corporations have sought to make the entire globe yield before the force of American patent law, with its predilection for private property in nature. In 1984, one Du Pont biotechnology executive called for "international conventions that would provide greater uniformity with respect to patentability." By the 1990s, the United States had largely succeeded, through a world trade agreement, in forcing other nations to grant at least some protection to patented plant species. Vandana Shiva, a prominent Indian environmental activist, has been one of the most outspoken critics of this trend. She observes that the word *patent* derives from the *letters patent* granted to Columbus and other explorers as they set off to conquer and colonize the "New World." The parallel she draws with the colonization process is especially apt. Recall that the European colonists found what they took to be vast stretches of empty lands when they first settled North America in the seventeenth century. That assumption allowed them to justify the conquest of Native American soil by assuming they were "improving" what had formerly been "waste." Such a view overlooked the ways in which native peoples made use of these lands, outside the private property framework. Now U.S. multinational companies are seeking, following in the footsteps of their colonial ancestors, to define Third World genetic material—the product of countless hours spent domesticating—as just another wasted resource in need of improvement. International conventions confirming this outlook, according to Shiva, amount to little more than "biopiracy."[51]

People in developing countries are not acquiescing to this assault on the fruits of their labor. In 1993, some half million Indian farmers gathered on Gandhi's birthday to protest the patenting of the neem seed by U.S. multinationals. Five years later, an Indian farm association, which claimed 10 million members, kicked off its "Cremate Monsanto" campaign. Nor is the opposition limited to India alone. Farmers in Brazil have destroyed fields filled with genetically modified soybeans, and the Mexican government has banned the importation of biotech corn altogether.

In Europe, where the opposition to genetically modified food has emerged the strongest, José Bové, the leader of a French farmers union, a man who in 1999 rammed his tractor into a McDonald's to symbolize his opposition to corporate America's takeover of the food supply, called genetically modified food "the symbol of a system of agriculture and a type of society that I refuse to accept." Bové makes clear that his opposition to "progress" in agriculture is not based on some romantic notion that life was better in the past. He objects, instead, he says, "because of concern for the future, and because of a will to have a say in future developments." In principle, he is not against research. Indeed, those who want to end biotechnology because they are seeking to preserve the integrity and purity of various organisms are in denial about the long-standing efforts to domesticate life forms for survival's sake. Bové rejects such starry-eyed and ahistorical notions as these. His concern is that by applying laboratory research at the ground level willy-nilly, without fully contemplating the tradeoffs, corporations risk leading us all down a one-way street, making it impossible to back up and respond to new ecological challenges as they arise.[52]

THE FUTURE

In 1994, when McDonald's opened up a restaurant in Kuwait, the line at the drive-up window stretched some seven miles down the road. In a country whose name is synonymous with oil, perhaps no one felt all that concerned about the traffic tie-up.

By the time it reached Kuwait, the American-based McDonald's Corporation had been exporting its stores abroad for almost three decades. In 1967, the fast food giant took its first steps in the direction of globalization, opening restaurants in Canada and Puerto Rico. By the late 1970s, the company had 5,000 stores in operation across the world, from Asia to Europe. A generation later, the number reached 21,000, as the chain sold hamburgers and French fries to people in over 100 countries. Noting the fabulous popularity of the Golden Arches outside the United States, the company's president for international operations observed that the hamburger franchises served "as a symbol of something—an economic maturity." It might also be said that the company signified the very embodiment of American consumer capitalism and the thorough commercialization of the world's food supply, with all its attendant social and ecological consequences.[53]

The amount of waste generated by this one corporation is sobering. According to the company's director of environmental affairs, by the 1990s each McDonald's restaurant disposed of 140 pounds of packaging waste each day, not counting the material used to wrap its burgers and fries and thrown out by customers themselves. Globally, that adds up to a total of a billion pounds of garbage per year.[54]

On the one hand, McDonald's added to the world's garbage woes; on the other, it put pressure on the planet's already stressed forest reserves. It takes, according to one calculation, 800 square miles of forest—that is, not woodland chopped down, but the amount of land in trees, some harvested, some still maturing—to supply the company's paper needs. That is an area equivalent in size to more than 450,000 football fields, all to supply paper to just one corporation. As it is, however, the company tapped forests across the globe from North America to Scandinavia to the Czech Republic, embattled woodlands all of them.[55]

It is one thing for people in a small country like Kuwait—population approximately two million—to pile into their cars and wait in line at a fast food restaurant. A more serious concern is what would happen, say, if the majority of the Chinese population—in excess of a billion—decided that they too want a chance at the American dream.

In fact, to a large extent, the Chinese are already headed down this path. The free market reforms put in place by Deng Xiaoping in the 1980s openly encouraged people to embrace American-style consumerism with its cars, refrigerators, and air conditioners. In the decade following 1986, Chinese consumption of substances damaging to the ozone layer increased from 3 to 18 percent of the worldwide total. The frenetic pace of economic growth over the last two decades is transforming China into one of the greatest polluters on the face of the earth. In 1995 alone, the burning of coal—the country's number one energy source—spewed more than 800 million tons of carbon dioxide into the air. One Chinese energy researcher no doubt spoke for many of his compatriots when he said: "It is just as hot in Beijing as it is in Washington DC. You try to tell the people of Beijing that they can't buy a car or an air-conditioner because of the global climate-change issue."[56]

But the news from overseas is not all gloom and doom. In 2001, U.S. researchers reported that since the mid-1990s, while China's gross domestic product surged 36 percent, its carbon dioxide emissions actually declined a full 17 percent. "There is good basis to argue," reads a report by one U.S. environmental group, "that China has done more to combat climate change over the past decade than has the United States."[57] The Chinese example is living proof that the royal road to consumption—for all its ecological problems—does not necessarily have to be paved with disaster.

CONCLUSION

DISNEY TAKES ON THE ANIMAL KINGDOM

On April 22, 1998, Earth Day, the Walt Disney Company, the same corporation that created Mickey Mouse, Bambi, and Dumbo, took a plunge into the real live world of nature. On 500 acres of erstwhile cow pasture in central Florida, the company opened Animal Kingdom, a nature theme park that transformed a landscape of palmettos and scrub into African savanna and other exotic terrains, replete with nearly four million new plants, including 1,800 different species of mosses, ferns, and perennials, hundreds of different kinds of grasses, plus more types of animals than most people encounter on a vacation to Africa, from antelopes to zebras. Indeed, Animal Kingdom offers such a realistic rendering of Africa's terrain that when South African ambassador Franklin Sonn visited it in 1998, he exclaimed, "This is the bush veldt. This is my home."[1]

Disney's Animal Kingdom is perhaps the logical end point of a culture that has been transforming various aspects of the natural world into commodities for some 400 years. The process began with the early American colonists who used the institution of private property, unknown in North America before then, to place a price on the land. In the centuries that followed, everything from beavers, trees, and pigeons to water, buffaloes, and garbage was drawn into the world of exchange. To a culture so bent on commodification, even the very concept of nature can be packaged up and sold to anyone with the 44 dollars that it takes to buy admission to the Disney wildlife park.

But do not for even a moment imagine that nature has come to an end in this supercharged commodity culture. The point of this book has been to show the ways in which nature figures as a force in American history. Even such a thoroughly contrived and artificial environment as the Animal Kingdom cannot escape the constraints imposed by nonhuman nature. Visitors pay to see animals, but Disney, try as it might, cannot guarantee its guests that the creatures will always perform on cue. The company may even be its own worst enemy, creating such a lush expanse of vegetation that the animals now have more places to hide. Worse still, local birds such as vultures and crows—not ones to turn down the offer of a free meal on Disney's tab—often horn in on the food that attendants spread liberally around the park. And what to do with all the animal droppings has proved a major headache. In one 18-month period, the park's wildlife produced 1,680 tons of manure. Gardeners carried off some for use as fertilizer, but Disney had to pay to have the remainder hauled away to a county landfill.[2] The Disney company has plenty of tricks up its sleeve for entertaining parkgoers, but it has yet to figure out a way to toilet train an elephant.

In a sense, the travails of Disney's Animal Kingdom are not all that different from the problems faced long ago by Indians practicing agriculture in New England, as they fended off crows and blackbirds, or the dilemmas that nineteenth-century southern rice planters encountered with bobolinks, or those of the suburban homeowner today, who awakens to find that a rabbit has eaten the leaves off a newly planted shrub. No culture is in complete control of its ecological destiny.

One of the central concerns of historians over the last two generations has involved the issue of agency, that is, the question of how much efficacy human beings have had in shaping their lives and that of society around them. Some of the best historical writing has shown that despite powerful social and economic forces—from the institution of slavery to the modern corporation—Americans have improvised in ways that have allowed them to make history on their own terms while reshaping, at least to some extent, the very same economic structures that constrained them in the first place. Examples of how Americans have dealt with larger structural forces in innovative ways range all the way from slaves singing songs in the fields to inspire community and combat racial oppression to modern-day wage workers doubling-up jobs to give themselves a brief respite from the monotony of the assembly line.[3]

But even these more sophisticated efforts at describing human agency have ignored the environment and implicitly conveyed the idea that people have always had their way with the natural world. For the last century, most historians have written books as if natural forces simply did not matter. Our journey here, from the Jamestown colonists blundering ashore in a time of severe drought to the wet spell that initially prompted droves of pioneers to take up farming in the American West to Henry Ford's failed Brazilian rubber project, suggests that, in fact, we need to rethink our assumptions about the role of nature in history. The stories that have unfolded across these pages demonstrate that it is quite simply wrong to view the natural world as an unchanging backdrop to the past. Nature can upset even the best-laid, most thoroughly orchestrated plans.

As historians and citizens we need to embrace a more humble view of human agency. We must acknowledge the unpredictability involved in incorporating nature into human designs and, in so doing, bring natural forces to the fore of the historical process. As Marx wrote, people "make their own history, but they do not make it just as they please."[4] They butt up against imposing social and economic forces, to be sure, but also ecological factors as formidable as the ones Marx called our attention to more than 100 years ago. When it comes to the human control of nature, beware: Things rarely turn out the way they are supposed to. The wind shifts, the earth moves, and, now and again, when you least expect it, a flock of birds swoops in for a meal.

PROLOGUE: ROCKS AND HISTORY

1. Alfred Crosby, *Ecological Imperialism: The Biological Expansion of Europe, 900–1900* (New York, 1986), 305–306.
2. Charles B. Hunt, *Natural Regions of the United States and Canada* (San Francisco, 1974), 203.
3. Quoted in Tim Flannery, *The Eternal Frontier: An Ecological History of North America and Its Peoples* (New York, 2001), 267.

CHAPTER 1: WILDERNESS UNDER FIRE

1. Jared Diamond, *The Third Chimpanzee: The Evolution and Future of the Human Animal* (New York, 1992), 339.
2. Tim Flannery, *The Eternal Frontier: An Ecological History of North America and Its Peoples* (New York, 2001), 176.
3. Ibid., 187; Shepard Krech, III, *The Ecological Indian: Myth and History* (New York, 1999), 38–39.
4. Krech, *The Ecological Indian*, 29–30, 40.
5. Jared Diamond, *Guns, Germs, and Steel: The Fates of Human Societies* (New York, 1997), 159, 355; idem, "Why Was Post-Pleistocene Development of Human Societies Slightly More Rapid in the Old World Than in the New World?" in *Americans before Columbus: Ice Age Origins*, comp. and ed. Ronald C. Carlisle (Pittsburgh, PA, 1988), 27.
6. John D. Daniels, "The Indian Population of North America in 1492," *William and Mary Quarterly*, 3d Ser., 49 (April 1992): 298–299, 300, 306, 310–311, 320.
7. Ibid., 314, 315, 317.
8. Krech, *The Ecological Indian*, 85, 92, 93.
9. William Cronon, *Changes in the Land: Indians, Colonists, and the Ecology of New England* (New York, 1983), 39–40, 53 (quotation).
10. Timothy Silver, *A New Face on the Countryside: Indians, Colonists, and Slaves in South Atlantic Forests, 1500–1800* (New York, 1990), 46–49.
11. Ibid., 43, 45, 51–52.
12. Richard White, *The Roots of Dependency: Subsistence, Environment, and Social Change among the Choctaws, Pawnees, and Navajos* (Lincoln, NE, 1983), 160, 165, 167, 170, 171.
13. M. Kat Anderson, Michael G. Barbour, and Valerie Whitworth, "A World of Balance and Plenty: Land, Plants, Animals, and Humans in a Pre-European California," in *Contested Eden: California before the Gold Rush*, ed. Ramón A. Gutiérrez and Richard J. Orsi (Berkeley, CA, 1998), 33; Cronon, *Changes in the Land*, 40–42; William Cronon and Richard White, "Indians in the Land," *American Heritage* 37 (August/September 1986): 21.
14. Quoted in Krech, *The Ecological Indian*, 201.
15. Ibid., 164–165, 170–171, quotation from p. 165.
16. Michael Williams, *Americans and Their Forests: A Historical Geography* (New York, 1989), 41–42 (1st quotation); Krech, *The Ecological Indian*, 103 (2d quotation).
17. Williams, *Americans and Their Forests*, 42, 44 (quotation).
18. Krech, *The Ecological Indian*, 104.
19. Quoted in ibid., 104–105.

20. White, *The Roots of Dependency*, 184–185.

21. Anderson, Barbour, and Whitworth, "A World of Balance," 19–20, 35.

22. White, *The Roots of Dependency*, 186; Silver, *A New Face on the Countryside*, 61, 62.

23. Williams, *Americans and Their Forests*, 46–48.

24. Mitchell T. Mulholland, "Territoriality and Horticulture: A Perspective for Prehistoric Southern New England," in *Holocene Human Ecology in Northeastern North America*, ed. George P. Nicholas (New York, 1988), 137–166.

25. Cronon and White, "Indians in the Land," 20.

CHAPTER 2: A TRULY NEW WORLD

1. David W. Stahle et al., "The Lost Colony and Jamestown Droughts," *Science* 280 (April 24, 1998): 564–567.

2. Tim Flannery, *The Eternal Frontier: An Ecological History of North America and Its Peoples* (New York, 2001), 83–84.

3. Quoted in Karen Ordahl Kupperman, "The Puzzle of the American Climate in the Early Colonial Period," *American Historical Review* 87 (December 1982): 1270.

4. Quoted in S. Max Edelson, "Planting the Lowcountry: Agricultural Enterprise and Economic Experience in the Lower South, 1695–1785" (Ph.D. diss., Johns Hopkins University, 1998), 13.

5. Kupperman, "The Puzzle of the American Climate," 1266; idem, "Fear of Hot Climates in the Anglo-American Colonial Experience," *William and Mary Quarterly*, 3d Ser., 42 (April 1984): 227.

6. Quoted in Carville Earle, *Geographical Inquiry and American Historical Problems* (Stanford, CA, 1992), 27.

7. Stahle et al., "The Lost Colony," 566.

8. Earle, *Geographical Inquiry*, 32–40.

9. Quoted in H. Roy Merrens and George D. Terry, "Dying in Paradise: Malaria, Mortality, and the Perceptual Environment in Colonial South Carolina," *Journal of Southern History* 50 (November 1984): 549.

10. Quoted in Kupperman, "The Puzzle of the American Climate," 1272.

11. Brian Fagan, *The Little Ice Age: How Climate Made History, 1300–1850* (New York, 2000), xiii.

12. Karen Ordahl Kupperman, "Climate and Mastery of the Wilderness in Seventeenth-Century New England," in *Seventeenth-Century New England*, ed. Colonial Society of Massachusetts (Boston, 1984), 31, 32 (quotation), 35–36.

13. Lenore A. Stiffarm and Phil Lane, Jr., "The Demography of Native North America: A Question of American Indian Survival," in *The State of Native America: Genocide, Colonization, and Resistance*, ed. M. Annette Jaimes (Boston, 1992), 37.

14. Elizabeth A. Fenn, "Biological Warfare in Eighteenth-Century North America: Beyond Jeffrey Amherst," *Journal of American History* 86 (March 2000): 1559 (quotation), 1560–1561.

15. Alfred Crosby, *Ecological Imperialism: The Biological Expansion of Europe, 900–1900* (New York, 1986), 202 (1st quotation); Timothy Silver, *A New Face on the Countryside: Indians, Colonists, and Slaves in South Atlantic Forests, 1500–1800* (New York, 1990), 74 (2d quotation).

16. Crosby, *Ecological Imperialism*, 208 (1st quotation); Colin G. Calloway, *New Worlds for All: Indians, Europeans, and the Remaking of Early America* (Baltimore, 1997), 39 (2d quotation).

17. Fenn, "Biological Warfare," 1552, 1558, 1573.

18. Alfred W. Crosby, Jr., *The Columbian Exchange: Biological and Cultural Consequences of 1492* (Westport, CT, 1972), 66, 107.

19. Judith A. Carney, Black Rice: The African Origins of Rice Cultivation in the Americas (Cambridge, MA, 2001), 7, 10–11, 38, 164–168.

20. Quoted in Calloway, New Worlds for All, 14.

21. Quotations in ibid., 52.

22. Quoted in Silver, A New Face on the Countryside, 190.

23. William Cronon, Changes in the Land: Indians, Colonists, and the Ecology of New England (New York, 1983), 65.

24. Quoted in ibid., 60.

25. Margaret Wickens Pearce, "Native Mapping in Southern New England Indian Deeds," in Cartographic Encounters: Perspectives on Native American Mapmaking and Map Use, ed. G. Malcolm Lewis (Chicago, 1998), 174–177.

26. Cronon, Changes in the Land, 75.

27. Calvin Martin, "The European Impact on the Culture of a Northeastern Algonquian Tribe: An Ecological Interpretation," William and Mary Quarterly, 3d Ser., 31 (January 1974): 25.

28. Cronon, Changes in the Land, 94–97.

29. Silver, A New Face on the Countryside, 94 (quotation), 97.

30. Charles F. Carroll, The Timber Economy of Puritan New England (Providence, RI, 1973), 8–11.

31. Silver, A New Face on the Countryside, 17–18, 121–123.

32. Quotations in Michael Williams, Americans and Their Forests: A Historical Geography (New York, 1989), 78, 79.

33. Silver, A New Face on the Countryside, 110–111.

34. Cronon, Changes in the Land, 124–126.

35. E. L. Jones, The European Miracle: Environments, Economics and Geopolitics in the History of Europe and Asia (Cambridge, UK, 1981), 84.

CHAPTER 3: REFLECTIONS FROM A WOODLOT

1. David R. Foster, Thoreau's Country: Journey through a Transformed Landscape (Cambridge, MA, 1999), 151.

2. Henry David Thoreau, Walden and Civil Disobedience, ed. Sherman Paul (1854 and 1849; reprint, Boston, 1960), 132; Foster, Thoreau's Country, 8, 9, 87 (last quotation).

3. Quotation in Michael Williams, Americans and Their Forests: A Historical Geography (New York, 1989), 57.

4. John R. Stilgoe, Common Landscape of America, 1580–1845 (New Haven, CT, 1982), 173–174, 181.

5. Quoted in ibid., 185.

6. Quoted in Robert A. Gross, "Culture and Cultivation: Agriculture and Society in Thoreau's Concord," Journal of American History 69 (June 1982): 47.

7. E. L. Jones, "Creative Disruptions in American Agriculture, 1620–1820," Agricultural History 48 (October 1974): 519.

8. Quoted in William Cronon, Changes in the Land: Indians, Colonists, and the Ecology of New England (New York, 1983), 133.

9. Quoted in James A. Henretta et al., America's History, 4th ed., 2 vols. (Boston, 2000), 1:111.

10. Carolyn Merchant, Ecological Revolutions: Nature, Gender, and Science in New England (Chapel Hill, NC, 1989), 187.

11. Brian Donahue, "Plowland, Pastureland, Woodland and Meadow: Husbandry in Concord, Massachusetts, 1635–1771" (Ph.D. diss., Brandeis University, 1995), 369.

12. Robert A. Gross, The Minutemen and Their World (New York, 1976), 107.

13. Sarah F. McMahon, " 'All Things in Their Proper Season:' Seasonal Rhythms of Diet in

Nineteenth Century New England," *Agricultural History* 63 (Spring 1989): 130, 132, 140–142, 145 (1st quotation), 146; idem, "A Comfortable Subsistence: The Changing Composition of Diet in Rural New England, 1620–1840," *William and Mary Quarterly*, 3d Ser., 42 (January 1985): 44; Diana Muir, *Reflections in Bullough's Pond: Economy and Ecosystem in New England* (Hanover, NH, 2000), 63 (2d quotation).

14. William R. Baron, "Eighteenth-Century New England Climate Variation and Its Suggested Impact on Society," *Maine Historical Society Quarterly* 21 (Spring 1982): 201.
15. Quoted in Alan Taylor, " 'The Hungry Year': 1789 on the Northern Border of Revolutionary America," in *Dreadful Visitations: Confronting Natural Catastrophe in the Age of Enlightenment*, ed. Alessa Johns (New York, 1999), 151.
16. Ibid., 153–161.
17. John D. Post, *The Last Great Subsistence Crisis in the Western World* (Baltimore, 1977), 4.
18. David M. Ludlum, *Early American Winters, 1604–1820* (Boston, 1966), 190 (1st and 2d quotations); Post, *The Last Great Subsistence Crisis*, 47 (3d quotation), 48.
19. Alan Taylor, "The Great Change Begins: Settling the Forest of Central New York," *New York History* (July 1995): 266.
20. Quoted in Post, *The Last Great Subsistence Crisis*, 106.
21. Ibid., 4.
22. Bettye Hobbs Pruitt, "Self-Sufficiency and the Agricultural Economy of Eighteenth-Century Massachusetts," *William and Mary Quarterly*, 3d Ser., 41 (July 1984): 333–364.
23. Winifred B. Rothenberg, "The Productivity Consequences of Market Integration: Agriculture in Massachusetts, 1771–1801," in *American Economic Growth and Standards of Living before the Civil War*, ed. Robert E. Gallman and John Joseph Wallis (Chicago, 1992), 335.
24. Christopher Clark, *The Roots of Rural Capitalism: Western Massachusetts, 1780–1860* (Ithaca, NY, 1990), 77–78.
25. Gross, "Culture and Cultivation," 49.
26. Peter D. McClelland, *Sowing Modernity: America's First Agricultural Revolution* (Ithaca, NY, 1997), 129, 162–164.
27. McMahon, "A Comfortable Subsistence," 47–48.
28. Foster, *Thoreau's Country*, 138–139.
29. Quoted in Lawrence Buell, *The Environmental Imagination: Thoreau, Nature Writing, and the Formation of American Culture* (Cambridge, MA, 1995), 515n.

CHAPTER 4: A WORLD OF COMMODITIES

1. Quoted in Leah Hager Cohen, *Glass, Paper, Beans: Revelations on the Nature and Value of Ordinary Things* (New York, 1997), 236.
2. John T. Cumbler, "The Early Making of an Environmental Consciousness: Fish, Fisheries Commissions, and the Connecticut River," *Environmental History Review* 15 (Winter 1991): 75 (quotation); Theodore Steinberg, *Nature Incorporated: Industrialization and the Waters of New England* (New York, 1991), 170; John T. Cumbler, *Reasonable Use: The People, the Environment, and the State: New England, 1790–1930* (New York, 2001), 15–16.
3. Gary Kulik, "Dams, Fish, and Farmers: Defense of Public Rights in Eighteenth-Century Rhode Island," in *The Countryside in the Age of Capitalist Transformation*, ed. Steven Hahn and Jonathan Prude (Chapel Hill, NC, 1985), 42–43.
4. Steinberg, *Nature Incorporated*, 85, 87.
5. Quoted in ibid., 147.
6. Quoted in Richard Manning, *Grassland: The History, Biology, Politics, and Promise of the American Prairie* (New York, 1995), 94.
7. William Cronon, *Nature's Metropolis: Chicago and the Great West* (New York, 1991), 111, 113, 116, 120, 125, 145.

8. Michael Williams, *Americans and Their Forests: A Historical Geography* (New York, 1989), 160–161.

9. Ibid., 130 (1st quotation); Edwin G. Burrows and Mike Wallace, *Gotham: A History of New York City to 1898* (New York, 1999), 450 (2d quotation).

10. Williams, *Americans and Their Forests*, 132; Thomas R. Cox et al., *This Well-Wooded Land: Americans and Their Forests from Colonial Times to the Present* (Lincoln, NE, 1985), 72; Cronon, *Nature's Metropolis*, 179.

11. Williams, *Americans and Their Forests*, 184–185, 188.

12. Ibid., 193–194; Cox et al., *This Well-Wooded Land*, 125.

13. Cronon, *Nature's Metropolis*, 159; Cox et al., *This Well-Wooded Land*, 158; Williams, *Americans and Their Forests*, 201–202.

14. Williams, *Americans and Their Forests*, 208–209.

15. Ibid., 211–212.

16. Ibid., 221.

17. Ibid., 217–218; James Willard Hurst, *Law and Economic Growth: The Legal History of the Lumber Industry in Wisconsin, 1836–1915*, rev. ed. (Madison, WI, 1984), 140, 141.

18. Hurst, *Law and Economic Growth*, 127.

19. Williams, *Americans and Their Forests*, 233–236.

20. Stephen J. Pyne, *Fire in America: A Cultural History of Wildland and Rural Fire*, rev. ed. (Seattle, 1997), 200, 201, 204, 205–206.

21. Quoted in ibid., 205.

22. James Fenimore Cooper, *The Pioneers* (1823; reprint, New York, 1959), 250; Jennifer Price, *Flight Maps: Adventures with Nature in Modern America* (New York, 1999), 1.

23. David R. Foster, *Thoreau's Country: Journey through a Transformed Landscape* (Cambridge, MA, 1999), 167 (quotation), 168, 171; David S. Wilcove, *The Condor's Shadow: The Loss and Recovery of Wildlife in America* (New York, 1999), 29.

24. Quoted in Price, *Flight Maps*, 41.

25. Wilcove, *The Condor's Shadow*, 30; Price, *Flight Maps*, 6, 18–19.

26. Wilcove, *The Condor's Shadow*, 28, 30.

27. Foster, *Thoreau's Country*, 169, 172.

28. Georg Simmel, *The Sociology of Georg Simmel*, ed. Kurt H. Wolf (1908; reprint, Glencoe, IL, 1950), 414; idem, *The Philosophy of Money*, trans. Tom Bottomore and David Frisby (1900; reprint, London, 1978), 427.

CHAPTER 5: KING CLIMATE IN DIXIE

1. David M. Ludlum, *Early American Winters, 1821–1870* (Boston, 1968), 106–107, 1st quotation from p. 107; Robert Croom Aldredge, *Weather Observers and Observations at Charleston, South Carolina, 1670–1871* (1936; reprint, Charleston, SC, 1940), 202 (2d quotation).

2. A. Cash Koeniger, "Climate and Southern Distinctiveness," *Journal of Southern History* 54 (February 1988): 21–44.

3. Albert E. Cowdrey, *This Land, This South: An Environmental History*, rev. ed. (Lexington, KY, 1996), 29, 30.

4. T. H. Breen, *Tobacco Culture: The Mentality of the Great Tidewater Planters on the Eve of Revolution* (Princeton, NJ, 1985), 46–49, 60 (quotation).

5. Quotations in Alan Kulikoff, *Tobacco and Slaves: The Development of Southern Cultures in the Chesapeake, 1680–1800* (Chapel Hill, NC, 1986), 47.

6. Carville Earle, *Geographical Inquiry and American Historical Problems* (Stanford, CA, 1992), 280–282.

7. Ibid., 283.

8. Henry M. Miller, "Transforming a 'Splendid and Delightsome Land': Colonists and

Ecological Change in the Chesapeake, 1607–1820," *Journal of the Washington Academy of Sciences* 76 (September 1986): 183; Stanley Wayne Trimble, *Man-Induced Soil Erosion on the Southern Piedmont, 1700–1970* (Ankeny, IA, 1974), 47 (quotation).

9. Lewis Cecil Gray, *History of Agriculture in the Southern United States to 1860*, 2 vols. (1932; reprint, Gloucester, MA, 1958), 1:446.

10. Quoted in S. Max Edelson, "Planting the Lowcountry: Agricultural Enterprise and Economic Experience in the Lower South, 1695–1785" (Ph.D. diss., Johns Hopkins University, 1998), 223.

11. Philip D. Morgan, "Work and Culture: The Task System and the World of Lowcountry Blacks, 1700 to 1880," *William and Mary Quarterly*, 3d Ser., 39 (October 1982): 577 (quotation).

12. Joyce E. Chaplin, "Tidal Rice Cultivation and the Problem of Slavery in South Carolina and Georgia, 1760–1815," *William and Mary Quarterly*, 3d Ser., 49 (January 1992): 47.

13. Judith A. Carney, *Black Rice: The African Origins of Rice Cultivation in the Americas* (Cambridge, MA, 2001), 91 (quotation), 93–94.

14. Morgan, "Work and Culture," 568–569, 575 (quotation).

15. Quoted in Edelson, "Planting the Lowcountry," 250.

16. Mart A. Stewart, *"What Nature Suffers to Groe:" Life, Labor, and Landscape on the Georgia Coast, 1680–1920* (Athens, GA, 1996), 104, 110.

17. Ibid., 161–162.

18. Ibid., 139–140; Chaplin, "Tidal Rice Cultivation," 60 (quotation).

19. Quoted in Stewart, *"What Nature Suffers to Groe,"* 155.

20. Harry L. Watson, " 'The Common Rights of Mankind': Subsistence, Shad, and Commerce in the Early Republican South," *Journal of American History* 83 (June 1996): 15 (quotation), 21.

21. Quoted in ibid., 33.

22. Quotations in ibid., 13, 14.

23. E. P. Thompson, "The Moral Economy of the English Crowd in the Eighteenth Century," in *Customs in Common: Studies in Traditional Popular Culture* (New York, 1991), 185–258.

24. Watson, " 'The Common Rights of Mankind,' " 19, 41–43.

25. James L. Watkins, *King Cotton: A Historical and Statistical Review, 1790 to 1908* (1908; reprint, New York, 1969), 13.

26. Gray, *History of Agriculture*, 2: 689, 705.

27. Michael Paul Rogin, *Fathers and Children: Andrew Jackson and the Subjugation of the American Indian* (New York, 1975), 180 (quotation); Richard White, *The Roots of Dependency: Subsistence, Environment, and Social Change among the Choctaws, Pawnees, and Navajos* (Lincoln, NE, 1983), 22–23.

28. Earle, *Geographical Inquiry*, 288; Trimble, *Man-Induced Soil Erosion*, 54 (quotation); Charles Reagan Wilson et al., eds., *Encyclopedia of Southern Culture* (Chapel Hill, NC, 1989), 319.

29. Stanley W. Trimble, "Perspectives on the History of Soil Erosion Control in the Eastern United States," *Agricultural History* 59 (April 1985): 174.

30. Gavin Wright, *Old South, New South: Revolutions in the Southern Economy Since the Civil War* (New York, 1986), 17–18, 19, 30–31.

31. Quoted in Eugene D. Genovese, *The Political Economy of Slavery: Studies in the Economy and Society of the Slave South* (New York, 1967), 95.

32. Ibid., 91 (quotation); Julius Rubin, "The Limits of Agricultural Progress in the Nineteenth-Century South," *Agricultural History* 49 (April 1975): 365, 366; Tamara Miner Haygood, "Cows, Ticks, and Disease: A Medical Interpretation of the Southern Cattle Industry," *Journal of Southern History* 52 (November 1986): 553, 563.

33. Jimmy M. Skaggs, *The Great Guano Rush: Entrepreneurs and American Overseas Expansion* (New York, 1994), 14, 71; Gray, *History of Agriculture*, 2: 805–806; Genovese, *The Political Economy of Slavery*, 94.

34. Earle, *Geographical Inquiry*, 288–290.

CHAPTER 6: THE GREAT FOOD FIGHT

1. David Madden, ed., *Beyond the Battlefield: The Ordinary Life and Extraordinary Times of the Civil War Soldier* (New York, 2000), 158 (quotation); James M. McPherson, *Battle Cry of Freedom: The Civil War Era* (New York, 1988), 850.

2. Quoted in George Brown Tindall and David E. Shi, *America: A Narrative History*, 5th ed., 2 vols. (New York, 1999), 1: 785.

3. Quoted in James M. McPherson, *Ordeal by Fire: The Civil War and Reconstruction* (New York, 1982), 191.

4. McPherson, *Battle Cry of Freedom*, 325.

5. Quoted in David M. Ludlum, *Early American Winters, 1821–1870* (Boston, 1968), 129.

6. Geoffrey C. Ward, *The Civil War* (New York, 1990), 158 (1st quotation), 159 (2d quotation); McPherson, *Battle Cry of Freedom*, 584 (3d quotation).

7. Reprinted in Ludlum, *Early American Winters*, 234.

8. Quoted in Ward, *The Civil War*, 275.

9. Quoted in Ludlum, *Early American Winters*, 134–135.

10. Quoted in ibid., 136.

11. Quotations in Madden, *Beyond the Battlefield*, 147, 158–159.

12. Quoted in Douglas Southall Freeman, *R. E. Lee: A Biography*, 4 vols. (New York, 1934–1935), 3: 247.

13. Ibid., 3: 252.

14. Ibid., 2: 491; 3: 252–253.

15. Quoted in Madden, *Beyond the Battlefield*, 155–156.

16. Gary B. Nash and Julie Roy Jeffrey, eds., *The American People: Creating a Nation and a Society*, 5th ed. (New York, 2001), 486 (1st quotation); John Solomon Otto, *Southern Agriculture during the Civil War Era, 1860–1880* (Westport, CT, 1994), 30 (2d quotation).

17. Christopher Clark et al., *Who Built America?: Working People and the Nation's Economy, Politics, Culture, and Society*, 2 vols. (New York, 2000), 1: 626 (1st quotation); McPherson, *Ordeal by Fire*, 370 (2d quotation).

18. Paul W. Gates, *Agriculture and the Civil War* (New York, 1965), 38–39.

19. Michael B. Chesson, "Harlots or Heroines? A New Look at the Richmond Bread Riot," *Virginia Magazine of History and Biography* 92 (April 1984): 134, 135, 144 (quotations).

20. Quotations in Drew Gilpin Faust, *The Creation of Confederate Nationalism* (Baton Rouge, LA, 1988), 54, 55.

21. Otto, *Southern Agriculture*, 23, 32.

22. Gates, *Agriculture and the Civil War*, 86, 116 (quotation).

23. Ibid., 120 (1st quotation); Tindall and Shi, *America*, 1: 773 (2d quotation); Ward, *The Civil War*, 197 (3d quotation).

24. Ludlum, *Early American Winters*, 133 (quotation); Gates, *Agriculture and the Civil War*, 86; Freeman, *R. E. Lee*, 3: 247.

25. Gates, *Agriculture and the Civil War*, 16 (quotations), 19.

26. Joseph P. Reidy, *From Slavery to Agrarian Capitalism in the Cotton Plantation South: Central Georgia, 1800–1880* (Chapel Hill, NC, 1992), 115–116 (quotation); Gates, *Agriculture and the Civil War*, 18.

27. Quoted in Reidy, *From Slavery to Agrarian Capitalism*, 117.

CHAPTER 7: EXTRACTING THE NEW SOUTH

1. Quoted in George Brown Tindall and David E. Shi, *America: A Narrative History*, 5th ed., 2 vols. (New York, 1999), 2: 793.

2. Gavin Wright, *Old South, New South: Revolutions in the Southern Economy Since the Civil War* (New York, 1986), 34; C. Vann Woodward, *Origins of the New South, 1877–1913* (Baton Rouge, LA, 1951), 182 (quotation).

3. Roger L. Ransom and Richard Sutch, *One Kind of Freedom: The Economic Consequences of Emancipation* (Cambridge, UK, 1977), 87, 89, 95, 98; Wright, *Old South, New South*, 91.

4. Steven Hahn, *The Roots of Southern Populism: Yeoman Farmers and the Transformation of the Georgia Upcountry, 1850–1890* (New York, 1983), 145; Gilbert C. Fite, *Cotton Fields No More: Southern Agriculture, 1865–1980* (Lexington, KY, 1984), 10 (quotation).

5. Ransom and Sutch, *One Kind of Freedom*, 101, 102.

6. Carville Earle, *Geographical Inquiry and American Historical Problems* (Stanford, CA, 1992), 295; David F. Weiman, "The Economic Emanipation of the Non-Slaveholding Class: Upcountry Farmers in the Georgia Cotton Economy," *Journal of Economic History* 45 (March 1985): 87; Ransom and Sutch, *One Kind of Freedom*, 187.

7. Earle, *Geographical Inquiry*, 295–296 (quotation); Stanley Wayne Trimble, *Man-Induced Soil Erosion on the Southern Piedmont, 1700–1970* (Ankeny, IA, 1974), 69–93.

8. Arvarh E. Strickland, "The Strange Affair of the Boll Weevil: The Pest as Liberator," *Agricultural History* 68 (Spring 1994): 166.

9. James R. Grossman, *Land of Hope: Chicago, Black Southerners, and the Great Migration* (Chicago, 1989), 14, 28–30, quotation from p. 30.

10. Strickland, "The Strange Affair of the Boll Weevil," 157; Kathryn Holland Braund, " 'Hog Wild' and 'Nuts: Billy Boll Weevil Comes to the Alabama Wiregrass," *Agricultural History* 63 (Summer 1989): 32.

11. Quoted in Paul Garon, *Blues and the Poetic Spirit* (1975; reprint, New York, 1979), 117.

12. Fite, *Cotton Fields No More*, 22 (quotations); Albert E. Cowdrey, *This Land, This South: An Environmental History*, rev. ed. (Lexington, KY, 1996), 106; Robert C. McMath, Jr., "Sandy Land and Hogs in the Timber: (Agri)cultural Origins of the Farmers' Alliance in Texas," in *The Countryside in the Age of Capitalist Transformation*, ed. Steven Hahn and Jonathan Prude (Chapel Hill, NC, 1985), 223.

13. Eugene D. Genovese, *Roll, Jordon, Roll: The World the Slaves Made* (New York, 1974), 486 (1st quotation); Charles Joyner, *Down by the Riverside: A South Carolina Slave Community* (Urbana, IL, 1984), 100 (2d quotation), 100–101 (3d quotation); Mart A. Stewart, *"What Nature Suffers to Groe:" Life, Labor, and Landscape on the Georgia Coast, 1680–1920* (Athens, GA, 1996),136.

14. Philip D. Morgan, "The Ownership of Property by Slaves in the Mid-Nineteenth-Century Low Country," *Journal of Southern History* 49 (August 1983): 411 (quotation).

15. Hahn, *The Roots of Southern Populism*, 60 (quotations); R. Ben Brown, "The Southern Range: A Study in Nineteenth Century Law and Society" (Ph.D. diss., University of Michigan, 1993), 7.

16. Hahn, *The Roots of Southern Populism*, 252 (1st quotation); Mart A. Stewart, " 'Whether Wast, Deodand, or Stray': Cattle, Culture, and the Environment in Early Georgia," *Agricultural History* 65 (Summer 1991): 24; Steven Hahn, "Hunting, Fishing, and Foraging: Common Rights and Class Relations in the Postbellum South," *Radical History Review* 26 (October 1982): 42 (2d quotation).

17. Hahn, "Hunting, Fishing, and Foraging," 44 (1st quotation), 39 (2d quotation); idem, *The Roots of Southern Populism*, 241 (3d quotation).

18. Hahn, *The Roots of Southern Populism*, 242; Brown, "The Southern Range," 190.

19. Cowdrey, *This Land, This South*, 115, 117; Jennifer Price, *Flight Maps: Adventures with Nature in Modern America* (New York, 1999), 59.

20. Stuart A. Marks, *Southern Hunting in Black and White: Nature, History, and Ritual in a Carolina Community* (Princeton, NJ, 1991), 48 (quotation), 49.

21. J. Crawford King, Jr., "The Closing of the Southern Range: An Exploratory Study," *Journal of Southern History* 48 (February 1982): 62, 68 (quotation).

22. Hahn, "Hunting, Fishing, and Foraging," 46 (1st quotation); Brown, "The Southern Range," 206 (2d quotation).

23. King, "The Closing of the Southern Range," 57.

24. Shawn Everett Kantor and J. Morgan Kousser, "Common Sense or Commonwealth? The Fence Law and Institutional Change in the Postbellum South," *Journal of Southern History* 59 (May 1993): 208 (quotation), 215.

25. Claire Strom, "Texas Fever and the Dispossession of the Southern Yeoman Farmer," *Journal of Southern History* 66 (February 2000): 73.

26. McMath, "Sandy Land and Hogs in the Timber," 205–229.

27. Michael Williams, *Americans and Their Forests: A Historical Geography* (New York, 1989), 238; Donald Edward Davis, *Where There Are Mountains: An Environmental History of the Southern Appalachians* (Athens, GA, 2000), 168 (quotation), 176.

28. Paul Wallace Gates, "Federal Land Policy in the South, 1866–1888," *Journal of Southern History* 6 (August 1940): 314; Williams, *Americans and Their Forests*, 242.

29. Williams, *Americans and Their Forests*, 242–243.

30. Ibid., 254; Ronald L. Lewis, *Transforming the Appalachian Countryside: Railroads, Deforestation, and Social Change in West Virginia, 1880–1920* (Chapel Hill, NC, 1998), 47 (1st quotation); Thomas R. Cox et al., *This Well-Wooded Land: Americans and Their Forests from Colonial Times to the Present* (Lincoln, NE, 1985), 164 (2d quotation).

31. Davis, *Where There Are Mountains*, 168; Lewis, *Transforming the Appalachian Countryside*, 265.

32. Stephen J. Pyne, *Fire in America: A Cultural History of Wildland and Rural Fire*, rev. ed. (Seattle, 1997), 148, 150, 155.

33. Davis, *Where There Are Mountains*, 176.

34. Quoted in ibid., 179.

35. J. R. McNeill, *Something New under the Sun: An Environmental History of the Twentieth-Century World* (New York, 2000), 256.

36. Davis, *Where There Are Mountains*, 194 (1st quotation), 195 (2d quotation), 197 (3d quotation).

37. Williams, *Americans and Their Forests*, 238.

38. Quoted in ibid., 281.

39. Paul Salstrom, *Appalachia's Path to Dependency: Rethinking a Region's Economic History, 1730–1940* (Lexington, KY, 1994), 21.

40. Ibid., 61, 82.

41. Harry M. Caudill, *Night Comes to the Cumberlands* (Boston, 1962), 151.

CHAPTER 8: THE UNFORGIVING WEST

1. Marc Reisner, *Cadillac Desert: The American West and Its Disappearing Water* (New York, 1986), 37 (1st quotation); John Opie, *Ogallala: Water for a Dry Land* (Lincoln, NE, 1993), 66 (2d quotation).

2. Donald Worster, *A River Running West: The Life of John Wesley Powell* (New York, 2001), 348–349; Reisner, *Cadillac Desert*, 47 (quotation).

3. Quotations in Gray Brechin, *Imperial San Francisco: Urban Power, Earthly Ruin* (Berkeley, CA, 1999), 30.

4. William Preston, "Serpent in the Garden: Environmental Change in Colonial California," in *Contested Eden: California before the Gold Rush*, ed. Ramón A. Gutiérrez and Richard J. Orsi (Berkeley, CA, 1998), 265, 273–274, 278.

5. Mary Hill, *Gold: The California Story* (Berkeley, CA, 1999), 18–19, 94–97; Brechin, *Imperial San Francisco*, 31, 32.

6. Hill, *Gold*, 72–73.

7. Brechin, *Imperial San Francisco*, 36 (1st quotation); Hill, *Gold*, 116, 118 (2d quotation).

8. Quoted in Brechin, *Imperial San Francisco*, 50.

9. Ibid., 48; Hill, *Gold*, 119–120.

10. Robert Kelley, *Battling the Inland Sea: American Political Culture, Public Policy, and the Sacramento Valley, 1850–1986* (Berkeley, CA, 1989), 74, 77, 107–108; Brechin, *Imperial San Francisco*, 52.

11. Elliott West, *The Way to the West: Essays on the Central Plains* (Albuquerque, NM, 1995), 30–32; Hill, *Gold*, 48.

12. West, *The Way to the West*, 15, 17.

13. Ibid., 21, 24–25, 26, 29 (quotation).

14. Ibid., 38–40; Elliott West, *The Contested Plains: Indians, Goldseekers, and the Rush to Colorado* (Lawrence, KS, 1998), 89.

15. West, *The Way to the West*, 43.

16. Ibid., 45–46; West, *The Contested Plains*, xv, 233 (quotation).

17. West, *The Way to the West*, 47.

18. Ibid., 11.

19. Quoted in David D. Smits, "The Frontier Army and the Destruction of the Buffalo: 1865–1883," *Western Historical Quarterly* 25 (Autumn 1994): 338.

20. William Cronon, *Nature's Metropolis: Chicago and the Great West* (New York, 1991), 215 (1st quotation); Shepard Krech, III, *The Ecological Indian: Myth and History* (New York, 1999), 124 (2d quotation).

21. Andrew C. Isenberg, *The Destruction of the Bison* (New York, 2000), 24–25, 106.

22. Ibid., 39–40, 47; West, *The Contested Plains*, 49–53.

23. Krech, *The Ecological Indian*, 127, 128 (quotation).

24. Isenberg, *The Destruction of the Bison*, 82 (1st quotation), 83; Krech, *The Ecological Indian*, 148 (2d quotation), 149.

25. West, *The Way to the West*, 61–63.

26. Quoted in Isenberg, *The Destruction of the Bison*, 112.

27. Ibid., 99–100, 131; Richard Manning, *Grassland: The History, Biology, Politics, and Promise of the American Prairie* (New York, 1995), 83.

28. Isenberg, *The Destruction of the Bison*, 136–137.

29. Smits, "The Frontier Army," 316 (1st quotation), 314 (2d quotation); Manning, *Grassland*, 85 (3d quotation).

30. Isenberg, *The Destruction of the Bison*, 141–142; Manning, *Grassland*, 87.

31. Quoted in Ernest Staples Osgood, *The Day of the Cattlemen* (Minneapolis, MN, 1929), 83.

32. Richard White, "Animals and Enterprise," in *The Oxford History of the American West*, ed. Clyde A. Milner, II, Carol A. O'Connor, and Martha A. Sandweiss (New York, 1994), 252–253; Terry G. Jordan, *North American Cattle-Ranching Frontiers: Origins, Diffusion, and Differentiation* (Albuquerque, NM, 1993), 220.

33. Jordan, *North American Cattle-Ranching Frontiers*, 222.

34. Ibid., 237.

35. Osgood, *The Day of the Cattlemen*, 99; Jeremy Rifkin, *Beyond Beef: The Rise and Fall of the Cattle Culture* (New York, 1993), 88–91.

36. Osgood, *The Day of the Cattlemen*, 190; David L. Wheeler, "The Blizzard of 1886 and Its Effect on the Range Cattle Industry in the Southern Plains," *Southwestern Historical Quarterly* 94 (1990–1991): 418–419.

37. Thadis W. Box, "Range Deterioration in West Texas," *Southwestern Historical Quarterly* 71 (1967–1968): 41 (1st quotation); Osgood, *The Day of the Cattlemen*, 193 (2d quotation).

38. Jordan, *North American Cattle-Ranching Frontiers,* 237, 238 (quotation).

39. Quoted in Box, "Range Deterioration in West Texas," 38.

40. Wheeler, "The Blizzard of 1886," 426.

41. Quoted in Edmund Morris, *The Rise of Theodore Roosevelt* (New York, 1979), 364–365.

42. Quoted in ibid., 365.

43. Richard L. Knight, "The Ecology of Ranching," in *Ranching West of the 100th Meridian,* ed. R. L. Knight, W. Gilgert, and E. Marston (Washington, DC, forthcoming).

44. Peter Iverson, *When Indians Became Cowboys: Native Peoples and Cattle Ranching in the American West* (Norman, OK, 1994), 82, 84; Carolyn Gilman and Mary Jane Schneider, *The Way to Independence: Memories of a Hidatsa Indian Family, 1840–1920* (St. Paul, MN, 1987), 242–243.

45. Opie, *Ogallala,* 67–68 (quotations).

46. Ibid., 93–95; Donald Worster, *Dust Bowl: The Southern Plains in the 1930s* (New York, 1979), 87–91.

47. Manning, *Grassland,* 172.

48. Worster, *Dust Bowl,* 4, 32 (quotation), 42.

CHAPTER 9: CONSERVATION RECONSIDERED

1. Quotations in Edmund Morris, *The Rise of Theodore Roosevelt* (New York, 1979), 372.

2. Ibid., 382–384.

3. Samuel P. Hays, *Conservation and the Gospel of Efficiency: The Progressive Conservation Movement, 1890–1920* (Cambridge, MA, 1959), 1–4, 265–266.

4. Donald Worster, *The Wealth of Nature: Environmental History and the Ecological Imagination* (New York, 1993), 190–196, 1st quotation from p. 193; John Mack Faragher et al., *Out of Many: A History of the American People,* 3d ed. (Upper Saddle River, NJ, 2000), 634 (2d quotation).

5. Nancy Langston, *Forest Dreams, Forest Nightmares: The Paradox of Old Growth in the Inland West* (Seattle, 1995), 93, 106–108, quotation from p. 107.

6. Gifford Pinchot, *The Fight for Conservation* (New York, 1910), 42, 43.

7. Patricia Nelson Limerick, *The Legacy of Conquest: The Unbroken Past of the American West* (New York, 1987), 298 (quotation).

8. Michael Williams, *Americans and Their Forests: A Historical Geography* (New York, 1989), 416, 433, 441 (quotation).

9. Donald Worster, *Nature's Economy: A History of Ecological Ideas* (1977; reprint, New York, 1985), 267 (1st quotation); Langston, *Forest Dreams, Forest Nightmares,* 112 (2d quotation).

10. Langston, *Forest Dreams, Forest Nightmares,* 151, 155.

11. Ibid., 151, 291.

12. Stephen J. Pyne, *Year of the Fires: The Story of the Great Fires of 1910* (New York, 2001), 196–197; Pinchot, *The Fight for Conservation,* 44–45.

13. Pyne, *Year of the Fires,* 80 (Pinchot quotation), 237.

14. Ibid., 257–258.

15. Quoted in Mike Davis, *Ecology of Fear: Los Angeles and the Imagination of Disaster* (New York, 1998), 229.

16. Peter Steinhart, *The Company of Wolves* (New York, 1995), 36–37.

17. Donald Worster, *An Unsettled Country: Changing Landscapes of the American West* (Albuquerque, NM, 1994), 79; Steinhart, *The Company of Wolves,* 37–38, 39 (quotation).

18. Worster, *Nature's Economy,* 270–271.

19. Thomas R. Dunlap, "Values for Varmints: Predator Control and Environmental Ideas, 1920–1939," *Pacific Historical Review* 53 (May 1984): 151; Davis, *Ecology of Fear,* 234–236, quotation from p. 234.

20. Alfred Runte, *National Parks: The American Experience*, rev. ed. (Lincoln, NE, 1987), 11, 48.

21. Chris J. Magoc, *Yellowstone: The Creation and Selling of an American Landscape, 1870–1903* (Albuquerque, NM, 1999), 19 (quotation); Runte, *National Parks*, 53.

22. Mark David Spence, *Dispossessing the Wilderness: Indian Removal and the Making of the National Parks* (New York, 1999), 37 (1st quotation); Magoc, *Yellowstone*, 93 (2d quotation).

23. Spence, *Dispossessing the Wilderness*, 4, 59 (quotation).

24. Magoc, *Yellowstone*, 141 (1st quotation), 146 (2d quotation).

25. Quoted in Spence, *Dispossessing the Wilderness*, 56.

26. Ibid., 45, 48, 50, 63; Karl Jacoby, *Crimes against Nature: Squatters, Poachers, Thieves, and the Hidden History of American Conservation* (Berkeley, CA, 2001), 88 (quotation).

27. Spence, *Dispossessing the Wilderness*, 63 (quotations), 65.

28. *Ward v. Race Horse*, 163 U.S. 504, 509, 518 (1896); Spence, *Dispossessing the Wilderness*, 67–68; David E. Wilkins, *American Indian Sovereignty and the U.S. Supreme Court: The Masking of Justice* (Austin, TX, 1997), 104.

29. Quoted in Jacoby, *Crimes against Nature*, 96.

30. Ibid., 2, 99 (quotation), 106–107, 118–119.

31. William T. Hornaday, *Our Vanishing Wild Life: Its Extermination and Preservation* (New York, 1913), 101; idem, *Wild Life Conservation in Theory and Practice* (New Haven, CT, 1914), 189.

32. Jacoby, *Crimes against Nature*, 134, 137 (1st and 2d quotations), 138 (3d quotation).

33. Mary Meagher and Douglas B. Houston, *Yellowstone and the Biology of Time: Photographs across a Century* (Norman, OK, 1998), 223–224.

34. David S. Wilcove, *The Condor's Shadow: The Loss and Recovery of Wildlife in America* (New York, 1999), 56; Michael B. Coughenour and Francis J. Singer, "The Concept of Overgrazing and Its Application to Yellowstone's Northern Range," in *The Greater Yellowstone Ecosystem: Redefining America's Wilderness Heritage*, ed. Robert B. Keiter and Mark S. Boyce (New Haven, CT, 1991), 211; Alston Chase, *Playing God in Yellowstone: The Destruction of America's First National Park* (San Diego, CA, 1987), 23 (quotation).

35. Steve W. Chadde and Charles E. Kay, "Tall-Willow Communities on Yellowstone's Northern Range: A Test of the 'Natural-Regulation' Paradigm," in *The Greater Yellowstone Ecosystem*, 236, 253–257.

36. Pinchot, *The Fight for Conservation*, 103.

37. Quoted in Chase, *Playing God in Yellowstone*, 125.

38. Andrew C. Isenberg, *The Destruction of the Bison* (New York, 2000), 179–180; Magoc, *Yellowstone*, 161.

39. Quoted in Isenberg, *The Destruction of the Bison*, 181.

40. Spence, *Dispossessing the Wilderness*, 69; Louis S. Warren, *The Hunter's Game: Poachers and Conservationists in Twentieth-Century America* (New Haven, CT, 1997), 144–145.

CHAPTER 10: DEATH OF THE ORGANIC CITY

1. R. Ben Brown, "The Southern Range: A Study in Nineteenth Century Law and Society" (Ph.D. diss., University of Michigan, 1993), 280–281, quotation from p. 281.

2. Upton Sinclair, *The Jungle* (1906; reprint, New York, 1981), 24, 25.

3. Quoted in Oscar Handlin, *This Was America: True Accounts of People and Places, Manners and Customs, As Recorded by European Travelers to the Western Shore in the Eighteenth, Nineteenth, and Twentieth Centuries* (Cambridge, MA, 1949), 217.

4. Quoted in Charles E. Rosenberg, *The Cholera Years: The United States in 1832, 1849, and 1866* (Chicago, 1962), 103.

5. Hendrik Hartog, "Pigs and Positivism," *Wisconsin Law Review* 1985 (July/August 1985): 905 (1st quotation), 908 (2d and 3d quotations).

6. Quotations in ibid., 910.
7. Edwin G. Burrows and Mike Wallace, Gotham: A History of New York City to 1898 (New York, 1999), 477.
8. Ibid., 747, 786; Rosenberg, The Cholera Years, 113; Susan Strasser, Waste and Want: A Social History of Trash (New York, 1999), 30.
9. Quoted in Burrows and Wallace, Gotham, 477.
10. Clay McShane and Joel A. Tarr, "The Centrality of the Horse in the Nineteenth-Century American City," in The Making of Urban America, 2d ed., ed. Raymond A. Mohl (Wilmington, DE, 1997), 105–106; Silas Farmer, The History of Detroit and Michigan . . . (Detroit, 1889), 892.
11. Joel A. Tarr, The Search for the Ultimate Sink: Urban Pollution in Historical Perspective (Akron, OH, 1996), 323–324, 326, 331.
12. Marc Linder and Lawrence S. Zacharias, Of Cabbages and Kings County: Agriculture and the Formation of Modern Brooklyn (Iowa City, IA, 1999), 35 (quotation); McShane and Tarr, "The Centrality of the Horse," 120.
13. Linder and Zacharias, Of Cabbages and Kings County, 6 (quotation), 29–31; table 5, p. 306.
14. Ibid., 45 (1st quotation), 46 (2d quotation).
15. Quoted in ibid., 4.
16. Joel A. Tarr, Search for the Ultimate Sink, 295, 299.
17. Ibid., 9.
18. Quoted in Norris Hundley, Jr., The Great Thirst: Californians and Water, 1770s–1990s (Berkeley, CA, 1992), 153.
19. Tarr, Search for the Ultimate Sink, 12; Burrows and Wallace, Gotham, 787; Elizabeth Blackmar, "Accountability for Public Health: Regulating the Housing Market in Nineteenth-Century New York City," in Hives of Sickness: Public Health and Epidemics in New York City, ed. David Rosner (New Brunswick, NJ, 1995), 52 (quotation), 53.
20. Edward K. Spann, The New Metropolis: New York City, 1840–1857 (New York, 1981), 130–131, 1st quotation from p. 131; Richard A. Wines, Fertilizer in America: From Waste Recycling to Resource Exploitation (Philadelphia, 1985), 32 (2d quotation).
21. Tarr, Search for the Ultimate Sink, 301–303.
22. William Ashworth, The Late, Great Lakes: An Environmental History (New York, 1986), 123 (quotation), 132, 134–135; Margaret Beattie Bogue, Fishing the Great Lakes: An Environmental History, 1783–1933 (Madison, WI, 2000), 169.
23. Charles Hardy, "Fish or Foul: A History of the Delaware River Basin through the Perspective of the American Shad, 1682 to the Present," Pennsylvania History 66 (Autumn 1999): 507, 518, 522–525, 533n.
24. Quoted in Judith Walzer Leavitt, The Healthiest City: Milwaukee and the Politics of Health Reform (Princeton, NJ, 1982), 124–125.
25. McShane and Tarr, "The Centrality of the Horse," 122; Martin V. Melosi, The Sanitary City: Urban Infrastructure in America from Colonial Times to the Present (Baltimore, 2000), 179.
26. Melosi, The Sanitary City, 176, 177; Strasser, Waste and Want, 125.
27. Suellen Hoy, Chasing Dirt: The American Pursuit of Cleanliness (New York, 1995), 72–75; Joel Tarr, e-mail with author, April 9, 2001.
28. Strasser, Waste and Want, 121–123.
29. Leavitt, The Healthiest City, 126 (1st quotation), 127 (2d quotation).
30. Benjamin Miller, Fat of the Land: Garbage of New York the Last Two Hundred Years (New York, 2000), photo caption, p. 73; Martin V. Melosi, Garbage in the Cities: Refuse, Reform, and the Environment, 1880–1980 (College Station, TX, 1981), 42.
31. Melosi, Garbage in the Cities, 169–170; idem, "Refuse Pollution and Municipal Reform: The Waste Problem in America, 1880–1917," in Pollution and Reform in American Cities,

1870–1930, ed. idem (Austin, TX, 1980), 127; Strasser, *Waste and Want*, 129 (quotation).

32. Strasser, *Waste and Want*, 12–15, 73, 91.

CHAPTER 11: MOVEABLE FEAST

1. Kevin Starr, *Inventing the Dream: California through the Progressive Era* (New York, 1985), 75–76, 83.
2. Quoted in Stephen Johnson, Robert Dawson, and Gerald Haslam, *The Great Central Valley: California's Heartland* (Berkeley, CA, 1993), 6.
3. Starr, *Inventing the Dream*, 131–132; Steven Stoll, *The Fruits of Natural Advantage: Making the Industrial Countryside in California* (Berkeley, CA, 1998), 28–29; Donald Worster, *Rivers of Empire: Water, Aridity, and the Growth of the American West* (New York, 1985), 99.
4. Ian Tyrrell, *True Gardens of the Gods: Californian-Australian Environmental Reform, 1860–1930* (Berkeley, CA, 1999), 223–224; Stoll, *The Fruits of Natural Advantage*, 60; Starr, *Inventing the Dream*, 133.
5. Worster, *Rivers of Empire*, 108–109; Tyrrell, *True Gardens of the Gods*, 106, 108 (quotation).
6. Stoll, *The Fruits of Natural Advantage*, xiii–xiv.
7. Marc Linder and Lawrence S. Zacharias, *Of Cabbages and Kings County: Agriculture and the Formation of Modern Brooklyn* (Iowa City, IA, 1999), 69–70.
8. David Vaught, *Cultivating California: Growers, Specialty Crops, and Labor, 1875–1920* (Baltimore, 1999), 49–50; Starr, *Inventing the Dream*, 134.
9. Vaught, *Cultivating California*, 50 (1st quotation); Harold Barger and Hans H. Landsberg, *American Agriculture, 1899–1939: A Study of Output, Employment and Productivity* (New York, 1942), 167–168 (2d quotation); Linder and Zacharias, *Of Cabbages and Kings County*, 71.
10. Vaught, *Cultivating California*, 109; Howard Seftel, "Government Regulation and the Rise of the California Fruit Industry: The Entrepreneurial Attack on Fruit Pests, 1880–1920," *Business History Review* 59 (Autumn 1985): 372; Stoll, *The Fruits of Natural Advantage*, 90 (quotation).
11. Stoll, *The Fruits of Natural Advantage*, 92–93.
12. Victoria Saker Woeste, *The Farmer's Benevolent Trust: Law and Agricultural Cooperation in Industrial America, 1865–1945* (Chapel Hill, NC, 1998), 30, 78, 81, 112, 113, 120–121; Starr, *Inventing the Dream*, 160–161; Charles C. Colby, "The California Raisin Industry—A Study in Geographic Interpretation," *Annals of the Association of American Geographers* 14 (June 1924): 103.
13. Linder and Zacharias, *Of Cabbages and Kings County*, 70 (quotation); Seftel, "Government Regulation," 386–388.
14. Douglas C. Sackman, *Orange Empire: Nature, Culture, and Growth in California, 1869–1939* (Berkeley, CA, forthcoming), manuscript copy in author's possession, 139, 146–149.
15. Ibid., 151–152, 160, 162; Stoll, *The Fruits of Natural Advantage*, 88 (quotation).
16. Sackman, *Orange Empire*, 180–225.
17. Quotations from ibid, 102.
18. Ibid., 94 (1st quotation); Jack Doyle, *Altered Harvest: Agriculture, Genetics, and the Fate of the World's Food Supply* (New York, 1985), 54 (2d quotation), 56.
19. Stoll, *The Fruits of Natural Advantage*, 95–97.
20. Ibid., 98, 104; Seftel, "Government Regulation," 377; Tyrrell, *True Gardens of the Gods*, 179–181, 195–196.
21. Stoll, *The Fruits of Natural Advantage*, 106, 108, 121; Seftel, "Government Regulation," 393.
22. Stoll, *The Fruits of Natural Advantage*, 123; Worster, *Rivers of Empire*, 317–318.

23. Stoll, *The Fruits of Natural Advantage*, 124; Worster, *Rivers of Empire*, 218–219; Don Mitchell, *The Lie of the Land: Migrant Workers and the California Landscape* (Minneapolis, MN, 1996), 59.

24. Worster, *Rivers of Empire*, 219; Sucheng Chan, *This Bitter-Sweet Soil: The Chinese in California Agriculture, 1860–1910* (Berkeley, CA, 1986), 114, 115.

25. Worster, *Rivers of Empire*, 220.

26. Ibid., 222; Mitchell, *The Lie of the Land*, 91; Sackman, *Orange Empire*, 188 (quotation).

27. Quotations in Carey McWilliams, *Factories in the Field: The Story of Migratory Farm Labor in California* (1939; reprint, Berkeley, CA, 1999), x, xiv.

28. Marc Reisner, *Cadillac Desert: The American West and Its Disappearing Water* (New York, 1986), 348; Worster, *Rivers of Empire*, 214.

29. Worster, *Rivers of Empire*, 234.

30. Ibid., 234–235; Reisner, *Cadillac Desert*, 348; Norris Hundley, Jr., *The Great Thirst: Californians and Water, 1770s–1990s* (Berkeley, CA, 1992), 235.

31. Worster, *Rivers of Empire*, 160–161, 240, 243; Hundley, *The Great Thirst*, 237, 252; Reisner, *Cadillac Desert*, 348–349.

32. Worster, *Rivers of Empire*, 246–247, quotation from p. 247; Reisner, *Cadillac Desert*, 350.

33. Worster, *Rivers of Empire*, 253–255; Hundley, *The Great Thirst*, 265–266.

34. Reisner, *Cadillac Desert*, 353–354.

35. Worster, *Rivers of Empire*, 256.

36. Reisner, *Cadillac Desert*, 13–14, 506, 510 (quotation); Worster, *Rivers of Empire*, 315.

37. Quoted in Vaught, *Cultivating California*, 186.

38. Stoll, *The Fruits of Natural Advantage*, 157.

CHAPTER 12: THE SECRET HISTORY OF MEAT

1. Quoted in John Vidal, *McLibel: Burger Culture on Trial* (New York, 1997), 30.

2. William Cronon, *Nature's Metropolis: Chicago and the Great West* (New York, 1991), 225, 226; Marvin Harris and Eric B. Ross, "How Beef Became King," *Psychology Today*, October 1978, 91.

3. Cronon, *Nature's Metropolis*, 228.

4. Ibid., 228–229, quotation from p. 229.

5. Timothy Cuff, "A Weighty Issue Revisited: New Evidence on Commercial Swine Weights and Pork Production in Mid-Nineteenth Century America," *Agricultural History* 66 (Fall 1992): table 1, p. 67.

6. Alexander Cockburn, "A Short, Meat-Oriented History of the World: From Eden to the Mattole," *New Left Review* 215 (January/February 1996): 24; Robert Aduddell and Louis Cain, "Location and Collusion in the Meat Packing Industry," in *Business Enterprise and Economic Change*, ed. Louis P. Cain and Paul J. Uselding (Kent, OH, 1973), 86.

7. Aduddell and Cain, "Location and Collusion," 91, 94–95.

8. Cronon, *Nature's Metropolis*, 233–234.

9. Richard J. Arnould, "Changing Patterns of Concentration in American Meat Packing, 1880–1963," *Business History Review* 45 (Spring 1971): 20.

10. Aduddell and Cain, "Location and Collusion," 95–96.

11. Upton Sinclair, *The Jungle* (1906; reprint, New York, 1981), 134–135.

12. Cronon, *Nature's Metropolis*, 236–237.

13. Arnould, "Changing Patterns of Concentration," 20; Jimmy M. Skaggs, *Prime Cut: Livestock Raising and Meatpacking in the United States, 1607–1983* (College Station, TX, 1986), 98–99.

14. Sinclair, *The Jungle*, 35, 109.

15. Cronon, *Nature's Metropolis*, 222–223; Aduddell and Cain, "Location and Collusion," 91–92; Edward Everett Dale, *The Range Cattle Industry: Ranching on the Great Plains from 1865 to 1925* (Norman, OK, 1960), 148.

16. Dale, *The Range Cattle Industry*, 153, 156.

17. Jack Doyle, *Altered Harvest: Agriculture, Genetics, and the Fate of the World's Food Supply* (New York, 1985), 120–121.

18. Harris and Ross, "How Beef Became King," table p. 91.

19. Skaggs, *Prime Cut*, 179–180.

20. Marvin Harris, *The Sacred Cow and the Abominable Pig: Riddles of Food and Culture* (New York, 1987), 119; Orville Schell, *Modern Meat* (New York, 1984), 19, 21–22, 23; J. R. McNeill, *Something New under the Sun: An Environmental History of the Twentieth-Century World* (New York, 2000), 202n.

21. Schell, *Modern Meat*, 189–190, 252.

22. Jon Lauck, *American Agriculture and the Problem of Monopoly: The Political Economy of Grain Belt Farming, 1953–1980* (Lincoln, NE, 2000), 54.

23. Skaggs, *Prime Cut*, 190–191; John Opie, *Ogallala: Water for a Dry Land* (Lincoln, NE, 1993), 153.

24. Skaggs, *Prime Cut*, 190–191 (quotation); Doyle, *Altered Harvest*, 131.

25. Lauck, *American Agriculture*, 56 (1st quotation); "Inside Big Meat," *CounterPunch* 6 (July 16–30, 1999), 1; Eric Schlosser, *Fast Food Nation: The Dark Side of the All-American Meal* (Boston, 2001), 172, 174; William Greider, "The Last Farm Crisis," *Nation*, November 20, 2000, 16 (2d quotation).

26. Skaggs, *Prime Cut*, 194; Harris and Ross, "How Beef Became King," table p. 91.

27. David Gerard Hogan, *Selling 'em by the Sack: White Castle and the Creation of American Food* (New York, 1997), 24, 38–39.

28. Vidal, *McLibel*, 24–25.

29. Ibid., 37 (observer quotation), 46; Schlosser, *Fast Food Nation*, 47.

30. Vidal, *McLibel*, 33.

31. Ibid., 38–40; Schlosser, *Fast Food Nation*, 76.

32. Margaret J. King, "Empires of Popular Culture: McDonald's and Disney," in *Ronald Revisited: The World of Ronald McDonald*, ed. Marshall William Fishwick (Bowling Green, OH, 1983), 107; Vidal, *McLibel*, 44, 183.

33. Harris, *The Sacred Cow*, 124–125.

34. Marion Nestle, "Food Lobbies, the Food Pyramid, and U.S. Nutrition Policy," in *The Nation's Health*, 5th ed., ed. Philip R. Lee and Carroll L. Estes (Sudbury, MA, 1997), 212–214, quotations from p. 214.

35. Ibid., 217–218.

36. Alan B. Durning and Holly B. Brough, *Taking Stock: Animal Farming and the Environment*, Worldwatch Paper 103, July 1991, 16–17, table 4, p. 17.

37. Ibid., 17–18; Cockburn, "A Short, Meat-Oriented History," 35; Opie, *Ogallala*, 5–6.

38. Donald Worster, *Under Western Skies: Nature and History in the American West* (New York, 1992), 43–44.

39. Denzel Ferguson and Nancy Ferguson, *Sacred Cows at the Public Trough* (Bend, OR, 1983), 36; Patricia Nelson Limerick, *The Legacy of Conquest: The Unbroken Past of the American West* (New York, 1987), 157 (quotation).

40. Durning and Brough, *Taking Stock*, 24.

41. Ferguson and Ferguson, *Sacred Cows*, 55, 94; Robert S. Devine, *Alien Invasion: America's Battle with Non-Native Animals and Plants* (Washington, DC, 1998), 52–53, 55, 59, 62.

42. Jeremy Rifkin, *Beyond Beef: The Rise and Fall of the Cattle Culture* (New York, 1993), 105–106; Ferguson and Ferguson, *Sacred Cows*, 84, 205, 216.

43. Glen E. Bugos, "Intellectual Property Protection in the American Chicken-Breeding Industry," *Business History Review* 66 (Spring 1992): 136–137, 147–148.

44. Ibid., 150–155.

45. Ibid., 155–156.

46. U.S. General Accounting Office, *Animal Agriculture: Information on Waste Management and Water Quality Issues*, GAO/RCED-95-200BR, June 1995, 47; Tim Flannery, *The Eternal Frontier: An Ecological History of North America and Its Peoples* (New York, 2001), 324.

47. Ken Silverstein, "Meat Factories," *Sierra*, January/February 1999, 31.

48. Quoted in Dale Miller, "Straight Talk from Smithfield's Joe Luter," *National Hog Farmer*, May 2000.

49. David Barboza, "Goliath of the Hog World," *New York Times*, April 7, 2000; Otis L. Graham, "Again the Backward Region? Environmental History in and of the American South," *Southern Cultures* 6 (Summer 2000): 56.

50. U.S. General Accounting Office, *Animal Agriculture: Waste Management Practices*, GAO/RCED-99-205, July 1999.

51. Quoted in Silverstein, "Meat Factories," 30.

52. Michael Satchell, "Hog Heaven—and Hell," *U.S. News & World Report*, January 22, 1996, 55.

53. Sharon Guynup, "Cell from Hell," *Sierra*, January/February 1999, 34.

CHAPTER 13: AMERICA IN BLACK AND GREEN

1. Quoted in Jamie Lincoln Kitman, "The Secret History of Lead," *Nation*, March 20, 2000, sidebar p. 18.

2. J. R. McNeill, *Something New under the Sun: An Environmental History of the Twentieth-Century World* (New York, 2000), 111.

3. Joseph Interrante, "You Can't Go to Town in a Bathtub: Automobile Movement and the Reorganization of Rural American Space, 1900–1930," *Radical History Review* 21 (Fall 1979): 151, 152 (quotation), 160; idem, "The Road to Autopia: The Automobile and the Spatial Transformation of American Culture," in *The Automobile and American Culture*, ed. David L. Lewis and Laurence Goldstein (Ann Arbor, MI, 1983), 98.

4. Interrante, "The Road to Autopia," 93.

5. Joseph Anthony Interrante, "A Moveable Feast: The Automobile and the Spatial Transformation of American Culture, 1890–1940" (Ph.D. diss., Harvard University, 1983), 12.

6. Tom McCarthy, "The Coming Wonder? Foresight and Early Concerns about the Automobile," *Environmental History* 6 (January 2001): 48 (1st quotation), 50 (2d quotation).

7. Ibid., 49–54.

8. Nelson Lichtenstein et al., *Who Built America? Working People and the Nation's Economy, Politics, Culture, and Society*, 2 vols. (New York, 2000), 2: 329–330, quotation from p. 330.

9. Alan P. Loeb, "Birth of the Kettering Doctrine: Fordism, Sloanism and the Discovery of Tetraethyl Lead," *Business and Economic History* 24 (Fall 1995): 77.

10. Ibid., 81; David Rosner and Gerald Markowitz, "A 'Gift of God'? The Public Health Controversy over Leaded Gasoline during the 1920s," *American Journal of Public Health* 75 (April 1985): 344; Kitman, "The Secret History of Lead," 16–17, 19–20.

11. Loeb, "Birth of the Kettering Doctrine," 82.

12. Quotations in Rosner and Markowitz, "A 'Gift of God'?," 345; Kitman, "The Secret History of Lead," 20.

13. Rosner and Markowitz, "A 'Gift of God'?," 345 (1st quotation), 346 (2d quotation).

14. Quoted in ibid., 349.

15. Ibid., 350 (quotation), 351; William Joseph Kovarik, "The Ethyl Controversy: The News Media and the Public Health Debate over Leaded Gasoline, 1924–1926" (Ph.D. diss., University of Maryland, College Park, 1993), 80, 91.

16. Kitman, "The Secret History of Lead," 14.

17. Glenn Yago, *The Decline of Transit: Urban Transportation in German and U.S. Cities, 1900–1970* (Cambridge, UK, 1984), 56–58.

18. Stephen B. Goddard, *Getting There: The Epic Struggle between Road and Rail in the American Century* (New York, 1994), 121–122; Martha Janet Bianco, "Private Profit versus Public Service: Competing Demands in Urban Transportation History and Policy, Portland, Oregon, 1872–1970" (Ph.D. diss., Portland State University, 1994), 27–55.

19. Bianco, "Private Profit versus Public Service," 453–454; Yago, *The Decline of Transit*, 58–59.

20. Ibid., 441.

21. Ibid., 441–442; Goddard, *Getting There*, 132, 134, 135; Yago, *The Decline of Transit*, 62.

22. Kenneth T. Jackson, *Crabgrass Frontier: The Suburbanization of the United States* (New York, 1985), 167; Jane Holtz Kay, *Asphalt Nation: How the Automobile Took over America and How We Can Take It Back* (New York, 1998), 199.

23. Kay, *Asphalt Nation*, 222–223; Interrante, "A Moveable Feast," 287.

24. Mike Davis, *Ecology of Fear: Los Angeles and the Imagination of Disaster* (New York, 1998), 73–74.

25. Robert A. Caro, *The Power Broker: Robert Moses and the Fall of New York* (New York, 1975), 895 (quotation).

26. Ibid., 897.

27. Ibid., 19, 838, 849 (quotations); Kay, *Asphalt Nation*, 230; Marshall Berman, *All That Is Solid Melts into Air: The Experience of Modernity* (New York, 1982), 294.

28. Caro, *The Power Broker*, 940, 943–944.

29. Ibid., 934–935, 944–949, quotation from p. 935.

30. Berman, *All That Is Solid*, 307.

31. Jackson, *Crabgrass Frontier*, 248–249; Kay, *Asphalt Nation*, 232.

32. Jackson, *Crabgrass Frontier*, 249; Kay, *Asphalt Nation*, 231; Caro, *The Power Broker*, 921.

33. Kay, *Asphalt Nation*, 233 (quotation), 243–244; Deborah Gordon, *Steering a New Course: Transportation, Energy, and the Environment* (Washington, DC, 1991), 12, 37; Davis, *Ecology of Fear*, 80.

34. Jackson, *Crabgrass Frontier*, 232–233, 293–294.

35. Ibid., 283–284.

36. Ibid., 234, 236; Adam Rome, *The Bulldozer in the Countryside: Suburban Sprawl and the Rise of American Environmentalism* (New York, 2001), 16 (quotation).

37. Rome, *The Bulldozer in the Countryside*, 120, 122; Eckbo, Dean, Austin, and Williams, *Open Space: The Choices before California: The Urban Metropolitan Open Space Study* (San Francisco, 1969), 15.

38. Rome, *The Bulldozer in the Countryside*, 121, 166 (quotation); John McPhee, *The Control of Nature* (New York, 1989), 203.

39. Stephen J. Pyne, *Fire in America: A Cultural History of Wildland and Rural Fire*, rev. ed. (Seattle, 1997), 405; Davis, *Ecology of Fear*, 141–146.

40. Rome, *The Bulldozer in the Countryside*, 46.

41. Ibid., 45–54, quotation from p. 52.

42. Ibid., 65–71; Raymond Arsenault, "The End of the Long Hot Summer: The Air Conditioner and Southern Culture," *Journal of Southern History* 50 (November 1984): 615.

43. Arsenault, "The End of the Long Hot Summer," 617.

44. F. Herbert Bormann, Diana Balmori, and Gordon T. Geballe, *Redesigning the American Lawn: A Search for Environmental Harmony* (New Haven, CT, 1993), 96.

45. Michael Pollan, "Why Mow? The Case against Lawns," *New York Times Magazine*, May 28, 1989 (1st quotation); Virginia Scott Jenkins, *The Lawn: A History of an American Obsession* (Washington, DC, 1994), 25, 53 (2d quotation).

46. Quoted in Jenkins, *The Lawn*, 80.

47. Quoted in Virginia Scott Jenkins, " 'Fairway Living': Lawncare and Lifestyle from Croquet to the Golf Course," in *The American Lawn*, ed. Georges Teyssot (New York, 1999), 127.

48. Mark Wigley, "The Electric Lawn," in *The American Lawn*, 155, 156.

49. Georges Teyssot, "The American Lawn: Surface of Everyday Life," in *The American Lawn*, 3.

50. Jenkins, *The Lawn*, 86–87, 142; Bormann, Balmori, and Geballe, *Redesigning the American Lawn*, 109.

51. Quoted in Jenkins, *The Lawn*, 146.

52. Edmund Russell, *War and Nature: Fighting Humans and Insects with Chemicals from World War I to Silent Spring* (New York, 2001), 95–144; Malcolm Gladwell, "The Mosquito Killer," *New Yorker*, July 2, 2001, 42, 48.

53. Beatriz Colomina, "The Lawn at War: 1941–1961," in *The American Lawn*, 138 (1st and 2d quotations); Jenkins, *The Lawn*, 154 (3d quotation).

54. Jenkins, *The Lawn*, 174–176; Bormann, Balmori, and Geballe, *Redesigning the American Lawn*, 33; Wigley, "The Electric Lawn," 191n.

55. Kay, *Asphalt Nation*, 91, 96.

56. Roy A. Rappaport, "Nature, Culture, and Ecological Anthropology," in *Man, Culture, and Society*, ed. Harry L. Shapiro (London, 1956), 263.

CHAPTER 14: THROWAWAY SOCIETY

1. Quoted in Eric Lipton, "The Long and Winding Road Now Followed by New York City's Trash," *New York Times*, March 24, 2001.

2. Quotations from ibid.

3. Jane Celia Busch, "The Throwaway Ethic in America" (Ph.D. diss., University of Pennsylvania, 1983), 335–336; Martin V. Melosi, *The Sanitary City: Urban Infrastructure in America from Colonial Times to the Present* (Baltimore, 2000), 340.

4. Thomas Hine, *The Total Package: The Evolution and Secret Meanings of Boxes, Bottles, Cans, and Tubes* (Boston, 1995), 154; James Brooke, "That Secure Feeling of a Printed Document," *New York Times*, April 21, 2000 (quotation).

5. Busch, "The Throwaway Ethic in America," 80–81; John T. Cumbler, *Reasonable Use: The People, the Environment, and the State: New England, 1790–1930* (New York, 2001), 56 (quotation); William Rathje and Cullen Murphy, *Rubbish: The Archeology of Garbage* (New York, 1992), 102.

6. William Cronon, *Nature's Metropolis: Chicago and the Great West* (New York, 1991), 336.

7. Susan Strasser, *Waste and Want: A Social History of Trash* (New York, 1999), 171–172.

8. Busch, "The Throwaway Ethic in America," table 8, p. 133, 138 (1st quotation), 138–139 (2d quotation).

9. Melosi, *The Sanitary City*, 350; Rathje and Murphy, *Rubbish*, 105, 128.

10. Melosi, *The Sanitary City*, 350; Rathje and Murphy, *Rubbish*, 206, 207.

11. Suellen Hoy, "The Garbage Disposer, the Public Health, and the Good Life," in *Technology and Choice: Readings from Technology and Culture*, ed. Marcel C. LaFollette and Jeffrey K. Stine (Chicago, 1991), 148, 160, 161; Susan Strasser, " 'The Convenience Is Out of This World': The Garbage Disposer and American Consumer Culture," in *Getting and Spending: European and American Consumer Societies in the Twentieth Century*, ed. Susan Strasser, Charles McGovern, and Matthias Judt (New York, 1998), 270 (quotation).

12. Melosi, *The Sanitary City*, table 17.1, p. 340; table 20.1, p. 398.

13. Jeffrey L. Meikle, "Material Doubts: The Consequences of Plastic," *Environmental History* 2 (July 1997): 279 (quotation); Malcolm W. Browne, "World Threat of Plastic Trash Defies Technological Solution," *New York Times*, September 6, 1987.

14. Melosi, *The Sanitary City*, table 17.1, p. 340; table 20.1, p. 398; Meikle, "Material Doubts," 290.

15. Rathje and Murphy, *Rubbish*, 101–102, 166 (quotations).

16. Browne, "World Threat of Plastic Trash."

17. U.S. Congress, House Committee on Small Business, *Scrap Tire Management and Recycling Opportunities*, 101st Cong., 2d sess., 1990, 131, 133–134; U.S. Congress, Office of Technology Assessment, *Facing America's Trash: What Next for Municipal Solid Waste?*, OTA-O-424, 1989, 118.

18. U.S. Congress, Office of Technology Assessment, *Facing America's Trash*, 339.

19. U.S. Congress, House Committee on Small Business, *Scrap Tire Management and Recycling Opportunities*, 71; Jane Holtz Kay, *Asphalt Nation: How the Automobile Took Over America and How We Can Take It Back* (New York, 1998), 87.

20. Donald Kennedy and Marjorie Lucks, "Rubber, Blight, and Mosquitoes: Biogeography Meets the Global Economy," *Environmental History* 4 (July 1999): 369, 376, 377; Chester G. Moore and Carl J. Mitchell, "Aedes Albopictus in the United States: Ten-Year Presence and Public Health Implication," *Emerging Infectious Diseases* 3 (July/September 1997), available online at http://www.cdc.gov/ncidod/EID/vol3no3/moore.htm.

21. Quoted in Chip Brown, "Blazing Tires: Virginia's Own Volcano," *Washington Post*, November 6, 1983.

22. Quoted in Reed Tucker, "What Will Happen To All Those Recalled Tires?" *Fortune*, October 16, 2000, 60.

23. Melosi, *The Sanitary City*, 339; figure 20.1, p. 397.

24. Benjamin Miller, *Fat of the Land: Garbage of New York the Last Two Hundred Years* (New York, 2000), 233; Rathje and Murphy, *Rubbish*, 85–86.

25. Rathje and Murphy, *Rubbish*, 4, 119, 120.

26. Hine, *The Total Package*, 240.

27. Quoted in Nancy Reckler, "New Yorkers Near World's Largest Landfill Say City Dumps on Them," *Washington Post*, August 7, 1996.

28. Miller, *Fat of the Land*, 282–284.

29. William L. Rathje, "Rubbish!," *Atlantic Monthly*, December 1989, 101–102.

30. Melosi, *The Sanitary City*, 401, 402.

31. Miller, *Fat of the Land*, 289–290.

32. Quoted in ibid., 290.

33. Ibid., 296.

34. Kirsten Engel, "Reconsidering the National Market in Solid Waste: Trade-Offs in Equity, Efficiency, Environmental Protection, and State Autonomy," *North Carolina Law Review* 73 (April 1995): 1495–1496.

35. Ibid., 1493–1495.

CHAPTER 15: SHADES OF GREEN

1. Quoted in "Oil Slick Fire Ruins Flats Shipyard," *Plain Dealer* (Cleveland, OH), November 2, 1952.

2. "Cuyahoga River on Fire," ibid., January 1, 1900.

3. "Oil Slick Fire Damages 2 River Spans," ibid. June 23, 1969; Roger Brown, "1969 River Blaze Scarred Image," ibid., June 18, 1989 (Barry quotation); "A Letter from the Publisher" and "The Cities: The Price of Optimism," *Time*, August 1, 1969, 41.

4. Kirkpatrick Sale, *The Green Revolution: The American Environmental Movement, 1962–1992* (New York, 1993), 80.

5. Joseph Anthony Interrante, "A Moveable Feast: The Automobile and the Spatial Transformation of American Culture, 1890–1940" (Ph.D. diss., Harvard University, 1983),

94–97, 98 (quotation); Paul Shriver Sutter, "Driven Wild: The Intellectual and Cultural Origins of Wilderness Advocacy during the Interwar Years" (Ph.D. diss., University of Kansas, 1997), 39.

6. Aldo Leopold, *A Sand County Almanac* (1949; reprint, New York, 1966), x, 240.

7. Sutter, "Driven Wild," 4, 9–10, 63, 66, 67, 431, 448.

8. Paul W. Hirt, *A Conspiracy of Optimism: Management of the National Forests Since World War Two* (Lincoln, NE, 1994), xx, xxiii, xxv, 162–163; Richard N. L. Andrews, *Managing the Environment, Managing Ourselves: A History of American Environmental Policy* (New Haven, CT, 1999), 194.

9. Hirt, *A Conspiracy of Optimism,* 164–165, 229–231; Andrews, *Managing the Environment,* 196; Sale, *The Green Revolution,* 15.

10. Marc Reisner, *Cadillac Desert: The American West and Its Disappearing Water* (New York, 1986), 140, 294.

11. Hal K. Rothman, *The Greening of a Nation? Environmentalism in the United States Since 1945* (Fort Worth, TX, 1998), 41 (quotation); Russell Martin, *A Story That Stands Like a Dam: Glen Canyon and the Struggle for the Soul of the West* (New York, 1989), 64–65, 69; Reisner, *Cadillac Desert,* 295.

12. Quoted in John McPhee, *Encounters with the Archdruid* (New York, 1971), 166.

13. Martin, *A Story That Stands Like a Dam,* 291; McPhee, *Encounters with the Archdruid,* 241 (Brower quotation).

14. Gregg Mitman, *Reel Nature: America's Romance with Wildlife on Film* (Cambridge, MA, 1999), 115 (quotation), 123.

15. Ibid., 126, 134.

16. Linda Lear, *Rachel Carson: Witness for Nature* (New York, 1997), 428; Andrews, *Managing the Environment,* 188; Rachel Carson, *Silent Spring* (1962; reprint, Boston, 1987), 189.

17. Robert Gottlieb, *Forcing the Spring: The Transformation of the American Environmental Movement* (Washington, DC, 1993), 85 (1st quotation); Stephen Fox, *John Muir and His Legacy: The American Conservation Movement* (Boston, 1981), 292.

18. Jerome Namias, "Nature and Possible Causes of the Northeastern United States Drought during 1962–65," *Monthly Weather Review* 94 (September 1966): 543–554.

19. William Ashworth, *The Late, Great Lakes: An Environmental History* (New York, 1986), 133, 142 (quotation); William McGucken, *Lake Erie Rehabilitated: Controlling Cultural Eutrophication, 1960s–1990s* (Akron, OH, 2000), 18–19.

20. Ashworth, *The Late, Great Lakes,* 136 (1st quotation), 143 (2d quotation).

21. Rothman, *The Greening of a Nation?,* 103.

22. Warren J. Belasco, *Appetite for Change: How the Counterculture Took on the Food Industry, 1966–1988* (New York, 1989), 21 (Rat quotation), 36–37; Sale, *The Green Revolution,* 23 (Heilbroner quotation).

23. Terry H. Anderson, *The Movement and the Sixties* (New York, 1995), 343–347, quotation from p. 343.

24. Howard E. McCurdy, *Space and the American Imagination* (Washington, DC, 1997), 227 (1st quotation), 229 (2d quotation).

25. J. Brooks Flippen, *Nixon and the Environment* (Albuquerque, NM, 2000), 227–228.

26. Andrews, *Managing the Environment,* 232–236.

27. Ibid., 236–237.

28. Quoted in Flippen, *Nixon and the Environment,* 15.

29. Sale, *The Green Revolution,* table p. 33; Andrews, *Managing the Environment,* 238.

30. Gottlieb, *Forcing the Spring,* 138–140; Mark Dowie, *Losing Ground: American Environmentalism at the Close of the Twentieth Century* (Cambridge, MA, 1995), 56.

31. Philip Shabecoff, *A Fierce Green Fire: The American Environmental Movement* (New York, 1993), 235, 237.

32. Gottlieb, *Forcing the Spring*, 209; Dowie, *Losing Ground*, 172 (quotation).

33. Robert R. M. Verchick, "In a Greener Voice: Feminist Theory and Environmental Justice," *Harvard Women's Law Journal* 19 (Spring 1996): 48.

34. Robert D. Bullard, ed., *Unequal Protection: Environmental Justice and Communities of Color* (San Francisco, 1994), 17.

35. Terence J. Centner, Warren Kriesel, and Andrew G. Keeler, "Environmental Justice and Toxic Releases: Establishing Evidence of Discriminatory Effect Based on Race and Not Income," *Wisconsin Environmental Law Journal* 3 (Summer 1996): 128–129, 143–146; Stephen Sandweiss, "The Social Construction of Environmental Justice," in *Environmental Injustices, Political Struggles: Race, Class, and the Environment*, ed. David E. Camacho (Durham, NC, 1998), 35.

36. Gottlieb, *Forcing the Spring*, 250–252; Harvey L. White, "Race, Class, and Environmental Hazards," in *Environmental Injustices, Political Struggles*, 69.

37. Dowie, *Losing Ground*, 134–135, quotations from p. 134.

38. James D. Proctor, "Whose Nature? The Contested Moral Terrain of Ancient Forests," in *Uncommon Ground: Rethinking the Human Place in Nature*, ed. William Cronon (New York, 1996), 275–276.

39. William Dietrich, *The Final Forest: The Battle for the Last Great Trees of the Pacific Northwest* (New York, 1992), 74.

40. Gottlieb, *Forcing the Spring*, 196–197; Sale, *The Green Revolution*, 66 (quotation).

41. John Bellamy Foster, "Capitalism and the Ancient Forest: Battle over Old Growth Forest in the Pacific Northwest," *Monthly Review* 43 (October 1991): 11 (1st quotation); Richard White, " 'Are You an Environmentalist or Do You Work for a Living?' Work and Nature," in *Uncommon Ground*, 171 (2d quotation).

42. Tarso Ramos, "Wise Use in the West: The Case of the Northwest Timber Industry," in *Let the People Judge: Wise Use and the Private Property Rights Movement*, ed. John Echeverria and Raymond Booth Eby (Washington, DC, 1995), 88.

43. Foster, "Capitalism and the Ancient Forest," 13 (quotation).

44. Alexis de Tocqueville, *Democracy in America*, ed. J. P. Mayer, trans. George Lawrence (1835–1839; reprint, Garden City, NY, 1969), 270; Shabecoff, *A Fierce Green Fire*, 134.

CHAPTER 16: PLANET U.S.A.

1. Richard P. Tucker, *The United States and the Ecological Degradation of the Tropical World* (Berkeley, CA, 2000), 232–233, 259–261.

2. Richard White, *The Organic Machine: The Remaking of the Columbia River* (New York, 1995), 81 (quotation); Valerie L. Kuletz, *The Tainted Desert: Environmental and Social Ruin in the American West* (New York, 1998), 44–45; Michael D'Antonio, *Atomic Harvest: Hanford and the Lethal Toll of America's Nuclear Arsenal* (New York, 1993), 1–2.

3. Carole Gallagher, *American Ground Zero: The Secret Nuclear War* (Cambridge, MA, 1993), xv, xvii, xxiii (quotation), xxv, 139.

4. J. R. McNeill, *Something New under the Sun: An Environmental History of the Twentieth-Century World* (New York, 2000), 343.

5. Quoted in Bruce Rich, *Mortgaging the Earth: The World Bank, Environmental Impoverishment, and the Crisis of Development* (Boston, 1994), 54.

6. Ibid., 232–234; William U. Chandler, *The Myth of the TVA: Conservation and Development in the Tennessee Valley, 1933–1983* (Cambridge, MA, 1984), 78.

7. Rich, *Mortgaging the Earth*, 9, 12.

8. Ibid., 14, 15, 17.

9. Ibid., 19.

10. Alan B. Durning and Holly B. Brough, *Taking Stock: Animal Farming and the Environment*, Worldwatch Paper 103, July 1991, 32–33, 38; Alexander Cockburn, "A Short, Meat-

Oriented History of the World: From Eden to the Mattole," *New Left Review* 215 (January/February 1996): 37.

11. Susan George, *A Fate Worse Than Debt* (New York, 1988), 162.

12. John Belamy Foster, " 'Let Them Eat Pollution': Capitalism and the World Environment," *Monthly Review* 44 (January 1993), 10, 11 (1st–3d quotations); "You Can Always Tell a Harvard Man . . . ," *Nation*, April 2, 2001, 8 (4th quotation).

13. John H. Perkins, *Geopolitics and the Green Revolution: Wheat, Genes, and the Cold War* (New York, 1997), 117, 119–120, 258.

14. Jack Doyle, *Altered Harvest: Agriculture, Genetics, and the Fate of the World's Food Supply* (New York, 1985), 35–40; Ruth Schwartz Cowan, *A Social History of American Technology* (New York, 1997), 303–310.

15. McNeill, *Something New under the Sun*, 220–221; Perkins, *Geopolitics and the Green Revolution*, 138–139; Doyle, *Altered Harvest*, 257.

16. Doyle, *Altered Harvest*, 258–261; McNeill, *Something New under the Sun*, 221–223.

17. Richard Manning, *Food's Frontier: The Next Green Revolution* (New York, 2000), 4–5.

18. Vandana Shiva, *The Violence of the Green Revolution: Third World Agriculture, Ecology and Politics* (London, 1991), 63–64.

19. Ibid., 74–75, 118; Doyle, *Altered Harvest*, 261 (quotation), 262; McNeill, *Something New under the Sun*, 224.

20. McNeill, *Something New under the Sun*, 223, 224; Vandana Shiva, *Stolen Harvest: The Hijacking of the Global Food Supply* (Cambridge, MA, 2000), 80.

21. Shiva, *The Violence of the Green Revolution*, 91; David Weir and Mark Schapiro, *Circle of Poison: Pesticides and People in a Hungry World* (Oakland, CA, 1981), 37.

22. James C. Scott, *Weapons of the Weak: Everyday Forms of Peasant Resistance* (New Haven, CT, 1985), 56, 80, 148; Weir and Schapiro, *Circle of Poison*, 37–38.

23. Tucker, *Ecological Degradation of the Tropical World*, 63–119, 157, 167, 176–178; Harvey A. Levenstein, *Revolution at the Table: The Transformation of the American Diet* (New York, 1988), 33.

24. Tucker, *Ecological Degradation of the Tropical World*, 250–258, 273, 275.

25. Ibid., 321–322, 328–331; McNeill, *Something New under the Sun*, 236.

26. George, *A Fate Worse Than Debt*, 31, 45; Pearce et al., "Debt and the Environment," *Scientific American* 272 (June 1995): 52–53; Susan George, *The Debt Boomerang: How Third World Debt Harms Us All* (Boulder, CO, 1992), 2.

27. George, *The Debt Boomerang*, xv.

28. Pearce et al., "Debt and the Environment," 53; George, *The Debt Boomerang*, 10, 13, 16; George, *A Fate Worse Than Debt*, 164–165; Rich, *Mortgaging the Earth*, 26–28.

29. Pearce et al., "Debt and the Environment," 53.

30. David E. Nye, *Consuming Power: A Social History of American Energies* (Cambridge, MA, 1999), 6.

31. Ibid., 187, 202, 205, 238.

32. McNeill, *Something New under the Sun*, 109.

33. Ibid., 109–110.

34. Andrew Ross, *Strange Weather: Culture, Science and Technology in the Age of Limits* (London, 1991), 201–202.

35. Ibid., 205 (1st quotation); Jack Doyle, *Taken for a Ride: Detroit's Big Three and the Politics of Pollution* (New York, 2000), 251 (2d quotation).

36. Daniel Sarewitz and Roger Pielke, Jr., "Breaking the Global-Warming Gridlock," *Atlantic Monthly*, July 2000, 57, 61; Andrew C. Revkin, "Study Faults Humans for Large Share of Global Warming," *New York Times*, July 14, 2000.

37. Ross Gelbspan, *The Heat Is On: The High Stakes Battle over Earth's Threatened Climate* (Reading, MA, 1997), 34 (quotation).

38. Doyle, *Taken for a Ride*, 240.

39. Ibid., 268, 373–374.

40. Ibid., 269, 375, 377–378, 386 (quotation).

41. Ibid., 394, 395.

42. Ibid., 396, 401, 402.

43. Ibid., 404, 417 (quotation), 418; Keith Bradsher, "Fuel Economy for New Cars Is at Lowest Level Since '80," *New York Times*, May 18, 2001.

44. Sarewitz and Pielke, "Breaking the Global-Warming Gridlock," 62; McNeill, *Something New under the Sun*, 16.

45. Quoted in Andrew C. Revkin, "Treaty Talks Fail to Find Consensus in Global Warming," *New York Times*, November 26, 2000.

46. Doyle, *Altered Harvest*, 71 (quotation).

47. Quoted in Shiva, *Stolen Harvest*, 11.

48. Marc Lappé and Britt Bailey, *Against the Grain: Biotechnology and the Corporate Takeover of Your Food* (Monroe, ME, 1998), 52–53; Rick Weiss, "Seeds of Discord: Mansanto's Gene Police Raise Alarm on Farmers' Rights, Rural Tradition," *Washington Post*, February 3, 1999.

49. Keith Aoki, "Neocolonialism, Anticommons Property, and Biopiracy in the (Not-So-Brave) New World Order of International Intellectual Property Protection," *Indiana Journal of Global Legal Studies* 6 (Fall 1998): 51; Naomi Roht-Arriaza, "Of Seeds and Shamans: The Appropriation of the Scientific and Technical Knowledge of Indigenous and Local Communities," *Michigan Journal of International Law* 17 (Summer 1996): 922 (quotation).

50. Jack Ralph Kloppenburg, Jr., *First the Seed: The Political Economy of Plant Biotechnology, 1492–2000* (Cambridge, UK, 1988), 152 (1st quotation), 185–186; Roht-Arriaza, "Of Seeds and Shamans," 932–933; Jeremy Rifkin, *The Biotech Century: Harnessing the Gene and Remaking the World* (New York, 1998), 52 (2d quotation).

51. Doyle, *Altered Harvest*, 313 (quotation); Vandana Shiva, "War against Nature and the People of the South," in *Views from the South: The Effects of Globalization and the WTO on Third World Countries*, ed. Sarah Anderson (np., 2000), 115; Laurie Anne Whitt, "Indigenous Peoples, Intellectual Property and the New Imperial Science," *Oklahoma City University Law Review* 23 (Spring/Summer 1998): 257.

52. Maria Margaronis, "The Politics of Food," *Nation*, December 27, 1999, 15 (1st quotation); "A Farmer for Our Time," *CounterPunch*, February 1–15, 2001, 1 (2d quotation).

53. John Vidal, *McLibel: Burger Culture on Trial* (New York, 1997), 35, 42 (quotation).

54. Ibid., 202.

55. Ibid., 206, 208.

56. Richard Smith, "Creative Destruction: Capitalist Development and China's Environment," *New Left Review* 222 (March/April 1997): 17, 25, 27 (quotation).

57. Quoted in Erik Eckholm, "China Said to Sharply Reduce Emissions of Carbon Dioxide," *New York Times*, June 15, 2001.

CONCLUSION: DISNEY TAKES ON THE ANIMAL KINGDOM

1. Quoted in Richard Corliss, "Beauty and the Beasts," *Time*, April 20, 1998, 66.

2. Dennis Blank, "A Mountain Grows in Orlando," *Business Week*, March 1, 1999, 8.

3. On agency, see William H. Sewell, Jr., "A Theory of Structure: Duality, Agency, and Transformation," *American Journal of Sociology* 98 (July 1992): 1–29; Sherry B. Ortner, "Theory in Anthropology Since the Sixties," *Comparative Studies in Society and History* 26 (January 1984): 126–166.

4. Karl Marx, "The Eighteenth Brumaire of Louis Bonaparte," in *The Marx-Engels Reader*, 2d ed., ed. Robert C. Tucker (New York, 1978), 595.

BIBLIOGRAPHY

Aduddell, Robert, and Louis Cain. "Location and Collusion in the Meat Packing Industry." In *Business Enterprise and Economic Change*, edited by Louis P. Cain and Paul J. Uselding. Kent, OH: Kent State Univ. Press, 1973.

Aiken, Charles S. *The Cotton Plantation South Since the Civil War.* Baltimore: Johns Hopkins Univ. Press, 1998.

Anderson, M. Kat, Michael G. Barbour, and Valerie Whitworth. "A World of Balance and Plenty: Land, Plants, Animals, and Humans in a Pre-European California." In *Contested Eden: California before the Gold Rush*, edited by Ramón A. Gutiérrez and Richard J. Orsi. Berkeley: Univ. of California Press, 1998.

Anderson, Terry H. *The Movement and the Sixties.* New York: Oxford Univ. Press, 1995.

Andrews, Richard N. L. *Managing the Environment, Managing Ourselves: A History of American Environmental Policy.* New Haven, CT: Yale Univ. Press, 1999.

Aoki, Keith. "Neocolonialism, Anticommons Property, and Biopiracy in the (Not-So-Brave) New World Order of International Intellectual Property Protection." *Indiana Journal of Global Legal Studies* 6 (Fall 1998): 11–58.

Armstrong, Ellis L., Michael C. Robinson, and Suellen M. Hoy, eds. *History of Public Works in the United States, 1776–1976.* Chicago: American Public Works Association, 1976.

Arnould, Richard J. "Changing Patterns of Concentration in American Meat Packing, 1880–1963." *Business History Review* 45 (Spring 1971): 18–34.

Arsenault, Raymond. "The End of the Long Hot Summer: The Air Conditioner and Southern Culture." *Journal of Southern History* 50 (November 1984): 597–628.

Ashworth, William. *The Late, Great Lakes: An Environmental History.* New York: Alfred A. Knopf, 1986.

Barger, Harold, and Hans H. Landsberg. *American Agriculture, 1899–1939: A Study of Output, Employment and Productivity.* New York: National Bureau of Economic Research, 1942.

Baron, William R. "Eighteenth-Century New England Climate Variation and Its Suggested Impact on Society." *Maine Historical Society Quarterly* 21 (Spring 1982): 201–218.

Baron, William, and Anne F. Bridges. "Making Hay in Northern New England: Maine as a Case Study, 1800–1850." *Agricultural History* 57 (April 1983): 165–180.

Belasco, Warren J. *Appetite for Change: How the Counterculture Took on the Food Industry, 1966–1988.* New York: Pantheon, 1989.

Bello, Walden. *Dark Victory: The United States and Global Poverty.* 2d ed. London: Pluto, 1999.

Berman, Marshall. *All That Is Solid Melts into Air: The Experience of Modernity.* New York: Penguin, 1982.

Bianco, Martha Janet. "Private Profit versus Public Service: Competing Demands in Urban Transportation History and Policy, Portland Oregon, 1872–1970." Ph.D. diss., Portland State Univ., 1994.

Blackmar, Elizabeth. "Accountability for Public Health: Regulating the Housing Market in Nineteenth-Century New York City." In *Hives of Sickness: Public Health and Epidemics in New York City*, edited by David Rosner. New Brunswick, NJ: Rutgers Univ. Press, 1995.

———. "Contemplating the Force of Nature." *Radical Historians Newsletter*, no. 70, May 1994.

Blumberg, Louis, and Robert Gottlieb. *War on Waste: Can America Win Its Battle with Garbage?* Washington, DC: Island Press, 1989.

Bogue, Margaret Beattie. *Fishing the Great Lakes: An Environmental History, 1783–1933.* Madison: Univ. of Wisconsin Press, 2000.

Bormann, F. Herbert, Diana Balmori, and Gordon T. Geballe. *Redesigning the American Lawn: A Search for Environmental Harmony.* New Haven, CT: Yale Univ. Press, 1993.

Bowden, Martyn J., Robert W. Kates, Paul A. Kay, William E. Riebsame, Richard A. Warrick, Douglas L. Johnson, Harvey A. Gould, and Daniel Weiner. "The Effect of Climate Fluctuations on Human Populations: Two Hypotheses." In *Climate and History*, edited by T. M. L. Wigley, M. J. Ingram, and G. Farmer. Cambridge: Cambridge Univ. Press, 1981.

Box, Thadis W. "Range Deterioration in West Texas." *Southwestern Historical Quarterly* 71 (1967–1968): 37–45.

Braund, Kathryn Holland. " 'Hog Wild' and 'Nuts: Billy Boll Weevil Comes to the Alabama Wiregrass." *Agricultural History* 63 (Summer 1989): 15–39.

Brechin, Gray. *Imperial San Francisco: Urban Power, Earthly Ruin.* Berkeley: Univ. of California Press, 1999.

Breen, T. H. *Tobacco Culture: The Mentality of the Great Tidewater Planters on the Eve of Revolution.* Princeton, NJ: Princeton Univ. Press, 1985.

Brick, Philip. "Taking Back the Rural West." In *Let the People Judge: Wise Use and the Private Property Rights Movement*, edited by John Echeverria and Raymond Booth Eby. Washington, DC: Island Press, 1995.

Brown, Lester R., Michael Renner, and Brian Halweil. *Vital Signs 2000: The Environmental Trends That Are Shaping Our Future.* New York: W. W. Norton, 2000.

Brown, R. Ben. "Closing the Southern Range: A Chapter in the Decline of the Southern Yeomanry." American Bar Foundation, Working Paper #9020, 1990.

———. "The Southern Range: A Study in Nineteenth Century Law and Society." Ph.D. diss., Univ. of Michigan, 1993.

Buell, Lawrence. *The Environmental Imagination: Thoreau, Nature Writing, and the Formation of American Culture.* Cambridge, MA: Harvard Univ. Press, 1995.

Bugos, Glen E. "Intellectual Property Protection in the American Chicken-Breeding Industry." *Business History Review* 66 (Spring 1992): 127–168.

Bullard, Robert D., ed. *Unequal Protection: Environmental Justice and Communities of Color.* San Francisco: Sierra Club Books, 1994.

Burrows, Edwin G., and Mike Wallace. *Gotham: A History of New York City to 1898.* New York: Oxford Univ. Press, 1999.

Busch, Jane Celia. "The Throwaway Ethic in America." Ph.D. diss., Univ. of Pennsylvania, 1983.

Bushman, Richard Lyman. "Markets and Composite Farms in Early America." *William and Mary Quarterly*, 3d Ser., 55 (July 1998): 351–374.

Callicott, J. Baird, ed. *Companion to A Sand County Almanac: Interpretive and Critical Essays.* Madison: Univ. of Wisconsin Press, 1987.

Calloway, Colin G. *New Worlds for All: Indians, Europeans, and the Remaking of Early America.* Baltimore: Johns Hopkins Univ. Press, 1997.

Carney, Judith A. *Black Rice: The African Origins of Rice Cultivation in the Americas.* Cambridge, MA: Harvard Univ. Press, 2001.

Caro, Robert A. *The Power Broker: Robert Moses and the Fall of New York.* New York: Vintage, 1975.

Carroll, Charles F. *The Timber Economy of Puritan New England.* Providence, RI: Brown Univ. Press, 1973.

Carson, Rachel. *Silent Spring.* 1962. Reprint. Boston: Houghton Mifflin, 1987.

Caudill, Harry M. *My Land Is Dying.* New York: Dutton, 1971.

———. *Night Comes to the Cumberlands.* Boston: Atlantic Monthly, 1962.

Centner, Terence J., Warren Kriesel, and Andrew G. Keeler. "Environmental Justice and

Toxic Releases: Establishing Evidence of Discriminatory Effect Based on Race and Not Income." *Wisconsin Environmental Law Journal* 3 (Summer 1996): 119–158.

Chadde, Steve W., and Charles E. Kay. "Tall-Willow Communities on Yellowstone's Northern Range: A Test of the 'Natural-Regulation' Paradigm." In *The Greater Yellowstone Ecosystem: Redefining America's Wilderness Heritage*, edited by Robert B. Keiter and Mark S. Boyce. New Haven, CT: Yale Univ. Press, 1991.

Chan, Sucheng. *This Bitter-Sweet Soil: The Chinese in California Agriculture, 1860–1910.* Berkeley: Univ. of California Press, 1986.

Chandler, William U. *The Myth of the TVA: Conservation and Development in the Tennessee Valley, 1933–1983.* Cambridge, MA: Ballinger, 1984.

Chaplin, Joyce E. *An Anxious Pursuit: Agricultural Innovation and Modernity in the Lower South, 1730–1815.* Chapel Hill: Univ. of North Carolina Press, 1993.

————. "Tidal Rice Cultivation and the Problem of Slavery in South Carolina and Georgia, 1760–1815." *William and Mary Quarterly*, 3d Ser., 49 (January 1992): 29–61.

Chase, Alston. *In a Dark Wood: The Fight over Forests and the Rising Tyranny of Ecology.* Boston: Houghton Mifflin, 1995.

————. *Playing God in Yellowstone: The Destruction of America's First National Park.* San Diego, CA: Harcourt Brace, 1987.

Chesson, Michael B. "Harlots or Heroines? A New Look at the Richmond Bread Riot." *Virginia Magazine of History and Biography* 92 (April 1984): 131–175.

Clark, Christopher. *The Roots of Rural Capitalism: Western Massachusetts, 1780–1860.* Ithaca, NY: Cornell Univ. Press, 1990.

Clements, Kendrick A. *Hoover, Conservation, and Consumerism: Engineering the Good Life.* Lawrence: Univ. Press of Kansas, 2000.

Cockburn, Alexander. "A Short, Meat-Oriented History of the World: From Eden to the Mattole." *New Left Review* 215 (January/February 1996): 16–42.

Cohen, Leah Hager. *Glass, Paper, Beans: Revelations on the Nature and Value of Ordinary Things.* New York: Doubleday, 1997.

Cohen, Michael P. *The Pathless Way: John Muir and American Wilderness.* Madison: Univ. of Wisconsin Press, 1984.

Colby, Charles C. "The California Raisin Industry—A Study in Geographic Interpretation." *Annals of the Association of American Geographers* 14 (June 1924): 49–108.

Colomina, Beatriz. "The Lawn at War: 1941–1961." In *The American Lawn*, edited by Georges Teyssot. New York: Princeton Architectural Press, 1999.

Commoner, Barry. *The Closing Circle: Nature, Man and Technology.* New York: Alfred A. Knopf, 1971.

————. *The Poverty of Power: Energy and the Economic Crisis.* New York: Bantam, 1977.

Conkin, Paul K. "Hot, Humid, and Sad." *Journal of Southern History* 64 (February 1998): 3–22.

Corbett, Katharine T. "Draining the Metropolis: The Politics of Sewers in Nineteenth Century St. Louis." In *Common Fields: An Environmental History of St. Louis*, edited by Andrew Hurley. St. Louis: Missouri Historical Society, 1997.

Coughenour, Michael B., and Francis J. Singer. "The Concept of Overgrazing and Its Application to Yellowstone's Northern Range." In *The Greater Yellowstone Ecosystem: Redefining America's Wilderness Heritage*, edited by Robert B. Keiter and Mark S. Boyce. New Haven, CT: Yale Univ. Press, 1991.

Cowan, Ruth Schwartz. *A Social History of American Technology.* New York: Oxford Univ. Press, 1997.

Cowdrey, Albert E. *This Land, This South: An Environmental History.* Revised Edition. Lexington: Univ. of Kentucky Press, 1996.

Cox, Thomas R., Robert S. Maxwell, Phillip Drennon Thomas, and Joseph J. Malone. *This*

Well-Wooded Land: Americans and Their Forests from Colonial Times to the Present. Lincoln: Univ. of Nebraska Press, 1985.

Craighead, John J. "Yellowstone in Transition." In *The Greater Yellowstone Ecosystem: Redefining America's Wilderness Heritage,* edited by Robert B. Keiter and Mark S. Boyce. New Haven, CT: Yale Univ. Press, 1991.

Craven, Avery Odelle. *Soil Exhaustion as a Factor in the Agricultural History of Virginia and Maryland, 1607–1860.* Urbana: Univ. of Illinois Press, 1926.

Cronon, William. *Changes in the Land: Indians, Colonists, and the Ecology of New England.* New York: Hill and Wang, 1983.

———. *Nature's Metropolis: Chicago and the Great West.* New York: W. W. Norton, 1991.

———, ed. *Uncommon Ground: Rethinking the Human Place in Nature.* New York: W. W. Norton, 1996.

———. "Modes of Prophecy and Production: Placing Nature in History." *Journal of American History* 76 (March 1990): 1122–1131.

———. "A Place for Stories: Nature, History, and Narrative." *Journal of American History* 78 (March 1992): 1347–1376.

———. "The Uses of Environmental History." *Environmental History Review* 17 (Fall 1993): 1–22.

Cronon, William, and Richard White. "Indians in the Land." *American Heritage* 37 (August/September 1986): 18–25.

Crosby, Alfred W., Jr. *The Columbian Exchange: Biological and Cultural Consequences of 1492.* Westport, CT: Greenwood, 1972.

———. *Ecological Imperialism: The Biological Expansion of Europe, 900–1900.* New York: Cambridge Univ. Press, 1986.

Cuff, Timothy. "A Weighty Issue Revisited: New Evidence on Commercial Swine Weights and Pork Production in Mid-Nineteenth Century America." *Agricultural History* 66 (Fall 1992): 55–74.

Cumbler, John T. *Reasonable Use: The People, the Environment, and the State: New England, 1790–1930.* New York: Oxford Univ. Press, 2001.

———. "The Early Making of an Environmental Consciousness: Fish, Fisheries Commissions, and the Connecticut River." *Environmental History Review* 15 (Winter 1991): 73–91.

D'Antonio, Michael. *Atomic Harvest: Hanford and the Lethal Toll of America's Nuclear Arsenal.* New York: Crown, 1993.

Dale, Edward Everett. *The Range Cattle Industry: Ranching on the Great Plains from 1865 to 1925.* Norman: Univ. of Oklahoma Press, 1960.

Daniels, John D. "The Indian Population of North America in 1492." *William and Mary Quarterly,* 3d Ser., 49 (April 1992): 298–320.

Dasmann, Raymond F. *The Destruction of California.* New York: Macmillan, 1965.

Davis, Donald Edward. *Where There Are Mountains: An Environmental History of the Southern Appalachians.* Athens: Univ. of Georgia Press, 2000.

Davis, John, and Dave Foreman, eds. *The Earth First! Reader: Ten Years of Radical Environmentalism.* Salt Lake City, UT: Peregrine Smith, 1991.

Davis, Mike. *Ecology of Fear: Los Angeles and the Imagination of Disaster.* New York: Metropolitan, 1998.

———. *Late Victorian Holocausts: El Niño Famines and the Making of the Third World.* London: Verso, 2001.

Davis, Susan G. *Spectacular Nature: Corporate Culture and the Sea World Experience.* Berkeley: Univ. of California Press, 1997.

Dawson, Robert, and Gray Brechin. *Farewell, Promised Land: Waking from the California Dream.* Berkeley: Univ. of California Press, 1999.

Dean, Warren. *Brazil and the Struggle for Rubber: A Study in Environmental History*. New York: Cambridge Univ. Press, 1987.

deBuys, William. *Salt Dreams: Land and Water in Low-Down California*. Albuquerque: Univ. of New Mexico Press, 1999.

Deloria, Vine, Jr. *Red Earth, White Lies: Native Americans and the Myth of Scientific Fact*. New York: Scribner, 1995.

Denevan, William M., ed. *The Native Population of the Americas in 1492*. Madison: Univ. of Wisconsin Press, 1976.

Devine, Robert S. *Alien Invasion: America's Battle with Non-Native Animals and Plants*. Washington, DC: National Geographic Society, 1998.

Diamond, Jared. *Guns, Germs, and Steel: The Fates of Human Societies*. New York: W. W. Norton, 1997.

———. *The Third Chimpanzee: The Evolution and Future of the Human Animal*. New York: Harper Collins, 1992.

———. "Why Was Post-Pleistocene Development of Human Societies Slightly More Rapid in the Old World Than in the New World?" In *Americans before Columbus: Ice Age Origins*, compiled and edited by Ronald C. Carlisle. Pittsburgh, PA: Univ. of Pittsburgh Press, 1988.

Di Chiro, Giovanna. "Nature as Community: The Convergence of Environment and Social Justice." In *Uncommon Ground: Rethinking the Human Place in Nature*, edited by William Cronon. New York: W. W. Norton, 1996.

Dietrich, William. *The Final Forest: The Battle for the Last Great Trees of the Pacific Northwest*. New York: Simon and Schuster, 1992.

Dobyns, Henry F. *Their Numbers Become Thinned: Native Population Dynamics in Eastern North America*. Knoxville: Univ. of Tennessee Press, 1983.

Donahue, Brian. "Plowland, Pastureland, Woodland and Meadow: Husbandry in Concord, Massachusetts, 1635–1771." Ph.D. diss., Brandeis Univ., 1995.

———. " 'Dammed at Both Ends and Cursed in the Middle': The 'Flowage' of the Concord River Meadows, 1798–1862." *Environmental Review* 13 (Fall/Winter 1989): 47–67.

———. "The Forests and Fields of Concord: An Ecological History, 1750–1850." *Chronos* 2 (Fall 1983): 15–63.

Dorman, Robert L. *A Word for Nature: Four Pioneering Environmental Advocates, 1845–1913*. Chapel Hill: Univ. of North Carolina Press, 1998.

Dowie, Mark. *Losing Ground: American Environmentalism at the Close of the Twentieth Century*. Cambridge, MA: MIT Press, 1995.

Doyle, Jack. *Altered Harvest: Agriculture, Genetics, and the Fate of the World's Food Supply*. New York: Viking, 1985.

———. *Taken for a Ride: Detroit's Big Three and the Politics of Pollution*. New York: Four Walls Eight Windows, 2000.

Duncan, Colin A. M. *The Centrality of Agriculture: Between Humankind and the Rest of Nature*. Montreal: McGill-Queen's Univ. Press, 1996.

Dunlap, Thomas R. *DDT: Scientists, Citizens, and Public Policy*. Princeton, NJ: Princeton Univ. Press, 1981.

———. "Values for Varmints: Predator Control and Environmental Ideas, 1920–1939." *Pacific Historical Review* 53 (May 1984): 141–161.

———. "Wildlife, Science, and the National Parks, 1920–1940." *Pacific Historical Review* 59 (May 1990): 187–202.

Durning, Alan B., and Holly B. Brough. *Taking Stock: Animal Farming and the Environment*. Worldwatch Paper 103, July 1991.

Earle, Carville. *Geographical Inquiry and American Historical Problems*. Stanford, CA: Stanford Univ. Press, 1992.

Easterbrook, Gregg. *A Moment on the Earth: The Coming Age of Environmental Optimism.* New York: Viking Penguin, 1995.

Eckbo, Dean, Austin, and Williams. *Open Space: The Choices before California: The Urban Metropolitan Open Space Study.* San Francisco, 1969.

Edelson, S. Max. "Planting the Lowcountry: Agricultural Enterprise and Economic Experience in the Lower South, 1695–1785." Ph.D. diss., Johns Hopkins Univ., 1998.

Elkind, Sarah S. *Bay Cities and Water Politics: The Battle for Resources in Boston and Oakland.* Lawrence: Univ. Press of Kansas, 1998.

Eller, Ronald D. *Miners, Millhands, and Mountaineers: Industrialization of the Appalachian South, 1880–1930.* Knoxville: Univ. of Tennessee Press, 1982.

Engel, Kirsten. "Reconsidering the National Market in Solid Waste: Trade-Offs in Equity, Efficiency, Environmental Protection, and State Autonomy." *North Carolina Law Review* 73 (April 1995): 1481–1566.

Ewens, Lara E. "Seed Wars: Biotechnology, Intellectual Property, and the Quest for High Yield Seeds." *Boston College International and Comparative Law Review* 23 (Spring 2000): 285–310.

Fagan, Brian. *The Little Ice Age: How Climate Made History, 1300–1850.* New York: Basic Books, 2000.

Faust, Drew Gilpin. *The Creation of Confederate Nationalism.* Baton Rouge: Louisiana State Univ. Press, 1988.

Fenn, Elizabeth A. "Biological Warfare in Eighteenth-Century North America: Beyond Jeffrey Amherst." *Journal of American History* 86 (March 2000): 1552–1580.

Ferguson, Denzel, and Nancy Ferguson. *Sacred Cows at the Public Trough.* Bend, OR: Maverick Publications, 1983.

Fischer, David Hackett. *Albion's Seed: Four British Folkways in America.* New York: Oxford Univ. Press, 1989.

Fite, Gilbert C. *Cotton Fields No More: Southern Agriculture, 1865–1980.* Lexington: Univ. of Kentucky Press, 1984.

Flader, Susan L. *Thinking Like a Mountain: Aldo Leopold and the Evolution of an Ecological Attitude toward Deer, Wolves, and Forests.* Columbia: Univ. of Missouri Press, 1974.

Flannery, Tim. *The Eternal Frontier: An Ecological History of North America and Its Peoples.* New York: Atlantic Monthly Press, 2001.

Flippen, J. Brooks. *Nixon and the Environment.* Albuquerque: Univ. of New Mexico Press, 2000.

Foster, David R. *Thoreau's Country: Journey through a Transformed Landscape.* Cambridge, MA: Harvard Univ. Press, 1999.

Foster, John Bellamy. "Capitalism and the Ancient Forest: Battle over Old Growth Forest in the Pacific Northwest." *Monthly Review* 43 (October 1991): 1–16.

———. " 'Let Them Eat Pollution': Capitalism and the World Environment." *Monthly Review* 44 (January 1993): 10–20.

Foster, John Bellamy, and Fred Magdoff. "Liebig, Marx, and the Depletion of Soil Fertility: Relevance for Today's Agriculture." In *Hungry for Profit: The Agribusiness Threat to Farmers, Food, and the Environment,* edited by Fred Magdoff, John Bellamy Foster, and Frederick H. Buttel. New York: Monthly Review Press, 2000.

Fox, Stephen. *John Muir and His Legacy: The American Conservation Movement.* Boston: Little, Brown and Company, 1981.

Frazier, Ian. *Great Plains.* New York: Farrar, Straus and Giroux, 1989.

Freeman, Douglas Southall. *R. E. Lee: A Biography.* 4 vols. New York: Charles Scribner's Sons, 1934–1935.

Freeze, R. Allan. *The Environmental Pendulum: A Quest for the Truth about Toxic Chemicals, Human Health, and Environmental Protection.* Berkeley: Univ. of California Press, 2000.

Freund, Peter, and George Martin. *The Ecology of the Automobile.* Montreal: Black Rose, 1993.

Friedberger, Mark. "Cattlemen, Consumers, and Beef." *Environmental History Review* 18 (Fall 1994): 37–57.

Gallagher, Carole. *American Ground Zero: The Secret Nuclear War.* Cambridge, MA: MIT Press, 1993.

Gates, Paul Wallace. *Agriculture and the Civil War.* New York: Alfred A. Knopf, 1965.

———. "Federal Land Policy in the South, 1866–1888." *Journal of Southern History* 6 (August 1940): 303–330.

Gelbspan, Ross. *The Heat Is On: The High Stakes Battle over Earth's Threatened Climate.* Reading, MA: Addison-Wesley, 1997.

Genovese, Eugene D. *The Political Economy of Slavery: Studies in the Economy and Society of the Slave South.* New York: Vintage, 1967.

———. *Roll, Jordon, Roll: The World the Slaves Made.* New York: Vintage, 1974.

George, Susan. *The Debt Boomerang: How Third World Debt Harms Us All.* Boulder, CO: Westview, 1992.

———. *A Fate Worse Than Debt.* New York: Grove Press, 1988.

Gilman, Carolyn, and Mary Jane Schneider. *The Way to Independence: Memories of a Hidatsa Indian Family, 1840–1920.* St. Paul: Minnesota Historical Society Press, 1987.

Goddard, Stephen B. *Getting There: The Epic Struggle between Road and Rail in the American Century.* New York: Basic Books, 1994.

Gordon, Deborah. *Steering a New Course: Transportation, Energy, and the Environment.* Washington, DC: Island Press, 1991.

Gottlieb, Robert. *Forcing the Spring: The Transformation of the American Environmental Movement.* Washington, DC: Island Press, 1993.

Graham, Otis L. "Again the Backward Region? Environmental History in and of the American South." *Southern Cultures* 6 (Summer 2000): 50–72.

Gray, Lewis Cecil. *History of Agriculture in the Southern United States to 1860.* 2 vols. Reprint Edition. Gloucester, MA: Peter Smith, 1958.

Greider, William. *One World, Ready or Not: The Manic Logic of Global Capitalism.* New York: Simon and Schuster, 1998.

Griffen, Keith. *The Political Economy of Agrarian Change: An Essay on the Green Revolution.* London: Macmillan, 1974.

Gross, Robert A. *The Minutemen and Their World.* New York: Hill and Wang, 1976.

———. "Culture and Cultivation: Agriculture and Society in Thoreau's Concord." *Journal of American History* 69 (June 1982): 42–61.

Grossman, James R. *Land of Hope: Chicago, Black Southerners, and the Great Migration.* Chicago: Univ. of Chicago Press, 1989.

Groves, R. H., and F. Di Castri, eds. *Biogeography of Mediterranean Invasions.* Cambridge: Cambridge Univ. Press, 1991.

Gutiérrez, Ramón A. *When Jesus Came, the Corn Mothers Went Away.* Stanford, CA: Stanford Univ. Press, 1991.

Hahn, Steven. *The Roots of Southern Populism: Yeoman Farmers and the Transformation of the Georgia Upcountry, 1850–1890.* New York: Oxford Univ. Press, 1983.

———. "Hunting, Fishing, and Foraging: Common Rights and Class Relations in the Postbellum South." *Radical History Review* 26 (October 1982): 37–64.

———. "A Response: Common Cents or Historical Sense?" *Journal of Southern History* 59 (May 1993): 243–258.

Handlin, Oscar. *This Was America: True Accounts of People and Places, Manners and Customs, As Recorded by European Travelers to the Western Shore in the Eighteenth, Nineteenth, and Twentieth Centuries.* Cambridge, MA: Harvard Univ. Press, 1949.

Hardy, Charles. "Fish or Foul: A History of the Delaware River Basin through the Perspective of the American Shad, 1682 to the Present." *Pennsylvania History* 66 (Autumn 1999): 506–534.

Harris, Marvin. *Cannibals and Kings: The Origins of Cultures.* New York: Random House, 1977.

———. *Cultural Materialism: The Struggle for a Science of Culture.* New York: Random House, 1979.

———. *The Sacred Cow and the Abominable Pig: Riddles of Food and Culture.* New York: Simon and Schuster, 1987.

Harris, Marvin, and Eric B. Ross. "How Beef Became King." *Psychology Today,* October 1978.

Hartog, Hendrik. "Pigs and Positivism." *Wisconsin Law Review* 1985 (July/August 1985): 899–935.

Harvey, David. *The Urban Experience.* Baltimore: Johns Hopkins Univ. Press, 1989.

Harvey, Mark W. T. *A Symbol of Wilderness: Echo Park and the American Conservation Movement.* Albuquerque: Univ. of New Mexico Press, 1994.

Haygood, Tamara Miner. "Cows, Ticks, and Disease: A Medical Interpretation of the Southern Cattle Industry." *Journal of Southern History* 52 (November 1986): 551–564.

Hays, Samuel P. *Beauty, Health, and Permanence: Environmental Politics in the United States, 1955–1985.* New York: Cambridge Univ. Press, 1987.

———. *Conservation and the Gospel of Efficiency: The Progressive Conservation Movement, 1890–1920.* Cambridge, MA: Harvard Univ. Press, 1959.

———. *A History of Environmental Politics Since 1945.* Pittsburgh, PA: Univ. of Pittsburgh Press, 2000.

Helms, John Douglas. "Just Lookin' for a Home: The Cotton Boll Weevil and the South." Ph.D. diss., Florida State Univ., 1977.

Henige, David. *Numbers from Nowhere: The American Indian Contact Population Debate.* Norman: Univ. of Oklahoma Press, 1998.

Hill, Mary. *Gold: The California Story.* Berkeley: Univ. of California Press, 1999.

Hilliard, Sam Bowers. *Hog Meat and Hoecake: Food Supply in the Old South, 1840–1860.* Carbondale: Southern Illinois Univ. Press, 1972.

———. "The Tidewater Rice Plantation: An Ingenious Adaptation to Nature." *Geoscience and Man* 12 (June 1975): 57–66.

Hine, Thomas. *The Total Package: The Evolution and Secret Meanings of Boxes, Bottles, Cans, and Tubes.* Boston: Little, Brown and Company, 1995.

Hirt, Paul W. *A Conspiracy of Optimism: Management of the National Forests Since World War Two.* Lincoln: Univ. of Nebraska Press, 1994.

Hogan, David Gerard. *Selling 'em by the Sack: White Castle and the Creation of American Food.* New York: New York Univ. Press, 1997.

Hornaday, William T. *Our Vanishing Wild Life: Its Extermination and Preservation.* New York: Charles Scribner's Sons, 1913.

———. *Wild Life Conservation in Theory and Practice.* New Haven, CT: Yale University Press, 1914.

Hoy, Suellen. *Chasing Dirt: The American Pursuit of Cleanliness.* New York: Oxford Univ. Press, 1995.

———. "The Garbage Disposer, the Public Health, and the Good Life." In *Technology and Choice: Readings from Technology and Culture,* edited by Marcel C. LaFollette and Jeffrey K. Stine. Chicago: Univ. of Chicago Press, 1991.

Hundley, Norris, Jr. *The Great Thirst: Californians and Water, 1770s–1990s.* Berkeley: Univ. of California Press, 1992.

Hunt, Charles B. *Natural Regions of the United States and Canada.* San Francisco: Freeman, 1974.

Hurley, Andrew. *Class, Race, and Industrial Pollution in Gary, Indiana, 1945–1980.* Chapel Hill: Univ. of North Carolina Press, 1995.

Hurst, James Willard. *Law and Economic Growth: The Legal History of the Lumber Industry in Wisconsin, 1836–1915.* Revised Edition. Madison: Univ. of Wisconsin Press, 1984.

Interrante, Joseph. "A Moveable Feast: The Automobile and the Spatial Transformation of American Culture, 1890–1940." Ph.D. diss., Harvard Univ., 1983.

————. "The Road to Autopia: The Automobile and the Spatial Transformation of American Culture." In *The Automobile and American Culture*, edited by David L. Lewis and Laurence Goldstein. Ann Arbor: Univ. of Michigan Press, 1983.

————. "You Can't Go to Town in a Bathtub: Automobile Movement and the Reorganization of Rural American Space, 1900–1930." *Radical History Review* 21 (Fall 1979): 151–168.

Isenberg, Andrew C. *The Destruction of the Bison.* New York: Cambridge Univ. Press, 2000.

Iverson, Peter. *When Indians Became Cowboys: Native Peoples and Cattle Ranching in the American West.* Norman: Univ. of Oklahoma Press, 1994.

Jackle, John A., and Keith A. Sculle. *Fast Food: Roadside Restaurants in the Automobile Age.* Baltimore: Johns Hopkins Univ. Press, 1999.

Jackson, Kenneth T. *Crabgrass Frontier: The Suburbanization of the United States.* New York: Oxford Univ. Press, 1985.

Jacoby, Karl. *Crimes against Nature: Squatters, Poachers, Thieves, and the Hidden History of American Conservation.* Berkeley: Univ. of California Press, 2001.

Jenkins, Virginia Scott. *The Lawn: A History of an American Obsession.* Washington, DC: Smithsonian Institution Press, 1994.

————. " 'Fairway Living': Lawncare and Lifestyle from Croquet to the Golf Course." In *The American Lawn*, edited by Georges Teyssot. New York: Princeton Architectural Press, 1999.

Jennings, Francis. *The Invasion of America: Indians, Colonialism, and the Cant of Conquest.* Chapel Hill: Univ. of North Carolina Press, 1975.

Johnson, Hildegard Binder. *Order upon the Land: The U.S. Rectangular Land Survey and the Upper Mississippi Country.* New York: Oxford Univ. Press, 1976.

Johnson, Stephen, Robert Dawson, and Gerald Haslam. *The Great Central Valley: California's Heartland.* Berkeley: Univ. of California Press, 1993.

Jones, E. L. *The European Miracle: Environments, Economics and Geopolitics in the History of Europe and Asia.* Cambridge: Cambridge Univ. Press, 1981.

————. "Creative Disruptions in American Agriculture, 1620–1820." *Agricultural History* 48 (October 1974): 510–528.

Jordan, Terry G. *North American Cattle-Ranching Frontiers: Origins, Diffusion, and Differentiation.* Albuquerque: Univ. of New Mexico Press, 1993.

Joyner, Charles. *Down by the Riverside: A South Carolina Slave Community.* Urbana: Univ. of Illinois Press, 1984.

Judd, Richard W. *Common Lands, Common People: The Origins of Conservation in Northern New England.* Cambridge, MA: Harvard Univ. Press, 1997.

Kantor, Shawn Everett, and J. Morgan Kousser. "Common Sense or Commonwealth? The Fence Law and Institutional Change in the Postbellum South." *Journal of Southern History* 59 (May 1993): 201–242.

Kay, Jane Holtz. *Asphalt Nation: How the Automobile Took over America and How We Can Take It Back.* Berkeley: Univ. of California Press, 1998.

Kelley, Robert. *Battling the Inland Sea: American Political Culture, Public Policy, and the Sacramento Valley, 1850–1986.* Berkeley: Univ. of California Press, 1989.

Kennedy, Donald, and Marjorie Lucks. "Rubber, Blight, and Mosquitoes: Biogeography Meets the Global Economy." *Environmental History* 4 (July 1999): 369–383.

King, J. Crawford, Jr. "The Closing of the Southern Range: An Exploratory Study." *Journal of Southern History* 48 (February 1982): 53–70.

King, Margaret J. "Empires of Popular Culture: McDonald's and Disney." In *Ronald Revisited: The World of Ronald McDonald*, edited by Marshall William Fishwick. Bowling Green, OH: Bowling Green Univ. Popular Press, 1983.

Kloppenburg, Jack Ralph, Jr. *First the Seed: The Political Economy of Plant Biotechnology, 1492–2000.* Cambridge: Cambridge Univ. Press, 1988.

Koeniger, A. Cash. "Climate and Southern Distinctiveness." *Journal of Southern History* 54 (February 1988): 21–44.

Kottak, Conrad P. "Rituals at McDonald's." In *Ronald Revisited: The World of Ronald McDonald*, edited by Marshall William Fishwick. Bowling Green, OH: Bowling Green Univ. Popular Press, 1983.

Kovarik, William Joseph. "The Ethyl Controversy: The News Media and the Public Health Debate over Leaded Gasoline, 1924–1926." Ph.D. diss., Univ. of Maryland, College Park, 1993.

Krech, Shepard, III. *The Ecological Indian: Myth and History.* New York: W. W. Norton, 1999.

Kuletz, Valerie L. *The Tainted Desert: Environmental and Social Ruin in the American West.* New York: Routledge, 1998.

Kulik, Gary. "Dams, Fish, and Farmers: Defense of Public Rights in Eighteenth-Century Rhode Island." In *The Countryside in the Age of Capitalist Transformation*, edited by Steven Hahn and Jonathan Prude. Chapel Hill: Univ. of North Carolina Press, 1985.

Kulikoff, Alan. *Tobacco and Slaves: The Development of Southern Cultures in the Chesapeake, 1680–1800.* Chapel Hill: Univ. of North Carolina Press, 1986.

Kunstler, James Howard. *The Geography of Nowhere: The Rise and Decline of America's Man-Made Landscape.* New York: Simon and Schuster, 1993.

Kupperman, Karen Ordahl. "Climate and Mastery of the Wilderness in Seventeenth-Century New England." In *Seventeenth-Century New England*, edited by the Colonial Society of Massachusetts. Boston: Colonial Society of Massachusetts, 1984.

———. "Fear of Hot Climates in the Anglo-American Colonial Experience." *William and Mary Quarterly*, 3d Ser., 42 (April 1984): 213–240.

———. "The Puzzle of the American Climate in the Early Colonial Period." *American Historical Review* 87 (December 1982): 1262–1289.

Langston, Nancy. *Forest Dreams, Forest Nightmares: The Paradox of Old Growth in the Inland West.* Seattle: Univ. of Washington Press, 1995.

———. "Forest Dreams, Forest Nightmares: An Environmental History of a Forest Health Crisis." In *American Forests: Nature, Culture, and Politics*, edited by Char Miller. Lawrence: Univ. Press of Kansas, 1997.

Laporte, Dominique. *History of Shit.* Translated by Nadia Benabid and Rodolphe el-Khoury. Cambridge, MA: MIT Press, 2000.

Lappé, Marc, and Britt Bailey. *Against the Grain: Biotechnology and the Corporate Takeover of Your Food.* Monroe, ME: Common Courage Press, 1998.

Lauck, Jon. *American Agriculture and the Problem of Monopoly: The Political Economy of Grain Belt Farming, 1953–1980.* Lincoln: Univ. of Nebraska Press, 2000.

Lear, Linda. *Rachel Carson: Witness for Nature.* New York: Henry Holt and Company, 1997.

Leavitt, Judith Walzer. *The Healthiest City: Milwaukee and the Politics of Health Reform.* Princeton, NJ: Princeton Univ. Press, 1982.

Leopold, Aldo. *A Sand County Almanac.* 1949. Reprint. New York: Oxford Univ. Press, 1966.

Levenstein, Harvey A. *Revolution at the Table: The Transformation of the American Diet.* New York: Oxford Univ. Press, 1988.

Lewis, Martin W. *Green Delusions: An Environmentalist Critique of Radical Environmentalism.* Durham, NC: Duke Univ. Press, 1992.

Lewis, Ronald L. *Transforming the Appalachian Countryside: Railroads, Deforestation, and Social Change in West Virginia, 1880–1920.* Chapel Hill: Univ. of North Carolina Press, 1998.

Limerick, Patricia Nelson. *The Legacy of Conquest: The Unbroken Past of the American West.* New York: W. W. Norton, 1987.

Linder, Marc, and Lawrence S. Zacharias. *Of Cabbages and Kings County: Agriculture and the Formation of Modern Brooklyn*. Iowa City: Univ. of Iowa Press, 1999.

Little, Charles E. *The Dying of the Trees: The Pandemic in America's Forests*. New York: Viking, 1995.

Lockridge, Kenneth. "Land, Population and the Evolution of New England Society, 1630–1790." *Past and Present* 39 (April 1968): 62–80.

Loeb, Alan P. "Birth of the Kettering Doctrine: Fordism, Sloanism and the Discovery of Tetraethyl Lead." *Business and Economic History* 24 (Fall 1995): 72–87.

Loewen, James W. *Lies My Teacher Told Me: Everything Your American History Textbook Got Wrong*. New York: Simon and Schuster, 1996.

Ludlum, David M. *Early American Winters, 1604–1820*. Boston: American Meteorological Society, 1966.

———. *Early American Winters, 1821–1870*. Boston: American Meteorological Society, 1968.

Luger, Stan. "Market Ideology and Administrative Fiat: The Rollback of Automotive Fuel Economy Standards." *Environmental History Review* 19 (Spring 1995): 76–93.

McCarthy, Tom. "The Coming Wonder? Foresight and Early Concerns about the Automobile." *Environmental History* 6 (January 2001): 46–74.

McCay, Bonnie J. *Oyster Wars and the Public Trust: Property, Law, and Ecology in New Jersey History*. Tucson: Univ. of Arizona Press, 1998.

McClelland, Peter D. *Sowing Modernity: America's First Agricultural Revolution*. Ithaca, NY: Cornell Univ. Press, 1997.

McEvoy, Arthur F. *The Fisherman's Problem: Ecology and Law in the California Fisheries*. New York: Cambridge Univ. Press, 1986.

McGucken, William. *Lake Erie Rehabilitated: Controlling Cultural Eutrophication, 1960s–1990s*. Akron, OH: Univ. of Akron Press, 2000.

McKibben, Bill. *The End of Nature*. New York: Random House, 1989.

MacLeish, William H. *The Day before America*. Boston: Houghton Mifflin, 1994.

McMahon, Sarah F. "A Comfortable Subsistence: The Changing Composition of Diet in Rural New England, 1620–1840." *William and Mary Quarterly*, 3d Ser., 42 (January 1985): 26–51.

———. " 'All Things in Their Proper Season': Seasonal Rhythms of Diet in Nineteenth Century New England." *Agricultural History* 63 (Spring 1989): 130–151.

McMath, Robert C., Jr. "Sandy Land and Hogs in the Timber: (Agri)cultural Origins of the Farmers' Alliance in Texas." In *The Countryside in the Age of Capitalist Transformation*, edited by Steven Hahn and Jonathan Prude. Chapel Hill: Univ. of North Carolina Press, 1985.

McNeill, J. R. *Something New under the Sun: An Environmental History of the Twentieth-Century World*. New York: W. W. Norton, 2000.

McPhee, John. *The Control of Nature*. New York: Farrar Straus Giroux, 1989.

———. *Encounters with the Archdruid*. New York: Farrar Straus and Giroux, 1971.

McPherson, James M. *Battle Cry of Freedom: The Civil War Era*. New York: Oxford Univ. Press, 1988.

———. *Ordeal by Fire: The Civil War and Reconstruction*. New York: Alfred A. Knopf, 1982.

McShane, Clay. *Down the Asphalt Path: The Automobile and the American City*. New York: Columbia Univ. Press, 1994.

McShane, Clay, and Joel A. Tarr. "The Centrality of the Horse in the Nineteenth-Century American City." In *The Making of Urban America*, 2d ed., edited by Raymond A. Mohl. Wilmington, DE: Scholarly Resources, 1997.

McWilliams, Carey. *California: The Great Exception*. 1949. Reprint. Westport, CT: Greenwood, 1971.

———. *Factories in the Field: The Story of Migratory Farm Labor in California*. 1939. Reprint. Berkeley: Univ. of California Press, 1999.

Madden, David, ed. *Beyond the Battlefield: The Ordinary Life and Extraordinary Times of the Civil War Soldier.* New York: Simon and Schuster, 2000.

Magoc, Chris J. *Yellowstone: The Creation and Selling of an American Landscape, 1870–1903.* Albuquerque: Univ. of New Mexico Press; Helena: Montana Historical Society, 1999.

Malin, James C. *The Grasslands of North America: Prolegomena to Its History.* Gloucester, MA: Peter Smith, 1967.

———. *History and Ecology: Studies of the Grassland.* Edited by Robert P. Swierenga. Lincoln: Univ. of Nebraska Press, 1984.

Manning, Richard. *Food's Frontier: The Next Green Revolution.* New York: North Point Press, 2000.

———. *Grassland: The History, Biology, Politics, and Promise of the American Prairie.* New York: Penguin, 1995.

Marden, Emily. "The Neem Tree Patent: International Conflict over the Commodification of Life." *Boston College International and Comparative Law Review* 22 (Spring 1999): 279–295.

Marks, Stuart A. *Southern Hunting in Black and White: Nature, History, and Ritual in a Carolina Community.* Princeton, NJ: Princeton Univ. Press, 1991.

Martin, Calvin. *Keepers of the Game: Indian-Animal Relationships and the Fur Trade.* Berkeley: Univ. of California Press, 1978.

———. *The Way of the Human Being.* New Haven, CT: Yale Univ. Press, 1999.

———. "The European Impact on the Culture of a Northeastern Algonquian Tribe: An Ecological Interpretation." *William and Mary Quarterly,* 3d Ser., 31 (January 1974): 3–26.

Martin, Russell. *A Story That Stands Like a Dam: Glen Canyon and the Struggle for the Soul of the West.* New York: Henry Holt and Company, 1989.

Matthiessen, Peter. *Wildlife in America.* Revised Edition. New York: Penguin, 1984.

Meagher, Mary, and Douglas B. Houston. *Yellowstone and the Biology of Time: Photographs across a Century.* Norman: Univ. of Oklahoma Press, 1998.

Meikle, Jeffrey L. "Material Doubts: The Consequences of Plastic." *Environmental History* 2 (July 1997): 278–300.

Melosi, Martin V. *Coping with Abundance: Energy and Environment in Industrial America.* Philadelphia: Temple Univ. Press, 1985.

———. *Garbage in the Cities: Refuse, Reform, and the Environment, 1880–1980.* College Station: Texas A&M Univ. Press, 1981.

———. *The Sanitary City: Urban Infrastructure in America from Colonial Times to the Present.* Baltimore: Johns Hopkins Univ. Press, 2000.

———, ed. *Pollution and Reform in American Cities, 1870–1930.* Austin: Univ. of Texas Press, 1980.

Merchant, Carolyn. *Ecological Revolutions: Nature, Gender, and Science in New England.* Chapel Hill: Univ. of North Carolina Press, 1989.

———. "Gender and Environmental History." *Journal of American History* 76 (March 1990): 1117–1121.

Merrens, H. Roy, and George D. Terry. "Dying in Paradise: Malaria, Mortality, and the Perceptual Environment in Colonial South Carolina." *Journal of Southern History* 50 (November 1984): 533–550.

Miller, Benjamin. *Fat of the Land: Garbage of New York the Last Two Hundred Years.* New York: Four Walls Eight Windows, 2000.

Miller, Henry M. "Transforming a 'Splendid and Delightsome Land': Colonists and Ecological Change in the Chesapeake, 1607–1820." *Journal of the Washington Academy of Sciences* 76 (September 1986): 173–187.

Mintz, Sidney W. *Sweetness and Power: The Place of Sugar in Modern History.* New York: Penguin, 1985.

Mitchell, Don. *The Lie of the Land: Migrant Workers and the California Landscape.* Minneapolis: Univ. of Minnesota Press, 1996.

Mitman, Gregg. *Reel Nature: America's Romance with Wildlife on Film.* Cambridge, MA: Harvard Univ. Press, 1999.

Morgan, Philip D. "The Ownership of Property by Slaves in the Mid-Nineteenth-Century Low Country." *Journal of Southern History* 49 (August 1983): 399–420.

———. "Work and Culture: The Task System and the World of Lowcountry Blacks, 1700 to 1880." *William and Mary Quarterly*, 3d Ser., 39 (October 1982): 563–599.

Morris, Edmund. *The Rise of Theodore Roosevelt.* New York: Coward, McCann, and Geoghegan, 1979.

Morrison, Samuel Eliot. *The Great Explorers: The European Discovery of America.* New York: Oxford Univ. Press, 1978.

Muir, Diana. *Reflections in Bullough's Pond: Economy and Ecosystem in New England.* Hanover, NH: Univ. Press of New England, 2000.

Mulholland, Mitchell T. "Territoriality and Horticulture: A Perspective for Prehistoric Southern New England." In *Holocene Human Ecology in Northeastern North America*, edited by George P. Nicholas. New York: Plenum, 1988.

Namias, Jerome. "Nature and Possible Causes of the Northeastern United States Drought during 1962–65." *Monthly Weather Review* 94 (September 1966): 543–554.

Nash, Roderick. *Wilderness and the American Mind.* 3d ed. New Haven, CT: Yale Univ. Press, 1982.

Nesson, Fern L. *Great Waters: A History of Boston's Water Supply.* Hanover, NH: Univ. Press of New England, 1983.

Nestle, Marion. "Food Lobbies, the Food Pyramid, and U.S. Nutrition Policy." In *The Nation's Health*, 5th ed., edited by Philip R. Lee and Carroll L. Estes. Sudbury, MA: Jones and Bartlett, 1997.

Nye, David E. *Consuming Power: A Social History of American Energies.* Cambridge, MA: MIT Press, 1999.

O'Brien, Jim. "Environmentalism as a Mass Movement: Historical Notes." *Radical America* 17 (March/June 1983): 7–27.

Ogle, Maureen. *All the Modern Conveniences: American Household Plumbing, 1840–1890.* Baltimore: Johns Hopkins Univ. Press, 1996.

———. "Water Supply, Waste Disposal, and the Culture of Privatism in the Mid-Nineteenth-Century American City." *Journal of Urban History* 25 (March 1999): 321–347.

Opie, John. *The Law of the Land: Two Hundred Years of American Farmland Policy.* Lincoln: Univ. of Nebraska Press, 1987.

———. *Nature's Nation: An Environmental History of the United States.* Fort Worth, TX: Harcourt Brace, 1998.

———. *Ogallala: Water for a Dry Land.* Lincoln: Univ. of Nebraska Press, 1993.

Osgood, Ernest Staples. *The Day of the Cattlemen.* Minneapolis: Univ. of Minnesota Press, 1929.

Otto, John Solomon. *Southern Agriculture during the Civil War Era, 1860–1880.* Westport, CT: Greenwood Press, 1994.

Paehlke, Robert C. *Environmentalism and the Future of Progressive Politics.* New Haven, CT: Yale Univ. Press, 1989.

Patterson, William A., III, and Kenneth E. Sassaman. "Indian Fires in the Prehistory of New England." In *Holocene Human Ecology in Northeastern North America*, edited by George P. Nicholas. New York: Plenum, 1988.

Pearce, David, Neil Adger, David Maddison, and Dominic Moran. "Debt and the Environment." *Scientific American* 272 (June 1995): 52–56.

Pearce, Margaret Wickens. "Native Mapping in Southern New England Indian Deeds." In *Cartographic Encounters: Perspectives on Native American Mapmaking and Map Use*, edited by G. Malcolm Lewis. Chicago: Univ. of Chicago Press, 1998.

Perkins, John H. *Geopolitics and the Green Revolution: Wheat, Genes, and the Cold War.* New York: Oxford Univ. Press, 1997.

Petersen, Shannon C. "The Modern Ark: A History of the Endangered Species Act." Ph.D. diss., Univ. of Wisconsin, Madison, 2000.

Pimentel, David, L. E. Hurd, A. C. Bellotti, M. J. Forster, I. N. Oka, O. D. Sholes, and R. J. Whitman. "Food Production and the Energy Crisis." In *Food: Politics, Economics, Nutrition, and Research*, edited by Philip H. Abelson. Washington, DC: American Association for the Advancement of Science, 1975.

Pimentel, David, P. A. Oltenacu, M. C. Nesheim, John Krummel, M. S. Allen, and Sterling Chick. "The Potential for Grass-Fed Livestock: Resource Constraints." *Science* 207 (February 22, 1980): 843–848.

Pinchot, Gifford. *The Fight for Conservation*. New York: Doubleday, Page and Company, 1910.

Pisani, Donald J. *From Family Farm to Agribusiness: The Irrigation Crusade in California and the West, 1850–1931*. Berkeley: Univ. of California Press, 1984.

Polanyi, Karl. *The Great Transformation: The Political and Economic Origins of Our Time*. Boston: Beacon, 1944.

Pollan, Michael. *Second Nature: A Gardener's Education*. New York: Atlantic Monthly, 1991.

Post, John D. *The Last Great Subsistence Crisis in the Western World*. Baltimore: Johns Hopkins Univ. Press, 1977.

Press, Frank, and Raymond Siever. *Understanding Earth*. New York: Freeman, 1994.

Preston, William. "Serpent in the Garden: Environmental Change in Colonial California." In *Contested Eden: California before the Gold Rush*, edited by Ramón A. Gutiérrez and Richard J. Orsi. Berkeley: Univ. of California Press, 1998.

Price, Jennifer. *Flight Maps: Adventures with Nature in Modern America*. New York: Basic Books, 1999.

Proctor, James D. "Whose Nature? The Contested Moral Terrain of Ancient Forests." In *Uncommon Ground: Rethinking the Human Place in Nature*, edited by William Cronon. New York: W. W. Norton, 1996.

Pruitt, Bettye Hobbs. "Self-Sufficiency and the Agricultural Economy of Eighteenth-Century Massachusetts." *William and Mary Quarterly*, 3d Ser., 41 (July 1984): 333–364.

Pulido, Laura. *Environmental and Economic Justice: Two Chicano Struggles in the Southwest*. Tucson: Univ. of Arizona Press, 1996.

Pyne, Stephen J. *Fire in America: A Cultural History of Wildland and Rural Fire*. Revised Edition. Seattle: Univ. of Washington Press, 1997.

———. *Year of the Fires: The Story of the Great Fires of 1910*. New York: Viking, 2001.

Raitz, Karl B., and Richard Ulack. *Appalachia: A Regional Geography: Land, People, and Development*. Boulder, CO: Westview, 1984.

Rakestraw, Lawrence. "Conservation Historiography: An Assessment." *Pacific Historical Review* 41 (August 1972): 271–288.

Ramos, Tarso. "Wise Use in the West: The Case of the Northwest Timber Industry." In *Let the People Judge: Wise Use and the Private Property Rights Movement*, edited by John Echeverria and Raymond Booth Eby. Washington, DC: Island Press, 1995.

Ransom, Roger L., and Richard Sutch. *One Kind of Freedom: The Economic Consequences of Emancipation*. Cambridge: Cambridge Univ. Press, 1977.

Rappaport, Roy A. *Ecology, Meaning, and Religion*. Berkeley, CA: North Atlantic Books, 1979.

———. *Pigs for the Ancestors: Ritual in the Ecology of a New Guinea People*. Revised Edition. New Haven, CT: Yale Univ. Press, 1984.

———. "The Flow of Energy in an Agricultural Society." In *Energy and Power*, edited by Dennis Flanagan et al. San Francisco: Freeman, 1971.

———. "Nature, Culture, and Ecological Anthropology." In *Man, Culture, and Society*, edited by Harry L. Shapiro. London: Oxford Univ. Press, 1956.

Rathje, William, and Cullen Murphy. *Rubbish: The Archeology of Garbage*. New York: Harper Collins, 1992.

Redfern, Ron. *The Making of a Continent*. New York: Times Books, 1983.

Reed, David, ed. *Structural Adjustment, the Environment, and Sustainable Development*. London: Earthscan, 1996.

Reidy, Joseph P. *From Slavery to Agrarian Capitalism in the Cotton Plantation South: Central Georgia, 1800–1880*. Chapel Hill: Univ. of North Carolina Press, 1992.

Reiger, John F. *American Sportsmen and the Origins of Conservation*. New York: Winchester, 1975.

Reisner, Marc. *Cadillac Desert: The American West and Its Disappearing Water*. New York: Penguin, 1986.

Rich, Bruce. *Mortgaging the Earth: The World Bank, Environmental Impoverishment, and the Crisis of Development*. Boston: Beacon, 1994.

Rifkin, Jeremy. *Beyond Beef: The Rise and Fall of the Cattle Culture*. New York: Plume, 1993.

———. *The Biotech Century: Harnessing the Gene and Remaking the World*. New York: Tarcher/Putnam, 1998.

Ritvoe, Harriet. *The Animal Estate: The English and Other Creatures in the Victorian Age*. Cambridge, MA: Harvard Univ. Press, 1987.

Robbins, William G. *Hard Times in Paradise: Coos Bay, Oregon, 1850–1986*. Seattle: Univ. of Washington Press, 1988.

Roberts, Neil. *The Holocene: An Environmental History*. Oxford: Basil Blackwell, 1989.

Rogin, Michael Paul. *Fathers and Children: Andrew Jackson and the Subjugation of the American Indian*. New York: Vintage, 1975.

Rohrbough, Malcolm J. *Days of Gold: The California Gold Rush and the American Nation*. Berkeley: Univ. of California Press, 1997.

Roht-Arriaza, Naomi. "Of Seeds and Shamans: The Appropriation of the Scientific and Technical Knowledge of Indigenous and Local Communities." *Michigan Journal of International Law* 17 (Summer 1996): 919–965.

Rome, Adam. *The Bulldozer in the Countryside: Suburban Sprawl and the Rise of American Environmentalism*. New York: Cambridge Univ. Press, 2001.

———. "Coming to Terms with Pollution: The Language of Environmental Reform, 1865–1915." *Environmental History* 3 (July 1996): 6–28.

———. "William Whyte, Open Space, and Environmental Activism." *Geographical Review* 88 (April 1998): 259–274.

Rose, Mark. *Interstate: Express Highway Politics, 1939–1989*. Revised Edition. Knoxville: Univ. of Tennessee Press, 1990.

Rosenberg, Charles E. *The Cholera Years: The United States in 1832, 1849 and 1866*. Chicago: Univ. of Chicago Press, 1962.

Rosenkrantz, Barbara Gutmann. *Public Health and the State: Changing Views in Massachusetts, 1842–1936*. Cambridge, MA: Harvard Univ. Press, 1972.

Rosner, David, and Gerald Markowitz. "A 'Gift of God'? The Public Health Controversy over Leaded Gasoline during the 1920s." *American Journal of Public Health* 75 (April 1985): 344–352.

Ross, Andrew. *Strange Weather: Culture, Science and Technology in the Age of Limits*. London: Verso, 1991.

Rothenberg, Winifred B. "The Productivity Consequences of Market Integration: Agriculture in Massachusetts, 1771–1801." In *American Economic Growth and Standards of Living before the Civil War*, edited by Robert E. Gallman and John Joseph Wallis. Chicago: Univ. of Chicago Press, 1992.

Rothman, Hal K. *Devil's Bargains: Tourism in the Twentieth-Century American West*. Lawrence: Univ. Press of Kansas, 1998.

———. *The Greening of a Nation? Environmentalism in the United States Since 1945*. Fort Worth, TX: Harcourt Brace, 1998.

Rowell, Andrew. *Green Backlash: Global Subversion of the Environmental Movement*. London: Routledge, 1996.

Rubin, Julius. "The Limits of Agricultural Progress in the Nineteenth-Century South." *Agricultural History* 49 (April 1975): 362–373.

Runte, Alfred. *National Parks: The American Experience*. Revised Edition. Lincoln: Univ. of Nebraska Press, 1987.

Russell, Edmund. *War and Nature: Fighting Humans and Insects with Chemicals from World War I to Silent Spring*. New York: Cambridge Univ. Press, 2001.

———. " 'Speaking of Annhihilation': Mobilizing for War against Human and Insect Enemies." *Journal of American History* 82 (March 1996): 1505–1529.

Sackman, Douglas C. *Orange Empire: Nature, Culture, and Growth in California, 1869–1939*. Berkeley: Univ. of California Press, forthcoming.

Sahlins, Marshall. *Stone Age Economics*. New York: Aldine de Gruyter, 1972.

Sale, Kirkpatrick. *The Green Revolution: The American Environmental Movement, 1962–1992*. New York: Hill and Wang, 1993.

Salstrom, Paul. *Appalachia's Path to Dependency: Rethinking a Region's Economic History, 1730–1940*. Lexington: Univ. of Kentucky Press, 1994.

Sandweiss, Stephen. "The Social Construction of Environmental Justice." In *Environmental Injustices, Political Struggles: Race, Class, and the Environment*, edited by David E. Camacho. Durham, NC: Duke Univ. Press, 1998.

Sauer, Carl Ortwin. *Sixteenth Century North America: The Land and the People as Seen by the Europeans*. Berkeley: Univ. of California Press, 1971.

Sawyer, Richard C. *To Make a Spotless Orange: Biological Control in California*. Ames: Iowa State Univ. Press, 1996.

Schell, Orville. *Modern Meat*. New York: Random House, 1984.

Schlosser, Eric. *Fast Food Nation: The Dark Side of the All-American Meal*. Boston: Houghton Mifflin, 2001.

Schrepfer, Susan R. *The Fight to Save the Redwoods: A History of Environmental Reform, 1917–1978*. Madison: Univ. of Wisconsin Press, 1983.

Scott, James C. *Weapons of the Weak: Everyday Forms of Peasant Resistance*. New Haven, CT: Yale Univ. Press, 1985.

Seftel, Howard. "Government Regulation and the Rise of the California Fruit Industry: The Entrepreneurial Attack on Fruit Pests, 1880–1920." *Business History Review* 59 (Autumn 1985): 369–402.

Sellars, Richard West. *Preserving Nature in the National Parks: A History*. New Haven, CT: Yale Univ. Press, 1997.

Sellers, Christopher C. *Hazards of the Job: From Industrial Disease to Environmental Health Science*. Chapel Hill: Univ. of North Carolina Press, 1997.

Shabecoff, Philip. *A Fierce Green Fire: The American Environmental Movement*. New York: Hill and Wang, 1993.

Sherow, James Earl. *Watering the Valley: Development along the High Plains Arkansas River, 1870–1950*. Lawrence: Univ. Press of Kansas, 1990.

Shiva, Vandana. *Stolen Harvest: The Hijacking of the Global Food Supply*. Cambridge, MA: South End, 2000.

———. *The Violence of the Green Revolution: Third World Agriculture, Ecology and Politics*. London: Zed, 1991.

———. "War against Nature and the People of the South." In *Views from the South: The Effects of Globalization and the WTO on Third World Countries*, edited by Sarah Anderson. np: Food First Books and the International Forum on Globalization, 2000.

Silver, Timothy. *A New Face on the Countryside: Indians, Colonists, and Slaves in South Atlantic Forests, 1500–1800*. New York: Cambridge Univ. Press, 1990.

Sinclair, Upton. *The Jungle*. 1906. Reprint. New York: Bantam, 1981.

Skaggs, Jimmy M. *The Great Guano Rush: Entrepreneurs and American Overseas Expansion*. New York: St. Martin's Press, 1994.

———. *Prime Cut: Livestock Raising and Meatpacking in the United States, 1607–1983*. College Station: Texas A&M Press, 1986.

Smith, David C., Harold W. Borns, W. R. Baron, and Anne E. Bridges. "Climatic Stress and Maine Agriculture, 1785–1885." In *Climate and History: Studies in Past Climates and Their Impact on Man*, edited by T. M. L. Wigley, M. J. Ingram, and G. Farmer. Cambridge: Cambridge Univ. Press, 1981.

Smith, David C., and Anne E. Bridges. "The Brighton Market: Feeding Nineteenth-Century Boston." *Agricultural History* 56 (January 1982): 3–21.

Smith, Henry Nash. *Virgin Land: The American West as Symbol and Myth*. Cambridge, MA: Harvard Univ. Press, 1950.

Smits, David D. "The Frontier Army and the Destruction of the Buffalo: 1865–1883." *Western Historical Quarterly* 25 (Autumn 1994): 313–338.

Spann, Edward K. *The New Metropolis: New York City, 1840–1857*. New York: Columbia Univ. Press, 1981.

Spence, Clark C. *The Rainmakers: American "Pluviculture" to World War II*. Lincoln: Univ. of Nebraska Press, 1980.

Spence, Mark David. *Dispossessing the Wilderness: Indian Removal and the Making of the National Parks*. New York: Oxford Univ. Press, 1999.

Stahle, David W., Malcolm K. Cleaveland, Dennis B. Blanton, Matthew D. Therrell, and David A.Gray. "The Lost Colony and Jamestown Droughts." *Science* 280 (April 24, 1998): 564–567.

Starr, Kevin. *Inventing the Dream: California through the Progressive Era*. New York: Oxford Univ. Press, 1985.

Stegner, Wallace. *Beyond the Hundredth Meridian: John Wesley Powell and the Second Opening of the West*. Boston: Houghton Mifflin, 1954.

Steinberg, Ted. *Acts of God: The Unnatural History of Natural Disaster in America*. New York: Oxford Univ. Press, 2000.

———. *Nature Incorporated: Industrialization and the Waters of New England*. New York: Cambridge Univ. Press, 1991.

———. *Slide Mountain, Or the Folly of Owning Nature*. Berkeley: Univ. of California Press, 1995.

———. "An Ecological Perspective on the Origins of Industrialization." *Environmental Review* 10 (Winter 1986): 261–276.

Steinhart, Peter. *The Company of Wolves*. New York: Vintage, 1995.

Stewart, Mart A. *"What Nature Suffers to Groe": Life, Labor, and Landscape on the Georgia Coast, 1680–1920*. Athens: Univ. of Georgia Press, 1996.

———. " 'Whether Wast, Deodand, or Stray': Cattle, Culture, and the Environment in Early Georgia." *Agricultural History* 65 (Summer 1991): 1–28.

Stiffarm, Lenore A., and Phil Lane, Jr. "The Demography of Native North America: A Question of American Indian Survival." In *The State of Native America: Genocide, Colonization, and Resistance*, edited by M. Annette Jaimes. Boston: South End, 1992.

Stilgoe, John R. *Common Landscape of America, 1580–1845*. New Haven, CT: Yale Univ. Press, 1982.

Stoll, Steven. *The Fruits of Natural Advantage: Making the Industrial Countryside in California*. Berkeley: Univ. of California Press, 1998.

Strasser, Susan. *Satisfaction Guaranteed: The Making of the American Mass Market*. New York: Pantheon, 1989.

———. *Waste and Want: A Social History of Trash*. New York: Metropolitan, 1999.

————. " 'The Convenience Is Out of This World': The Garbage Disposer and American Consumer Culture." In *Getting and Spending: European and American Consumer Societies in the Twentieth Century*, edited by Susan Strasser, Charles McGovern, and Matthias Judt. New York: Cambridge Univ. Press, 1998.

Strickland, Arvarh E. "The Strange Affair of the Boll Weevil: The Pest as Liberator." *Agricultural History* 68 (Spring 1994): 157–168.

Strickland, John Scott. "Traditional Culture and Moral Economy: Social and Economic Change in the South Carolina Low Country, 1865–1910." In *The Countryside in the Age of Capitalist Transformation*, edited by Steven Hahn and Jonathan Prude. Chapel Hill: Univ. of North Carolina Press, 1985.

Strom, Claire. "Texas Fever and the Dispossession of the Southern Yeoman Farmer." *Journal of Southern History* 66 (February 2000): 49–74.

Sullivan, Robert. *The Meadowlands: Wilderness Adventures at the Edge of a City.* New York: Scribner, 1998.

Sutter, Paul Shriver. "Driven Wild: The Intellectual and Cultural Origins of Wilderness Advocacy during the Interwar Years." Ph.D. diss., Univ. of Kansas, 1997.

Tarr, Joel A. *The Search for the Ultimate Sink: Urban Pollution in Historical Perspective.* Akron, OH: Univ. of Akron Press, 1996.

————. "A Note on the Horse as an Urban Power Source." *Journal of Urban History* 25 (March 1999): 434–448.

Taylor, Alan. " 'The Hungry Year': 1789 on the Northern Border of Revolutionary America." In *Dreadful Visitations: Confronting Natural Catastrophe in the Age of Enlightenment*, edited by Alessa Johns. New York: Routledge, 1999.

————. "Unnatural Inequalities: Social and Environmental Histories." *Environmental History* 1 (October 1996): 6–19.

————. " 'Wasty Ways': Stories of American Settlement." *Environmental History* 3 (July 1998): 291–310.

Taylor, Joseph E., III. *Making Salmon: An Environmental History of the Northwest Fisheries Crisis.* Seattle: Univ. of Washington Press, 1999.

Terrie, Philip G. "Recent Work in Environmental History." *American Studies International* 27 (October 1989): 42–65.

Teyssot, Georges, ed. *The American Lawn.* New York: Princeton Architectural Press, 1999.

Thompson, E. P. *Customs in Common: Studies in Traditional Popular Culture.* New York: New Press, 1991.

Tober, James A. *Who Owns the Wildlife? The Political Economy of Conservation in Nineteenth Century America.* Westport, CT: Greenwood, 1981.

Trimble, Stanley Wayne. *Man-Induced Soil Erosion on the Southern Piedmont, 1700–1970.* Ankeny, IA: Soil Conservation Society of America, 1974.

————. "Perspectives on the History of Soil Erosion Control in the Eastern United States." *Agricultural History* 59 (April 1985): 162–180.

Tucker, Richard P. *The United States and the Ecological Degradation of the Tropical World.* Berkeley: Univ. of California Press, 2000.

Tyrrell, Ian. *True Gardens of the Gods: Californian-Australian Environmental Reform, 1860–1930.* Berkeley: Univ. of California Press, 1999.

Vaught, David. *Cultivating California: Growers, Specialty Crops, and Labor, 1875–1920.* Baltimore: Johns Hopkins Univ. Press, 1999.

Verchick, Robert R. M. "The Commerce Clause, Environmental Justice, and the Interstate Garbage Wars." *Southern California Law Review* 70 (July 1997): 1239–1310.

————. "In a Greener Voice: Feminist Theory and Environmental Justice." *Harvard Women's Law Journal* 19 (Spring 1996): 23–88.

Vidal, John. *McLibel: Burger Culture on Trial.* New York: New Press, 1997.

Vileisis, Ann. *Discovering the Unknown Landscape: A History of America's Wetlands.* Washington, DC: Island Press, 1997.

Wallock, Leonard. "The Myth of the Master Builder: Robert Moses, New York, and the Dynamics of Metropolitan Development Since World War II." *Journal of Urban History* 17 (August 1991): 339–362.

Ward, G. M, P. L. Knox, and B. W. Hobson. "Beef Production Options and Requirements for Fossil Fuel." *Science* 198 (October 21, 1977): 265–271.

Ward, Geoffrey C. *The Civil War.* New York: Vintage, 1990.

Warren, Louis S. *The Hunter's Game: Poachers and Conservationists in Twentieth-Century America.* New Haven, CT: Yale Univ. Press, 1997.

Warrick, Richard A. "Drought in the US Great Plains: Shifting Social Consequences?" In *Interpretations of Calamity,* edited by K. Hewitt. Boston: Allen and Unwin, 1983.

Watkins, James L. *King Cotton: A Historical and Statistical Review, 1790 to 1908.* Reprint Edition. New York: Negro Universities Press, 1969.

Watson, Harry L. " 'The Common Rights of Mankind': Subsistence, Shad, and Commerce in the Early Republican South." *Journal of American History* 83 (June 1996): 13–43.

Webb, Walter Prescott. *The Great Plains.* Boston: Ginn, 1931.

Weiman, David F. "The Economic Emanipation of the Non-Slaveholding Class: Upcountry Farmers in the Georgia Cotton Economy." *Journal of Economic History* 45 (March 1985): 71–93.

Weir, David, and Mark Schapiro. *Circle of Poison: Pesticides and People in a Hungry World.* Oakland, CA: Institute for Food and Development Policy, 1981.

West, Elliott. *The Contested Plains: Indians, Goldseekers, and the Rush to Colorado.* Lawrence: Univ. Press of Kansas, 1998.

———. *The Way to the West: Essays on the Central Plains.* Albuquerque: Univ. of New Mexico Press, 1995.

Wheeler, David L. "The Blizzard of 1886 and Its Effect on the Range Cattle Industry in the Southern Plains." *Southwestern Historical Quarterly* 94 (1990–1991): 415–432.

White, Harvey L. "Race, Class, and Environmental Hazards." In *Environmental Injustices, Political Struggles: Race, Class, and the Environment,* edited by David E. Camacho. Durham, NC: Duke Univ. Press, 1998.

White, Richard. *"It's Your Misfortune and None of My Own": A New History of the American West.* Norman: Univ. of Oklahoma Press, 1991.

———. *Land Use, Environment, and Social Change: The Shaping of Island County, Washington.* Seattle: Univ. of Washington Press, 1980.

———. *The Organic Machine: The Remaking of the Columbia River.* New York: Hill and Wang, 1995.

———. *The Roots of Dependency: Subsistence, Environment, and Social Change among the Choctaws, Pawnees, and Navajos.* Lincoln: Univ. of Nebraska Press, 1983.

———. "American Environmental History: The Development of a New Historical Field." *Pacific Historical Review* 54 (August 1985): 297–335.

———. "Animals and Enterprise." In *The Oxford History of the American West,* edited by Clyde A. Milner, II, Carol A. O'Connor, and Martha A. Sandweiss. New York: Oxford Univ. Press, 1994.

———. " 'Are You an Environmentalist or Do You Work for a Living?' Work and Nature." In *Uncommon Ground: Rethinking the Human Place in Nature,* edited by William Cronon. New York: W. W. Norton, 1996.

———. "Environmental History, Ecology, and Meaning." *Journal of American History* 76 (March 1990): 1111–1116.

White, Richard, and William Cronon. "Ecological Change and Indian-White Relations." In

Handbook of North American Indians, edited by William C. Sturtevant. Washington, DC: Smithsonian Institution Press, 1988.

Whitt, Laurie Anne. "Indigenous Peoples, Intellectual Property and the New Imperial Science." *Oklahoma City Univ. Law Review* 23 (Spring/Summer 1998): 211–259.

Whyte, William H. *The Last Landscape*. Garden City, NY: Doubleday, 1968.

Wicander, Reed, and James S. Monroe. *Historical Geology: Evolution of the Earth and Life through Time*. 2d ed. Minneapolis, MN: West, 1993.

Wigley, Mark. "The Electric Lawn." In *The American Lawn*, edited by Georges Teyssot. New York: Princeton Architectural Press, 1999.

Wilcove, David S. *The Condor's Shadow: The Loss and Recovery of Wildlife in America*. New York: Freeman, 1999.

Wilkins, David E. *American Indian Sovereignty and the U.S. Supreme Court: The Masking of Justice*. Austin: Univ. of Texas Press, 1997.

Williams, Michael. *Americans and Their Forests: A Historical Geography*. New York: Cambridge Univ. Press, 1989.

Willis, Susan. *A Primer for Daily Life*. London: Routledge, 1991.

Wilson, Alexander. *The Culture of Nature: North American Landscape from Disney to the Exxon Valdez*. Cambridge, MA: Blackwell, 1992.

Wines, Richard A. *Fertilizer in America: From Waste Recycling to Resource Exploitation*. Philadelphia: Temple Univ. Press, 1985.

Wirth, John D. *Smelter Smoke in North America: The Politics of Transborder Pollution*. Lawrence: Univ. Press of Kansas, 2000.

Woeste, Victoria Saker. *The Farmer's Benevolent Trust: Law and Agricultural Cooperation in Industrial America, 1865–1945*. Chapel Hill: Univ. of North Carolina Press, 1998.

Wood, Peter H. *Black Majority: Negroes in Colonial South Carolina from 1670 through the Stono Rebellion*. New York: Alfred A. Knopf, 1974.

Woodward, C. Vann. *Origins of the New South, 1877–1913*. Baton Rouge: Louisiana State Univ. Press, 1951.

Worster, Donald. *Dust Bowl: The Southern Plains in the 1930s*. New York: Oxford Univ. Press, 1979.

———. *Nature's Economy: A History of Ecological Ideas*. 1977. Reprint. New York: Cambridge Univ. Press, 1985.

———. *A River Running West: The Life of John Wesley Powell*. New York: Oxford Univ. Press, 2001.

———. *Rivers of Empire: Water, Aridity, and the Growth of the American West*. New York: Pantheon, 1985.

———. *Under Western Skies: Nature and History in the American West*. New York: Oxford Univ. Press, 1992.

———. *An Unsettled Country: Changing Landscapes of the American West*. Albuquerque: Univ. of New Mexico Press, 1994.

———. *The Wealth of Nature: Environmental History and the Ecological Imagination*. New York: Oxford Univ. Press, 1993.

———, ed. *The Ends of the Earth: Perspectives on Modern Environmental History*. New York: Cambridge Univ. Press, 1988.

———. "History as Natural History: An Essay on Theory and Method." *Pacific Historical Review* 53 (February 1984): 1–19.

———. "Seeing beyond Culture." *Journal of American History* 76 (March 1990): 1142–1147.

———. "A Tapestry of Change: Nature and Culture on the Prairie." In *The Inhabited Prairie*, photographed and compiled by Terry Evans. Lawrence: Univ. Press of Kansas, 1998.

———. "Transformations of the Earth: Toward an Agroecological Perspective in History." *Journal of American History* 76 (March 1990): 1087–1106.

Wright, Gavin. *Old South, New South: Revolutions in the Southern Economy Since the Civil War*. New York: Basic Books, 1986.

———. *The Political Economy of the Cotton South: Households, Markets, and Wealth in the Nineteenth Century*. New York: W. W. Norton, 1978.

Wright, Susan. *Molecular Politics: Developing American and British Regulatory Policy for Genetic Engineering, 1972–1982*. Chicago: Univ. of Chicago Press, 1994.

Yago, Glenn. *The Decline of Transit: Urban Transportation in German and U.S. Cities, 1900–1970*. Cambridge: Cambridge Univ. Press, 1984.

Page numbers in *italics* refer to illustrations.